Ship Stability for Masters and Mates

Ship Stability for Masters and Mates

Fifth edition

Captain D. R. Derrett

Revised by Dr C. B. Barrass

ELSEVIER
BUTTERWORTH
HEINEMANN

AMSTERDAM BOSTON HEIDELBERG LONDON NEW YORK OXFORD
PARIS SAN DIEGO SAN FRANCISCO SINGAPORE SYDNEY TOKYO

Elsevier Butterworth-Heinemann
Linacre House, Jordan Hill, Oxford OX2 8DP
200 Wheeler Road, Burlington, MA 01803

First published by Stanford Maritime Ltd 1964
Third edition (metric) 1972
Reprinted 1973, 1975, 1977, 1979, 1982
Fourth edition 1984
Reprinted 1985
Fourth edition by Butterworth-Heinemann Ltd 1990
Reprinted 1990 (twice), 1991, 1993, 1997, 1998, 1999
Fifth edition 1999
Reprinted 2000 (twice), 2001, 2002, 2003, 2004

British Library Cataloguing in Publication Data
A catalogue record for this book is available from the British Library

Library of Congress Cataloguing in Publication Data
A catalogue record for this book is available from the Library of Congress

ISBN 0 7506 4101 0

For information on all Elsevier Butterworth-Heinemann
publications visit our web site at www.bh.com

Typesetting and artwork creation by David Gregson Associates, Beccles, Suffolk
Printed and bound in Great Britain by Biddles Ltd, King's Lynn, Norfolk

Contents

Preface

This book was written primarily to meet the needs of the UK students when studying, either in their spare time at sea or ashore, for Department of Transport Certificates of Competency for Deck Officers and Engineering Officers. It will, however, also prove extremely useful to Maritime Studies degree students when studying the subject and will prove a ready and handy reference for those persons responsible for the stability of ships. I trust that this book, which is printed to include up-to-date syllabuses and specimen examination papers, will offer assistance to all of these persons.

Acknowledgement is made to the Controller of Her Majesty's Stationery Office for permission to reproduce Crown copyright material, being the Ministry of Transport Notice No. M375, *Carriage of Stability Information*, Forms M.V. 'Exna' (1) and (2), Merchant Shipping Notice No. M1122, *Simplified Stability Information*, Maximum Permissible Deadweight Diagram, and extracts from the Department of Transport Examination Syllabuses.

Specimen examination papers given in Appendix VI are reproduced by kind permission of the Scottish Qualifications Authority (SQA), based in Glasgow.

Note:

Throughout this book, when dealing with Transverse Stability, BM, GM and KM will be used. When dealing with Longitudinal Stability, i.e. Trim, then BM_L, GM_L and KM_L will be used to denote the longitudinal considerations. Hence no suffix 'T' for Transverse Stability, but suffix 'L' for the Longitudinal Stability text and diagrams.

C. B. Barrass

Introduction

Captain D. R. Derrett wrote the standard text book, *Ship Stability for Masters and Mates*. In this 1999 edition, I have revised several areas of his book and introduced new areas/topics in keeping with developments over the last nine years within the shipping industry.

This book has been produced for several reasons. The main aims are as follows:

1. To provide knowledge at a basic level for those whose responsibilities include the loading and safe operation of ships.
2. To give maritime students and Marine Officers an awareness of problems when dealing with stability and strength and to suggest methods for solving these problems if they meet them in the day-to-day operation of ships.
3. To act as a good, quick reference source for those officers who obtained their Certificates of Competency a few months/years prior to joining their ship, port authority or drydock.
4. To help Masters, Mates and Engineering Officers prepare for their SQA/MSA exams.
5. To help students of naval architecture/ship technology in their studies on ONC, HNC, HND and initial years on undergraduate degree courses.
6. When thinking of maritime accidents that have occurred in the last few years as reported in the press and on television, it is perhaps wise to pause and remember the proverb 'Prevention is better than cure'. If this book helps in preventing accidents in the future then the efforts of Captain Derrett and myself will have been worthwhile.

Finally, I thought it would be useful to have a table of ship types (see next page) showing typical deadweights, lengths, breadths, C_b values and designed service speeds. It gives an awareness of just how big these ships are, the largest moving structures made by man.

It only remains for me to wish you, the student, every success with your Maritime studies and best wishes in your chosen career. Thank you.

C. B. Barrass

Ship types and general characteristics

The table below indicates the characteristics relating to several merchant ships operating today.

The first indicator for a ship is usually her deadweight; closely followed by her LBP and C_b values.

Type of ship or name	Typical DWT (tonnes or m^3)	LBP (m)	BR. MLD (m)	Typical C_b fully loaded	Service speed (knots)
ULCC, VLCC and supertankers	565 000 to 100 000	440 to 250	70 to 40	0.85 to 0.82	13 to $15\frac{3}{4}$
Medium sized oil tankers	100 000 to 50 000	250 to 175	40 to 25	0.82 to 0.80	15 to $15\frac{3}{4}$
OBO carriers	up to 173 000	200 to 300	up to 45	0.78 to 0.80	15 to 16
Ore carriers	up to 323 000	200 to 320	up to 58	0.79 to 0.83	$14\frac{1}{2}$ to $15\frac{1}{2}$
General cargo ships	3000 to 15 000	100 to 150	15 to 25	0.700	14 to 16
Liquefied natural gas (LNG) and liquefied petroleum (LPG) ships	130 000 m^3 to 75 000 m^3	up to 280	46 to 25	0.66 to 0.68	$20\frac{3}{4}$ to 16
Passenger liners (2 examples below)	5000 to 20 000	200 to 300	20 to 40	0.60 to 0.64	24 to 30
QE2 (built (1970)	15 520	270	32	0.600	$28\frac{1}{2}$
Oriana (built 1994)	7270	224	32.2	0.625	24
Container ships	10 000 to 72 000	200 to 300	30 to 45	0.56 to 0.60	20 to 28
Roll on/roll off car and passenger ferries	2000 to 5000	100 to 180	21 to 28	0.55 to 0.57	18 to 24

Chapter 1
Forces and moments

The solution of many of the problems concerned with ship stability involves an understanding of the resolution of forces and moments. For this reason a brief examination of the basic principles will be advisable.

Forces

A *force* can be defined as any push or pull exerted on a body. The S.I. unit of force is the Newton, one Newton being the force required to produce in a mass of one kilogram an acceleration of one metre per second per second. When considering a force the following points regarding the force must be known:

(a) The magnitude of the force,
(b) The direction in which the force is applied, and
(c) The point at which the force is applied.

The resultant force. When two or more forces are acting at a point, their combined effect can be represented by one force which will have the same effect as the component forces. Such a force is referred to as the 'resultant force', and the process of finding it is called the 'resolution of the component forces'.

The resolution of forces. When resolving forces it will be appreciated that a force acting towards a point will have the same effect as an equal force acting away from the point, so long as both forces act in the same direction and in the same straight line. Thus a force of 10 Newtons (N) pushing to the right on a certain point can be substituted for a force of 10 Newtons (N) pulling to the right from the same point.

(a) *Resolving two forces which act in the same straight line*
If both forces act in the same straight line and in the same direction the resultant is their sum, but if the forces act in opposite directions the resultant is the difference of the two forces and acts in the direction of the larger of the two forces.

Example 1

Whilst moving an object one man pulls on it with a force of 200 Newtons, and another pushes in the same direction with a force of 300 Newtons. Find the resultant force propelling the object.

Component forces $\underrightarrow{300\,N}$ A $\underrightarrow{200\,N}$

The resultant force is obviously 500 Newtons, the sum of the two forces, and acts in the direction of each of the component forces.

Resultant force $\underrightarrow{500\,N}$ A   *or*   A $\underrightarrow{500\,N}$

Example 2

A force of 5 Newtons is applied towards a point whilst a force of 2 Newtons is applied at the same point but in the opposite direction. Find the resultant force.

Component forces $\underrightarrow{5\,N}$ A $\underleftarrow{2\,N}$

Since the forces are applied in opposite directions, the magnitude of the resultant is the difference of the two forces and acts in the direction of the 5 N force.

Resultant force $\underrightarrow{3\,N}$ A   *or*   A $\underrightarrow{3\,N}$

(b) *Resolving two forces which do not act in the same straight line*
When the two forces do not act in the same straight line, their resultant can be found by completing a parallelogram of forces.

Example 1

A force of 3 Newtons and a force of 5 N act towards a point at an angle of 120 degrees to each other. Find the direction and magnitude of the resultant.

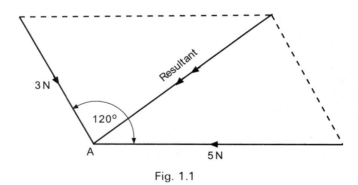

Fig. 1.1

Ans. Resultant 4.36 N at $36° \, 34\frac{1}{2}'$ to the 5 N force.

Note. Notice that each of the component forces and the resultant all act towards the point A.

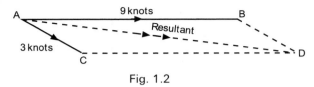

Fig. 1.2

Example 2

A ship steams due east for an hour at 9 knots through a current which sets 120 degrees (T) at 3 knots. Find the course and distance made good.

The ship's force would propel her from A to B in one hour and the current would propel her from A to C in one hour. The resultant is AD, $0.97\frac{1}{2}^\circ \times 11.6$ miles and this will represent the course and distance made good in one hour. *Note.* In the above example both of the component forces and the resultant force all act away from the point A.

Example 3

A force of 3 N acts downwards towards a point whilst another force of 5 N acts away from the point to the right as shown in Figure 1.3. Find the resultant.

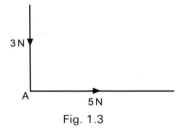

Fig. 1.3

In this example one force is acting towards the point and the second force is acting away from the point. Before completing the parallelogram, substitute either a force of 3 N acting away from the point for the force of 3 N towards the point as shown in Figure 1.4, or a force of 5 N towards the point for the

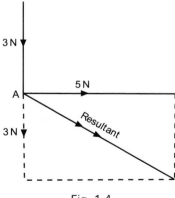

Fig. 1.4

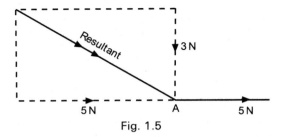

Fig. 1.5

force of 5 N away from the point as shown in Figure 1.5. In this way both of the forces act either towards or away from the point. The magnitude and direction of the resultant is the same whichever substitution is made; i.e. 5.83 N at an angle of 59° to the vertical.

(c) *Resolving two forces which act in parallel directions*
When two forces act in parallel directions, their combined effect can be represented by one force whose magnitude is equal to the algebraic sum of the two component forces, and which will act through a point about which their moments are equal.

The following two examples may help to make this clear.

Example 1
In Figure 1.6 the parallel forces W and P are acting upwards through A and B respectively. Let W be greater than P. Their resultant, (W + P), acts upwards through the point C such that $P \times y = W \times x$. Since W is greater than P, the point C will be nearer to B than to A.

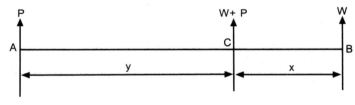

Fig. 1.6

Example 2
In Figure 1.7 the parallel forces W and P act in opposite directions through A and B respectively. If W is again greater than P, their resultant, (W − P), acts through point C on AB produced such that $P \times y = W \times x$.

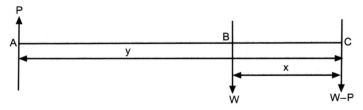

Fig. 1.7

Moments of Forces

The moment of a force is a measure of the turning effect of the force about a point. The turning effect will depend upon the following:

(a) The magnitude of the force, and
(b) The length of the lever upon which the force acts, the lever being the perpendicular distance between the line of action of the force and the point about which the moment is being taken.

The magnitude of the moment is the product of the force and the length of the lever. Thus, if the force is measured in Newtons and the length of the lever in metres, the moment found will be expressed in Newton-metres (Nm).

Resultant moment. When two or more forces are acting about a point their combined effect can be represented by one imaginary moment called the 'Resultant Moment'. The process of finding the resultant moment is referred to as the 'Resolution of the Component Moments'.

Resolution of moments. To calculate the resultant moment about a point, find the sum of the moments to produce rotation in a clockwise direction about the point, and the sum of the moments to produce rotation in an anti-clockwise direction. Take the lesser of these two moments from the greater and the difference will be the magnitude of the resultant. The direction in which it acts will be that of the greater of the two component moments.

Example 1

A capstan consists of a drum 2 metres in diameter around which a rope is wound, and four levers at right angles to each other, each being 2 metres long. If a man on the end of each lever pushes with a force of 500 Newtons, what strain is put on the rope? (See Figure 1.8(a).)

Moments are taken about O, the centre of the drum.

$$\text{Total moment in an anti-clockwise direction} = 4 \times (2 \times 500) \text{ Nm}$$

$$\text{The resultant moment} = 4000 \text{ Nm (Anti-clockwise)}$$

$$\text{Let the strain on the rope} = P \text{ Newtons}$$

$$\text{The moment about O} = (P \times 1) \text{ Nm}$$

$$\therefore P \times 1 = 4000$$

$$\text{or } P = 4000 \text{ N}$$

Ans. <u>The strain is 4000 N.</u>

Note. For a body to remain at rest, the resultant force acting on the body must be zero and the resultant moment about its centre of gravity must also be zero, if the centre of gravity be considered a fixed point.

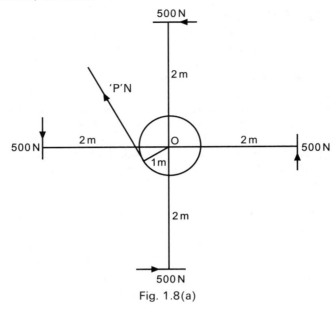

Fig. 1.8(a)

Mass

In the S.I. system of units it is most important to distinguish between the mass of a body and its weight. Mass is the fundamental measure of the quantity of matter in a body and is expressed in terms of the kilogram and the tonne, whilst the weight of a body is the force exerted on it by the Earth's gravitational force and is measured in terms of the Newton (N) and kilo-Newton (kN).

Weight and mass are connected by the formula:

$$\text{Weight} = \text{Mass} \times \text{Acceleration}$$

Example 2

Find the weight of a body of mass 50 kilograms at a place where the acceleration due to gravity is 9.81 metres per second per second.

$$\text{Weight} = \text{Mass} \times \text{Acceleration}$$
$$= 50 \times 9.81$$

Ans. Weight = 490.5 N

Moments of Mass

If the force of gravity is considered constant then the weight of bodies is proportional to their mass and the resultant moment of two or more weights about a point can be expressed in terms of their mass moments.

Example 3

A uniform plank is 3 metres long and is supported at a point under its mid-length. A load having a mass of 10 kilograms is placed at a distance of 0.5

metres from one end and a second load of mass 30 kilograms is placed at a distance of one metre from the other end. Find the resultant moment about the middle of the plank.

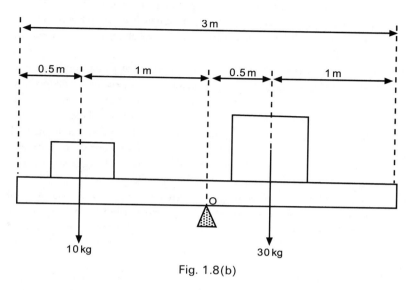

Fig. 1.8(b)

Moments are taken about O, the middle of the plank.

$$\text{Clockwise moment} = 30 \times 0.5$$
$$= 15 \, \text{kg m}$$
$$\text{Anti-clockwise moment} = 10 \times 1$$
$$= 10 \, \text{kg m}$$
$$\text{Resultant moment} = 15 - 10$$

Ans. Resultant moment $= 5 \, \text{kg m clockwise}$

Exercise 1

1   A capstan bar is 3 metres long. Two men are pushing on the bar, each with a force of 400 Newtons. If one man is placed half-way along the bar and the other at the extreme end of the bar, find the resultant moment about the centre of the capstan.

2   A uniform plank is 6 metres long and is supported at a point under its mid-length. A 10 kg mass is placed on the plank at a distance of 0.5 metres from one end and a 20 kg mass is placed on the plank 2 metres from the other end. Find the resultant moment about the centre of the plank.

3   A uniform plank is 5 metres long and is supported at a point under its mid-length. A 15 kg mass is placed 1 metre from one end and a 10 kg mass is placed 1.2 metres from the other end. Find where a 13 kg mass must be placed on the plank so that the plank will not tilt.

4   A weightless bar 2 metres long is suspended from the ceiling at a point which is 0.5 metres in from one end. Suspended from the same end is a mass of 110 kg. Find the mass which must be suspended from a point 0.3 metres in from the other end of the bar so that the bar will remain horizontal.

5   Three weights are placed on a plank. One of 15 kg mass is placed 0.6 metres in from one end, the next of 12 kg mass is placed 1.5 metres in from the same end, and the last of 18 kg mass is placed 3 metres from this end. If the mass of the plank be ignored, find the resultant moment about the end of the plank.

Chapter 2
Centroids and the centre of gravity

The centroid of an area is situated at its geometrical centre. In each of the following figures 'G' represents the centroid, and if each area was suspended from this point it would balance.

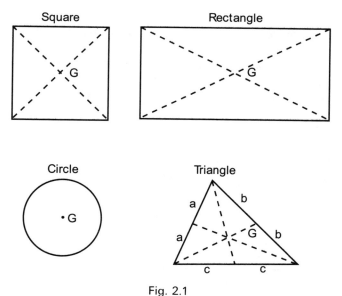

Fig. 2.1

The centre of gravity of a body is the point at which all the mass of the body may be assumed to be concentrated and is the point through which the force of gravity is considered to act vertically downwards, with a force equal to the weight of the body. It is also the point about which the body would balance.

The centre of gravity of a homogeneous body is at its geometrical centre. Thus the centre of gravity of a homogeneous rectangular block is half-way along its length, half-way across its breadth and at half its depth.

Let us now consider the effect on the centre of gravity of a body when the distribution of mass within the body is changed.

Effect of removing or discharging mass

Consider a rectangular plank of homogeneous wood. Its centre of gravity will be at its geometrical centre — that is, half-way along its length, half-way across its breadth, and at half depth. Let the mass of the plank be W kg and let it be supported by means of a wedge placed under the centre of gravity as shown in Figure 2.2. The plank will balance.

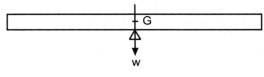

Fig. 2.2

Now let a short length of the plank, of mass w kg, be cut from one end such that its centre of gravity is d metres from the centre of gravity of the plank. The other end, now being of greater mass, will tilt downwards. Figure 2.3(a) shows that by removing the short length of plank a resultant moment of $w \times d$ kg m has been created in an anti-clockwise direction about G.

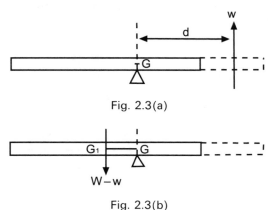

Fig. 2.3(a)

Fig. 2.3(b)

Now consider the new length of plank as shown in Figure 2.3(b). The centre of gravity will have moved to the new half-length indicated by the distance G to G_1. The new mass, $(W - w)$ kg, now produces a tilting moment of $(W - w) \times GG_1$ kg m about G.

Since these are simply two different ways of showing the same effect, the moments must be the same. i.e.

$$(W - w) \times GG_1 = w \times d$$

or

$$GG_1 = \frac{w \times d}{W - w} \text{ metres}$$

From this it may be concluded that when mass is removed from a body, the centre of gravity of the body will move directly away from the centre of gravity of the mass removed, and the distance it moves will be given by the formula:

$$GG_1 = \frac{w \times d}{\text{Final mass}} \text{ metres}$$

where GG_1 is the shift of the centre of gravity of the body, w is the mass removed, and d is the distance between the centre of gravity of the mass removed and the centre of gravity of the body.

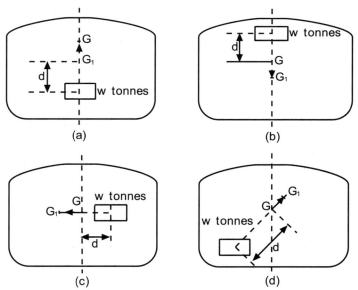

Fig. 2.4.   Discharging a mass w.

Application to ships

In each of the above figures, G represents the centre of gravity of the ship with a mass of w tonnes on board at a distance of d metres from G. G to G_1 represents the shift of the ship's centre of gravity due to discharging the mass.

In Figure 2.4(a), it will be noticed that the mass is vertically below G, and that when discharged G will move vertically upwards to G_1.

In Figure 2.4(b), the mass is vertically above G and the ship's centre of gravity will move directly downwards to G_1.

In Figure 2.4(c), the mass is directly to starboard of G and the ship's centre of gravity will move directly to port from G to G_1.

In Figure 2.4(d), the mass is below and to port of G, and the ship's centre of gravity will move upwards and to starboard.

In each case:

$$GG_1 = \frac{w \times d}{\text{Final displacement}} \text{ metres}$$

Effect of adding or loading mass

Once again consider the plank of homogeneous wood shown in Figure 2.2. Now add a piece of plank of mass w kg at a distance of d metres from G as shown in Figure 2.5(a).

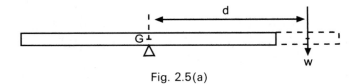

Fig. 2.5(a)

The heavier end of the plank will again tilt downwards. By adding a mass of w kg at a distance of d metres from G a tilting moment of $w \times d$ kg m. about G has been created.

Now consider the new plank as shown in Figure 2.5(b). Its centre of gravity will be at its new half-length (G_1), and the new mass, (W + w) kg, will produce a tilting moment of $(W + w) \times GG_1$ kg m about G.

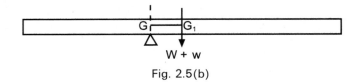

Fig. 2.5(b)

These tilting moments must again be equal, i.e.

$$(W + w) \times GG_1 = w \times d$$

or

$$GG_1 = \frac{w \times d}{W + w} \text{ metres}$$

From the above it may be concluded that when mass is added to a body, the centre of gravity of the body will move directly towards the centre of gravity of the mass added, and the distance which it moves will be given by the formula:

$$GG_1 = \frac{w \times d}{\text{Final mass}} \text{ metres}$$

where GG_1 is the shift of the centre of gravity of the body, w is the mass added, and d is the distance between the centres of gravity.

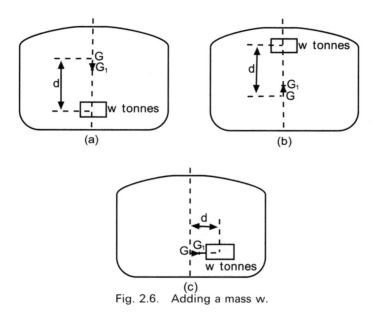

Fig. 2.6.   Adding a mass w.

Application to ships

In each of the above figures, G represents the position of the centre of gravity of the ship before the mass of w tonnes has been loaded. After the mass has been loaded, G will move directly towards the centre of gravity of the added mass (i.e. from G to G_1).

Also, in each case:

$$GG_1 = \frac{w \times d}{\text{Final displacement}} \text{ metres}$$

Effect of shifting weights

In Figure 2.7, G represents the original position of the centre of gravity of a ship with a weight of 'w' tonnes in the starboard side of the lower hold having its centre of gravity in position g_1. If this weight is now discharged the ship's centre of gravity will move from G to G_1 directly away from g_1. When the same weight is reloaded on deck with its centre of gravity at g_2 the ship's centre of gravity will move from G_1 to G_2.

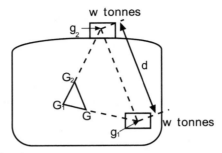

Fig. 2.7.   Discharging, adding and moving a mass w.

From this it can be seen that if the weight had been shifted from g_1 to g_2 the ship's centre of gravity would have moved from G to G_2.

It can also be shown that GG_2 is parallel to $g_1 \, g_2$ and that

$$GG_2 = \frac{w \times d}{W} \text{ metres}$$

where w is the mass of the weight shifted, d is the distance through which it is shifted, and W is the ship's displacement.

The centre of gravity of the body will always move parallel to the shift of the centre of gravity of any weight moved within the body.

Effect of suspended weights

The centre of gravity of a body is the point through which the force of gravity may be considered to act vertically downwards. Consider the centre of gravity of a weight suspended from the head of a derrick as shown in Figure 2.8.

It can be seen from Figure 2.8 that whether the ship is upright or inclined in either direction, the point in the ship through which the force of gravity may be considered to act vertically downwards is g_1, the point of suspension. Thus the centre of gravity of a suspended weight is considered to be at the point of suspension.

Conclusions

1. The centre of gravity of a body will move directly *towards* the centre of gravity of any *weight added*.
2. The centre of gravity of a body will move directly *away* from the centre of gravity of any *weight removed*.
3. The centre of gravity of a body will *move parallel* to the shift of the centre of gravity of any *weight moved* within the body.

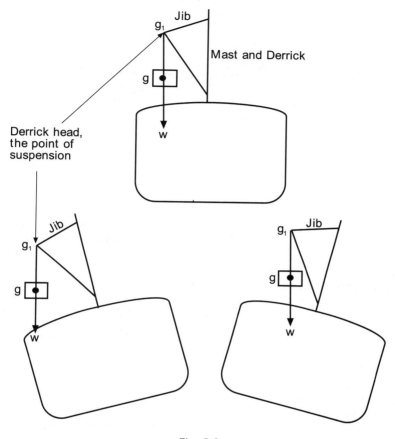

Fig. 2.8

4. The *shift of the centre of gravity* of the body in each case is given by the formula:

$$GG_1 = \frac{w \times d}{W} \text{ metres}$$

where w is the mass of the weight added, removed, or shifted, W is the *final* mass of the body, and d is, in 1 and 2, the distance between the centres of gravity, and in 3, the distance through which the weight is shifted.

5. When a weight is *suspended* its centre of gravity is considered to be at the *point of suspension*.

Example 1
A hold is partly filled with a cargo of bulk grain. During the loading, the ship takes a list and a quantity of grain shifts so that the surface of the grain remains parallel to the waterline. Show the effect of this on the ship's centre of gravity.

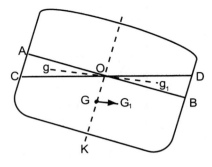

Fig. 2.9

In Figure 2.9, G represents the original position of the ship's centre of gravity when upright. AB represents the level of the surface of the grain when the ship was upright and CD the level when inclined. A wedge of grain AOC with its centre of gravity at g has shifted to ODB with its centre of gravity at g_1. The ship's centre of gravity will shift from G to G_1, such that GG_1 is parallel to gg_1, and the distance

$$GG_1 = \frac{w \times d}{W} \text{ metres}$$

Example 2

A ship is lying starboard side to a quay. A weight is to be discharged from the port side of the lower hold by means of the ship's own derrick. Describe the effect on the position of the ship's centre of gravity during the operation.

Note. When a weight is suspended from a point, the centre of gravity of the weight appears to be at the point of suspension regardless of the distance between the point of suspension and the weight. Thus, as soon as the weight is clear of the deck and is being borne at the derrick head, the centre of gravity of the weight appears to move from its original position to the derrick head. For example, it does not matter whether the weight is 0.6 metres or 6.0 metres above the deck, or whether it is being raised or lowered; its centre of gravity will appear to be at the derrick head.

In Figure 2.10, G represents the original position of the ship's centre of gravity, and g represents the centre of gravity of the weight when lying in the lower hold. As soon as the weight is raised clear of the deck, its centre of gravity will appear to move vertically upwards to g_1. This will cause the ship's centre of gravity to move upwards from G to G_1, parallel to gg_1. The centres of gravity will remain at G_1 and g_1 respectively during the whole of the time the weight is being raised. When the derrick is swung over the side, the derrick head will move from g_1 to g_2, and since the weight is suspended from the derrick head, its centre of gravity will also appear to move from g_1 to g_2. This will cause the ship's centre of gravity to move from G_1 to G_2. If the weight is now landed on the quay it is in effect being discharged from the derrick head

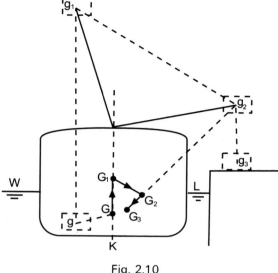

Fig. 2.10

and the ship's centre of gravity will move from G_2 to G_3 in a direction directly
away from g_2. G_3 is therefore the final position of the ship's centre of gravity
after discharging the weight.

From this it can be seen that the net effect of discharging the weight is a shift
of the ship's centre of gravity from G to G_3, directly away from the centre of
gravity of the weight discharged. This would agree with the earlier conclusions
which have been reached in Figure 2.4.

Note. The only way in which the position of the centre of gravity of a ship can
be altered is by changing the distribution of the weights within the ship, i.e. by
adding, removing, or *shifting* weights.

Students find it hard sometimes to accept that the weight, when suspended
from the derrick, acts at its point of suspension.

However, it can be proved, by experimenting with ship models or
observing full-size ship tests. The final angle of heel when measured verifies
that this assumption is indeed correct.

Exercise 2

1 A ship has displacement of 2400 tonnes and KG = 10.8 metres. Find the new KG if a weight of 50 tonnes mass already on board is raised 12 metres vertically.

2 A ship has displacement of 2000 tonnes and KG = 10.5 metres. FInd the new KG if a weight of 40 tonnes mass already on board is shifted from the 'tween deck to the lower hold. through a distance of 4.5 metres vertically.

3 A ship of 2000 tonnes displacement has KG = 4.5 metres. A heavy lift of 20 tonnes mass is in the lower hold and has KG = 2 metres. This weight is then raised 0.5 metres clear of the tank top by a derrick whose head is 14 metres above the keel. Find the new KG of the ship.

4 A ship has a displacement of 7000 tonnes and KG = 6 metres. A heavy lift in the lower hold has KG = 3 metres and mass 40 tonnes. Find the new KG when this weight is raised through 1.5 metres vertically and is suspended by a derrick whose head is 17 metres above the keel.

5 Find the shift in the centre of gravity of a ship of 1500 tonnes displacement when a weight of 25 tonnes mass is shifted from the starboard side of the lower hold to the port side on deck through a distance of 15 metres.

Chapter 3
Density and specific gravity

Density is defined as 'mass per unit volume'. e.g.

The mass density of FW $= 1000$ kg per cubic metre or 1.000 tonne/m^3
The mass density of SW $= 1025$ kg per cubic metre or 1.025 tonne/m^3

The specific gravity (SG) or relative density of a substance is defined as the ratio of the weight of the substance to the weight of an equal volume of fresh water.

If a volume of one cubic metre is considered, then the SG or relative density of a substance is the ratio of the density of the substance to the density of fresh water. i.e.

$$\text{SG or relative density of a substance} = \frac{\text{Density of the substance}}{\text{Density of fresh water}}$$

The density of FW $= 1000$ kg per cu. m

$$\therefore \text{SG of a substance} = \frac{\text{Density of the substance in kg per cu. m}}{1000}$$

or

$$\text{Density in kg per cu. m} = 1000 \times \text{SG}$$

Example 1
Find the relative density of salt water whose density is 1025 kg per cu. m

$$\text{Relative density} = \frac{\text{Density of SW in kg per cu. m}}{1000}$$

$$= \frac{1025}{1000}$$

$\therefore$ relative density of salt water $= 1.025$

Example 2

Find the density of a fuel oil whose relative density is 0.92

$$\text{Density in kg per cu.m} = 1000 \times SG$$
$$= 1000 \times 0.92$$
$$\therefore \text{Density} = 920 \text{ kg per cu.m}$$

Example 3

When a double-bottom tank is full of fresh water it holds 120 tonnes. Find how many tonnes of oil of relative density 0.84 it will hold.

$$\text{Relative density} = \frac{\text{Mass of oil}}{\text{Mass of FW}}$$

or

$$\text{Mass of oil} = \text{Mass of FW} \times \text{relative density}$$
$$= 120 \times 0.84 \text{ tonnes}$$
$$\text{Mass of oil} = 100.8 \text{ tonnes}$$

Example 4

A tank measures $20\,m \times 24\,m \times 10.5\,m$ and contains oil of relative density 0.84. Find the mass of oil it contains when the ullage is 2.5 m. An ullage is the distance from the surface of the liquid in the tank to the top of the tank. A sounding is the distance from the surface of the liquid to the base of the tank or sounding pad.

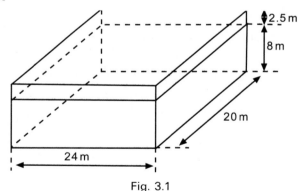

Fig. 3.1

$$\text{Volume of oil} = L \times B \times D$$
$$= 20 \times 24 \times 8 \text{ cu.m}$$
$$\text{Density of oil} = SG \times 1000$$
$$= 840 \text{ kg per cu.m or } 0.84 \text{ t/m}^3$$
$$\text{Mass of oil} = \text{Volume} \times \text{density}$$
$$= 20 \times 24 \times 8 \times 0.84$$
$$\text{Mass of oil} = 3225.6 \text{ tonnes}$$

Example 5

A tank will hold 153 tonnes when full of fresh water. Find how many tonnes of oil of relative density 0.8 it will hold allowing 2% of the oil loaded for expansion.

$$\text{Mass of freshwater} = 153 \text{ tonnes}$$
$$\therefore \text{ Volume of the tank} = 153 \text{ m}^3$$
$$\text{Volume of oil} + 2\% \text{ of volume of oil} = \text{Volume of the tank}$$
$$\text{or } 102\% \text{ of volume of the oil} = 153 \text{ m}^3$$
$$\therefore \text{ volume of the oil} = 153 \times \frac{100}{102} \text{ m}^3$$
$$= 150 \text{ m}^3$$
$$\text{Mass of the oil} = \text{Volume} \times \text{Density}$$
$$= 150 \times 0.8 \text{ tonnes}$$

Ans. = <u>120 tonnes</u>

Exercise 3

1   A tank holds 120 tonnes when full of fresh water. Find how many tonnes of oil of relative density 0.84 it will hold, allowing 2% of the volume of the tank for expansion in the oil.

2   A tank when full will hold 130 tonnes of salt water. Find how many tonnes of oil relative density 0.909 it will hold, allowing 1% of the volume of the tank for expansion.

3   A tank measuring $8 \text{ m} \times 6 \text{ m} \times 7 \text{ m}$ is being filled with oil of relative density 0.9. Find how many tonnes of oil in the tank when the ullage is 3 metres.

4   Oil of relative density 0.75 is run into a tank measuring $6 \text{ m} \times 4 \text{ m} \times 8 \text{ m}$ until the ullage is 2 metres. Calculate the number of tonnes of oil the tank then contains.

5   A tank will hold 100 tonnes when full of fresh water. Find how many tonnes of oil of relative density 0.85 may be loaded if 2% of the volume of the oil loaded is to be allowed for expansion.

6   A deep tank 10 metres long, 16 metres wide and 6 metres deep has a coaming 4 metres long, 4 metres wide and 25 cm deep. (Depth of tank does not include depth of coaming). How may tonnes of oil, of relative density 0.92, can it hold if a space equal to 3% of the oil loaded is allowed for expansion?

Chapter 4
Laws of flotation

Archimedes' Principle states that when a body is wholly or partially immersed in a fluid it appears to suffer a loss in mass equal to the mass of the fluid it displaces.

The mass density of fresh water is 1000 kg per cu. m. Therefore, when a body is immersed in fresh water it will appear to suffer a loss in mass of 1000 kg for every 1 cu. m of water it displaces.

When a box measuring 1 cu. m and of 4000 kg mass is immersed in fresh water it will appear to suffer a loss in mass of 1000 kg. If suspended from a spring balance the balance would indicate a mass of 3000 kg.

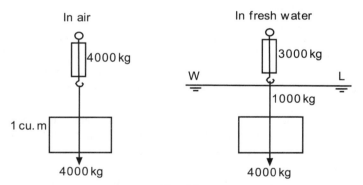

Fig. 4.1

Since the actual mass of the box is not changed, there must be a force acting vertically upwards to create the apparent loss of mass of 1000 kg. This force is called the *force of buoyancy*, and is considered to act vertically upwards through a point called the *centre of buoyancy*. The centre of buoyancy is the centre of gravity of the underwater volume.

Now consider the box shown in Figure 4.2(a) which also has a mass of 4000 kg, but has a volume of 8 cu. m. If totally immersed in fresh water it will displace 8 cu. m of water, and since 8 cu. m of fresh water has a mass of

8000 kg, there will be an upthrust or force of buoyancy causing an apparent loss of mass of 8000 kg. The resultant apparent loss of mass is 4000 kg. When released, the box will rise until a state of equilibrium is reached, i.e. when the buoyancy is equal to the mass of the box. To make the buoyancy produce a loss of mass of 4000 kg the box must be displacing 4 cu m of water. This will occur when the box is floating with half its volume immersed, and the resultant force then acting on the box will be zero. This is shown in Figure 4.2(c).

Now consider the box to be floating in fresh water with half its volume immersed as shown in Figure 4.2(c). If a mass of 1000 kg be loaded on deck as shown in Figure 4.3(a) the new mass of the body will be 5000 kg, and since this exceeds the buoyancy by 1000 kg, it will move downwards.

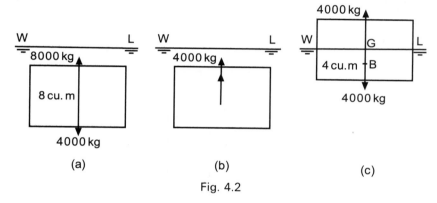

Fig. 4.2

The downwards motion will continue until buoyancy is equal to the mass of the body. This will occur when the box is displacing 5 cu. m of water and the buoyancy is 5000 kg, as shown in Figure 4.3(b).

The conclusion which may be reached from the above is that for a body to float at rest in still water, it must be displacing its own weight of water and the centre of gravity must be vertically above or below the centre of buoyancy.

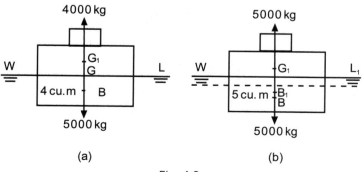

Fig. 4.3

The variable immersion hydrometer

The variable immersion hydrometer is an instrument, based on the Law of Archimedes, which is used to determine the density of liquids. The type of hydrometer used to find the density of the water in which a ship floats is usually made of a non-corrosive material and consists of a weighted bulb with a narrow rectangular stem which carries a scale for measuring densities between 1000 and 1025 kilograms per cubic metre, i.e. 1.000 and 1.025 t/m^3.

The position of the marks on the stem are found as follows. First let the hydrometer, shown in Figure 4.4, float upright in fresh water at the mark X. Take the hydrometer out of the water and weigh it. Let the mass be M_x kilograms. Now replace the hydrometer in fresh water and add lead shot in the bulb until it floats with the mark Y, at the upper end of the stem, in the

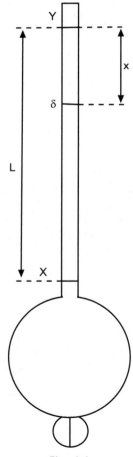

Fig. 4.4

waterline. Weigh the hydrometer again and let its mass now be M_y kilograms.

The mass of water displaced by the stem between X and Y is therefore equal to $M_y - M_x$ kilograms. Since 1000 kilograms of fresh water occupy one cubic metre, the volume of the stem between X and Y is equal to $\dfrac{M_y - M_x}{1000}$ cu. m.

Let L represent the length of the stem between X and Y, and let 'a' represent the cross-sectional area of the stem.

$$a = \frac{\text{Volume}}{\text{Length}}$$

$$= \frac{M_y - M_x}{1000\,L} \text{ sq m}$$

Now let the hydrometer float in water of density $\delta\,\text{kg/m}^3$ with the waterline 'x' metres below Y.

$$\text{Volume of water displaced} = \frac{M_y}{1000} - x\,a$$

$$= \frac{M_y}{1000} - x\left(\frac{M_y - M_x}{1000\,L}\right) \qquad \text{(I)}$$

But

$$\text{Volume of water displaced} = \frac{\text{Mass of water displaced}}{\text{Density of water displaced}}$$

$$= \frac{M_y}{1000\,\delta} \qquad \text{(II)}$$

Equate (I) and (II) $\therefore \dfrac{M_y}{1000\,\delta} = \dfrac{M_y}{1000} - x\left(\dfrac{M_y - M_x}{1000\,L}\right)$

or

$$\delta = \frac{M_y}{M_y - x\left(\dfrac{M_y - M_x}{L}\right)}$$

In this equation, M_y, M_x and L are known constants whilst δ and x are variables. Therefore, to mark the scale it is now only necessary to select various values of δ and to calculate the corresponding values of x.

Tonnes per Centimetre Immersion (TPC)

The TPC for any draft is the mass which must be loaded or discharged to change a ship's mean draft in salt water by one centimetre, where

$$\text{TPC} = \frac{\text{water-plane area}}{100} \times \text{density of water}$$

$$\therefore \text{TPC} = \frac{\text{WPA}}{100} \times \rho$$

WPA is in m^2.
ρ is in t/m^3.

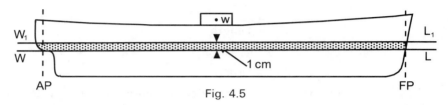

Fig. 4.5

Consider a ship floating in *salt water* at the waterline WL as shown in Figure 4.5. Let 'A' be the area of the water-plane in square metres.

Now let a mass of 'w' tonnes be loaded so that the mean draft is increased by one centimetre. The ship then floats at the waterline $W_1 L_1$. Since the draft has been increased by one centimetre, the mass loaded is equal to the TPC for this draft. Also, since an extra mass of water equal to the mass loaded must be displaced, then the mass of water in the layer between WL and $W_1 L_1$ is also equal to the TPC.

$$\text{Mass} = \text{Volume} \times \text{Density}$$

$$= A \times \frac{1}{100} \times \frac{1025}{1000} \text{ tonnes} = \frac{1.025\,A}{100} \text{ tonnes}$$

$$\therefore \text{TPC}_{sw} = \frac{1.025\,A}{100} = \frac{\text{WPA}}{97.56}. \quad \text{Also, TPC}_{fw} = \frac{\text{WPA}}{100}$$

TPC in dock water

Note. When a ship is floating in dock water of a relative density other than 1.025 the weight to be loaded or discharged to change the mean draft by 1 centimetre (TPC_{dw}) may be found from the TPC in salt water (TPC_{sw}) by simple proportion as follows:

$$\frac{\text{TPC}_{dw}}{\text{TPC}_{sw}} = \frac{\text{relative density of dock water } (\text{RD}_{dw})}{\text{relative density of salt water } (\text{RD}_{sw})}$$

or

$$\text{TPC}_{dw} = \frac{\text{RD}_{dw}}{1.025} \times \text{TPC}_{sw}$$

Reserve buoyancy

It has already been shown that a floating vessel must displace its own weight of water. Therefore, it is the submerged portion of a floating vessel which provides the buoyancy. The volume of the enclosed spaces above the waterline are not providing buoyancy but are being held in reserve. If extra weights are loaded to increase the displacement, these spaces above the waterline are there to provide the extra buoyancy required. Thus, *reserve buoyancy* may be defined as the volume of the enclosed spaces above the waterline. It may be expressed as a volume or as a percentage of the total volume of the vessel.

Example 1

A box-shaped vessel 105 m long, 30 m beam, and 20 m deep, is floating upright in fresh water. If the displacement is 19 500 tonnes, find the volume of reserve buoyancy.

$$\text{Volume of water displaced} = \frac{\text{Mass}}{\text{Density}} = 19\,500 \text{ cu. m}$$

$$\text{Volume of vessel} = 105 \times 30 \times 20 \text{ cu. m}$$

$$= 63\,000 \text{ cu. m}$$

$$\text{Reserve buoyancy} = \text{Volume of vessel} - \text{volume of water displaced}$$

Ans. Reserve buoyancy $= 43\,500$ cu. m

Example 2

A box-shaped barge 16 m × 6 m × 5 m is floating alongside a ship in fresh water at a mean draft of 3.5 m. The barge is to be lifted out of the water and loaded on to the ship with a heavy-lift derrick. Find the load in tonnes borne by the purchase when the draft of the barge has been reduced to 2 metres.

Note. By Archimedes' Principle the barge suffers a loss in mass equal to the mass of water displaced. The mass borne by the purchase will be the difference between the actual mass of the barge and the mass of water displaced at any draft, or the difference between the mass of water originally displaced by the barge and the new mass of water displaced.

$$\text{Mass of the barge} = \text{Original mass of water displaced}$$
$$= \text{Volume} \times \text{density}$$
$$= 16 \times 6 \times 3.5 \times 1 \text{ tonnes}$$
$$\text{Mass of water displace at 2 m draft} = 16 \times 6 \times 2 \times 1 \text{ tonnes}$$
$$\therefore \text{ Load borne by the purchase} = 16 \times 6 \times 1 \times (3.5 - 2) \text{ tonnes}$$

Ans. $= 144$ tonnes

Example 3

A cylindrical drum 1.5 m long and 60 cm in diameter has mass 20 kg when empty. Find its draft in water of density 1024 kg per cu. m if it contains 200 litres of paraffin of relative density 0.6, and is floating with its axis perpendicular to the waterline (Figure 4.6).

Note. The drum must displace a mass of water equal to the mass of the drum plus the mass of the paraffin.

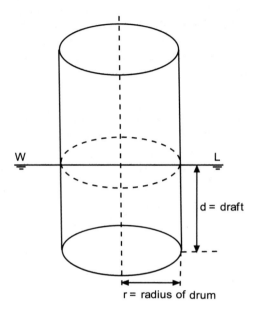

r = radius of drum

Fig. 4.6

$$\text{Density of the paraffin} = \text{SG} \times 1000 \text{ kg per cu. m}$$
$$= 600 \text{ kg per cu. m}$$
$$\text{Mass of the paraffin} = \text{Volume} \times \text{density} = 0.2 \times 600 \text{ kg}$$
$$= 120 \text{ kg}$$
$$\text{Mass of the drum} = 20 \text{ kg}$$
$$\text{Total mass} = 140 \text{ kg}$$

Therefore the drum must displace 140 kg of water.

$$\text{Volume of water displaced} = \frac{\text{Mass}}{\text{Density}} = \frac{140}{1024} \text{ cu. m}$$

$$\text{Volume of water displaced} = 0.137 \text{ cu. m}$$

Let d = draft, and r = radius of the drum, where $r = \dfrac{60}{2} = 30 \text{ cm} = 0.3 \text{ m}$.

$$\text{Volume of water displaced (V)} = \pi r^2 \, d$$

or

$$d = \frac{V}{\pi r^2}$$

$$= \frac{0.137}{\dfrac{22}{7} \times 0.3 \times 0.3} \; m$$

$$= 0.484 \, m$$

Ans. Draft $= 0.484 \, m$

Homogeneous logs of rectangular section

The draft at which a rectangular homogeneous log will float may be found as follows:

$$\text{Mass of log} = \text{Volume} \times \text{density}$$
$$= L \times B \times D \times SG \text{ of } \log \times 1000 \, kg$$
$$\text{Mass of water displaced} = \text{Volume} \times \text{density}$$
$$= L \times B \times d \times SG \text{ of water} \times 1000 \, kg$$
$$\text{But Mass of water displaced} = \text{Mass of log}$$
$$\therefore \; L \times B \times d \times SG \text{ of water} \times 1000 = L \times B \times D \times SG \text{ of } \log \times 1000$$

or

$$d \times SG \text{ of water} = D \times SG \text{ of log}$$

$$\frac{\text{Draft}}{\text{Depth}} = \frac{SG \text{ of log}}{SG \text{ of water}} \quad \text{or} \quad \frac{\text{relative density of log}}{\text{relative density of water}}$$

Example 4

Find the distance between the centres of gravity and buoyancy of a rectangular log 1.2 m wide, 0.6 m deep, and of relative density 0.8 when floating in fresh water with two of its sides parallel to the waterline.

If BM is equal to $\dfrac{b^2}{12 \, d}$ determine if this log will float with two of its sides parallel to the waterline.

Note. The centre of gravity of a homogeneous log is at its geometrical centre. See Figure 4.7

$$\frac{\text{Draft}}{\text{Depth}} = \frac{\text{Relative density of log}}{\text{Relative density of water}}$$

$$\text{Draft} = \frac{0.6 \times 0.8}{1}$$

$$\left.\begin{array}{l} \text{Draft} = 0.48 \, m \\[4pt] KB = 0.24 \, m \\[4pt] KG = 0.30 \, m \end{array}\right\} \text{see Figure 4.8}$$

Ans. BG $= 0.06 \, m$

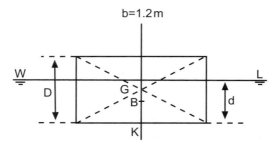

Fig. 4.7

$$BM = \frac{b^2}{12 \times d} = \frac{1.2^2}{12 \times 0.48} = 0.25 \text{ m}$$

$$KB \text{ as above} = +0.24 \text{ m}$$

$$KM = KB + BM = +0.49 \text{ m}$$

$$-KG = -0.30 \text{ m}$$

$$GM = 0.19 \text{ m}$$

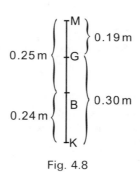

Fig. 4.8

Conclusion

Because G is below M, this homogeneous log is in stable equilibrium. Consequently, it *will* float with two of its sides parallel to the waterline.

Exercise 4

1   A drum of mass 14 kg when empty, is 75 cm long, and 60 cm in diameter. Find its draft in salt water if it contains 200 litres of paraffin of relative density 0.63.

2   A cube of wood of relative density 0.81 has sides 30 cm long. If a mass of 2 kg is placed on the top of the cube with its centre of gravity vertically over that of the cube, find the draft in salt water.

3   A rectangular tank (3 m × 1.2 m × 0.6 m) has no lid and is floating in fresh water at a draft of 15 cm. Calculate the minimum amount of fresh water which must be poured into the tank to sink it.

4   A cylindrical salvage buoy is 5 metres long, 2.4 metres in diameter, and floats on an even keel in salt water with its axis in the water-plane. Find the upthrust which this buoy will produce when fully immersed.

5   A homogeneous log of rectangular cross-section is 30 cm wide and 25 cm deep. The log floats at a draft of 17 cm. Find the reserve buoyancy and the distance between the centre of buoyancy and the centre of gravity.

6   A homogeneous log of rectangular cross-section is 5 m. long, 60 cm wide, 40 cm deep, and floats in fresh water at a draft of 30 cm. Find the mass of the log and its relative density.

7   A homogeneous log is 3 m long, 60 cm wide, 60 cm deep, and has relative density 0.9. Find the distance between the centres of buoyancy and gravity when the log is floating in fresh water.

8   A log of square section is 5 m × 1 m × 1 m. The relative density of the log is 0.51 and it floats half submerged in dock water. Find the relative density of the dock water.

9   A box-shaped vessel 20 m × 6 m × 2.5 m floats at a draft of 1.5 m in water of density 1013 kg per cu. m. Find the displacement in tonnes, and the height of the centre of buoyancy above the keel.

10 An empty cylindrical drum 1 metre long and 0.6 m. in diameter has mass 20 kg. Find the mass which must be placed in it so that it will float with half of its volume immersed in (a) salt water, and (b) fresh water.

11 A lifeboat, when fully laden, displaces 7.2 tonnes. Its dimensions are 7.5 m × 2.5 m × 1 m, and its block coefficient 0.6. Find the percentage of its volume under water when floating in fresh water.

12 A homogeneous log of relative density 0.81 is 3 metres long, 0.5 metres square cross-section, and is floating in fresh water. Find the displacement of the log, and the distance between the centres of gravity and buoyancy.

13 A box-shaped barge 55 m × 10 m × 6 m. is floating in fresh water on an even keel at 1.5 m draft. If 1800 tonnes of cargo is now loaded, find the difference in the height of the centre of buoyancy above the keel.

14 A box-shaped barge 75 m × 6 m × 4 m displaces 180 tonnes when light. If

360 tonnes of iron are loaded while the barge is floating in fresh water, find her final draft and reserve buoyancy.

15   A drum 60 cm in diameter and 1 metre long has mass 30 kg when empty. If this drum is filled with oil of relative density 0.8, and is floating in fresh water, find the percentage reserve buoyancy.

Chapter 5
Effect of density on draft and displacement

Effect of change of density when the displacement is constant

When a ship moves from water of one density to water of another density, without there being a change in her mass, the draft will change. This will happen because the ship must displace the same mass of water in each case. Since the density of the water has changed, the volume of water displaced must also change. This can be seen from the formula:

$$\text{Mass} = \text{Volume} \times \text{Density}$$

If the density of the water increases, then the volume of water displaced must decrease to keep the mass of water displaced constant, and vice versa.

The effect on box-shaped vessels

$$\text{New mass of water displaced} = \text{Old mass of water displaced}$$
$$\therefore \text{New volume} \times \text{new density} = \text{Old volume} \times \text{Old density}$$
$$\frac{\text{New volume}}{\text{Old volume}} = \frac{\text{Old density}}{\text{New density}}$$
$$\text{But volume} = \text{L} \times \text{B} \times \text{draft}$$
$$\therefore \frac{\text{L} \times \text{B} \times \text{New draft}}{\text{L} \times \text{B} \times \text{Old draft}} = \frac{\text{Old density}}{\text{New density}}$$

or

$$\frac{\text{New draft}}{\text{Old draft}} = \frac{\text{Old density}}{\text{New density}}$$

Example 1

A box-shaped vessel floats at a mean draft of 2.1 metres, in dock water of density 1020 kg per cu. m. Find the mean draft for the same mass displacement in salt water of density 1025 kg per cubic metre.

$$\frac{\text{New draft}}{\text{Old draft}} = \frac{\text{Old density}}{\text{New density}}$$

$$\text{New draft} = \frac{\text{Old density}}{\text{New density}} \times \text{Old draft}$$

$$= \frac{1020}{1025} \times 2.1\,\text{m}$$

$$= 2.09\,\text{m}$$

Ans. New draft = 2.09 m

Example 2

A box-shaped vessel floats upright on an even keel as shown in fresh water of density 1000 kg per cu. m, and the centre of buoyancy is 0.50 m above the keel. Find the height of the centre of buoyancy above the keel when the vessel is floating in salt water of density 1025 kg per cubic metre.

Note. The centre of buoyancy is the geometric centre of the underwater volume and for a box-shaped vessel must be at half draft, i.e. $KB = \frac{1}{2}$ draft.

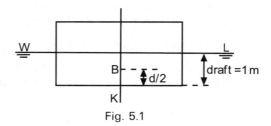

Fig. 5.1

In Fresh Water

$$KB = 0.5\,\text{m, and since } KB = \tfrac{1}{2} \text{ draft, then draft} = 1\,\text{m}$$

In Salt Water

$$\frac{\text{New draft}}{\text{Old draft}} = \frac{\text{Old density}}{\text{New density}}$$

$$\text{New draft} = \text{Old draft} \times \frac{\text{Old density}}{\text{New density}}$$

$$= 1 \times \frac{1000}{1025}$$

$$\text{New draft} = 0.976\,\text{m}$$

$$\text{New } KB = \tfrac{1}{2} \text{ new draft}$$

Ans. New KB = 0.488 m, say 0.49 m.

The effect on ship-shaped vessels

It has already been shown that when the density of the water in which a vessel floats is changed the draft will change, but the mass of water in kg or tonnes displaced will be unchanged. i.e.

$$\text{New displacement} = \text{Old displacement}$$

or

$$\text{New volume} \times \text{new density} = \text{Old volume} \times \text{old density}$$

$$\therefore \frac{\text{New volume}}{\text{Old volume}} = \frac{\text{Old density}}{\text{New density}}$$

With ship-shapes this formula should not be simplified further as it was in the case of a box-shape because the underwater volume is not rectangular. To find the change in draft of a ship-shape due to change of density a quantity known as the 'Fresh Water Allowance' must be known.

The *Fresh Water Allowance* is the number of millimetres by which the mean draft changes when a ship passes from salt water to fresh water, or vice versa, whilst floating at the loaded draft. It is found by the formula:

$$\text{FWA (in mm)} = \frac{\text{Displacement (in tonnes)}}{4 \times \text{TPC}}$$

The proof of this formula is as follows:

$$\text{To show that FWA (in mm)} = \frac{\text{Displacement (in tonnes)}}{4 \times \text{TPC}}$$

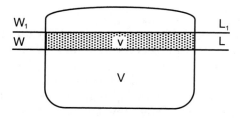

Fig. 5.2

Consider the ship shown in Figure 5.2 to be floating at the load Summer draft in salt water at the waterline WL. Let V be the volume of salt water displaced at this draft.

Now let W_1L_1 be the waterline for the ship when displacing the same mass of fresh water. Also, let 'v' be the extra volume of water displaced in fresh water.

The total volume of fresh water displaced is then $V + v$.

$$\text{Mass} = \text{Volume} \times \text{density}$$

$$\therefore \text{ Mass of SW displaced} = 1025\,V$$

$$\text{and mass of FW displaced} = 1000\,(V + v)$$

$$\text{but mass of FW displaced} = \text{mass of SW displaced}$$

$$\therefore \ 1000\,(V + v) = 1025\,V$$

$$1000\,V + 1000\,v = 1025\,V$$

$$1000\,v = 25\,V$$

$$v = V/40$$

Now let w be the mass of salt water in volume v, in tonnes and let W be the mass of salt water in volume V, in tonnes.

$$\therefore w = W/40$$

$$\text{but } w = \frac{\text{FWA}}{10} \times \text{TPC}$$

$$\frac{\text{FWA}}{10} \times \text{TPC} = W/40$$

or

$$\text{FWA} = \frac{W}{4 \times \text{TPC}} \text{ mm}$$

where

$$W = \text{Loaded salt water displacement in tonnes}$$

Figure 5.3 shows a ship's load line marks. The centre of the disc is at a distance below the deck line equal to the ship's Statutory Freeboard. Then 540 mm forward of the disc is a vertical line 25 mm thick, with horizontal lines measuring 230×25 mm on each side of it. The upper edge of the one marked 'S' is in line with the horizontal line through the disc and indicates the draft to which the ship may be loaded when floating in salt water in a Summer Zone. Above this line and pointing aft is another line marked 'F', the upper edge of which indicates the draft to which the ship may be loaded when floating in fresh water in a Summer Zone. If loaded to this draft in fresh water the ship will automatically rise to 'S' when she passes into salt water. The perpendicular distance in millimetres between the upper edges of these two lines is therefore the ship's Fresh Water Allowance.

When the ship is loading in dock water which is of a density between these two limits 'S' may be submerged such a distance that she will automatically rise to 'S' when the open sea and salt water is reached. The

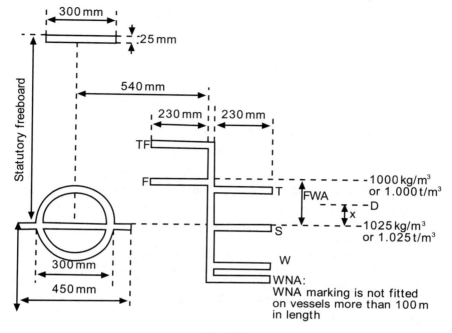

Fig. 5.3

distance by which 'S' can be submerged, called the *Dock Water Allowance*, is found in practice by simple proportion as follows:

$$\text{Let } x = \text{The Dock Water Allowance}$$

$$\text{Let } \rho_{DW} = \text{Density of the dock water}$$

Then

$$\frac{x \, mm}{FWA \, mm} = \frac{1025 - \rho_{DW}}{1025 - 1000}$$

or

$$\text{Dock Water Allowance} = \frac{FWA \, (1025 - \rho_{DW})}{25}$$

Example 3

A ship is loading in dock water of density 1010 kg per cu. m. FWA = 150 mm. Find the change in draft on entering salt water.

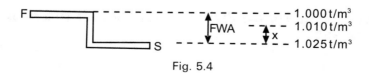

Fig. 5.4

$$\text{Let } x = \text{The change in draft in millimetres}$$

$$\text{Then } \frac{x}{\text{FWA}} = \frac{1025 - 1010}{25}$$

$$x = 150 \times \frac{15}{25}$$

$$x = 90 \, \text{mm}$$

Ans. Draft will decrease by 90 mm, i.e. 9 cm

Example 4

A ship is loading in a Summer Zone in dock water of density 1005 kg per cu. m. FWA = 62.5 mm, TPC = 15 tonnes. The lower edge of the Summer load line is in the waterline to port and is 5 cm above the waterline to starboard. Find how much more cargo may be loaded if the ship is to be at the correct load draft in salt water.

Note. This ship is obviously listed to port and if brought upright the lower edge of the 'S' load line on each side would be 25 mm above the waterline. Also, it is the upper edge of the line which indicates the 'S' load draft and, since the line is 25 mm thick, the ship's draft must be increased by 50 mm to bring her to the 'S' load line in dock water. In addition 'S' may be submerged by x mm.

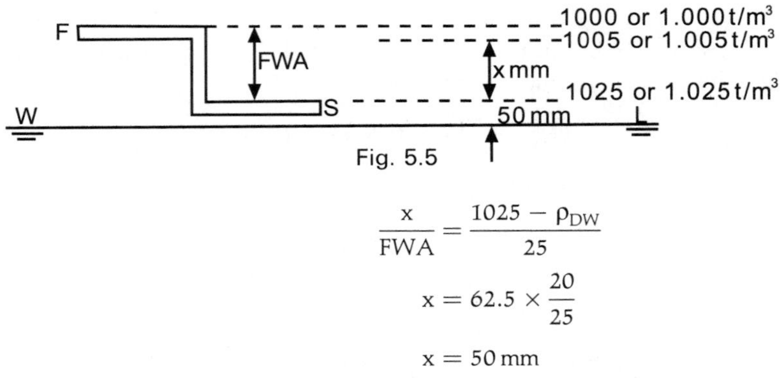

Fig. 5.5

$$\frac{x}{\text{FWA}} = \frac{1025 - \rho_{DW}}{25}$$

$$x = 62.5 \times \frac{20}{25}$$

$$x = 50 \, \text{mm}$$

$$\therefore \text{ Total increase in draft required} = 100 \, \text{mm or } 10 \, \text{cm}$$

$$\text{and cargo to load} = \text{Increase in draft} \times \text{TPC}$$

$$= 10 \times 15$$

Ans. Cargo to load = 150 tonnes

Effect of density on displacement when the draft is constant

Should the density of the water in which a ship floats be changed without the ship altering her draft, then the mass of water displaced must have changed. The change in the mass of water displaced may have been brought about by bunkers and stores being loaded or consumed during a sea passage, or by cargo being loaded or discharged.

In all cases:

New volume of water displaced = Old volume of water displaced

or

$$\frac{\text{New displacement}}{\text{New density}} = \frac{\text{Old displacement}}{\text{Old density}}$$

or

$$\frac{\text{New displacement}}{\text{Old displacement}} = \frac{\text{New density}}{\text{Old density}}$$

Example 1

A ship displaces 7000 tonnes whilst floating in fresh water. Find the displacement of the ship when floating at the same draft in water of density 1015 kg per cubic metre, i.e. 1.015 t/m³.

$$\frac{\text{New displacement}}{\text{Old displacement}} = \frac{\text{New density}}{\text{Old density}}$$

$$\text{New displacement} = \text{Old displacement} \times \frac{\text{New density}}{\text{Old density}}$$

$$= 7000 \times \frac{1015}{1000}$$

Ans. New displacement = 7105 tonnes

Example 2

A ship of 6400 tonnes displacement is floating in salt water. The ship has to proceed to a berth where the density of the water is 1008 kg per cu. m. Find how much cargo must be discharged if she is to remain at the salt water draft.

$$\frac{\text{New displacement}}{\text{Old displacement}} = \frac{\text{New density}}{\text{Old density}}$$

or

$$\text{New displacement} = \text{Old displacement} \times \frac{\text{New density}}{\text{Old density}}$$

$$= 6400 \times \frac{1008}{1025}$$

New displacement = 6293.9 tonnes

Old displacement = 6400.0 tonnes

Ans. Cargo to discharge = 106.1 tonnes

Example 3

A ship 120 m × 17 m × 10 m has a block coefficient 0.800 and is floating at the load Summer draft of 7.2 metres in fresh water. Find how much more cargo can be loaded to remain at the same draft in salt water.

$$\text{Old displacement} = L \times B \times \text{draft} \times C_b \times \text{density}$$

$$= 120 \times 17 \times 7.2 \times 0.800 \times 1000 \text{ tonnes}$$

$$\text{Old displacement} = 11\,750 \text{ tonnes}$$

$$\frac{\text{New displacement}}{\text{Old displacement}} = \frac{\text{New density}}{\text{Old density}}$$

$$\text{New displacement} = \text{Old displacement} \times \frac{\text{New density}}{\text{Old density}}$$

$$= 11,750 \times \frac{1025}{1000}$$

$$\text{New displacement} = 12\,044 \text{ tonnes}$$

$$\text{Old displacement} = 11\,750 \text{ tonnes}$$

Ans. Cargo to load = 294 tonnes

Note. This problem should not be attempted as one involving TPC and FWA.

Exercise 5

Density and draft

1   A ship displaces 7500 cu. m of water of density 1000 kg per cu. m. Find the displacement in tonnes when the ship is floating at the same draft in water of density 1015 kg per cu. m.

2   When floating in fresh water at a draft of 6.5 m a ship displaces 4288 tonnes. Find the displacement when the ship is floating at the same draft in water of density 1015 kg per cu. m.

3   A box-shaped vessel 24 m × 6 m × 3 m displaces 150 tonnes of water. Find the draft when the vessel is floating in salt water.

4   A box-shaped vessel draws 7.5 m in dock water of density 1006 kg per cu. m. Find the draft in salt water of density 1025 kg per cu. m.

5   The KB of a rectangular block which is floating in fresh water is 50 cm. Find the KB in salt water.

6   A ship is lying at the mouth of a river in water of density 1024 kg per cu. m and the displacement is 12 000 tonnes. The ship is to proceed up river and to berth in dock water of density 1008 kg per cu. m with the same draft as at present. Find how much cargo must be discharged.

7   A ship arrives at the mouth of a river in water of density 1016 kg per cu. m with a freeboard of 'S' m. She then discharges 150 tonnes of cargo, and proceeds up river to a second port, consuming 14 tonnes of bunkers. When she arrives at the second port the freeboard is again 'S' m., the density of the water being 1004 kg per cu. m. Find the ship's displacement on arrival at the second port.

8   A ship loads in fresh water to her salt water marks and proceeds along a river to a second port consuming 20 tonnes of bunkers. At the second port, where the density is 1016 kg per cu. m, after 120 tonnes of cargo have been loaded, the ship is again at the load salt water marks. Find the ship's load displacement in salt water.

The TPC and FWA etc.

9   A ship's draft is 6.40 metres forward, and 6.60 metres aft. FWA = 180 mm. Density of the dock water is 1010 kg per cu. m. If the load mean draft in salt water is 6.7 metres, find the final drafts F and A in dock water if this ship is to be loaded down to her marks and trimmed 0.15 metres by the stern. (Centre of flotation is amidships).

10   A ship floating in dock water of density 1005 kg per cu. m has the lower edge of her Summer load line in the waterline to starboard and 50 mm above the waterline to port. FWA = 175 mm and TPC = 12 tonnes. Find the amount of cargo which can yet be loaded in order to bring the ship to the load draft in salt water.

11   A ship is floating at 8 metres mean draft in dock water of relative density 1.01. TPC = 15 tonnes, and FWA = 150 mm. The maximum permissible draft in salt water is 8.1 m. Find the amount of cargo yet to load.

12   A ship's light displacement is 3450 tonnes and she has on board 800 tonnes of bunkers. She loads 7250 tonnes of cargo, 250 tonnes of bunkers, and 125 tonnes of fresh water. The ship is then found to be 75 mm from the load draft. TPC = 12 tonnes. Find the ship's deadweight and load displacement.

13   A ship has a load displacement of 5400 tonnes, TPC = 30 tonnes. If she loads to the Summer load line in dock water of density 1010 kg per cu. m, find the change in draft on entering salt water of density 1025 kg per cu. m.

14   A ship's FWA is 160 mm, and she is floating in dock water of density 1012 kg per cu. m. Find the change in draft when she passes from dock water to salt water.

Chapter 6
Transverse statical stability

Recapitulation

1. The centre of gravity of a body 'G' is the point through which the force of gravity is considered to act vertically downwards with a force equal to the weight of the body. KG is VCG of the ship.
2. The centre of buoyancy 'B' is the point through which the force of buoyancy is considered to act vertically upwards with a force equal to the weight of water displaced. It is the centre of gravity of the underwater volume. KB is VCB of the ship.
3. To float at rest in still water, a vessel must displace her own weight of water, and the centre of gravity must be in the same vertical line as the centre of buoyancy.
4. $KM = KB + BM$. Also $KM = KG + GM$.

Definitions

1. *Heel.* A ship is said to be heeled when she is inclined by an external force. For example, when the ship is inclined by the action of the waves or wind.
2. *List.* A ship is said to be listed when she is inclined by forces within the ship. For example, when the ship is inclined by shifting a weight transversely within the ship. This is a fixed angle of heel.

The metacentre

Consider a ship floating upright in still water as shown in Figure 6.1(a). The centres of gravity and buoyancy are at G and B respectively. Figure 6.1(c) shows the righting couple. GZ is the righting lever.

Now let the ship be inclined by an external force to a small angle (θ) as shown in Figure 6.1(b). Since there has been no change in the distribution of weights the centre of gravity will remain at G and the weight of the ship (W) can be considered to act vertically downwards through this point.

When heeled, the wedge of buoyancy WOW_1 is brought out of the water and an equal wedge LOL_1 becomes immersed. In this way a wedge of buoyancy having its centre of gravity at g is transferred to a position with its

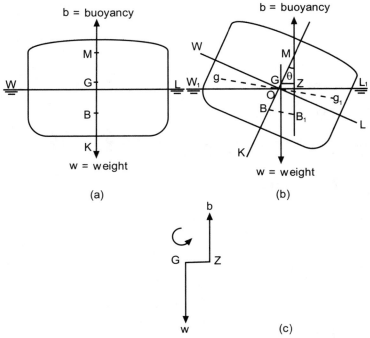

Righting couple where b = w

Fig. 6.1.   Stable equilibrium

centre of gravity at g_1. The centre of buoyancy, being the centre of gravity of the underwater volume, must shift from B to the new position B_1, such that BB_1 is parallel to gg_1, and $BB_1 = \dfrac{v \times gg_1}{V}$ where v is the volume of the transferred wedge, and V is the ship's volume of displacement.

The verticals through the centres of buoyancy at two consecutive angles of heel intersect at a point called the *metacentre*. For angles of heel up to about 15° the vertical through the centre of buoyancy may be considered to cut the centre line at a fixed point called the initial metacentre (M in Figure 6.1(b)). The height of the initial metacentre above the keel (KM) depends upon a ship's underwater form. Figure 6.2 shows a typical curve of KM's for a ship plotted against draft.

The vertical distance between G and M is referred to as the *metacentric height*. If G is below M the ship is said to have positive metacentric height, and if G is above M the metacentric height is said to be negative.

Equilibrium

Stable equilibrium

A ship is said to be in stable equilibrium if, when inclined, she tends to return to the initial position. For this to occur the centre of gravity must be

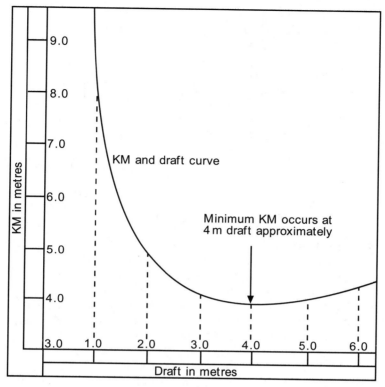

Fig. 6.2

below the metacentre, that is, the ship must have positive initial metacentric height. Figure 6.1(a) shows a ship in the upright position having a positive GM. Figure 6.1(b) shows the same ship inclined to a small angle. The position of G remains unaffected by the heel and the force of gravity is considered to act vertically downwards through this point. The centre of buoyancy moves out to the low side from B to B_1 to take up the new centre of gravity of the underwater volume, and the force of buoyancy is considered to act vertically upwards through B_1 and the metacentre M. If moments are taken about G there is a moment to return the ship to the upright. This moment is referred to as the *Moment of Statical Stability* and is equal to the product of the force 'W' and the length of the lever GZ. i.e.

Moment of Statical Stability $= W \times GZ$ *tonnes-metres.*

The lever GZ is referred to as the *righting lever* and is the perpendicular distance between the centre of gravity and the vertical through the centre of buoyancy.

At a small angle of heel (less than 15°):

$GZ = GM \times \sin\theta$ and Moment of Statical Stability $= W \times GM \times \sin\theta$

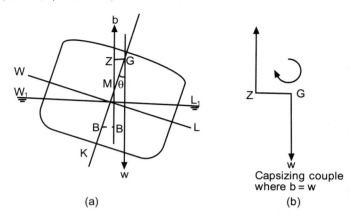

Fig. 6.3.   Unstable equilibrium.

Unstable equilibrium

When a ship which is inclined to a small angle tends to heel over still further, she is said to be in unstable equilibrium. For this to occur the ship must have a negative GM. Note how G is above M.

Figure 6.3(a) shows a ship in unstable equilibrium which has been inclined to a small angle. The moment of statical stability, $W \times GZ$, is clearly a capsizing moment which will tend to heel the ship still further.

Note. A ship having a very small negative initial metacentric height GM need not necessarily capsize. This point will be examined and explained later. This situation produces an angle of loll.

Neutral equilibrium

When G coincides with M as shown in Figure 6.4(a), the ship is said to be in neutral equilibrium, and if inclined to a small angle she will tend to remain

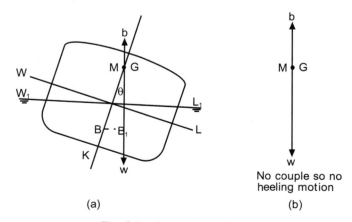

Fig. 6.4.   Neutral equilibrium.

at that angle of heel until another external force is applied. The ship has zero GM. Note that KG = KM.

Moment of Statical Stability = W × GZ, but in this case GZ = 0

∴ Moment of Statical Stability = 0 see Figure 6.4(b)

Therefore there is no moment to bring the ship back to the upright or to heel her over still further. The ship will move vertically up and down in the water at the fixed angle of heel until further external or internal forces are applied.

Correcting unstable and neutral equilibrium

When a ship in unstable or neutral equilibrium is to be made stable, the effective centre of gravity of the ship should be lowered. To do this one or more of the following methods may be employed:

1. weights already in the ship may be lowered,
2. weights may be loaded below the centre of gravity of the ship,
3. weights may be discharged from positions above the centre of gravity, or
4. free surfaces within the ship may be removed.

The explanation of this last method will be found in Chapter 7.

Stiff and tender ships

The *time period* of a ship is the time taken by the ship to roll from one side to the other and back again to the initial position.

When a ship has a comparatively large GM, for example 2 m to 3 m, the righting moments at small angles of heel will also be comparatively large. It will thus require larger moments to incline the ship. When inclined she will tend to return more quickly to the initial position. The result is that the ship will have a comparatively short time period, and will roll quickly – and perhaps violently – from side to side. A ship in this condition is said to be 'stiff', and such a condition is not desirable. The time period could be as low as 8 seconds. The effective centre of gravity of the ship should be raised within that ship.

When the GM is comparatively small, for example 0.16 m to 0.20 m the righting moments at small angles of heel will also be small. The ship will thus be much easier to incline and will not tend to return so quickly to the initial position. The time period will be comparatively long and a ship, for example 30 to 35 seconds, in this condition is said to be 'tender'. As before, this condition is not desirable and steps should be taken to increase the GM by lowering the effective centre of gravity of the ship.

The officer responsible for loading a ship should aim at a happy medium between these two conditions whereby the ship is neither too stiff nor too tender. A time period of 20 to 25 seconds would generally be acceptable for those on board a ship at sea.

Negative GM and angle of loll

It has been shown previously that a ship having a negative initial metacentric height will be unstable when inclined to a small angle. This is shown in Figure 6.5(a).

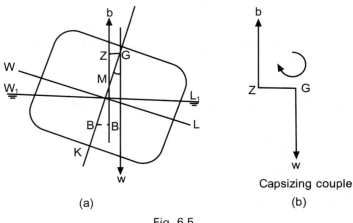

Capsizing couple

(a)   (b)

Fig. 6.5

As the angle of heel increases, the centre of buoyancy will move out still further to the low side. If the centre of buoyancy moves out to a position vertically under G, the capsizing moment will have disappeared as shown in Figure 6.5(b). The angle of heel at which this occurs is called the *angle of loll*. It will be noticed that at the angle of loll, the GZ is zero. G remains on the centre line.

If the ship is heeled beyond the angle of loll from θ_1 to θ_2, the centre of buoyancy will move out still further to the low side and there will be a moment to return her to the angle of loll as shown in Figure 6.5(c).

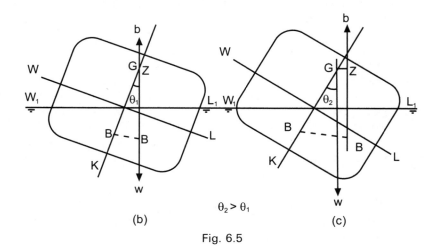

$\theta_2 > \theta_1$

(b)   (c)

Fig. 6.5

From this it can be seen that the ship will oscillate about the angle of loll instead of about the vertical. If the centre of buoyancy does not move out far enough to get vertically under G, the ship will capsize.

The angle of loll will be to port or starboard and back to port depending on external forces such as wind and waves. One minute it may flop over to 3° P and then suddenly flop over to 3° S.

There is always the danger that G will rise above M and create a situation of unstable equilibrium. This will cause capsizing of the ship.

Exercise 6

1 Define the terms 'heel', 'list', 'initial metacentre' and 'initial metacentric height'.
2 Sketch transverse sections through a ship, showing the positions of the centre of gravity, centre of buoyancy, and initial metacentre, when the ship is in (a) Stable equilibrium, (b) Unstable equilibrium, and (c) Neutral equilibrium.
3 Explain what is meant by a ship being (a) tender and, (b) stiff;
4 With the aid of suitable sketches, explain what is meant by 'angle of loll'.
5 A ship of 10 000 t displacement has an initial metacentric height of 1.5 m. What is the moment of statical stability when the ship is heeled 10 degrees?

The GM value

GM is crucial to ship stability. The table below shows *typical* working values for GM for several ship-types all at *fully-loaded* drafts.

Ship type	GM at fully-loaded condition
General cargo ships	0.30–0.50 m
Oil tankers to VLCCs	0.30–1.00 m
Container ships	1.50 m approx.
Ro-Ro vessels	1.50 m approx.
Bulk ore carriers	2–3 m

At drafts below the fully-loaded draft, due to KM tending to be larger in value it will be found that corresponding GM values will be *higher* than those listed in the table above. For all conditions of loading the D.Tp stipulate that the GM must never be less than 0.15 m.

Chapter 7
Effect of free surface of liquids on stability

When a tank is completely filled with a liquid, the liquid cannot move within the tank when the ship heels. For this reason, as far as stability is concerned, the liquid may be considered a static weight having its centre of gravity at the centre of gravity of the liquid within the tank.

Figure 7.1(a) shows a ship with a double-bottom tank filled with a liquid having its centre of gravity at g. The effect when the ship is heeled to a small angle θ is shown in Figure 7.1(b). No weights have been moved within the ship, therefore the position of G is not affected. The centre of buoyancy will move out to the low side indicated by BB_1.

$$\text{Moment of statical stability} = W \times GZ$$
$$= W \times GM \times \sin \theta$$

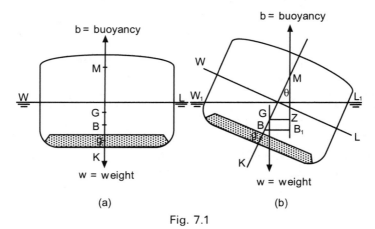

Fig. 7.1

Now consider the same ship floating at the same draft and having the same KG, but increase the depth of the tank so that the liquid now only partially fills it as shown in Figures 7.1(c) and 7.1(d).

When the ship heels, as shown in Figure 7.2, the liquid flows to the low side of the tank such that its centre of gravity shifts from g to g_1. This will cause the ship's centre of gravity to shift from G to G_1, parallel to gg_1.

$$\text{Moment of statical stability} = W \times G_1Z_1$$
$$= W \times G_vZ_v$$
$$= W \times G_vM \times \sin\theta$$

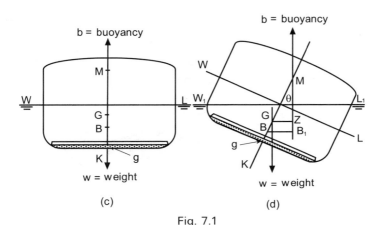

Fig. 7.1

This indicates that the effect of the free surface is to reduce the effective metacentric height from GM to G_vM. GG_v is therefore the virtual loss of GM due to the free surface. Any loss in GM is a loss in stability.

If free surface be created in a ship with a small initial metacentric height, the virtual loss of GM due to the free surface may result in a negative metacentric height. This would cause the ship to take up an angle of loll which may be dangerous and in any case is undesirable. This should be borne in mind when considering whether or not to run water ballast into tanks to correct an angle of loll, or to increase the GM. Until the tank is full there will be a virtual loss of GM due to the free surface effect of the liquid. It should also be noted from Figure 7.2 that even though the distance GG_1 is fairly small it produces a relatively large virtual loss in GM (GG_v).

Correcting an angle of loll

If a ship takes up an angle of loll due to a very small negative GM it should be corrected as soon as possible. GM may be, for example −0.05 to −0.10 m, well below the D.Tp. minimum stipulation of 0.15 m.

First make sure that the heel is due to a negative GM and not due to uneven distribution of the weights on board. For example, when bunkers are burned from one side of a divided double bottom tank it will obviously cause G to move to G_1, away from the centre of gravity of the burned bunkers, and will result in the ship listing as shown in Figure 7.3.

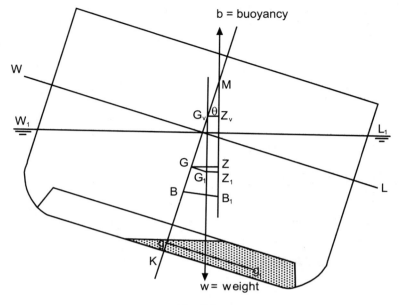

Fig. 7.2

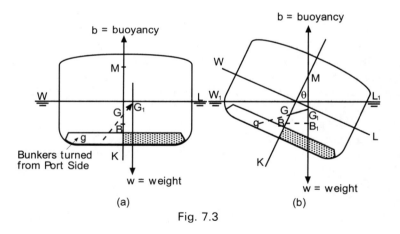

Fig. 7.3

Having satisfied oneself that the weights within the ship are uniformly distributed, one can assume that the list is probably due to a very small negative GM. To correct this it will be necessary to lower the position of the effective centre of gravity sufficiently to bring it below the initial metacentre. Any slack tanks should be topped up to eliminate the virtual rise of G due to free surface effect. If there are any weights which can be lowered within the ship, they should be lowered. For example, derricks may be lowered if any are topped; oil in deep tanks may be transferred to double bottom tanks, etc.

Assume now that all the above action possible has been taken and that the ship is still at an angle of loll. Assume also that there are double bottom tanks which are empty. Should they be filled, and if so, which ones first?

Before answering these questions consider the effect on stability during the filling operation. Free surfaces will be created as soon as liquid enters an empty tank. This will give a virtual rise of G which in turn will lead to an increased negative GM and an increased angle of loll. Therefore, if it is decided that it is safe to use the tanks, those which have the smallest area can be filled first so that the increase in list is cut to a minimum. Tanks should be filled one at a time.

Next, assume that it is decided to start by filling a tank which is divided at the centre line. Which side is to be filled first? If the high side is filled first the ship will start to right herself but will then roll suddenly over to take up a larger angle of loll on the other side, or perhaps even capsize. Now consider filling the low side first. Weight will be added low down in the vessel and G will thus be lowered, but the added weight will also cause G to move out of the centre line to the low side, increasing the list. Free surface is also being created and this will give a virtual rise in G, thus causing a loss in GM, which will increase the list still further.

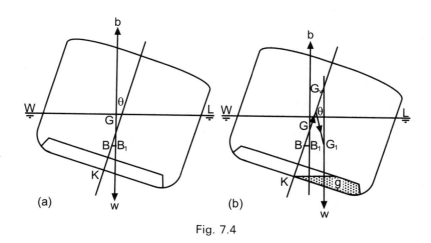

Fig. 7.4

Figure 7.4(a) shows a ship at an angle of loll with the double bottom tanks empty and in Figure 7.4(b) some water has been run into the low side. The shift of the centre of gravity from G to G_v is the virtual rise of G due to the free surface, and the shift from G_v to G_1 is due to the weight of the added water.

It can be seen from the figure that the net result is a moment to list the ship over still further, but the increase in list is a gradual and controlled increase. When more water is now run into the tank the centre of gravity of the ship will gradually move downwards and the list will start to decrease.

As the list decreases, water may be run into the other side of the tank. The water will then be running in much more quickly, causing G to move downwards more quickly. The ship cannot roll suddenly over to the other side as there is more water in the low side than in the high side. If sufficient weight of water is loaded to bring G on the centre line below M, the ship should complete the operation upright.

To summarize:

(a) Check that the list is due to a very small negative GM, for example −0.05 to −0.10 m.
(b) Top up any slack tanks and lower weights within the ship if possible.
(c) If the ship is still listed and it is decided to fill double-bottom tanks, start by filling the low side of a tank which is adequately sub-divided.
(d) The list is bound to be increased in the initial stages.
(e) Never start by filling tanks on the high side first.
(f) Always *calculate the effects first* before *authorizing action* to be taken to ballast any tanks.

Exercise 7

1   With the aid of suitable sketches, show the effect of slack tanks on a ship's stability.
2   A ship leaves port upright with a full cargo of timber, and with timber on deck. During the voyage, bunkers, stores and fresh water are consumed evenly from each side. If the ship arrives at her destination with a list, explain the probable cause of the list and how this should be remedied.
3   A ship loaded with timber and with timber on deck, berths with an angle of loll away from the quay. From which side should the timber on deck be discharged first and why?

Chapter 8
TPC and displacement curves

Recapitulation

The TPC is the mass which must be loaded or discharged to change the ship's mean draft by 1 cm. When the ship is floating in salt water it is found by using the formula:

$$TPC_{SW} = \frac{WPA}{97.56}$$

where

WPA = the area of the water-plane in sq metres.

The area of the water-plane of a box-shaped vessel is the same for all drafts if the trim be constant, and so the TPC will also be the same for all drafts.

In the case of a ship the area of the water-plane is not constant for all drafts, and therefore the TPC will reduce at lower drafts, as shown in Figure 8.1. The TPC's are calculated for a range of drafts extending beyond the light and loaded drafts and these are then tabulated or plotted on a graph. From the table or graph the TPC at intermediate drafts may be found.

TPC curves

When constructing a TPC curve the TPC's are plotted against the corresponding drafts. It is usually more convenient to plot the drafts on the vertical axis and the TPC' on the horizontal axis.

Example

(a) Construct a graph from the following information:

Mean draft (m)	3.0	3.5	4.0	4.5
TPC (tonnes)	8.0	8.5	9.2	10.0

(b) From this graph find the TPC's at drafts of 3.2 m; 3.7 m; and 4.3 m.

(c) If the ship is floating at a mean draft of 4 m and then loads 50 tonnes of cargo, 10 tonnes of fresh water, and 25 tonnes of bunkers, whilst 45 tonnes of ballast are discharged, find the final mean draft.

(a) For the graph see Figure 8.1
(b) TPC at 3.2 m draft   = 8.17 tonnes
     TPC at 3.7 m draft   = 8.77 tonnes
     TPC at 4.3 m draft   = 9.68 tonnes
(c) TPC at 4 m draft   = 9.2 tonnes

Loaded Cargo	50 tonnes
Fresh water	10 tonnes
Bunkers	25 tonnes
Total	85 tonnes

Discharged ballast   45 tonnes
Net loaded   40 tonnes

$$\text{Increase in draft} = \frac{W}{\text{TPC}}$$

$$= \frac{40}{9.2}$$

$$= 4.35 \text{ cm}$$

Increase in draft   = 0.044 m
Original draft   = 4.000 m
New mean draft = 4.044 m

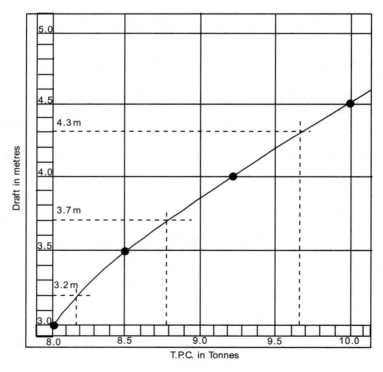

Fig. 8.1

Note. If the net weight loaded or discharged is very large, there is likely to be a considerable difference between the TPC's at the original and the new drafts, in which case to find the change in draft the procedure is as follows:

First find an approximate new draft using the TPC at the original draft, then find the TPC at the approximate new draft. Using the mean of these two TPC's find the actual increase or decrease in draft.

Displacement curves

A displacement curve is one from which the displacement of the ship at any particular draft can be found, and vice versa. The draft scale is plotted on the vertical axis and the scale of displacements on a horizontal axis. As a general rule the largest possible scale should be used to ensure reasonable accuracy. When the graph paper is oblong in shape, the length of the paper should be used for the displacement scale and the breadth for the drafts. It is quite unnecessary in most cases to start the scale from zero as the information will only be required for drafts between the light and load displacements (known as the boot-topping area).

Example

(a) Construct a displacement curve from the following data:

Draft (m)	3	3.5	4	4.5	5.0	5.5
Displacement (tonnes)	2700	3260	3800	4450	5180	6060

(b) If this ship's light draft is 3 m, and the load draft is 5.5 m, find the deadweight.

(c) Find the ship's draft when there are 500 tonnes of bunkers, and 50 tonnes of fresh water and stores on board.

(d) When at 5.13 m mean draft the ship discharges 2100 tonnes of cargo and loads 250 tonnes of bunkers. Find the new mean draft.

(e) Find the approximate TPC at 4.4 m mean draft.

(f) If the ship is floating at a mean draft of 5.2 m, and the load mean draft is 5.5 m, find how much more cargo may be loaded.

(a) See Figure 8.2 for the graph

(b) Load   Draft 5.5 m   Displacement   6060 tonnes
    Light   Draft 3.0 m   Displacement   2700 tonnes
    Deadweight = 3360 tonnes

(c) Light displacement   2700 tonnes
    Bunkers   +500 tonnes
    Fresh water and stores   +50 tonnes
    New displacement   3250 tonnes
    ∴ Draft = 3.48 m

(d) Displacement at 5.13 m   5380 tonnes
    Cargo discharged   −2100 tonnes
                               3280 tonnes
    Bunkers loaded   250 tonnes

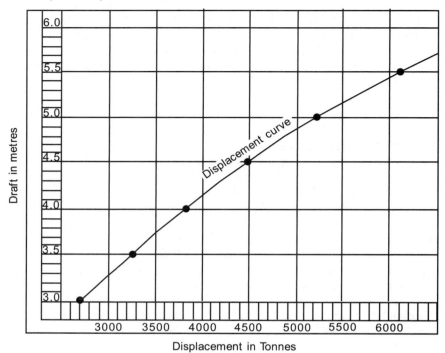

Fig. 8.2

New displacement   3530 tonnes
∴ New draft = 3.775 m

(e) At 4.5 m draft the displacement is   4450 tonnes
    At 4.3 m draft the displacement is   −4175 tonnes
    Difference to change the draft 0.2 m   275 tonnes

    Difference to change the draft 1 cm $\dfrac{275}{20}$ tonnes
∴ TPC = 13.75 tonnes

(f) Load draft 5.5 m   Displacement   6060 tonnes
    Present draft 5.2 m   Displacement   −5525 tonnes
                          Difference   535 tonnes
∴ Load 535 tonnes

In fresh water, the TPC is calculated as follows

$$TPC_{FW} = \frac{WPA}{100}$$

$$\text{or} \quad TPC_{FW} = TC_{SW} \times \frac{1.000}{1.025}.$$

Exercise 8

TPC curves

1 (a) Construct a TPC curve from the following data:

Mean draft (m)	1	2	3	4	5
TPC (tonnes)	3.10	4.32	5.05	5.50	5.73

   (b) From this curve find the TPC at drafts of 1.5 m and 2.1 m.

   (c) If this ship floats at 2.2 m mean draft and then discharges 45 tonnes of ballast, find the new mean draft.

2 (a) From the following information construct a TPC curve:

Mean draft (m)	1	2	3	4	5
Area of water-plane (sq m)	336	567	680	743	777

   (b) From this curve find the TPC's at mean drafts of 2.5 m and 4.5 m.

   (c) If, while floating at a draft of 3.8 m, the ship discharges 380 tonnes of cargo and loads 375 tonnes of bunkers, 5 tonnes of stores, and 125 tonnes of fresh water, find the new mean draft.

3 From the following information construct a TPC curve:

Mean draft (m)	1	3	5	7
TPC (tonnes)	4.7	10.7	13.6	15.5

Then find the new mean draft if 42 tonnes of cargo is loaded whilst the ship is floating at 4.5 m mean draft.

Displacement curves

4 (a) From the following information construct a displacement curve:

Displacement (tonnes)	376	736	1352	2050	3140	4450
Mean draft (m)	1	2	3	4	5	6

   (b) From this curve find the displacement at a draft of 2.3 m.

   (c) If this ship floats at 2.3 m mean draft and then loads 850 tonnes of cargo and discharges 200 tonnes of cargo, find the new mean draft.

   (d) Find the approximate TPC at 2.5 m mean draft.

5 The following information is taken from a ship's displacement scale:

Displacement (tonnes)	335	1022	1949	2929	3852	4841
Mean draft (m)	1	1.5	2	2.5	3	3.5

   (a) Construct the displacement curve for this ship and from it find the draft when the displacement is 2650 tonnes.

   (b) If this ship arrived in port with a mean draft of 3.5 m, discharged her cargo, loaded 200 tonnes of bunkers, and completed with a mean draft of 2 m, find how much cargo she discharged.

   (c) Assuming that the ship's light draft is 1 m, find the deadweight when the ship is floating in salt water at a mean draft of 1.75 m.

6 (a) From the following information construct a displacement curve:

Displacement (tonnes)	320	880	1420	2070	2800	3680
Draft (m)	1	1.5	2	2.5	3	3.5

   (b) If this ship's light draft is 1.1 m, and the load draft 3.5 m, find the deadweight.

   (c) If the vessel had on board 300 tonnes of cargo, 200 tonnes of ballast, and 60 tonnes of fresh water and stores, what would be the salt water mean draft.
7 (a) Construct a displacement curve from the following data:

Draft (m)	1	2	3	4	5	6
Displacement (tonnes)	335	767	1270	1800	2400	3100

   (b) The ship commenced loading at 3 m mean draft and, when work ceased for the day, the mean draft was 4.2 m. During the day 85 tonnes of salt water ballast had been pumped out. Find how much cargo had been loaded.
   (c) If the ship's light draft was 2 m find the mean draft after she had taken in 870 tonnes of water ballast and 500 tonnes of bunkers.
   (d) Find the TPC at 3 m mean draft.
8 (a) From the following information construct a displacement curve:

Draft (m)	1	2	3	4	5	6
Displacement (tonnes)	300	1400	3200	5050	7000	9000

   (b) If the ship is floating at a mean draft of 3.2 m, and then loads 1800 tonnes of cargo and 200 tonnes of bunkers, and also pumps out 450 tonnes of water ballast, find the new displacement and final mean draft.
   (c) At a certain draft the ship discharged 1700 tonnes of cargo and loaded 400 tonnes of bunkers. The mean draft was then found to be 4.5 m. Find the original mean draft.

Chapter 9
Form coefficients

The coefficient of fineness of the water-plane area (C_w)

The coefficient of fineness of the water-plane area is the ratio of the area of the water-plane to the area of a rectangle having the same length and maximum breadth.

In Figure 9.1 the area of the ship's water-plane is shown shaded and ABCD is a rectangle having the same length and maximum breadth.

$$\text{Coefficient of fineness } (C_w) = \frac{\text{Area of water-plane}}{\text{Area of rectangle ABCD}}$$

$$= \frac{\text{Area of water-plane}}{L \times B}$$

$$\therefore \text{ Area of the water-plane} = L \times B \times C_w$$

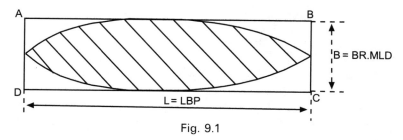

Fig. 9.1

Example 1

Find the area of the water-plane of a ship 36 metres long, 6 metres beam, which has a coefficient of fineness of 0.8.

$$\text{Area of water-plane} = L \times B \times C_w$$
$$= 36 \times 6 \times 0.8$$

Ans. Area of water-plane $= 172.8\,\text{sq m}$

Example 2

A ship 128 metres long has a maximum beam of 20 metres at the waterline, and coefficient of fineness of 0.85. Calculate the TPC at this draft.

$$\text{Area of water-plane} = L \times B \times C_w$$

$$= 128 \times 20 \times 0.85$$

$$= 2176 \text{ sq metres}$$

$$\text{TPC}_{SW} = \frac{\text{WPA}}{97.56}$$

$$= \frac{2176}{97.56}$$

Ans. $\underline{\text{TPC}_{SW} = 22.3 \text{ tonnes}}$

The block coefficient of fineness of displacement (C_b)

The block coefficient of a ship at any particular draft is the ratio of the volume of displacement at that draft to the volume of a rectangular block having the same overall length, breadth, and depth.

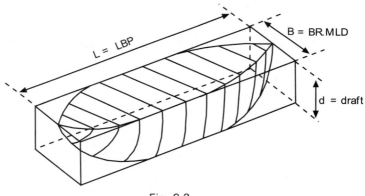

Fig. 9.2

In Figure 9.2 the shaded portion represents the volume of the ship's displacement at the draft concerned, enclosed in a rectangular block having the same overall length, breadth, and depth.

$$\text{Block coefficient } (C_b) = \frac{\text{Volume of displacement}}{\text{Volume of the block}}$$

$$= \frac{\text{Volume of displacement}}{L \times B \times \text{draft}}$$

$$\therefore \text{ Volume of displacement} = L \times B \times \text{draft} \times C_b$$

Ship's lifeboats

The cubic capacity of a lifeboat should be determined by Simpson's rules or by any other method giving the same degree of accuracy. The accepted C_b for a ship's lifeboat constructed of wooden planks is 0.6 and this is the figure to be used in calculations unless another specific value is given. Thus, the cubic capacity of a wooden lifeboat can be found using the formula:

$$\text{Volume} = (L \times B \times \text{Depth} \times 0.6) \text{ cubic metres.}$$

The number of persons which a lifeboat may be certified to carry is equal to the greatest whole number obtained by the formula V/x where 'V' is the cubic capacity of the lifeboat in cubic metres and 'x' is the volume in cubic metres for each person. 'x' is 0.283 for a lifeboat 7.3 metres in length or over, and 0.396 for a lifeboat 4.9 metres in length. For intermediate lengths of lifeboats, the value of 'x' is determined by interpolation.

Example 1

Find the number of persons which a wooden lifeboat 10 metres long, 2.7 metres wide, and 1 metre deep may be certified to carry.

$$\text{Volume of the boat} = (L \times B \times D \times 0.6) \text{ cu. m}$$
$$= 10 \times 2.7 \times 1 \times 0.6$$
$$= 16.2 \text{ cu. m}$$
$$\text{Number of persons} = V/x$$
$$= 16.2/0.283$$

Ans. Number of persons = 57

Example 2

A ship 64 metres long, 10 metres maximum beam, has a light draft of 1.5 metres and a load draft of 4 metres. The block coefficient of fineness is 0.6 at the light draft and 0.75 at the load draft. Find the deadweight.

$$\text{Light displacement} = L \times B \times \text{draft} \times C_b \text{ cu. m}$$
$$= 64 \times 10 \times 1.5 \times 0.6$$
$$= 576 \text{ cu. m}$$
$$\text{Load displacement} = L \times B \times \text{draft} \times C_b \text{ cu. m}$$
$$= 64 \times 10 \times 4 \times 0.75$$
$$= 1920 \text{ cu. m}$$
$$\text{Deadweight} = \text{Load displacement} - \text{Light displacement}$$
$$= (1920{-}576) \text{ cu. m}$$
$$\text{Deadweight} = 1344 \text{ cu. m}$$
$$= 1344 \times 1.025 \text{ tonnes}$$

Ans. Deadweight = 1377.6 tonnes

The midships coefficient (C$_m$)

The midships coefficient to any draft is the ratio of the transverse area of the midships Section (A$_m$) to a rectangle having the same breadth and depths.

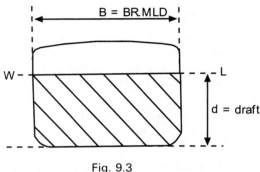

Fig. 9.3

In Figure 9.3 the shaded portion represents the area of the midships section to the waterline WL, enclosed in a rectangle having the same breadth and depth.

$$\text{Midships coefficient } (C_m) = \frac{\text{Midships area } (A_m)}{\text{Area of rectangle}}$$

$$= \frac{\text{Midships area } (A_m)}{B \times d}$$

or

$$\text{Midships area } (A_m) = B \times d \times C_m$$

The prismatic coefficient (C$_p$)

The prismatic coefficient of a ship at any draft is the ratio of the volume of displacement at that draft to the volume of a prism having the same length as the ship and the same cross-sectional area as the ship's midships area. The prismatic coefficient is used mostly by ship-model researchers.

In Figure 9.4 the shaded portion represents the volume of the ship's displacement at the draft concerned, enclosed in a prism having the same length as the ship and a cross-sectional area equal to the ship's midships area (A$_m$).

$$\text{Prismatic coefficient } (C_p) = \frac{\text{Volume of ship}}{\text{Volume of prism}}$$

$$= \frac{\text{Volume of ship}}{L \times A_m}$$

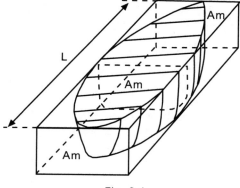

Fig. 9.4

or

$$\text{Volume of ship} = L \times A_m \times C_p$$

Note

$$C_m \times C_p = \frac{A_m}{B \times d} \times \frac{\text{Volume of ship}}{L \times A_m}$$

$$= \frac{\text{Volume of ship}}{L \times B \times d}$$

$$= C_b$$

$$\therefore C_m \times C_p = C_b$$

or

$$C_p = \frac{C_B}{C_m}$$

Note. C_p is always slightly higher than C_B at each waterline.

Having described exactly what C_w, C_b, C_w and C_p are, it would be useful to know what their values would be for several ship types.

First of all it must be remembered that all of these form coefficients will never be more than unity.

For the C_b values at *fully loaded drafts* the following table gives good typical values:

Ship type	Typical C_b fully loaded	Ship type	Typical C_b fully loaded
ULCC	0.850	General cargo ship	0.700
Supertanker	0.825	Passenger liner	0.625
Oil tanker	0.800	Container ship	0.575
Bulk carrier	0.750	Coastal tug	0.500

medium form ships (C_b approx. 0.700), full-form ships ($C_b > 0.700$), fine-form ships ($C_b < 0.700$).

To extimate a value for C_w for these ship types at their *fully loaded* drafts, it is useful to use the following rule-of-thumb approximation.

$$C_w = (\tfrac{2}{3} \times C_b) + \tfrac{1}{3} @ \text{ Draft Mld only!}$$

Hence, for the oil tanker, C_w would be 0.867, for the general cargo ship C_w would be 0.800 and for the tug C_w would be 0.667 in fully loaded conditions.

For merchant ships, the midships coefficient or midship area coefficient is 0.980 to 0.990 at fully loaded draft. It depends on the rise-of-floor and the bilge radius. Rise of floor is almost obsolete nowadays.

As shown before;

$$C_p = \frac{C_b}{C_m}$$

Hence for the bulk carrier, when C_b is 0.750 with a C_m of 0.985, the C_p will be:

$$C_p = \frac{0.750}{0.985} = 0.761 @ \text{ Draft Mld}$$

C_p is used mainly by researchers at ship-model tanks carrying out tests to obtain the least resistance for particular hull forms of prototypes.

C_b and C_w change as the drafts move from fully loaded to light-ballast to lightship conditions. The diagram (Figure 9.5) shows the curves at drafts below the fully loaded draft for a general cargo ship of 135.5 m LBP.

'K' is calculated for the fully loaded condition and is *held constant* for all remaining drafts down to the ship's lightship (empty ship) waterline.

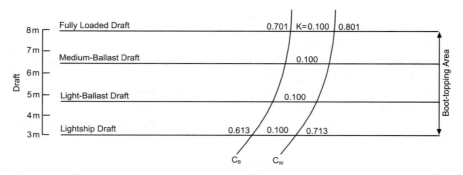

Fig. 9.5.   Variation of C_b and C_w values with draft. (Note how the two curves are parallel at a distance of 0.100 apart).

Exercise 9

1 (a) Define 'coefficient of fineness of the water-plane'.
   (b) The length of a ship at the waterline is 100 m, the maximum beam is 15 m, and the coefficient of fineness of the water-plane is 0.8. Find the TPC at this draft.

2 (a) Define 'block coefficient of fineness of displacement'.
   (b) A ship's length at the waterline is 120 m when floating on an even keel at a draft of 4.5 m. The maximum beam is 20 m. If the ship's block coefficient is 0.75, find the displacement in tonnes at this draft in salt water.

3 A ship is 150 m long, has 20 m beam, load draft 8 m, light draft 3 m. The block coefficient at the load draft is 0.766, and at the light draft is 0.668. Find the ship's deadweight.

4 A ship 120 m long × 15 m beam has a block coefficient of 0.700 and is floating at the load draft of 7 m in fresh water. Find how much more cargo can be loaded if the ship is to float at the same draft in salt water.

5 A ship 100 m long, 15 m beam, and 12 m deep, is floating on an even keel at a draft ot 6 m, block coefficient 0.8. The ship is floating in salt water. Find the cargo to discharge so that the ship will float at the same draft in fresh water.

6 A ship's lifeboat is 10 m long, 3 m beam, and 1.5 m deep. Find the number of persons which may be carried.

7 A ship's lifeboat measures 10 m × 2.5 m × 1 m. Find the number of persons which may be carried.

Chapter 10
Simpson's Rules for areas and centroids

Areas and volumes

Simpson's Rules may be used to find the areas and volumes of irregular figures. The rules are based on the assumption that the boundaries of such figures are curves which follow a definite mathematical law. When applied to ships they give a good approximation of areas and volumes. The accuracy of the answers obtained will depend upon the spacing of the ordinates and upon how near the curve follows the law.

Simpson's First Rule

This rule assumes that the curve is a parabola of the second order. A parabola of the second order is one whose equation, referred to co-ordinate axes, is of the form $y = a_0 + a_1x + a_2x^2$, where a_0, a_1, and a_2 are constants.

Let the curve in Figure 10.1 be a parabola of the second order. Let y_1, y_2 and y_3 be three ordinates equally spaced at 'h' units apart.

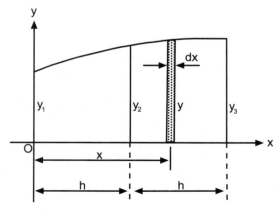

Fig. 10.1

The area of the elementary strip is ydx. Then the area enclosed by the curve and the axes of reference is given by

$$\text{Area of figure} = \int_O^{2h} y\,dx$$

$$\text{But } y = a_0 + a_1x + a_2x^2$$

$$\therefore \text{Area of figure} = \int_O^{2h} \left(a_0 + a_1x + a_2x^2\right) dx$$

$$= \left[a_0x + \frac{a_1x^2}{2} + \frac{a_2x^3}{3}\right]_O^{2h}$$

$$= 2a_0h + 2a_1h^2 + \tfrac{8}{3}a_2h^3$$

Assume that the area of figure $= Ay_1 + By_2 + Cy_3$

Using the equation of the curve and substituting 'x' for O, h and 2h respectively:

$$\text{Area of figure} = Aa_0 + B(a_0 + a_1h + a_2h^2)$$

$$+ C(a_0 + 2a_1h + 4a_2h^2)$$

$$= a_0(A + B + C) + a_1h(B + 2C)$$

$$+ a_2h^2(B + 4C)$$

$$\therefore 2a_0h + 2a_1h^2 + \tfrac{8}{3}a_2h^3 = a_0(A + B + C) + a_1h(B + 2C)$$

$$+ a_2h^2(B + 4C)$$

Equating coefficients:

$$A + B + C = 2h, \ B + 2C = 2h, \text{ and } B + 4C = \tfrac{8}{3}h$$

From which:

$$A = \frac{h}{3}, \ B = \frac{4h}{3}, \text{ and } C = \frac{h}{3}$$

$$\therefore \text{Area of figure} = \frac{h}{3}(y_1 + 4y_2 + y_3)$$

This is *Simpson's First Rule*.

It should be noted that Simpson's First Rule can also be used to find the area under a curve of the third order, i.e., a curve whose equation, referred to the co-ordinate axes, is of the form $y = a_0 + a_1x + a_2x^2 + a_3x^3$, where a_0, a_1, a_2 and a_3 are constants.

Summary:
A coefficient of $\frac{1}{3}$ with multipliers of 1, 4, 1 etc.

Simpson's Second Rule

This rule assumes that the equation of the curve is of the third order, i.e. of a curve whose equation, referred to the co-ordinate axes, is of the form $y = a_0 + a_1x + a_2x^2 + a_3x^3$, where a_0, a_1, a_2 and a_3 are constants.

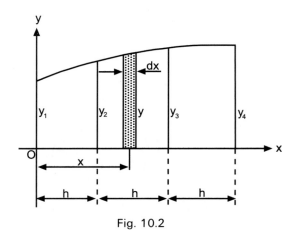

Fig. 10.2

In Figure 10.2:

Area of elementary strip $= y\,dx$

$$\text{Area of the figure} = \int_O^{3h} y\,dx$$

$$= \int_O^{3h} (a_0 + a_1x + a_2x^2 + a_3x^3)\,dx$$

$$= \left[a_0x + \tfrac{1}{2} a_1x^2 + \tfrac{1}{3} a_2x^3 + \tfrac{1}{4} a_3x^4\right]_O^{3h}$$

$$= 3a_0h + \tfrac{9}{2} a_1h^2 + 9a_2h^3 + \tfrac{81}{4} a_3h^4$$

Let the area of the figure $= Ay_1 + By_2 + Cy_3 + Dy_4$

$$= Aa_0 + B(a_0 + a_1h + a_2h^2 + a_3h^3)$$
$$+ C(a_0 + 2a_1h + 4a_2h^2 + 8a_3h^3)$$
$$+ D(a_0 + 3a_1h + 9a_2h^2 + 27a_3h^3)$$
$$= a_0(A + B + C + D) + a_1h(B + 2C + 3D)$$
$$+ a_2h^2(B + 4C + 9D) + a_3h^3(B + 8C + 27D)$$

Equating coefficients:

$$A + B + C + D = 3h$$

$$B + 2C + 3D = \frac{9}{2}h$$

$$B + 4C + 9D = 9h$$

$$B + 8C + 27D = \frac{81}{4}h$$

From which:

$$A = \tfrac{3}{8}h, \ B = \tfrac{9}{8}h, \ C = \tfrac{9}{8}h, \ \text{and} \ D = \tfrac{3}{8}h$$

$$\therefore \text{Area of figure} = \tfrac{3}{8}hy_1 + \tfrac{9}{8}hy_2 + \tfrac{9}{8}hy_3 + \tfrac{3}{8}hy_4$$

or

$$\text{Area of figure} = \tfrac{3}{8}h(y_1 + 3y_2 + 3y_3 + y_4)$$

This is *Simpson's Second Rule.*

Summary:
A coefficient of $\frac{3}{8}$ with multipliers of 1, 3, 3, 1 etc.

Simpson's Third Rule
In Figure 10.3:

$$\text{Area of the elementary strip} = ydx$$

$$\text{Area between } y_1 \text{ and } y_2 \text{ in figure} = \int_O^h ydx$$

$$= a_0h + \tfrac{1}{2}a_1h^2 + \tfrac{1}{3}a_2h^3$$

Let the area between y_1 and $y_2 = Ay_1 + By_2 + Cy_3$

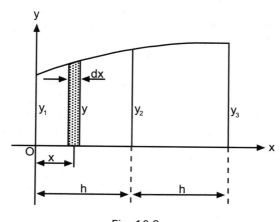

Fig. 10.3

$$\text{Then area} = Aa_0 + B(a_0 + a_1h + a_2h^2)$$
$$+ C(a_0 + 2a_1h + 4a_2h^2)$$
$$= a_0(A + B + C) + a_1h(B + 2C)$$
$$+ a_2h^2(B + 4C)$$

Equating coefficients:

$$A + B + C = h, \; B + 2C = h/2, \; B + 4C = h/3$$

From which:

$$A = \frac{5h}{12}, \; B = \frac{8h}{12}, \; \text{and } C = -\frac{h}{12}$$

∴ Area of figure between y_1 and $y_2 = \frac{5}{12}hy_1 + \frac{8}{12}hy_2 + \left(-\frac{1}{12}hy_3\right)$

or

$$\text{Area} = \frac{h}{12}(5y_1 + 8y_2 - y_3)$$

This is the *Five/eight (or Five/eight minus one) rule, and is used to find the area between two consecutive ordinates when three consecutive ordinates are known.*

Summary:
A coefficient of $\frac{1}{12}$ with multipliers of 5, 8, −1 etc.

Areas of water-planes and similar figures using extensions of Simpson's Rules

Since a ship is uniformly built about the centre line it is only necessary to calculate the area of half the water-plane and then double the area found to obtain the area of the whole water-plane.

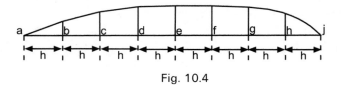

Fig. 10.4

Figure 10.4 represents the starboard side of a ship's water-plane area. To find the area, the centre line is divided into a number of equal lengths each 'h' m. long. The length 'h' is called the *common interval*. The half-breadths, a, b, c, d, etc., are then measured and each of these is called a *half-ordinate*.

Using Simpson's First Rule
This rule can be used to find areas when there are an odd number of ordinates.

$$\text{Area of Figure 10.5(a)} = \frac{h}{3}(a + 4b + c)$$

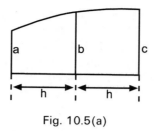

Fig. 10.5(a)

If the common interval and the ordinates are measured in metres, the area found will be in square metres.

Let this rule now be applied to a water-plane area such as that shown in Figure 10.5(b).

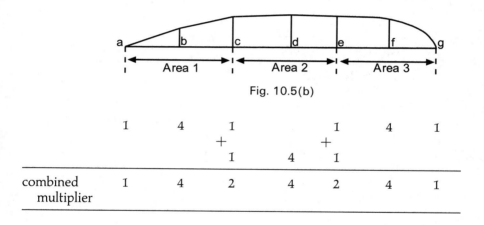

Fig. 10.5(b)

	1	4	1		1	4	1
			+		+		
			1	4	1		
combined multiplier	1	4	2	4	2	4	1

The water-plane is divided into three separate areas and Simpson's First Rule is used to find each separate area.

$$\text{Area } 1 = h/3(a + 4b + c)$$
$$\text{Area } 2 = h/3(c + 4d + e)$$
$$\text{Area } 3 = h/3(e + 4f + g)$$
$$\text{Area of } \tfrac{1}{2} \text{ WP} = \text{Area } 1 + \text{Area } 2 + \text{Area } 3$$

$$\therefore \text{ Area of } \tfrac{1}{2} \text{ WP} = h/3(a + 4b + c) + h/3(c + 4d + e)$$
$$+ h/3(e + 4f + g)$$
$$\text{or Area of } \tfrac{1}{2} \text{ WP} = h/3(a + 4b + 2c + 4d + 2e + 4f + g)$$

This is the form in which the formula should be used. Within the brackets the half-ordinates appear in their correct sequence from forward to aft. The coefficients of the half-ordinates are referred to as Simpson's Multipliers and they are in the form: 1424241. Had there been nine half-ordinates, the Multipliers would have been: 142424241. It is usually much easier to set out that part of the problem within the brackets in tabular form. Note how the Simpson's multipliers begin and end with 1, as shown in Figure 10.5(b).

Example

A ship 120 metres long at the waterline has equidistantly spaced half-ordinates commencing from forward as follows:

$$0, 3.7, 5.9, 7.6, 7.5, 4.6, 0.1 \text{ metres respectively.}$$

Find the area of the water-plane and the TPC at this draft.
Note. There is an odd number of ordinates in the water-plane and therefore the First Rule can be used.

No.	$\frac{1}{2}$ ord.	SM	Area function
a	0	1	0
b	3.7	4	14.8
c	5.9	2	11.8
d	7.6	4	30.4
e	7.5	2	15.0
f	4.6	4	18.4
g	0.1	1	0.1
			$90.5 = \Sigma_1$

Σ_1 is used because it is a total; using Simpson's First Rule:

$$h = \frac{120}{6} = \text{the common interval CI}$$

$$\therefore \text{CI} = 20 \text{ metres}$$

$$\text{Area of WP} = \tfrac{1}{3} \times \text{CI} \times \Sigma_1 \times 2 \text{ (for both sides)}$$

$$= \tfrac{1}{3} \times 20 \times 90.5 \times 2$$

Ans. Area of WP = 1207 sq m

$$\text{TPC}_{SW} = \frac{\text{WPA}}{97.56} = \frac{1207}{97.56}$$

Ans. TPC = 12.37 tonnes

Note. If the half-ordinates are used in these calculations, then the area of half the water-plane is found. If however the whole breadths are used, the total area of the water-plane will be found. If half-ordinates are given and the WPA is requested, simply multiply by 2 at the end of the formula as shown above.

Using the extension of Simpson's Second Rule

This rule can be used to find the area when the number of ordinates is such that if one be subtracted from the number of ordinates the remainder is divisible by 3.

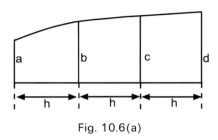

Fig. 10.6(a)

$$\text{Area of Figure } 10.6(a) = \tfrac{3}{8}\, h(a + 3b + 3c + d)$$

Now consider a water-plane area which has been divided up using seven half-ordinates as shown in Figure 10.6(b).

The water-plane can be split into two sections as shown, each section having four ordinates.

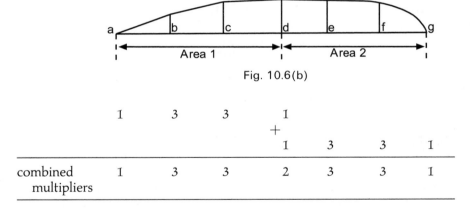

Fig. 10.6(b)

1	3	3	1			
			+			
			1	3	3	1

combined multipliers	1	3	3	2	3	3	1

$$\text{Area } 1 = \tfrac{3}{8}\, h(a + 3b + 3c + d)$$

$$\text{Area } 2 = \tfrac{3}{8}\, h(d + 3e + 3f + g)$$

$$\text{Area of } \tfrac{1}{2}\, \text{WP} = \text{Area } 1 + \text{Area } 2$$

$$\therefore \text{Area of } \tfrac{1}{2}\, \text{WP} = \tfrac{3}{8}\, h(a + 3b + 3c + d) + \tfrac{3}{8}\, h(d + 3e + 3f + g)$$

or

$$\text{Area of } \tfrac{1}{2}\, \text{WP} = \tfrac{3}{8}\, h(a + 3b + 3c + 2d + 3e + 3f + g)$$

This is the form in which the formula should be used. As before, all of the ordinates appear in their correct order within the brackets. The multipliers are now 1332331. Had there been ten ordinates the multipliers would have been 1332332331. Note how the Simpson's multipliers begin and end with 1, as shown in Figure 10.6(b).

Example

Find the area of the water-plane described in the first example using Simpson's Second Rule.

No.	$\frac{1}{2}$ ord.	SM	Area function
a	0	1	0
b	3.7	3	11.1
c	5.9	3	17.7
d	7.6	2	15.2
e	7.5	3	22.5
f	4.6	3	13.8
g	0.1	1	0.1
			$80.4 = \Sigma_2$

Σ_2 is used because it is a total; using Simpson's Second Rule:

$$\text{Area WP} = \tfrac{3}{8} \times \text{CI} \times \Sigma_2 \times 2 \text{ (for both sides)}$$

$$= \tfrac{3}{8} \times 20 \times 80.4 \times 2$$

Ans. Area WP = 1206 sq m   (compared to 1207 sq. m previous answer)

The small difference in the two answers shows that the area found can only be a close approximation to the correct area.

The Five/Eight Rule (Simpson's Third Rule)

This rule may be used to find the area between two consecutive ordinates when three consecutive ordinates are known.

The rule states that the area between two consecutive ordinates is equal to five times the first ordinate plus eight times the middle ordinate minus the external ordinate, all multiplied by $\frac{1}{12}$ of the common interval.

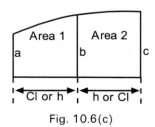

Fig. 10.6(c)

$$\text{Thus: Area 1} = \frac{h}{12}(5a + 8b - c) \text{ or } \frac{1}{12} \times CI \times \Sigma_3$$

$$\text{Also: Area 2} = \frac{h}{12}(5c + 8b - a) \text{ or } \frac{1}{12} \times CI \times \Sigma_3$$

Σ_3 is used because it is a total; using Simpson's Third Rule. Consider the next example.

Example

Three consecutive ordinates in a ship's water-plane, spaced 6 metres apart, are 14 m, 15 m, and 15.5 m respectively. Find the area between the last two ordinates.

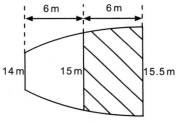

Fig. 10.6(d)

$$\text{Shaded Area} = \frac{h}{12}(5a + 8b - c)$$

$$= \frac{6}{12}(77.5 + 120 - 14)$$

Ans. Area = 91.75 sq m

Volumes of ship shapes and similar figures

Let the area of the elementary strip in Figures 10.7(a) and (b) be 'Y' square metres. Then the volume of the strip in each case is equal to Y dx and the volume of each ship is equal to $\int_O^{4h} Y \, dx$.

The value of the integral in each case is found by Simpson's Rules using the areas at equidistant intervals as ordinates. i.e.

$$\text{Volume} = \frac{h}{3}(A + 4B + 2C + 4D + E)$$

or

$$\frac{CI}{3} \times \Sigma_1$$

Thus the volume of displacement of a ship to any particular draft can be found first by calculating the areas of water-planes or transverse areas at equidistant intervals and then using these areas as ordinates to find the volume by Simpson's Rules.

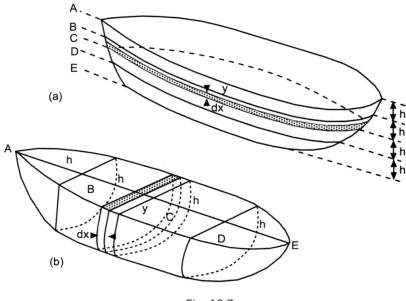

Fig. 10.7

Example

The areas of a ship's water-planes are as follows:

Draft (m)	0	1	2	3	4
Area of WP (sq m)	650	660	662	661	660

Calculate the ship's displacement in tonnes when floating in salt water at 4 metres draft. Also, if the ship's load draft is 4 metres. find the FWA.

Draft (m)	Area	SM	Volume function
0	650	1	650
1	660	4	2640
2	662	2	1324
3	661	4	2644
4	660	1	660
			$7918 = \Sigma_1$

Σ_1 is used because it is a total; using Simpson's First Rule:

$$\text{Underwater volume} = \tfrac{1}{3} \times CI \times \Sigma_1 = \tfrac{1}{3} \times 1.0 \times 7918$$

$$= 2639\,\tfrac{1}{3}\,\text{Cu. m}$$

$$\text{SW displacement} = 2639\,\tfrac{1}{3} \times 1.025\,\text{tonnes}$$

Ans. SW displacement = 2705.3 tonnes

$$\text{Load TPC}_{SW} = \frac{\text{WPA}}{97.56}$$

$$= \frac{660}{97.56}$$

$$= 6.77\,\text{tonnes}$$

$$\text{FWA} = \frac{\text{Displacement}}{4 \times \text{TPC}}$$

$$= \frac{2705.3}{4 \times 6.77}$$

Ans. FWA = 99.9 mm or 9.99 cm

Appendages and intermediate ordinates

Appendages

It has been mentioned previously that areas and volumes calculated by the use of Simpson's Rules depend for their accuracy on the curvature of the sides following a definite mathematical law. It is very seldom that the ship's sides do follow one such curve. Consider the ship's water-plane area shown in Figure 10.8. The sides from the stem to the quarter form one curve but from this point to the stern is part of an entirely different curve. To obtain an answer which is as accurate as possible, the area from the stem to the quarter may be calculated by the use of Simpson's Rules and then the remainder of the area may be found by a second calculation. The remaining area mentioned above is referred to as an *appendage*.

Similarly, in Figure 10.9 the side of the ship forms a reasonable curve from the waterline down to the turn of the bilge, but below this point the curve is one of a different form.

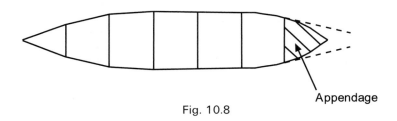

Appendage

Fig. 10.8

In this case the volume of displacement between the waterline (WL) and the water-plane XY could be found by use of Simpson's Rules and then the volume of the appendage found by means of a second calculation.

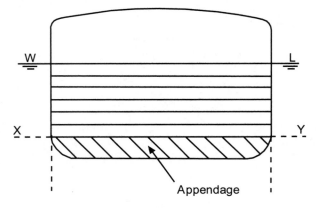

Fig. 10.9

Example
A ship's breadths, at 9 m intervals commencing from forward are as follows:

0, 7.6, 8.7, 9.2, 9.5, 9.4, and 8.5 metres respectively.

Abaft the last ordinate is an appendage of 50 sq m. Find the total area of the water-plane.

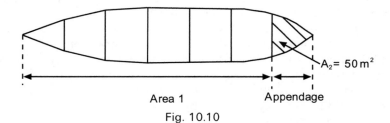

Fig. 10.10

Ord.	SM	Product for area
0	1	0
7.6	4	30.4
8.7	2	17.4
9.2	4	36.8
9.5	2	19.0
9.4	4	37.6
8.5	1	8.5
		$149.7 = \Sigma_1$

$$\text{Area } 1 = \tfrac{1}{3} \times CI \times \Sigma_1$$

$$\text{Area } 1 = \tfrac{2}{3} \times 149.7$$

$$\text{Area } 1 = 449.1 \, \text{sq. m}$$

$$\text{Appendage} = 50.0 \, \text{sq. m} = \text{Area } 2$$

$$\underline{\text{Area of WP} = 499.1 \, \text{sq. m}}$$

Subdivided common intervals

The area or volume of an appendage may be found by the introduction of intermediate ordinates. Referring to the water-plane area shown in Figure 10.11, the length has been divided into seven equal parts and the half ordinates have been set up. Also, the side is a smooth curve from the stem to the ordinate 'g'.

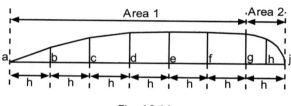

Fig. 10.11

If the area of the water-plane is found by putting the eight half-ordinates directly through the rules, the answer obtained will obviously be an erroneous one. To reduce the error the water-plane may be divided into two parts as shown in the figure.

Then,

$$\text{Area No. } 1 = h/3(a + 4b + 2c + 4d + 2e + 4f + g)$$

To find Area No. 2, an intermediate semi-ordinate is set up midway between the semi-ordinates g and j. The common interval for this area is $h/2$.

Then,

$$\text{Area No. } 2 = h/2 \times \tfrac{1}{3} \times (g + 4h + j)$$

or,

$$\text{Area No. } 2 = h/3(\tfrac{1}{2} g + 2h + \tfrac{1}{2} j)$$

If CI is halved, then multipliers are halved, i.e. from 1, 4, 1 etc. to $\tfrac{1}{2}$, 2, $\tfrac{1}{2}$.

$$\begin{aligned}
\text{Area of } \tfrac{1}{2} \text{WP} &= \text{Area } 1 + \text{Area } 2 \\
&= h/3(a + 4b + 2c + 4d + 2e + 4f + g) \\
&\quad + h/3(\tfrac{1}{2} g + 2h + \tfrac{1}{2} j) \\
&= h/3(a + 4b + 2c + 4d + 2e + 4f + g + \tfrac{1}{2} g \\
&\quad + 2h + \tfrac{1}{2} j)
\end{aligned}$$

$$\therefore \text{ Area of } \tfrac{1}{2} \text{WP} = h/3(a + 4b + 2c + 4d + 2e + 4f + 1\tfrac{1}{2}\,g$$
$$+ 2h + \tfrac{1}{2}\,j) \quad \text{or} \quad \tfrac{1}{3} \times h \times \Sigma_1$$

Example 1

The length of a ship's water-plane is 100 metres. The lengths of the half-ordinates commencing from forward are as follows:

0, 3.6, 6.0, 7.3, 7.7, 7.6, 4.8, 2.8 and 0.6 metres respectively.

Midway between the last two half-ordinates is one whose length is 2.8 metres. Find the area of the waterplane.

$\tfrac{1}{2}$ ord.	SM	Area function
0	1	0
3.6	4	14.4
6.0	2	12.0
7.3	4	29.2
7.7	2	15.4
7.6	4	30.4
4.8	$1\tfrac{1}{2}$	7.2
2.8	2	5.6
0.6	$\tfrac{1}{2}$	0.3
		$114.5 = \Sigma_1$

$$\text{Area} = \tfrac{2}{3} \times \text{CI} \times \Sigma_1$$
$$\text{CI} = 100/7 = 14.29\,\text{m}$$
$$\text{Area of WP} = \tfrac{2}{3} \times 14.29 \times 114.5$$

Ans. Area of WP = 1, 090.5 sq m

Note how the CI used was the *Largest* CI in the ship's water-plane.

In some cases an even more accurate result may be obtained by dividing the water-plane into three separate areas as shown in Figure 10.12 and introducing intermediate semi-ordinates at the bow and the stern.

$$\text{Area 1} = h/2 \times \tfrac{1}{3} \times (a + 4b + c)$$
$$= h/3(\tfrac{1}{2}\,a + 2b + \tfrac{1}{2}\,c)$$
$$\text{Area 2} = h/3(c + 4d + 2e + 4f + g)$$
$$\text{Area 3} = h/2 \times \tfrac{1}{3}(g + 4h + j)$$
$$= h/3(\tfrac{1}{2}\,g + 2h + \tfrac{1}{2}\,j)$$

Area $\frac{1}{2}$ WP = Area 1 + Area 2 + Area 3

$$= h/3(\tfrac{1}{2}a + 2b + \tfrac{1}{2}c) + c + 4d + 2e + 4f + g$$

$$+ \tfrac{1}{2}g + 2h + \tfrac{1}{2}j$$

Area $\frac{1}{2}$ WP = $h/3(\tfrac{1}{2}a + 2b + 1\tfrac{1}{2}c + 4d + 2e + 4f + 1\tfrac{1}{2}g$

$$+ 2h + \tfrac{1}{2}j)$$ or $h/3 \times \Sigma_I$

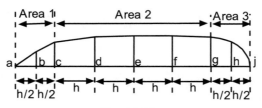

Fig. 10.12

	$\frac{1}{2}$	2	$\frac{1}{2}$		1	4	1			
			+				+			
			1	4	1		$\frac{1}{2}$	2	$\frac{1}{2}$	
combined multipliers	$\frac{1}{2}$	2	$1\frac{1}{2}$	4	2	4	$1\frac{1}{2}$	2	$\frac{1}{2}$	

Example 2

A ship's water-plane is 72 metres long and the lengths of the half-ordinates commencing from forward are as follows:

0.2, 2.2, 4.4, 5.5, 5.8, 5.9. 5.9, 5.8, 4.8, 3.5 and 0.2 metres respectively.

$\frac{1}{2}$ ord.	SM	Area function
0.2	$\frac{1}{2}$	0.1
2.2	2	4.4
4.4	$1\frac{1}{2}$	6.6
5.5	4	22.0
5.8	2	11.6
5.9	4	23.6
5.9	2	11.8
5.8	4	23.2
4.8	$1\frac{1}{2}$	7.2
3.5	2	7.0
0.2	$\frac{1}{2}$	0.1
		$117.6 = \Sigma_I$

The spacing between the first three and the last three half-ordinates is half of the spacing between the other half-ordinates. Find the area of the water-plane.

$$\text{Area} = \tfrac{1}{3} \times \text{CI} \times \Sigma_1 \times 2$$

$$\text{CI} = 72/8 = 9\,\text{m}$$

$$\text{Area of WP} = \tfrac{1}{3} \times 9 \times 117.6 \times 2$$

Ans. Area of WP = 705.6 sq. m

Note. It will be seen from this table that the effect of halving the common interval is to halve the Simpson's Multipliers.

Σ_1 is because it is using Simpson's First Rule.

Areas and volumes having an awkward number of ordinates

Occasionally the number of ordinates used is such that the area or volume concerned cannot be found directly by use of either the First or the Second Rule. In such cases the area or volume should be divided into two parts, the area of each part being calculated separately, and the total area found by adding the areas of the two parts together.

Example 1

Show how the area of a water-plane may be found when using six semi-ordinates. Neither the First nor the Second Rule can be applied directly to the whole area but the water-plane can be divided into two parts as shown in Figure 10.13 Area No. 1 can be calculated using the First Rule and area No. 2 by the Second Rule. The areas of the two parts may then be added together to find the total area.

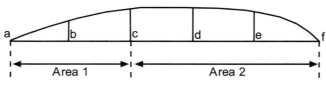

Fig. 10.13

An alternative method would be to find the area between the half-ordinates a and e by the First Rule and then find the area between the half-ordinates e and f by the 'five-eight' Rule.

Example 2

Show how the area may be found when using eight semi-ordinates.

Divide the area up as shown in Figure 10.14. Find area No. 1 using the Second Rule and area No. 2 using the First Rule.

An alternative method is again to find the area between the half-ordinates a

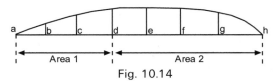

Fig. 10.14

and g by the first rule and the area between the half-ordinates g and h by the 'five-eight' rule.

In practice, the naval architect divides the ship's length into 10 stations and then subdivides the forward and aft ends in order to obtain extra accuracy with the calculations.

In doing so, the calculations can be made using Simpson's First and Second Rules, perhaps as part of a computer package.

Centroids and centres of gravity

To find the centre of flotation

The *centre of flotation* is the centre of gravity or *centroid* of the water-plane area, and is the point about which a ship heels and trims. It must lie on the longitudinal centre line but may be slightly forward or aft of amidships (from say 3 per cent L forward of amidships for oil tankers to say 3 per cent L aft of amidships for container ships).

To find the area of a water-plane by Simpson's Rules, the half-breadths are used as ordinates. If the moments of the half-ordinates about any point are used as ordinates, then the total moment of the area about that point will be found. If the total moment is now divided by the total area, the quotient will give the distance of the centroid of the area from the point about which the moments were taken. This may be shown as follows:

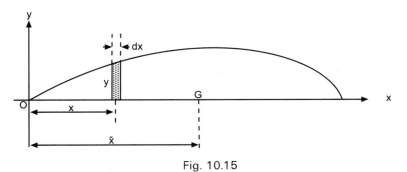

Fig. 10.15

In Figure 10.15:

$$\text{Area of strip} = y \cdot dx$$

$$\text{Area of the } \tfrac{1}{2} \text{ WP} = \int_{O}^{L} y \cdot dx$$

$$\text{Area of the WP} = 2 \cdot \int_O^L y \cdot dx$$

The value of the integral is found using the formula:

$$\int_O^L y \cdot dx = \frac{h}{3}(a + 4b + 2c + 4d + e)$$

Thus, the value of the integral is found by Simpson's Rules using values of the variable y as ordinates.

$$\text{Moment of strip about OY} = x \cdot y \cdot dx$$

$$\text{Moment of } \tfrac{1}{2} \text{ WP about OY} = \int_O^L x \cdot y \cdot dx$$

$$\text{Moment of WP about OY} = 2 \cdot \int_O^L x \cdot y \cdot dx$$

The value of this integral is found by Simpson's Rules using values of the product $x \cdot y$ as ordinates.

Let the distance of the centre of flotation be $\bar{X}$ from OY, then:

$$\bar{X} = \frac{\text{Moment}}{\text{Area}}$$

$$= \frac{2 \cdot \int_O^L x \cdot y \cdot dx}{2 \cdot \int_O^L y \cdot dx} = \frac{\Sigma_2}{\Sigma_1} \times CI$$

Example 1

A ship 150 metres long has half-ordinate commencing from aft as follows:

0, 5, 9, 9, 9, 7 and 0 metres respectively.

Find the distance of the centre of flotation from forward (see Fig. 10.16).
Note. To avoid using large numbers the levers used are in terms of CI the common interval. It is more efficient than using levers in metres (see table on facing page).

$$\text{Area of the water-plane} = \tfrac{2}{3} \times CI \times \Sigma_1$$

$$= \tfrac{2}{3} \times 25 \times 376 \text{ sq. m}$$

$$\text{Distance of C. F. from aft} = \frac{\Sigma_2}{\Sigma_1} \times CI$$

$$= \frac{376}{120} \times CI$$

$$= 78.33 \text{ m}$$

Ans. C. F. is 78.33 m from aft

½ Ordinate		SM	Products for area	Levers from A*	Moment function
Aft	0	1	0	0	0
	5	4	20	1	20
	9	2	18	2	36
⊗	9	4	36	3	108
	9	2	18	4	72
	7	4	28	5	140
Forward	0	1	0	6	0
			$\overline{120 = \Sigma_1}$		$\overline{376 = \Sigma_2}$

*The Levers are in terms of the number of CI from the aft ordinate through to the foremost ordinate.

Σ_1, because it is the first total.

Σ_2, because it is the second total.

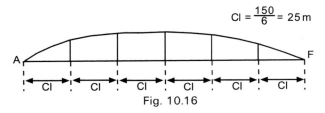

$$CI = \frac{150}{6} = 25\,m$$

Fig. 10.16

This problem can also be solved by taking the moments about amidships as in the following example:

Example 2

A ship 75 m long has half-ordinates at the load water-plane commencing from aft as follows:

0, 1, 2, 4, 5, 5, 5, 4, 3, 2 and 0 metres respectively.

The spacing between the first three semi-ordinates and the last three semi-ordinates is half of that between the other semi-ordinates. Find the position of the Centre of Flotation relative to amidships.

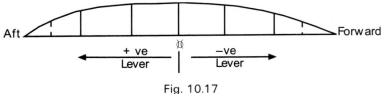

Fig. 10.17

Use +ve the sign for levers and moments AFT of amidships (⊗).

Use −ve sign for levers and moments FORWARD of amidships (⊗).

$\frac{1}{2}$ Ordinate		SM	Area function	Levers	Moment function
Aft	0	$\frac{1}{2}$	0	+4	0
	1	2	2	$+3\frac{1}{2}$	+7
	2	$1\frac{1}{2}$	3	+3	+9
	4	4	16	+2	+32
	5	2	10	+1	+10
⟨⟩	5	4	20	0	0
	5	2	10	−1	−10
	4	4	16	−2	−32
	3	$1\frac{1}{2}$	4.5	−3	−13.5
	2	2	4.0	$-3\frac{1}{2}$	−14
Forward	0	$\frac{1}{2}$	0	−4	0
			$85.5 = \Sigma_1$		$-11.5 = \Sigma_2$

$$CI = \frac{75}{8} = 9.375 \, m$$

Σ_1 denotes first total.
Σ_2 denotes second algebriac total.
The point having a lever of zero is the fulcrum point. All other levers +ve and
−ve are then relative to this point.

$$\text{Distance of C. F. from admidships} = \frac{\Sigma_2}{\Sigma_1} \times CI$$

$$= \frac{-11.5}{85.5} \times 9.375$$

$$= -1.26 \, m$$

The −ve sign shows it is forward of ⟨⟩.
Ans. C. F. is 1.26 metres forward of amidships

To find the KB
The centre of buoyancy is the three-dimensional centre of gravity of the
underwater volume and Simpson's Rules may be used to determine its
height above the keel.

First, the areas of water-planes are calculated at equidistant intervals of
draft between the keel and the waterline. Then the volume of displacement
is calculated by using these areas as ordinates in the rules. The moments of
these areas about the keel are then taken to find the total moment of the
underwater volume about the keel. The KB is then found by dividing the
total moment about the keel by the volume of displacement.

It will be noted that this procedure is similar to that for finding the position of the Centre of Flotation, which is the two-dimensional centre of gravity of each water-plane.

Example 1

A ship is floating upright on an even keel at 6.0 m draft F and A. The areas of the water-planes are as follows:

Draft (m)	0	1	2	3	4	5	6
Area (sq. m)	5000	5600	6020	6025	6025	6025	6025

Find the ship's KB at this draft.

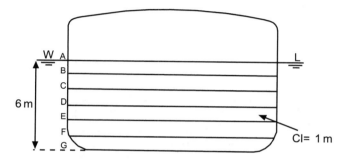

Fig. 10.18

Water-plane	Area	SM	Volume function	Levers	Moment function
A	6025	1	6025	6	36 150
B	6025	4	24 100	5	120 500
C	6025	2	12 050	4	48 200
D	6025	4	24 100	3	72 300
E	6020	2	12 040	2	24 080
F	5600	4	22 400	1	22 400
G	5000	1	5000	0	0
			$105\,715 = \Sigma_1$		$323\,630 = \Sigma_2$

$$KB = \frac{\text{Moment about keel}}{\text{volume of displacement}}$$

$$\therefore KB = \frac{\Sigma_2}{\Sigma_1} \times CI$$

$$= \frac{323\,630}{105\,715} \times 1.0$$

Ans. <u>KB</u> = <u>3.06 metres</u>

$$= 0.51 \times d \text{ approximately.}$$

The lever of zero was at the keel so the final answer was relative to this point, i.e. above base.

If we Simpsonize $\frac{1}{2}$ ords we will obtain *areas.*

If we Simpsonize areas we will obtain *volumes.*

Example 2

A ship is floating upright in S.W. on an even keel at 7 m draft F And A. The TPC's are as follows:

Draft (m)	1	2	3	4	5	6	7
TPC (tonnes)	60	60.3	60.5	60.5	60.5	60.5	60.5

The volume between the outer bottom and 1 m draft is 3044 cu. m, and its centre of gravity is 0.5 m above the keel. Find the ship's KB.

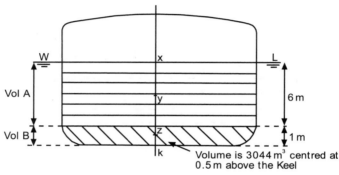

Fig. 10.19

In Figure 10.19:

Let KY represent the height of the centre of gravity of volume A above the keel, and KZ represent the height of the centre of gravity of volume B above the keel.

Let $X = \dfrac{100}{1.025}$ then the area of each water-plane is equal to TPC $\times$ X sq m

Σ_1 denotes the first total.
Σ_2 denotes the second total. $\Big\}$ see Table below

Draft	Area	SM	Volume function	Levers 1 m	Moment function
7	60.5	1	60.5	0	0
6	60.5	4	242.0	1	242.0
5	60.5	2	121.0	2	242.0
4	60.5	4	242.0	3	726.0
3	60.5	2	121.0	4	484.0
2	60.3	4	241.2	5	1206.0
1	60.0	1	60.0	6	360.0
			$1087.7 = \Sigma_1$		$3260.0 = \Sigma_2$

$$\text{Volume A} = \frac{1}{3} \times CI \times \Sigma_1 \times X$$

$$= \frac{1}{3} \times 1.0 \times 1087.7 \times \frac{100}{1.025} = 35372$$

Volume A = 35372 cu. m

Volume B = +3044 cu. m

Total Volume = 38416 cu. m

$$XY = \frac{\Sigma_2}{\Sigma_1} \times CI = \frac{\text{Moment}}{\text{Volume A}}$$

$$= \frac{3260}{1087.7} \times 1.0 = 3 \text{ m below } 7 \text{ m waterline}$$

XY = 3 m

KX = 7 m

KX − XY = KY, so KY = 4 m

Moments about the keel

Volume	KG_{keel}	Moments about keel
35 372	4	141 488
+ 3 044	0.5	+ 1 522
38 416		143 010

$$KB = \frac{\text{Total moment}}{\text{Total volume}} = \frac{143\,010}{38\,416} = 3.72 \text{ metres}$$

$$= 0.531 \times d$$

Summary

When using Simpson's Rules for ship calculations always use the following procedure

1 Make a sketch using the given information.
2 Insert values into a *table* as shown in worked examples.
3 Use tabulated summations to finally *calculate* requested values.

Exercise 10

1 A ship's load water-plane is 60 m long. The lengths of the half-ordinates commencing from forward are as follows:

   0.1, 3.5, 4.6, 5.1, 5.2, 5.1, 4.9, 4.3 and 0.1 m respectively.

   Calculate the area of the water-plane, the TPC in salt water, and the position of the centre of flotation, from amidships.

2 The half-ordinates of a ship's water-plane, which is 60 m long, commencing from forward, are as follows:

   0, 3.8, 4.3, 4.6, 4.7, 4.7, 4.5, 4.3, and 1 m respectively.

   Find the area of the water-plane, the TPC, the coefficient of fineness of the water-plane area, and the position of the centre of flotation, from amidships.

3 The breadths at the load water-plane of a ship 90 metres long, measured at equal intervals from forward, are as follows:

   0, 3.96, 8.53, 11.58, 12.19, 12.5, 11.58, 5.18, 3.44, and 0.30 m respectively.

   If the load draft is 5 metres, and the block coefficient is 0.6, find the FWA and the position of the centre of flotation, from amidships.

4 The areas of a ship's water-planes, commencing from the load draft of 24 metres, and taken at equal distances apart, are:

   2000, 1950, 1800, 1400, 800, 400, and 100 sq m respectively.

   The lower area is that of the ship's outer bottom. Find the displacement in salt water, the Fresh Water Allowance, and the height of the centre of buoyancy above the keel.

5 The areas of vertical transverse sections of a forward hold, spaced equidistantly between bulkheads, are as follows:

   800, 960, 1100, and 1120 sq m respectively.

   The length of the hold is 20 m. Find how many tonnes of coal (stowing at 4 cu. m per tonne) it will hold.

6 A ship 90 metres long is floating on an even keel at 6 m draft. The half-ordinates, commencing from forward, are as follows:

   0, 4.88, 6.71, 7.31, 7.01, 6.40, and 0.9 m respectively.

   The half-ordinates 7.5 metres from bow and stern are 2.13 m. and 3.35 m respectively. Find the area of the water-plane and the change in draft if 153 tonnes of cargo is loaded with its centre of gravity vertically over the centre of flotation. Find also the position of the centre of flotation.

7 The areas of a ship's water-planes commencing from the load water-plane and spaced at equidistant intervals down to the inner bottom, are:

   2500, 2000, 1850, 1550, 1250, 900 and 800 sq m respectively.

Below the inner bottom is an appendage 1 metre deep which has a mean area of 650 sq m. The load draft is 7 metres. Find the load displacement in salt water, the Fresh Water Allowance, and the height of the centre of buoyancy above the keel.

8 A ship's water-plane is 80 metres long. The breadths commencing from forward are as follows:

0, 3.05, 7.1, 9.4, 10.2, 10.36, 10.3, 10.0, 8.84, 5.75 and 0 m respectively.

The space between the first three and the last three ordinates is half of that between the other ordinates. Calculate the area of the water-plane, and the position of the centre of flotation.

9 Three consecutive ordinates in a ship's water-plane area are:

6.3, 3.35, and 0.75 m respectively.

The common interval is 6 m. Find the area contained between the last two ordinates.

10 The transverse horizontal ordinates of a ship's midships section commencing from the load waterline and spaced at 1 metre intervals are as follows:

16.30, 16.30, 16.30, 16.00, 15.50, 14.30, and 11.30 m respectively.

Below the lowest ordinate there is an appendage of 8.5 sq m. Find the area of the transverse section.

11 The following table gives the area of a ship's water-plane at various drafts:

Draft(m)	6	7	8
Area(sq m)	700	760	800

Find the volume of displacement and approximate mean TPC between the drafts of 7 and 8 m.

12 The areas of a ship's water-planes, commencing from the load water-plane and spaced 1 metre apart, are as follows:

800, 760, 700, 600, 450, and 10 sq m respectively.

Midway between the lowest two water-planes the area is 180 sq m. Find the load displacement in salt water, and the height of the centre of buoyancy above the keel.

Chapter 11
Final KG

When a ship is completed by the builders, certain written stability information must be handed over to the shipowner with the ship. Details of the information required are contained in the load line Rules, parts of which are reproduced in Appendix I of this book. The information includes details of the ship's Lightweight, the Lightweight VCG and LCG, and also the positions of the centres of gravity of cargo and bunker spaces. This gives an initial condition from which the displacement and KG for any condition of loading may be calculated. The final KG is found by taking the moments of the weights loaded or discharged, about the keel. For convenience, when taking the moments, consider the ship to be on her beam ends.

In Figure 11.1(a), KG represents the original height of the centre of gravity above the keel, and W represents the original displacement. The original moment about the keel is therefore $W \times KG$.

Now load a weight w_1 with its centre of gravity at g_1 and discharge w_2 from g_2. This will produce moments about the keel of $w_1 \times Kg_1$ and

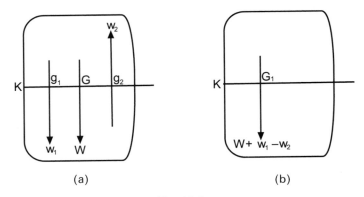

(a)   (b)

Fig. 11.1

$w_2 \times Kg_2$ in directions indicated in the figure. The final moment about the keel will be equal to the original moment plus the moment of the weight added minus the moment of the weight discharged. But the final moment must also be equal to the final displacement multiplied by the final KG as shown in Figure 11.1(b). i.e.

$$\text{Final moment} = \text{Final KG} \times \text{Final displacement}$$

or

$$\text{Final KG} = \frac{\text{Final moment}}{\text{Final displacement}}$$

Example 1

A ship of 6000 tonnes displacement has $KG = 6\,m$ and $KM = 7.33\,m$. The following cargo is loaded:

$$1000 \text{ tonnes},\quad KG\ 2.5\ m$$

$$500 \text{ tonnes},\quad KG\ 3.5\ m$$

$$750 \text{ tonnes},\quad KG\ 9.0\ m$$

The following is then discharged:

$$450 \text{ tonnes of cargo } KG\ 0.6\ m$$

$$\text{and } 800 \text{ tonnes of cargo } KG\ 3.0\ m$$

Find the final GM.

Weight	KG	Moment about the keel
+6000	6.0	+36 000
+1000	2.5	+2500
+500	3.5	+1750
+750	9.0	+6750
+8250		+47 000
−450	0.6	−270
−800	3.0	−2400
+7000		+44 330

$$\text{Final KG} = \frac{\text{Final moment}}{\text{Final displacement}}$$

$$= \frac{44\,330}{7000} = 6.33 \text{ m}$$

$$\text{GM} = \text{KM} - \text{KG}$$

$$\text{KM} = 7.33 \text{ m, as given}$$

$$\text{Final KG} = \underline{6.33} \text{ m, as calculated}$$

Ans. Final GM = 1.00 m

Note. KM was assumed to be similar value at 6000 tonnes and 7000 tonnes displacement. This is feasible. As can be seen on Figure 6.2, it is possible to have the same KM at two different drafts.

Example 2

A ship of 5000 tonnes displacement has KG 4.5 m, KM 5.3 m. The following cargo is loaded:

2000 tonnes KG 3.7 m,   and 1000 tonnes KG 7.5 m.

Find how much deck cargo (KG 9 m) may now be loaded if the ship is to sail with a minimum GM of 0.3 m.

Let 'x' tonnes of deck cargo be loaded, so that the vessel sails with GM = 0.3 m.

$$\text{Final KM} = 5.3 \text{ m}$$

$$\text{Final GM} = 0.3 \text{ m}$$

$$\underline{\text{Final KG} = 5.0 \text{ m}}$$

$$\text{Final KG} = \frac{\text{Final moment}}{\text{Final displacement}} = 5.0 \text{ m}$$

$$\therefore 5 = \frac{37\,400 + 9x}{8000 + x}$$

$$40\,000 + 5x = 37\,400 + 9x$$

$$2600 = 4x$$

$$x = 650 \text{ tonnes}$$

Ans. Maximum to load = 650 tonnes

Weight	KG	Moment about the keel
5000	4.5	22 500
2000	3.7	7400
1000	7.5	7500
x	9.0	9x
8000 + x		37 400 + 9x

Exercise 11

1 A ship has a displacement of 1800 tonnes and KG = 3 m. She loads 3400 tonnes of cargo (KG = 2.5 m), and 400 tonnes of bunkers (KG = 5.0 m). Find the final KG.

2 A ship has a light displacement of 2000 tonnes and light KG = 3.7 m. She then loads 2500 tonnes of cargo (KG = 2.5 m), and 300 tonnes of bunkers (KG = 3 m). Find the new KG.

3 A ship sails with displacement 3420 tonnes and KG = 3.75 m. During the voyage bunkers were consumed as follows: 66 tonnes (KG = 0.45 m) and 64 tonnes (KG = 2 m). Find the KG at the end of the voyage.

4 A ship has displacement 2000 tonnes and KG = 4 m. She loads 1500 tonnes of cargo (KG = 6 m), 3500 tonnes of cargo (KG = 5 m), and 1520 tonnes of bunkers (KG = 1 m). She then discharges 2000 tonnes of cargo (KG = 2.5 m) and consumes 900 tonnes of oil fuel (KG = 0.5 m) during the voyage. Find the final KG on arrival at the port of destination.

5 A ship has a light displacement of 2000 tonnes (KG = 3.6 m). She loads 2500 tonnes of cargo (KG = 5 m) and 300 tonnes of bunkers (KG = 3 m). The GM is then found to be 0.15 m. Find the GM with the bunkers empty.

6 A ship has a displacement of 3200 tonnes (KG = 3 m, and KM = 5.5 m) She then loads 5200 tonnes of cargo (KG = 5.2 m). Find how much deck cargo having a KG = 10 m may now be loaded if the ship is to complete loading with a positive GM of 0.3 m.

7 A ship of 5500 tonnes displacement has KG 5 m, and she proceeds to load the following cargo:

> 1000 tonnes KG 6 m
> 700 tonnes KG 4 m
> 300 tonnes KG 5 m

She then discharges 200 tonnes of ballast KG 0.5 m. Find how much deck cargo (KG = 10 m) can be loaded so that the ship may sail with a positive GM of 0.3 metres. The load KM is 6.3 m.

8 A ship of 3500 tonnes light displacement and light KG 6.4 m has to load 9600 tonnes of cargo. The KG of the lower hold is 4.5 m, and that of the tween deck is 9 m. The load KM is 6.2 m and, when loading is completed, the righting moment at 6 degrees of heel is required to be 425 tonnes m. Calculate the amount of cargo to be loaded into the lower hold and tween deck respectively (Righting moment = W × GM × sin heel.)

9 A ship arrives in port with displacement 6000 tonnes and KG 6 m. She then discharges and loads the following quantities:

Discharge	1250 tonnes of cargo	KG 4.5 metres
	675 tonnes of cargo	KG 3.5 metres
	420 tonnes of cargo	KG 9.0 metres
Load	980 tonnes of cargo	KG 4.25 metres
	550 tonnes of cargo	KG 6.0 metres

700 tonnes of bunkers KG 1.0 metre

70 tonnes of FW   KG 12.0 metres

During the stay in port 30 tonnes of oil (KG 1 m) are consumed. If the final KM is 6.8 m, find the GM on departure.

10 A ship has light displacement 2800 tonnes and light KM 6.7 m. She loads 400 tonnes of cargo (KG 6 m) and 700 tonnes (KG 4.5 m). The KG is then found to be 5.3 m. Find the light GM.

11 A ship's displacement is 4500 tonnes and KG 5 m. The following cargo is loaded:

450 tonnes KG 7.5 m

120 tonnes KG 6.0 m

650 tonnes KG 3.0 m.

Find the amount of cargo to load in a 'tween deck (KG 6 m) so that the ship sails with a GM of 0.6 m. (The load KM is 5.6 m)

12 A ship of 7350 tonnes displacement has KG 5.8 m and GM 0.5 m. Find how much deck cargo must be loaded (KG 9 m) if there is to be a metacentric height of not less than 0.38 m when loading is completed.

13 A ship is partly loaded and has a displacement of 9000 tonnes, KG 6 m, and KM 7.3 m. She is to make a 19-day passage consuming 26 tonnes of oil per day (KG 0.5 m). Find how much deck cargo she may load (KG 10 m) if the GM on arrival at the destination is to be not less than 0.3 m.

Chapter 12
Calculating KB, BM, and metacentric diagrams

THE method used to determine the final position of the centre of gravity was examined in the previous chapter. To ascertain the GM for any condition of loading it is necessary also to calculate the KB and BM (i.e. KM) for any draft.

To find KB

The centre of buoyancy is the centre of gravity of the underwater volume.

For a box-shaped vessel on an even keel, the underwater volume is rectangular in shape and the centre of buoyancy will be at the half-length, on the centre line, and at half the draft as shown in Figure 12.1(a).

Therefore, for a box-shaped vessel on an even keel: $KB = \frac{1}{2}$ draft.

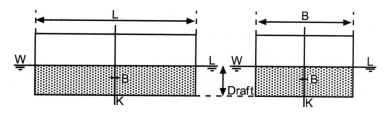

Fig. 12.1(a).   Box-shaped vessel

For a vessel which is in the form of a triangular prism as shown in Figure 12.1(b) the underwater section will also be in the form of a triangular prism. The centroid of a triangle is at 2/3 of the median from the apex. Therefore the centre of buoyancy will be at the half-length, on the centre line, but the KB = 2/3 draft.

For an ordinary ship the KB may be found fairly accurately by Simpson's Rules as explained in Chapter 10. The approximate depth of the centre of buoyancy of a ship *below* the waterline usually lies between 0.44 × draft

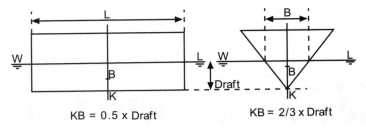

KB = 0.5 x Draft   KB = 2/3 x Draft

Fig. 12.1(b).   Triangular-shaped vessel

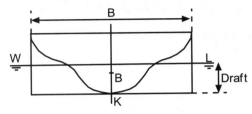

KB ≈ 0.535 x Draft

Fig. 12.1(c).   Ship-shaped vessel

and 0.49 × draft. A closer approximation of thus depth can be obtained by using Morrish's Formula, which states:

$$\text{Depth of centre of buoyancy } below \text{ waterline} = \frac{1}{3}\left(\frac{d}{2}+\frac{V}{A}\right)$$

where

d = Mean draft

V = Volume of displacement

and

A = Area of the water-plane

The derivation of this formula is as follows:

In Figure 12.2, let ABC be the curve of water-plane areas plotted against drafts to the load waterline. Let DE = V/A and draw EG parallel to the base cutting the diagonal FD in H.

It must first be shown that area DAHC is equal to area DABC.

Rectangle AH = Rectangle HC

∴ Triangle AGH = Triangle HEC

and

Area AHCD = Area AGED

Area AGED = V/A × A

= V

but

Area DABC = V

∴ Area DAHC = Area DABC

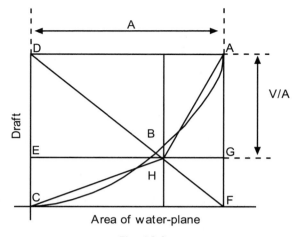

Fig. 12.2

The distance of the centroid of DABC below AD is the distance of the centre of buoyancy below the load waterline. It is now assumed that the centroid of the area DAHC is the same distance below the load waterline as the centroid of area DABC.

To find the distance of the centroid of area DAHC below AD.

$$\frac{\text{Area AGH}}{\text{Area AGED}} = \frac{\frac{1}{2}\text{AG} \cdot \text{GH}}{\text{AG} \cdot \text{AD}}$$

$$= \frac{1}{2}\frac{\text{GH}}{\text{AD}}$$

$$= \frac{1}{2}\frac{\text{GF}}{\text{AF}}$$

$$= \frac{1}{2}\frac{\text{AF} - \text{AG}}{\text{AF}}$$

$$= \frac{1}{2}\left(\frac{\text{d} - \text{AG}}{\text{d}}\right)$$

$$\therefore \text{Area AGH} = \frac{1}{2}\frac{(\text{d} - \text{V/A})}{\text{d}} \times \text{Area AGED}$$

The centroid of AGED is $\frac{1}{2}\frac{\text{V}}{\text{A}}$ from AD.

Now let triangle AGH be shifted to HEC.

The centroid of AGED will move parallel to the shift of the centroid of AGH and the vertical component of this shift (x) is given by:

$$x = \frac{AGH \times d/3}{AGED}$$

$$= \frac{\frac{1}{2}\left(\frac{d - V/A}{d}\right) \times \frac{d}{3} \times AGED}{AGED}$$

$$= \frac{1}{2}\left(\frac{d - V/A}{d}\right) \times \frac{d}{3}$$

$$= \frac{1}{6}(d - V/A)$$

The new vertical distance of the centroid *below* AD will now be given by:

$$\text{Distance } below \text{ AD} = \frac{1}{2}\frac{V}{A} + \frac{1}{6}\left(d - \frac{V}{A}\right)$$

$$= \frac{1}{3}\frac{V}{A} + \frac{1}{6}d$$

$$= \frac{1}{3}\left(\frac{d}{2} + \frac{V}{A}\right)$$

Therefore the distance of the centre of buoyancy *below* the load waterline is given by the formula:

$$\text{Distance } below \text{ LWL} = \frac{1}{3}\left(\frac{d}{2} + \frac{V}{A}\right)$$

This is known as *Morrish's* or *Normand's formula* and will give very good results for merchant ships.

To find Transverse BM

The Transverse BM is the height of the transverse metacentre above the centre of buoyancy and is found by using the formula:

$$BM = \frac{1}{V}$$

where

1 = The second moment of the water-plane area about the centre line,

and

V = The ship's volume of displacement

The derivation of this formula is as follows:

Consider a ship inclined to a small angle (θ) as shown in Figure 12.3(a) Let 'y' be the half-breadth.

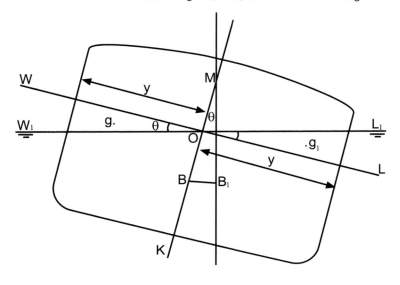

Fig. 12.3(a)

Since θ is a small angle then arc WW_1 = arc LL_1

$$= \theta y$$

Also:

Area of wedge WOW_1 = Area of wedge LOL_1

$$= \tfrac{1}{2} \theta y^2$$

Consider an elementary wedge of longitudinal length dx as in Figure 12.3(b).

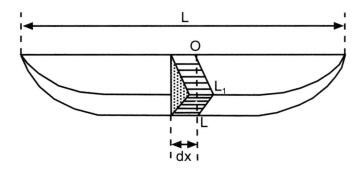

Fig. 12.3(b)

$$\text{The volume of this wedge} = \tfrac{1}{2}\,\theta\,y^2\,dx$$

$$\text{The moment of the wedge about the centre line} = \tfrac{1}{2}\,\theta\,y^2\,dx \times \tfrac{2}{3}\,y$$

$$= \tfrac{1}{3}\,\theta\,y^3\,dx$$

$$\begin{array}{l}\text{The total moment of both wedges} \\ \text{about the centre line}\end{array} = \tfrac{2}{3}\,\theta\,y^3\,dx$$

$$\text{The sum of the moments of all such wedges} = \int_{O}^{L} \tfrac{2}{3}\,\theta\,y^3\,dx$$

$$= \theta \int_{O}^{L} \tfrac{2}{3}\,y^3\,dx$$

But

$$\left.\int_{O}^{L} \tfrac{2}{3}\,y^3\,dx = \begin{array}{l}\text{The second moment} \\ \text{of the water-plane} \\ \text{area about the ship's centre line}\end{array}\right\} = I$$

$$\begin{array}{l}\therefore\,\text{The sum of the moments} \\ \text{of the wedges}\end{array} = I \times \theta$$

$$\begin{array}{l}\text{But the sum of} \\ \text{the moments}\end{array} = v \times gg_1$$

where v is the volume of the immersed or emerged wedge.

$$\therefore\ I \times \theta = v \times gg_1$$

or

$$I = \frac{v \times gg_1}{\theta} \qquad\qquad (I)$$

Now:

$$BB_1 = \frac{v \times gg_1}{V}$$

and

$$BB_1 = BM \times \theta$$

$$\therefore\ BM \times \theta = \frac{v \times gg_1}{V}$$

or

$$BM \times V = \frac{v \times gg_1}{\theta}$$

Substituting in (I) above:

$$BM \times V = I$$

$$\therefore\ BM = \frac{I}{V}$$

For a rectangular water-plane area the second moment about the centre line is found by the formula:

$$I = \frac{LB^3}{12}$$

where L = the length of the water-plane, and B = the breadth of the water-plane, (the derivation of this formula is shown in Chapter 29).

Thus, for a vessel having a rectangular water-plane area:

$$BM = \frac{LB^3}{12V}$$

For a box-shaped vessel:

$$BM = \frac{I}{V}$$

$$= \frac{LB^3}{12V}$$

$$= \frac{L \times B^3}{12 \times L \times B \times draft}$$

$$\therefore BM = \frac{B^2}{12d}$$

where B = the beam of the vessel, and d = any draft of the vessel. B is a constant, d is a variable.

For a triangular-shaped prism:

$$BM = \frac{I}{V}$$

$$= \frac{LB^3}{12V}$$

$$= \frac{L \times B^3}{12(\frac{1}{2} \times L \times B \times draft)}$$

$$\therefore BM = \frac{B^2}{6d}$$

where B is the breadth *at the waterline* and d is the corresponding draft. B and d are variables.

Example 1

A box-shaped vessel is 24 m × 5 m × 5 m and floats on an even keel at 2 m draft. KG = 1.5 m. Calculate the initial metacentric height.

$$KB = \frac{1}{2} \text{ draft} \qquad BM = \frac{B^2}{12d} \qquad KB = \quad 1.00\,m$$

$$BM = +1.04\,m$$

$$KB = 1\,m \qquad BM = \frac{5^2}{12 \times 2} \qquad KM = \quad 2.04\,m$$

$$KG = -1.50\,m$$

$$BM = 1.04\,m \qquad GM = \quad \underline{0.54\,m}$$

Ans. $\underline{GM = +0.54\,m}$

Example 2

A vessel is in the form of a triangular prism 32 m long, 8 m wide at the top, and 5 m deep. KG = 3.7 m. Find the initial metacentric height when floating on even keel at 4 m draft F and A.

Let 'x' be the half-breadth *at the waterline*, as shown in Figure 12.4. Then

$$\frac{x}{4} = \frac{4}{5}$$

$$x = \frac{16}{5}$$

$$x = 3.2\,m$$

$$\therefore \text{ The breadth at the waterline} = 6.4\,m$$

$$KB = 2/3 \text{ draft} \qquad BM = \frac{B^2}{6d} \qquad KB = \quad 2.67\,m$$

$$= 2/3 \times 4 \qquad\qquad\qquad BM = +1.71\,m$$

$$KB = 2.67\,m \qquad = \frac{6.4 \times 6.4}{6 \times 4} \qquad KM = \quad 4.38\,m$$

$$KG = -3.70\,m$$

$$BM = 1.71\,m \qquad GM = \quad \underline{0.68\,m}$$

Ans. $\underline{GM = +0.68\,m}$

Note how the breadth 'B' would decrease at the lower drafts. See also Figure 12.6(b).

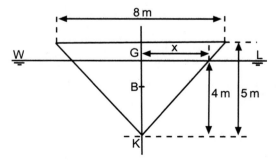

Fig. 12.4

Example 3

The second moment of a ship's water-plane area about the centre line is $20\,000\,\text{m}^4$ units. The displacement is 7000 tonnes whilst floating in dock water of density 1008 kg per cu. m. KB $= 1.9\,\text{m}$, and KG $= 3.2\,\text{m}$. Calculate the initial metacentric height.

$$\text{Volume of water displaced} = \frac{7000 \times 1000}{1008}\,\text{cu. m} = 6944\,\text{cu. m}$$

$$\text{BM} = \frac{\text{I}}{\text{V}}$$

$$\therefore \text{BM} = \frac{20\,000}{6944}$$

$$\text{BM} = \quad 2.88\,\text{m}$$

$$\text{KB} = +1.90\,\text{m}$$

$$\overline{\text{KM} = \quad 4.78\,\text{m}}$$

$$\text{KG} = \quad 3.20\,\text{m}$$

Ans. $\underline{\text{GM} = +1.58\,\text{m}}$

Metacentric diagrams

It has been mentioned in Chapter 6 that the officer responsible for loading a ship should aim to complete the loading with a GM which is neither too large nor too small. See table of typical GM values on p. 49 for merchant ships when fully loaded. A metacentric diagram is a figure in graph form from which the KB, BM, and thus the KM can be found for any draft by inspection. If the KG is known and the KM is found from the diagram, the difference will give the GM. Also, if a final GM be decided upon, the KM can be taken from the graph and the difference will give the required final KG.

The diagram is usually drawn for drafts between the light and loaded displacements, i.e. 3 m and 13 m respectively overpage.

Figure 12.5 shows a metacentric diagram drawn for a ship having the following particulars:

Draft (m)	KB (m)	KM (m)
13	6.65	11.60
12	6.13	11.30
11	5.62	11.14
10	5.11	11.10
9	4.60	11.15
8	4.10	11.48
7	3.59	11.94
6	3.08	12.81
5	2.57	14.30
4	2.06	16.63
3	1.55	20.54
–	–	–

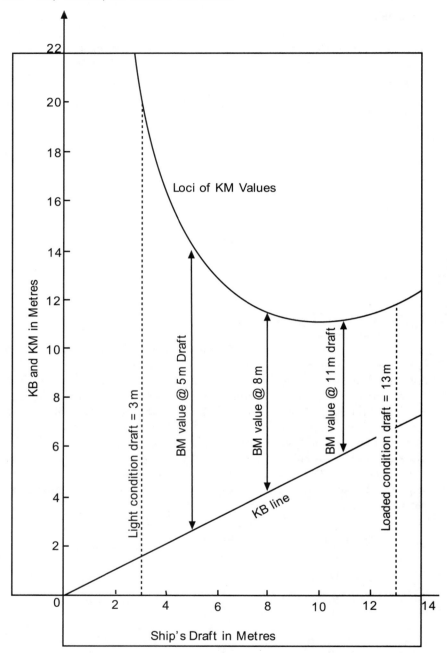

Fig. 12.5.   Metacentric diagram for a ship-shaped vessel.

The following is a description of the method used in constructing this diagram. The scale on the left-hand side represents a scale of metres, and it is from this scale that all measurements are to be taken.

First the curve of the Centres of Buoyancy is plotted.

For each draft plot the corresponding KB. For example, plot 6.65 m @ 13 m, 6.13 m @ 12 m draft and so on to 1.55 m @ 3 m draft.

Join these points together to form the KB curve. In practice it will be very close to being a straight line because the curvature will be so small. See Figure 12.5.

Next the KM curve or Locus of Metacentres. For each draft plot the corresponding KM value given in the table.

At 13 m plot 11.60 m. At 12 m plot 11.30 m and so on down to plotting 20.54 m KM @ 3 m draft.

These points are then joined by a smooth curve as shown in Figure 12.5.

Note how it is possible for two different drafts to have the same value of KM in the range of drafts from 7 m to 13 m approximately.

For any draft being considered, the vertical distance between the KB line and the KM curve gives the BM value.

To find the KB's and KM's the vertical distances are measured from the base line to the curves.

Example 1

Construct the metacentric diagram for a box-shaped vessel 64 m long, 10 m beam, and 6 m deep, for even keel drafts at 0.5 m intervals between the light draft 1 metre and the load draft 5 m. Also, from the diagram find:

(a) The minimum KM and the draft at which it occurs, and
(b) The BM at 3.5 m.

Draft	$KB = \frac{1}{2} \, draft$	$BM = B^2/12d$	$KM = KB + BM$
1 m	0.5 m	8.33 m	8.83 m
1.5 m	0.75 m	5.56 m	6.31 m
2 m	1.0 m	4.17 m	5.17 m
2.5 m	1.25 m	3.33 m	4.58 m
3.0 m	1.5 m	2.78 m	4.28 m
3.5 m	1.75 m	2.38 m	4.13 m
4.0 m	2.00 m	2.08 m	4.08 m
4.5 m	2.25 m	1.85 m	4.10 m
5.0 m	2.5 m	1.67 m	4.17 m

See Figure 12.6(a) for KB and KM plotted against draft.

Explanation. To find the minimum KM, draw a horizontal tangent to the lowest point of the curve of metacentres, i.e. through A. The point where the tangent cuts the scale will give the minimum KM and the draft at which it occurs.

Note. It is shown below that for a box-shaped vessel the minimum KM and the draft at which it occurs are both given by $B/\sqrt{6}$, where B is the beam.

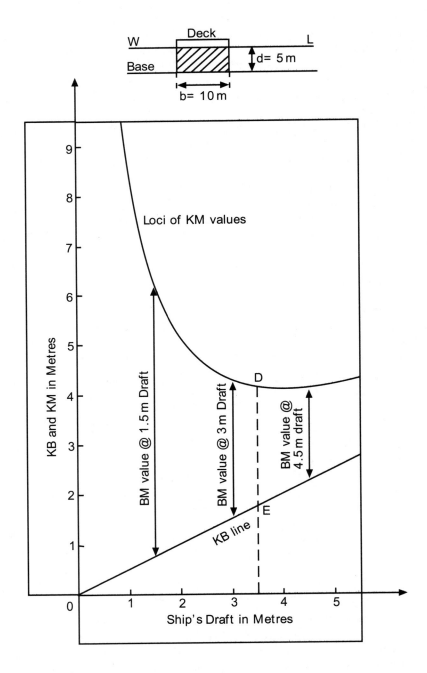

Fig. 12.6(a).   Metacentric diagram for a box-shaped vessel.

Therefore, the answer to part (a) of the question is:

$$\text{Minimum KM} = 4.08 \text{ m occurring at } 4.08 \text{ m draft}$$

To find the BM at 3.5 m draft, measure the distance DE on the scale and it will give the BM (2.38 m).

Therefore, the answer to part (b) of the question is:

$$\text{BM at } 3.5 \text{ m draft} = 2.38 \text{ m}$$

To show that, for a box-shaped vessel, the minimum KM and the draft at which it occurs are both given by the expression $B/\sqrt{6}$, where B is equal to the vessel's beam.

$$KM = KB + BM$$

For a box-shaped vessel:

$$KM = \frac{d}{2} + \frac{B^2}{12d} \quad \text{------------ (I)}$$

$$\frac{dKM}{dd} = \frac{1}{2} + \frac{B^2}{12d^2}$$

For minimum KM:

$$\frac{dKM}{dd} = O$$

$$\therefore O = \frac{1}{2} + \frac{B^2}{12d^2}$$

$$B^2 = 6d^2$$

and

$$d = B/\sqrt{6}$$

Substituting in equation (I) above:

$$\text{minimum KM} = \frac{B}{2\sqrt{6}} + \frac{B^2\sqrt{6}}{12B}$$

$$= \frac{6B + 6B}{12\sqrt{6}}$$

$$\text{minimum KM} = B/\sqrt{6}$$

Figure 12.6(b) shows a metacentric diagram for a triangular-shaped underwater form with apex at the base. Note how the KM values have produced a straight line instead of the parabolic curve of the rectangular hull form. Note also how BM increases with *every increase* in *draft*.

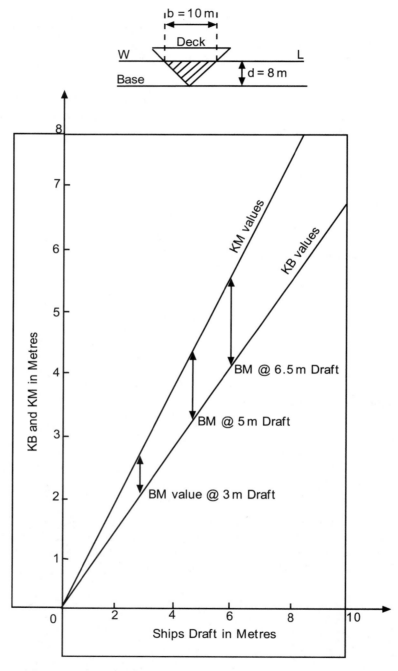

Fig. 12.6(b).   Metacentric diagram for triangular-shaped vessel.

Exercise 12

1 A box-shaped vessel 75 m long, 12 m beam and 7 m deep, is floating on an even keel at 6 m draft. Calculate the KM.

2 Compare the initial metacentric heights of two barges, each 60 m. long, 10 m beam at the waterline, 6 m deep, floating upright on an even keel at 3 m draft, and having KG = 3 m. One barge is in the form of a rectangular prism and the other is in the form of a triangular prism, floating apex downwards.

3 Two box-shaped vessels are each 100 m long, 4 m deep, float at 3 m draft, and have KG = 2.5 m. Compare their initial Metacentric Heights if one has 10 m beam and the other has 12 m beam.

4 Will a homogeneous log of square cross-section and relative density 0.7 have a positive initial Metacentric Height when floating in fresh water with one side parallel to the waterline? Verify your answer by means of a calculation.

5 A box-shaped vessel 60 m × 12 m × 5 m is floating on an even keel at a draft of 4 m. Construct a metacentric diagram for drafts between 1 m and 4 m. From the diagram find:
(a) the KM's at drafts of 2.4 m and 0.9 m, and
(b) the draft at which the minimum KM occurs.

6 Construct a metacentric diagram for a box-shaped vessel 65 m × 12 m × 6 m for drafts between 1 m and 6 m. From the diagram find:
(a) the KM's at drafts of 1.2 m and 3.6 m, and
(b) the minimum KM and the draft at which it occurs.

7 Construct a metacentric diagram for a box-shaped vessel 70 m long and 10 m beam, for drafts between 1 m and 6 m. From the diagram find:
(a) the KM's at drafts of 1.5 m and 4.5 m, and
(b) the draft at which the minimum KM occurs.

8 A box-shaped vessel is 60 m long, 13.73 m wide and floats at 8 m even-keel draft in salt water.
(a) Calculate the KB, BM and KM values for drafts 3 m to 8 m at intervals of 1 m. From your results draw the Metacentric Diagram.
(b) At 3.65 m draft even keel, it is known that the VCG is 4.35 m above base. Using your diagram, estimate the transverse GM for this condition of loading.
(c) At 5.60 m draft even keel, the VCG is also 5.60 m above base. Using your diagram, estimate the GM for this condition of loading. What state of equilibrium is the ship in?

Draft (m)	3	4	5	6	7	8
KM (m)	6.75	5.94	5.64	5.62	5.75	5.96

Chapter 13
List

Consider a ship floating upright as shown in Figure 13.1. The centres of gravity and buoyancy are on the centre line. The resultant force acting on the ship is zero, and the resultant moment about the centre of gravity is zero.

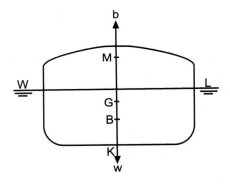

Fig. 13.1

Now let a weight already on board the ship be shifted transversely such that G moves to G_1 as in Figure 13.2(a). This will produce a listing moment of $W \times GG_1$ and the ship will list until G_1 and the centre of buoyancy are in the same vertical line as in Figure 13.2(b).

In this position G_1 will also lie vertically under M so long as the angle of list is small. Therefore, if the final positions of the metacentre and the centre of gravity are known, the final list can be found, using trigonometry, in the triangle GG_1M which is right-angled at G.

The final position of the centre of gravity is found by taking moments about the keel and about the centre line.

Note. It will be found more convenient in calculations, when taking moments, to consider the ship to be upright throughout the operation.

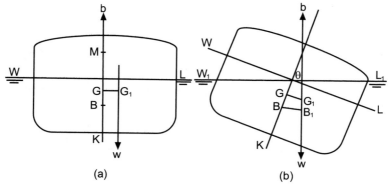

Fig. 13.2

Example 1

A ship of 6000 tonnes displacement has KM = 7.3 m, and KG = 6.7 m, and is floating upright. A weight of 60 tonnes already on board is shifted 12 m transversely. Find the resultant list.

Figure 13.3(a) shows the initial position of G before the weight was shifted and Figure 13.3(b) shows the final position of G after the weight has been shifted.

When the weight is shifted transversely the ship's centre of gravity will also shift transversely, from G to G_1. The ship will then list θ degrees to bring G_1 vertically under M the metacentre.

$$GG_1 = \frac{w \times d}{W}$$

$$= \frac{60 \times 12}{6000}$$

$$GG_1 = 0.12\,\text{m}$$

$$GM = KM - KG = 7.3 - 6.7 = 0.6\,\text{m}$$

In triangle GG_1M:

$$\tan\theta = \frac{GG_1}{GM}$$

$$= \frac{0.12}{0.60} = 0.20$$

Ans. List $= 11° \, 18\frac{1}{2}'$

Example 2

A ship of 8000 tonnes displacement has KM = 8.7 m, and KG = 7.6 m. The following weights are then loaded and discharged:

Load 250 tonnes cargo KG 6.1 m and centre of gravity 7.6 m to starboard of the centre line.

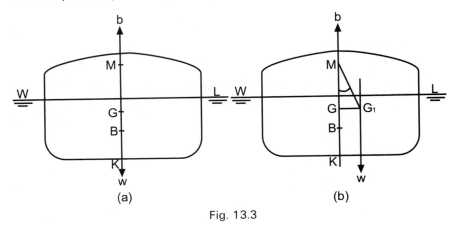

Fig. 13.3

Load 300 tonnes fuel oil KG 0.6 m and centre of gravity 6.1 m to port of the centre line.

Discharge 50 tonnes of ballast KG 1.2 m and centre of gravity 4.6 m to port of the centre line.

Find the final list.

Note. In this type of problem find the final KG by taking moments about the keel, and the final distance of the centre of gravity from the centre line by taking moments about the centre line.

Moments about the keel

Weight	KG	Moments about keel
8000	7.6	60 800
250	6.1	1 525
300	0.6	180
8550		62 505
−50	1.2	−60
8500		62 445

$$\text{Final KG} = \frac{\text{Final moment}}{\text{Final displacement}}$$

$$= \frac{62\,445}{8500}$$

Final KG = 7.35 m

KM =   8.70 m

Final KG = −7.35 m

Final GM =   1.35 m

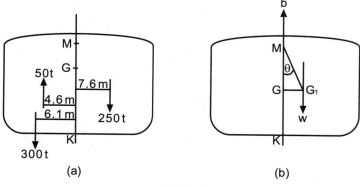

Fig. 13.4

Moments about the centre line (as in Figure 13.4(a))

For levers to port, use + ve sign.
For levers to starboard, use − ve sign.

w	d	Listing moment	
		to port + ve	to starboard − ve
+250	−7.6	−	−1900
−50	+4.6	−	−230
+300	+6.1	+1830	−
		+1830	−2130
			+1830
	final moment		−300

Let the final position of the centre of gravity be as shown in Figure 13.4(b)

$$\therefore \text{ Final listing moment} = W \times GG_1$$

or

$$GG_1 = \frac{\text{Final moment}}{\text{Final displacement}}$$

$$= \frac{-300}{8500} = -0.035 \text{ m}$$

$GG_1 = 0.035$ m to starboard, because of the − ve sign used in table.

Since the final position of the centre of gravity must lie vertically under M, it follows that the ship will list θ degrees to starboard.

$$\tan \theta = \frac{GG_1}{GM}$$

$$= \frac{-0.035}{1.35} = -0.0259$$

$$\therefore \theta = 1° 29'$$

Ans. Final list = 1° 29′ to starboard

Example 3

A ship of 8000 tonnes displacement has a GM = 0.5 m. A quantity of grain in the hold, estimated at 80 tonnes, shifts and, as a result, the centre of gravity of this grain moves 6.1 m horizontally and 1.5 m vertically. Find the resultant list.

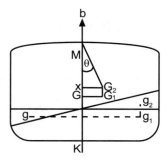

Fig. 13.5

Referring to Figure 13.5, let the centre of gravity of the grain shift from g to g_2. This will cause the ship's centre of gravity to shift from G to G_2 in a direction parallel to gg_2. The horizontal components of these shifts are g to g_1 and G to G_1 respectively, whilst the vertical components are g_1g_2 and G_1G_2.

$$GG_1 = \frac{w \times d}{W} \qquad G_1G_2 = \frac{w \times d}{W}$$

$$= \frac{80 \times 6.1}{8000} \qquad = \frac{80 \times 1.5}{8000}$$

$$GG_1 = 0.061 \text{ m} \qquad G_1G_2 = 0.015 \text{ m}$$

In Figure 13.5

$$GX = G_1G_2 \qquad XG_2 = GG_1 \qquad \tan \theta = \frac{XG_2}{MX}$$

$$GX = 0.015 \text{ m} \qquad XG_2 = 0.061 \text{ m}$$

$$GM = 0.500 \text{ m} \qquad \tan \theta = \frac{0.061}{0.485} = 0.126$$

$$XM = 0.485 \text{ m} \qquad \tan \theta = 0.126$$

Ans. List = 7° 12′

Example 4

A ship of 13 750 tonnes displacement, GM $= 0.75$ m, is listed $2\frac{1}{2}$ degrees to starboard and has yet to load 250 tonnes of cargo. There is space available in each side of No 3 between deck (centre of gravity, 6.1 m out from the centre line). Find how much cargo to load on each side if the ship is to be upright on completion of loading.

Load 'w' tonnes to port, and $(250 - w)$ tonnes to starboard.

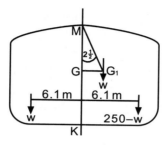

Fig. 13.6

In triangle $GG_1 M$:

$$GG_1 = GM \tan \theta$$
$$= 0.75 \tan 2\frac{1}{2}^\circ$$
$$= 0.75 \times 0.0437$$
$$GG_1 = 0.0328 \text{ m}$$

Moments about the centre line

w	d	Listing moment	
		to port	*to starboard*
w	6.1	6.1 w	—
13 750	0.0328	—	451
250 − w	6.1	—	1525 − 6.1 w
		6.1 w	1976 − 6.1 w

If the ship is to complete loading upright, then:

$$\text{Moment to port} = \text{Moment to starboard}$$

$$6.1 w = 1976 - 6.1 w$$

$$w = 161.97 \text{ tonnes}$$

Ans. Load 161.97 tonnes to port and 88.03 tonnes to starboard

Example 5

A ship of 9900 tonnes displacement has KM $= 7.3$ m, and KG $= 6.4$ m. She has yet to load two 50 tonne lifts with her own gear and the first lift is to be placed on deck on the inshore side (KG 9 m and centre of gravity 6 m out from the centre line). When the derrick plumbs the quay its head is 15 m above the keel and 12 m out from the centre line. Calculate the maximum list during the operation.

Note. The maximum list will obviously occur when the first lift is in place on the deck and the second weight is suspended over the quay as shown in Figure 13.7.

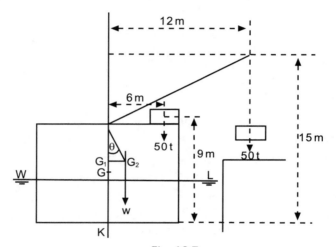

Fig. 13.7

Moments about the keel

Weight	KG	Moment
9900	6.4	63 360
50	9.0	450
50	15.0	750
10 000		64 560

$$\text{Final KG} = \frac{\text{Final moment}}{\text{Final displacement}}$$

$$= \frac{64.560}{10\,000}$$

Final KG $= 6.456$ m (KG$_1$)

i.e. a rise of 0.056 m above the original KG of 6.4 m.

Moment about the centre line

w	d	Listing moment	
		to port	to starboard
50	12	–	600
50	6	–	300
			900

$$\text{Listing moment} = 900 \text{ tonnes m}$$

$$\text{But listing moment} = W \times G_1G_2$$

$$\therefore W \times G_1G_2 = 900$$

$$G_1G_2 = \frac{900}{10\,000}$$

$$G_1G_2 = 0.09 \text{ m}$$

$$GG_1 = KG_1 - KG = 6.456 - 6.400 = 0.056 \text{ m}$$

$$GM = KM - KG = 7.3 - 6.4$$

$$\therefore GM = 0.9 \text{ m}$$

In the triangle $G_1 G_2 M$

$$G_1M = GM - GG_1$$

$$= 0.9 \text{ m} - 0.056 \text{ m}$$

$$G_1M = 0.844 \text{ m}$$

$$\tan\theta = \frac{G_1G_2}{G_1M}$$

$$= \frac{0.09}{0.844}$$

$$\tan\theta = 0.1066$$

Ans. Maximum list $= 6° 6'$

Summary
1 Always make a *sketch* from the given information.
2 Use a moment of weight table.
3 Use values from table to *calculate* the final requested data.

Exercise 13

1 A ship of 5000 tonnes displacement has KG 4.2 m, KM 4.5 m, and is listed 5 degrees to port. Assuming that the KM remains constant, find the final list if 80 tonnes of bunkers are loaded in No. 2 starboard tank whose centre of gravity is 1 metre above the keel and 4 metres out from the centre line.

2 A ship of 4515 tonnes displacement is upright and has KG 5.4 m, and KM 5.8 m. It is required to list the ship 2 degrees to starboard and a weight of 15 tonnes is to be shifted transversely for this purpose. Find the distance through which it must be shifted.

3 A ship of 7800 tonnes displacement has a mean draft of 6.8 m and is to be loaded to a mean draft of 7 metres. GM = 0.7 m TPC = 20 tonnes. The ship is at present listed 4 degrees to starboard. How much more cargo can be shipped in the port and starboard tween deck, centres of gravity 6 m and 5 m respectively from the centre line, for the ship to complete loading and finish upright.

4 A ship of 1500 tonnes displacement has KB 2.1 m, KG 2.7 m, and KM 3.1 m, and is floating upright in salt water. Find the list if a weight of 10 tonnes is shifted transversely across the deck through a distance of 10 metres.

5 A weight of 12 tonnes, when moved transversely across the deck through a distance of 12 m, causes a ship of 4000 tonnes displacement to list 3.8 degrees to starboard. KM = 6 m. Find the KG.

6 A quantity of grain, estimated at 100 tonnes, shifts 10 m horizontally and 1.5 m vertically in a ship of 9000 tonnes displacement. If the ship's original GM was 0.5 m, find the resulting list.

7 A ship of 7500 tonnes displacement has KM 8.6 m, KG 7.8 m and 20 m beam. A quantity of deck cargo is lost from the starboard side (KG 12 m, and centre of gravity 6 m in from the rail). If the resulting list is 3 degrees 20 minutes to port, find how much deck cargo was lost.

8 A ship of 12 500 tonnes displacement, KM 7 m, KG 6.4 m, has a 3 degree list to starboard and has yet to load 500 tonnes of cargo. There is space available in the tween decks, centres of gravity 6 m each side of the centre line. Find how much cargo to load on each side if the ship is to complete loading upright.

9 A ship is listed 2½ degrees to port. The displacement is 8500 tonnes KM 5.5 m, and KG 4.6 m. The ship has yet to load a locomotive of 90 tonnes mass on deck on the starboard side (centre of gravity 7.5 m from the centre line), and a tender of 40 tonnes. Find how far from the centre line the tender must be placed if the ship is to complete loading upright, and also find the final GM. (KG of the deck cargo is 7 m)

10 A ship of 9500 tonnes displacement is listed 3½ degrees to starboard and has KM 9.5 m and KG 9.3 m. She loads 300 tonnes of bunkers in No. 3 double-bottom tank port side (KG 0.6 m and centre of gravity 6 m from the centre line), and discharges two parcels of cargo each of 50 tonnes from the

port side of No. 2 Shelter Deck (KG 11 m and centre of gravity 5 m from the centre line). Find the final list.

11 A ship of 6500 tonnes displacement is floating upright and has $GM = 0.15$ m. A weight of 50 tonnes, already on board, is moved 1.5 m vertically downwards and 5 m transversely to starboard. Find the list.

12 A ship of 5600 tonnes displacement is floating upright. A weight of 30 tonnes is lifted from the port side of No. 2 tween deck to the starboard side of No. 2 shelter deck (10 m. horizontally). Find the weight of water to be transferred in No. 3 double-bottom tank from starboard to port to keep the ship upright. The distance between the centres of gravity of the tanks is 6 m.

13 A ship is just about to lift a weight from a jetty and place it on board. Using the data given below, calculate the angle of heel after the weight has just been lifted from this jetty. Weight to be lifted is 140 t with an outreach of 9.14 m. Displacement of ship prior to the lift is 10 060 tonnes. Prior to lift-off, the KB is 3.4 m. KG is 3.66 m, TPC_{SW} is 20, I_{NA} is 22 788 m^4, draft is 6.7 m in salt water. Height to derrick head is 18.29 m above the keel.

Chapter 14
Moments of statical stability

When a ship is inclined by an external force, such as wind and wave action, the centre of buoyancy moves out to the low side, parallel to the shift of the centre of gravity of the immersed and emerged wedges, to the new centre of gravity of the under-water volume. The force of buoyancy is considered to act vertically upwards through the centre of buoyancy, whilst the weight of the ship is considered to act vertically downwards through the centre of gravity. These two equal and opposite forces produce a moment or couple which may tend to right or capsize the ship. The moment is referred to as the *moment of statical stability* and may be defined as the moment to return the ship to the initial position when inclined by an external force.

A ship which has been inclined by an external force is shown in Figure 14.1.

The centre of buoyancy has moved from B to B_1 parallel to gg_1, and the force of buoyancy (W) acts vertically upwards through B_1. The weight of the ship (W) acts vertically downwards through the centre of gravity (G).

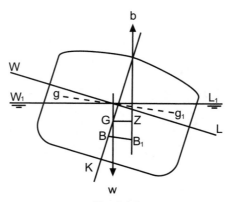

Fig. 14.1

The perpendicular distance between the lines of action of the forces (GZ) is called the *righting lever*. Taking moments about the centre of gravity, the moment of statical stability is equal to the product of the righting lever and the displacement, or:

$$\text{Moment of statical stability} = W \times GZ$$

The moment of statical stability at a small angle of heel

At small angles of heel the force of buoyancy may be considered to act vertically upwards through a fixed point called the initial metacentre (M). This is shown in Figure 14.2, in which the ship is inclined to a small angle (θ degrees).

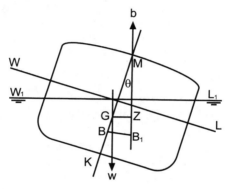

Fig. 14.2

$$\text{Moment of statical stability} = W \times GZ$$

$$\text{But in triangle GZM: } GZ = GM \sin \theta°$$

$$\therefore \text{ Moment of statical stability} = W \times GM \times \sin \theta°$$

From this formula it can be seen that for any particular displacement at small angles of heel, the righting moments will vary directly as the initial metacentric height (GM). Hence, if the ship has a comparatively large GM she will tend to be 'stiff', whilst a small GM will tend to make her 'tender'. It should also be noticed, however, that the stability of a ship depends not only upon the size of the GM or GZ but also upon the displacement. Thus two similar ships may have identical GM's, but if one is at the light displacement and the other at the load displacement, their respective states of stability will be vastly different. The ship which is at the load displacement will be much more 'stiff' than the other.

Example 1

A ship of 4000 tonnes displacement has KG 5.5 m and KM 6.0 m. Calculate the moment of statical stability when heeled 5 degrees.

$$GM = KM - KG = 6.0 - 5.5 = 0.5 \, m$$

$$\text{Moment of statical stability} = W \times GM \times \sin \theta°$$

$$= 4000 \times 0.5 \times \sin 5°$$

$$\underline{\text{Moment of statical stability} = 174.4 \, \text{tonnes m}}$$

Example 2

When a ship of 12 000 tonnes displacement is heeled $6\frac{1}{2}$ degrees the moment of statical stability is 600 tonnes m. Calculate the initial metacentric height.

$$\text{Moment of statical stability} = W \times GM \times \sin \theta°$$

$$\therefore GM = \frac{\text{Moment of statical stability}}{W \times \sin \theta°}$$

$$= \frac{600}{12\,000 \sin 6\frac{1}{2}°}$$

$$\underline{GM = 0.44 \, m}$$

The moment of statical stability at a large angle of heel

At a large angle of heel the force of buoyancy can no longer be considered to act vertically upwards through the initial metacentre (M). This is shown in Figure 14.3, where the ship is heeled to an angle of more than 15 degrees. The centre of buoyancy has moved further out to the low side, and the vertical through B_1 no longer passes through (M), the initial metacentre. The righting lever (GZ) is once again the perpendicular distance between the vertical through G and the vertical through B_1, and the moment of statical stability is equal to $W \times GZ$.

But GZ is no longer equal to $GM \sin \theta°$. Up to the angle at which the

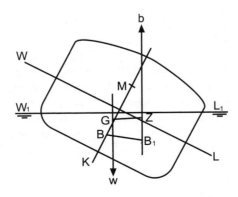

Fig. 14.3

deck edge is immersed, it may be found by using a formula known as the *Wall-sided formula*. i.e.

$$GZ = (GM + \tfrac{1}{2} BM \tan^2 \theta) \sin \theta$$

The derivation of this formula is as follows:

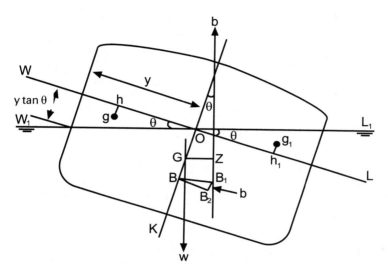

Fig. 14.4

Refer to the ship shown in Figure 14.4. When inclined the wedge WOW_1 is transferred to LOL_1 such that its centre of gravity shifts from g to g_1. This causes the centre of buoyancy to shift from B to B_1. The horizontal components of these shifts are hh_1 and BB_2 respectively, the vertical components being $(gh + g_1h_1)$ and B_1B_2 respectively.

Let BB_2 be 'a' units and let B_1B_2 be 'b' units.

Now consider the wedge LOL_1:

$$\text{Area} = \tfrac{1}{2}\, y^2 \tan \theta$$

Consider an elementary strip longitudinally of length dx as in Figure 14.5(b).

$$\text{Volume} = \tfrac{1}{2}\, y^2 \tan \theta\, dx$$

The total horizontal shift of the wedge (hh_1), is $2/3 \times 2y$ or $4/3 \times y$.

$$\therefore \text{ Moment of shifting this wedge} = \tfrac{4}{3}\, y \times \tfrac{1}{2}\, y^2 \tan \theta\, dx$$

$$= \tfrac{2}{3}\, y^3 \tan \theta\, dx$$

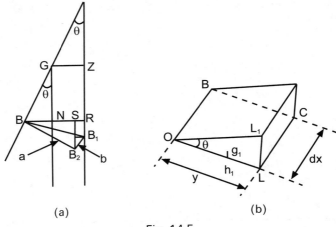

Fig. 14.5

The sum of the moment of all such wedges $= \int_O^L \frac{2}{3} y^3 \tan \theta \, dx$

$$= \tan \theta \int_O^L \frac{2}{3} y^3 \, dx$$

But the second moment of the water-plane area about the centre-line (I) $\quad = \int_O^L \frac{2}{3} y^3 \, dx$

$\therefore$ Sum of the moment of all such wedges $= I \tan \theta$

$$BB_2 = \frac{v \times hh_1}{V}$$

or

$$V \times BB_2 = v \times hh_1$$

But, the sum of the moments of the wedges $= v \times hh_1$

$$\therefore V \times BB_2 = I \tan \theta$$

$$BB_2 = \frac{I}{V} \tan \theta$$

$$BB_2 = BM \tan \theta \quad ------ \text{'a'}$$

The vertical shift of the wedge $= gh + g_1h_1$

$$= 2gh$$

$\therefore$ The vertical moment of the shift $= v \times 2gh$

$$= 2vgh$$

In Figure 14.5(b):

$$OL = y \text{ and } Oh_1 = \frac{2}{3} y$$

But
$$LL_1 = y \tan \theta$$

$$\therefore g_1 h_1 = \tfrac{1}{3} y \tan \theta$$

The volume of the wedge $= \tfrac{1}{2} y^2 \tan \theta \, dx$

The moment of the vertical shift $= \tfrac{1}{2} y^2 \tan \theta \, dx \times \tfrac{2}{3} y \tan \theta$

$$= \tfrac{1}{3} y^3 \tan^2 \theta \, dx$$

The vertical moment of all such wedges $= \displaystyle\int_O^L \tfrac{1}{3} y^3 \tan^2 \theta \, dx$

$$= \tfrac{1}{2} I \tan^2 \theta$$

$\therefore$ The moment of the vertical shift $= \tfrac{1}{2} I \tan^2 \theta$

Also
$$B_1 B_2 = \frac{v \times 2gh}{V}$$

or
$$V \times b = 2vgh$$

but

$$2vgh = \text{The vertical moment of the shift}$$

$$\therefore V \times b = \tfrac{1}{2} I \tan^2 \theta$$

or

$$b = \frac{I}{V} \times \frac{\tan^2 \theta}{2}$$

$$B_1 B_2 = \frac{BM \tan^2 \theta}{2} \quad {-\,-\,-\,-\,-\,-\,-\,-\,-\,-\,-\,-}\; 'b'$$

Referring to Figure 14.5(a)

$GZ = NR$

$\quad = BR - BN$

$\quad = (BS + SR) - BN$

$\quad = a \cos \theta + b \sin \theta - BG \sin \theta$

$\quad = BM \tan \theta \cos \theta + \tfrac{1}{2} BM \tan^2 \theta \sin \theta - BG \sin \theta \qquad \text{[from 'a' and 'b']}$

$\quad = BM \sin \theta + \tfrac{1}{2} BM \tan^2 \theta \sin \theta - BG \sin \theta$

$\quad = \sin \theta \, (BM + \tfrac{1}{2} BM \tan^2 \theta - BG)$

$GZ = \sin \theta \, (GM + \tfrac{1}{2} BM \tan^2 \theta) \qquad\qquad \text{[for } \theta \text{ up to } 25°]$

This is the *Wall-sided formula*.

Note. This formula may be used to obtain the GZ at any angle of heel so long as the ship's side at WW_1 is parallel to LL_1, but for small angles of heel (θ up to 5°), the term $\frac{1}{2} BM \tan^2 \theta$ may be omitted.

Example 1

A ship of 6000 tonnes displacement has KB 3 m, KM 6 m, and KG 5.5 m. Find the moment of statical stability at 25 degrees heel.

$$GZ = (GM + \tfrac{1}{2} BM \tan^2 \theta) \sin \theta$$

$$= (0.5 + \tfrac{1}{2} \times 3 \times \tan^2 25°) \sin 25°$$

$$= 0.8262 \sin 25°$$

$$GZ = 0.35 \, m$$

$$\text{Moment of statical stability} = W \times GZ$$

$$= 6000 \times 0.35$$

$$\underline{\text{Moment of statical stability} = \underline{2100 \text{ tonnes m}}}$$

Example 2

A box-shaped vessel $65 \, m \times 12 \, m \times 8 \, m$ has KG 4 m, and is floating in salt water upright on an even keel at 4 m draft F and A. Calculate the moments of statical stability at *(a)*, 5 degrees and *(b)*, 25 degrees heel.

$$W = L \times B \times draft \times 1.025 \qquad KB = \tfrac{1}{2} \, draft \qquad BM = \frac{B^2}{12d}$$

$$= 65 \times 12 \times 4 \times 1.025 \text{ tonnes} \qquad KB = 2 \, m \qquad = \frac{12 \times 12}{12 \times 4}$$

$$W = 3198 \text{ tonnes} \qquad\qquad\qquad\qquad\qquad\qquad BM = 3 \, m$$

$$
\begin{array}{rr}
KB = & 2 \, m \\
BM = & +3 \, m \\
\hline
KM = & 5 \, m \\
KG = & -4 \, m \\
\hline
GM = & 1 \, m \\
\hline
\end{array}
$$

At 5° heel

$$GZ = GM \sin \theta$$

$$= 1 \times \sin 5°$$

$$GZ = 0.0872$$

$$\text{Moment of statical stability} = W \times GZ$$

$$= 3198 \times 0.0872$$

$$= 278.9 \text{ tonnes m}$$

At 25° heel

$$GZ = (GM + \tfrac{1}{2} BM \tan^2 \theta) \sin \theta$$

$$= (1 + \tfrac{1}{2} \times 3 \times \tan^2 25°) \sin 25°$$

$$= (1 + 0.3262) \sin 25°$$

$$= 1.3262 \sin 25°$$

$$GZ = 0.56 \text{ metres}$$

$$\text{Moment of statical stability} = W \times GZ$$

$$= 3198 \times 0.56$$

$$= 1790.9 \text{ tonnes m}$$

Ans. (a) 278.9 tonnes m and (b) 1790.9 tonnes m.

The moment of statical stability at a large angle of heel may also be calculated using a formula known as *Attwood's formula*: i.e.

$$\text{Moment of statical stability} = W \left(\frac{v \times hh_1}{V} - BG \sin \theta \right)$$

The derivation of this formula is as follows:

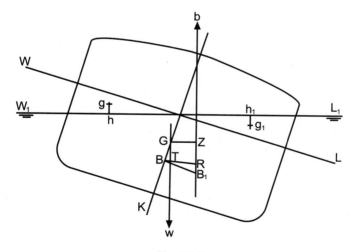

Fig. 14.6

$$\text{Moment of statical stability} = W \times GZ$$

$$= W(BR - BT)$$

Let v = the volume of the immersed or emerged wedge,

hh_1 = the horizontal component of the shift of the centre of gravity of the wedge,

V = the underwater volume of the ship, and

BR = the horizontal component of the shift of the centre of buoyancy.

$$BT = BG \sin \theta$$

also

$$BR = \frac{v \times hh_1}{V}$$

$$\therefore \text{ Moment of statical stability} = W \left(\frac{v \times hh_1}{V} - BG \sin \theta \right)$$

Exercise 14

1   A ship of 10 000 tonnes displacement has GM 0.5 m. Calculate the moment of statical stability when the ship is heeled $7\frac{3}{4}$ degrees.

2   When a ship of 12 000 tonnes displacement is heeled $5\frac{1}{4}$ degrees the moment of statical stability is 300 tonnes m KG 7.5 m. Find the height of the metacentre above the keel.

3   Find the moment of statical stability when a ship of 10 450 tonnes displacement is heeled 6 degrees if the GM is 0.5 m.

4   When a ship of 10 000 tonnes displacement is heeled 15 degrees, the righting lever is 0.2 m, KM 6.8 m. Find the KG and the moment of statical stability.

5   A box-shaped vessel 55 m × 7.5 m × 6 m has KG 2.7 m, and floats in salt water on an even keel at 4 m draft F and A. Calculate the moments of statical stability at (a) 6 degrees heel and (b) 24 degrees heel.

6   A ship of 10 000 tonnes displacement has KG 5.5 m, KB 2.8 m, and BM 3 m. Calculate the moments of statical stability at (a) 5 degrees heel and (b) 25 degrees heel.

7   A box-shaped vessel of 3200 tonnes displacement has GM 0.5 m, and beam 15 m, and is floating at 4 m draft. Find the moments of statical stability at 5 degrees and 25 degrees heel.

8   A ship of 11 000 tonnes displacement has a moment of statical stability of 500 tonnes m when heeled 5 degrees. Find the initial metacentric height.

9   (a) Write a brief description on the characteristics associated with an 'Angle of Loll'.

   (b) For a box-shaped barge, the breadth is 6.4 m and the draft is 2.44 m even keel, with a KG of 2.67 m.

Using the given wall-sided formula, calculate the GZ ordinates up to an angle of heel of 20°, in 4° increments. From the results construct a Statical Stability curve up to 20° angle of heel. Label the important points on this constructed curve.

$$GZ = \sin \theta (GM + \tfrac{1}{2} BM \tan^2 \theta)$$

Chapter 15
Trim

Trim may be considered as the longitudinal equivalent of list. Trim is also known as 'longitudinal stability'. It is in effect transverse stability turned through 90°. Instead of trim being measured in degrees it is measured as the difference between the drafts forward and aft. If difference is zero then the ship is on even keel. If forward draft is greater than aft draft, the vessel is trimming *by the bow*. If aft draft is greater than the forward draft, the vessel is trimming *by the stern*.

Consider a ship to be floating at rest in still water and on an even keel as shown in Figure 15.1.

The centre of gravity (G) and the centre of buoyancy (B) will be in the same vertical line and the ship will be displacing her own weight of water. So $W = b$.

Now let a weight 'w', already on board, be shifted aft through a distance 'd', as shown in Figure 15.1. This causes the centre of gravity of the ship to shift from G to G_1, parallel to the shift of the centre of gravity of the weight shifted, so that:

$$GG_1 = \frac{w \times d}{W}$$

or

$$W \times GG_1 = w \times d$$

A trimming moment of $W \times GG_1$ is thereby produced.
But

$$W \times GG_1 = w \times d$$

$$\therefore \text{ The trimming moment} = w \times d$$

The ship will now trim until the centres of gravity and buoyancy are again in the same vertical line, as shown in Figure 15.2. When trimmed, the wedge of buoyancy LFL_1 emerges and the wedge WFW_1 is immersed. Since the ship, when trimmed, must displace the same weight of water as

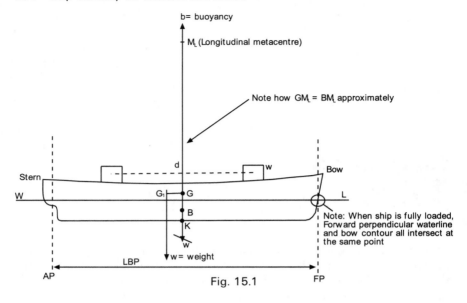

Fig. 15.1

when on an even keel, the volume of the immersed wedge must be equal to the volume of the emerged wedge and F, the point about which the ship trims, is the centre of gravity of the water-plane area. The point F is called the 'Centre of Flotation' or 'Tipping Centre'.

A vessel with a rectangular water-plane has its centre of flotation on the centre line amidships but, on a ship, it may be a little forward or abaft amidships, depending upon the shape of the water-plane. In trim problems, unless stated otherwise, it is to be assumed that the centre of flotation is situated amidships.

Trimming moments are taken about the centre of flotation since this is the point about which rotation takes place.

The longitudinal metacentre (M_L) is the point of intersection between the verticals through the longitudinal positions of the centres of buoyancy. The vertical distance between the centre of gravity and the longitudinal metacentre (GM_L) is called the longitudinal metacentric height.

BM_L is the height of the longitudinal metacentre above the centre of buoyancy and is found for any shape of vessel by the formula:

$$BM_L = \frac{I_L}{V}$$

where

$I_L =$ the longitudinal second moment of the water-plane about the centre of flotation

and

$V =$ the vessel's volume of displacement

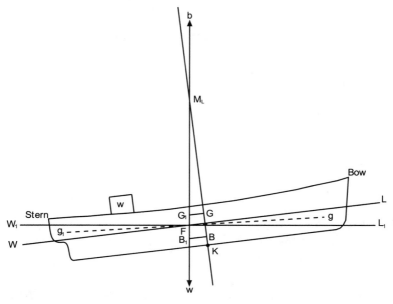

Fig. 15.2

The derivation of this formula is similar to that for finding the transverse BM.

For a rectangular water-plane area:

$$I_L = \frac{BL^3}{12}$$

where

L = the length of the water-plane

and

B = the breadth of the water-plane

Thus, for a vessel having a rectangular water-plane:

$$BM_L = \frac{BL^3}{12V}$$

For a box-shaped vessel:

$$BM_L = \frac{I_L}{V}$$

$$= \frac{BL^3}{12V}$$

$$= \frac{BL^3}{12 \times L \times B \times d}$$

$$BM_L = \frac{L^2}{12d}$$

where

L = the length of the vessel, and $\left.\vphantom{\begin{matrix}a\\b\end{matrix}}\right\}$ Hence, BM_L is independent

d = the draft of the vessel $\qquad$ of ships Br. Mld.

For a triangular prism:

$$BM_L = \frac{I_L}{V}$$

$$= \frac{BL^3}{12 \times \frac{1}{2} \times L \times B \times d}$$

$$BM_L = \frac{L^2}{6d}, \text{ so again is independent of Br. Mld.}$$

It should be noted that the distance BG is small when compared with BM_L or GM_L and, for this reason, BM_L may, without appreciable error, be substituted for GM_L in the formula for finding MCT 1 cm.

The Moment to Change Trim one centimetre (MCT 1 cm or MCTC)

The MCT 1 cm, or MCTC, is the moment required to change trim by 1 cm, and may be calculated by using the formula:

$$MCT\ 1\ cm = \frac{W \times GM_L}{100L}$$

where

W = the vessel's displacement in tonnes

GM_L = the longitudinal metacentric height in metres, and

L = the vessel's length in metres.

The derivation of this formula is as follows:

Consider a ship floating on an even keel as shown in Figure 15.3(a). The ship is in equilibrium.

Now shift the weight 'w' forward through a distance of 'd' metres. The ship's centre of gravity will shift from G to G_1, causing a trimming moment of $W \times GG_1$, as shown in Figure 15.3(b).

The ship will trim to bring the centres of buoyancy and gravity into the same vertical line as shown in Figure 15.3(c). The ship is again in equilibrium.

Let the ship's length be L metres and let the tipping centre (F) be l metres from aft.

The longitudinal metacentre (M_L) is the point of intersection between the verticals through the centre of buoyancy when on an even keel and when trimmed.

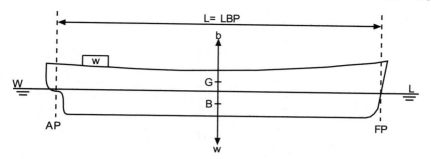

Fig. 15.3(a)

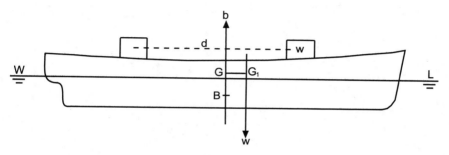

Fig. 15.3(b)

$$GG_I = \frac{w \times d}{W} \text{ and } GG_I = GM_L \tan \theta$$

$$\therefore \tan \theta = \frac{w \times d}{W \times GM_L}$$

but

$$\tan \theta = \frac{t}{L} \text{ (See Figure 15.4(b))}$$

Let the change of trim due to shifting the weight be 1 cm. Then $w \times d$ is the moment to change trim 1 cm.

$$\therefore \tan \theta = \frac{1}{100L}$$

but

$$\tan \theta = \frac{w \times d}{W \times GM_L}$$

$$\therefore \tan \theta = \frac{MCT \ 1 \ cm}{W \times GM_L}$$

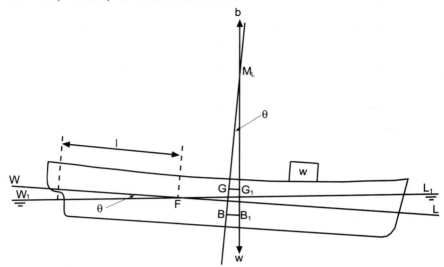

Fig. 15.3(c)

or

$$\frac{\text{MCT } 1 \text{ cm}}{\text{W} \times \text{GM}_L} = \frac{1}{100\text{L}}$$

and

$$\text{MCT } 1 \text{ cm} = \frac{\text{W} \times \text{GM}_L}{100\text{L}} \text{ tonnes m/cm.}$$

To find the change of draft forward and aft due to change of trim

When a ship changes trim it will obviously cause a change in the drafts forward and aft. One of these will be increased and the other decreased. A formula must now be found which will give the change in drafts due to change of trim.

Consider a ship floating upright as shown in Figure 15.4(a). F_1 represents

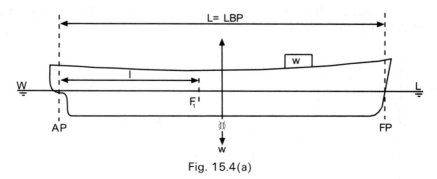

Fig. 15.4(a)

the position of the centre of flotation which is l metres from aft. The ship's length is L metres and a weight 'w' is on deck forward.

Let this weight now be shifted aft a distance of 'd' metres. The ship will trim about F_1 and change the trim 't' cms by the stern as shown in Figure 15.4(b).

W_1C is a line drawn parallel to the keel.

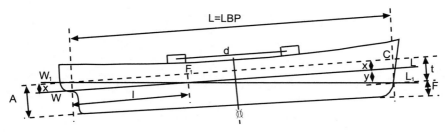

Fig. 15.4(b)

'A' represents the new draft aft and 'F' the new draft forward. The trim is therefore equal to A − F and, since the original trim was zero, this must also be equal to the change of trim.

Let 'x' represent the change of draft aft due to the change of trim and let 'y' represent the change forward.

In the triangles WW_1F_1 and W_1L_1C, using the property of similar triangles:

$$\frac{x\,cm}{l\,m} = \frac{t\,cm}{L\,m}$$

or

$$x\,cm = \frac{l\,m \times t\,cm}{L\,m}$$

∴ Change of draft aft in cm $= \dfrac{l}{L} \times$ Change of trim in cm

where

l = the distance of centre of flotation from aft in metres, and

L = the ship's length in metres

It will also be noticed that $x + y = t$

∴ Change of draft F in cm = Change of trim − Change of draft A.

The effect of shifting weights already on board

Example 1

A ship 126 m long is floating at drafts of 5.5 m F and 6.5 m A. The centre of flotation is 3 m aft of amidships. MCT 1 cm = 240 tonnes m. Displacement =

6000 tonnes. Find the new drafts if a weight of 120 tonnes already on board is shifted forward a distance of 45 metres.

$$\text{Trimming moment} = w \times d$$

$$= 120 \times 45$$

$$= 5400 \text{ tonnes m by the head}$$

$$\text{Change of trim} = \frac{\text{Trimming moment}}{\text{MCT 1 cm}}$$

$$= \frac{5400}{240}$$

$$= 22.5 \text{ cm by the head}$$

$$\text{Change of draft aft} = \frac{l}{L} \times \text{Change of trim}$$

$$= \frac{60}{126} \times 22.5$$

$$= 10.7 \text{ cm}$$

$$\text{Change of draft forward} = \frac{66}{126} \times 22.5$$

$$= 11.8 \text{ cm}$$

Original drafts	6.500 m A	5.500 m F
Change due to trim	−0.107 m	+0.118 m
Ans. New drafts	6.393 m A	5.618 m F

Example 2

A box-shaped vessel 90 m × 10 m × 6 m floats in salt water on an even keel at 3 m draft F and A. Find the new drafts if a weight of 64 tonnes already on board is shifted a distance of 40 metres aft.

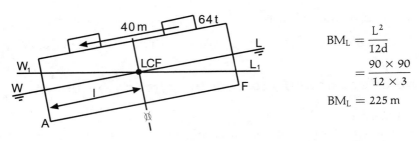

$$BM_L = \frac{L^2}{12d}$$

$$= \frac{90 \times 90}{12 \times 3}$$

$$BM_L = 225 \text{ m}$$

Fig. 15.5

$$W = L \times B \times d \times 1.025$$

$$= 90 \times 10 \times 3 \times 1.025$$

$$W = 2767.5 \text{ tonnes}$$

$$\text{MCT 1 cm} = \frac{W \times GM_L}{100L}$$

Since BG is small compared with GM_L:

$$\text{MCT 1 cm} \simeq \frac{W \times BM_L}{100L}$$

$$= \frac{2767.5 \times 225}{100 \times 90}$$

$$\text{MCT 1 cm} = 69.19 \text{ tonnes m/cm}$$

$$\text{Change of trim} = \frac{w \times d}{\text{MCT 1 cm}}$$

$$= \frac{64 \times 40}{69.19}$$

$$\text{Change of trim} = 37 \text{ cm by the stern}$$

$$\text{Change of draft aft} = \frac{l}{L} \times \text{Change of trim}$$

$$= \tfrac{1}{2} \times 37 \text{ cm}$$

$$\text{Change of draft aft} = 18.5 \text{ cm}$$

$$\text{Change of draft forward} = 18.5 \text{ cm.}$$

Original drafts	3.000 m A	3.000 m F
Change due to trim	+0.185 m	−0.185 m
Ans. <u>New drafts</u>	3.185 m A	2.815 m F

The effect of loading and/or discharging weights

When a weight is loaded at the centre of flotation it will produce no trimming moment, but the ship's drafts will increase uniformly so that the ship displaces an extra weight of water equal to the weight loaded. If the weight is now shifted forward or aft away from the centre of flotation, it will cause a change of trim. From this it can be seen that when a weight is loaded away from the centre of flotation, it will cause both a bodily sinkage and a change of trim.

Similarly, when a weight is being discharged, if the weight is first shifted to the centre of flotation it will produce a change of trim, and if it is then discharged from the centre of flotation the ship will rise bodily. Thus, both a change of trim and bodily rise must be considered when a weight is being discharged away from the centre of flotation.

Example 1

A ship 90 m long is floating at drafts 4.5 m F and 5.0 m A. The centre of flotation is 1.5 m aft of amidships. TPC 10 tonnes. MCT 1 cm. 120 tonnes m. Find the new drafts if a total weight of 450 tonnes is loaded in a position 14 m forward of amidships.

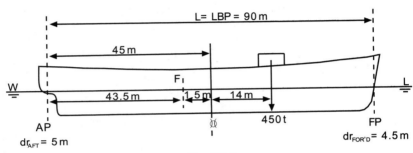

Fig. 15.6

$$\text{Bodily sinkage} = \frac{w}{\text{TPC}}$$

$$= \frac{450}{10}$$

$$\text{Bodily sinkage} = 45 \text{ cm}$$

$$\text{Change of trim} = \frac{\text{Trim moment}}{\text{MCT 1 cm}}$$

$$= \frac{450 \times 15.5}{120}$$

$$\text{Change of trim} = 58.12 \text{ cm by the head}$$

$$\text{Change of draft aft} = \frac{l}{L} \times \text{Change of trim}$$

$$= \frac{43.5}{90} \times 58.12$$

$$\text{Change of draft aft} = 28.09 \text{ cm}$$

$$\text{Change of draft forward} = \frac{46.5}{90} \times 58.12$$

$$\text{Change of draft forward} = 30.03 \text{ cm}$$

Original drafts	5.000 m A	4.500 m F
Bodily sinkage	+0.450 m	+0.450 m
	5.450 m	4.950 m
Change due trim	−0.281 m	+0.300 m
Ans. <u>New drafts</u>	5.169 m A	5.250 m F

Note. In the event of more than one weight being loaded or discharged, the net weight loaded or discharged is used to find the net bodily increase or decrease in draft, and the resultant trimming moment is used to find the change of trim.

Also, when the net weight loaded or discharged is large, it may be necessary to use the TPC and MCT 1 cm at the original draft to find the approximate new drafts, and then rework the problem using the TPC and MCT 1 cm for the mean of the old and the new drafts to find a more accurate result.

Example 2

A box-shaped vessel 40 m × 6 m × 3 m is floating in salt water on an even keel at 2 m draft F and A. Find the new drafts if a weight of 35 tonnes is discharged from a position 6 m from forward. MCT 1 cm = 8.4 tonnes m.

$$TPC = \frac{WPA}{97.56}$$

$$= \frac{40 \times 6}{97.56}$$

$$TPC = 2.46 \text{ tonnes}$$

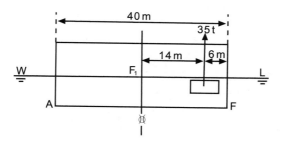

Fig. 15.7

$$\text{Bodily rise} = \frac{w}{TPC}$$

$$= \frac{35}{2.46}$$

$$\text{Bodily rise} = 14.2 \text{ cm}$$

$$\text{Change of trim} = \frac{w \times d}{MCT \ 1 \ cm}$$

$$= \frac{35 \times 14}{8.4}$$

$$\text{Change of trim} = 58.3\,\text{cm by the stern}$$

$$\text{Change of draft aft} = \frac{1}{L} \times \text{Change of trim}$$

$$= \tfrac{1}{2} \times 58.3\,\text{cm}$$

$$\text{Change of draft aft} = 29.15\,\text{cm}$$

$$\text{Change of draft forward} = \tfrac{1}{2} \times 58.3$$

$$\text{Change of draft forward} = 29.15\,\text{cm}$$

Original drafts	2.000 m A	2.000 m F
Bodily rise	−0.140 m	−0.140 m
	1.860 m	1.860 m
Change due trim	+0.290 m	−0.290 m
Ans. New drafts	2.150 m A	1.570 m F

Example 3

A ship 100 m long arrives in port with drafts 3 m F and 4.3 m A. TPC 10 tonnes. MCT 1 cm 120 tonnes m. The centre of flotation is 3 m aft of amidships. If 80 tonnes of cargo is loaded in a position 24 m forward of amidships and 40 tonnes of cargo is discharged from 12 m aft of amidships, what are the new drafts?

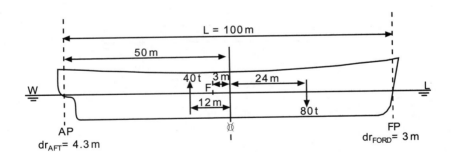

Fig. 15.8

		Bodily sinkage $= \dfrac{w}{\text{TPC}}$
Cargo loaded	80 tonnes	
Cargo discharged	40 tonnes	$= \dfrac{40}{10}$
Net loaded	40 tonnes	Bodily sinkage $= 4\,\text{cm}$

To find the change of trim take moments about the centre of flotation.

Weight	Distance from C.F.	Moment to change trim by	
		head	stern
+80	−27	2160	−
−40	+9	360	−
		2520	−

$$\text{Change of trim} = \frac{\text{Trim moment}}{\text{MCT 1 cm}}$$

$$= \frac{2520}{120}$$

$$\text{Change of trim} = 21 \text{ cm by the head}$$

$$\text{Change of draft aft} = \frac{l}{L} \times \text{Change of trim}$$

$$= \frac{47}{100} \times 21$$

$$\text{Change of draft aft} = 9.87 \text{ cm}$$

$$\text{Change of draft forward} = \frac{53}{100} \times 21$$

$$\text{Change of draft forward} = 11.13 \text{ cm}$$

Original drafts	4.300 m A	3.000 m F
Bodily sinkage	+0.040 m	+0.040 m
	4.340 m	3.040 m
Change due trim	−0.099 m	+0.111 m
Ans. New drafts	4.241 m A	3.151 m F

Example 4

A ship of 6000 tonnes displacement has drafts 7 m F and 8 m A. MCT 1 cm 100 tonnes m, TPC 20 tonnes, centre of flotation is amidships. 500 tonnes of cargo is discharged from each of the following four holds:

No. 1 hold, centre of gravity 40 m forward of amidships
No. 2 hold, centre of gravity 25 m forward of amidships
No. 3 hold, centre of gravity 20 m aft of amidships
No. 4 hold, centre of gravity 50 m aft of amidships

The following bunkers are also loaded:

150 tonnes at 12 m forward of amidships
50 tonnes at 15 m aft of amidships

Find the new drafts forward and aft.

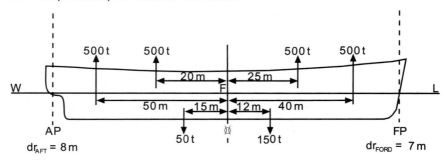

Fig. 15.9

Total cargo discharged	2000 tonnes	Bodily rise $= \dfrac{w}{\text{TPC}}$	
Total bunkers loaded	200 tonnes	$= \dfrac{1800}{20}$	
Net weight discharged	1800 tonnes	Bodily rise $= 90$ cm	

Assume levers and moments aft of LCF are +ve.
Assume levers and moments forward of LCF are −ve.

Weight	Distance from C.F.	Moments
−500	−40	+20 000
−500	−25	+12 500
−500	+20	−10 000
−500	+50	−25 000
+150	−12	−1800
+50	+15	+750
		−3550

Resultant moment 3550 tonnes m by the head because of the −ve sign.

$$\text{Change of trim} = \frac{\text{Trim moment}}{\text{MCT 1 cm}}$$

$$= \frac{3550}{100}$$

Change of trim = 35.5 cm by the head

Since centre of flotation is amidships,

$$\text{Change of draft aft} = \text{Change of draft forward}$$

$$= \tfrac{1}{2} \text{ change of trim}$$

$$= 17.75 \text{ cm say } 0.18 \text{ m}$$

Original drafts	8.000 m A	7.000 m F
Bodily rise	−0.900 m	−0.900 m
	7.100 m	6.100 m
Change due trim	−0.180 m	+0.180 m
Ans. <u>New drafts</u>	6.920 m A	6.280 m F

Example 5

A ship arrives in port trimmed 25 cm by the stern. The centre of flotation is amidships. MCT 1 cm 100 tonnes m. A total of 3800 tonnes of cargo is to be discharged from 4 holds, and 360 tonnes of bunkers loaded in No. 4 double bottom tank. 1200 tonnes of the cargo is to be discharged from No. 2 hold and 600 tonnes from No. 3 hold. Find the amount to be discharged from Nos. 1 and 4 holds if the ship is to complete on an even keel.

Centre of gravity of No. 1 hold is 50 m forward of the centre of flotation
Centre of gravity of No. 2 hold is 30 m forward of the centre of flotation
Centre of gravity of No. 3 hold is 20 m abaft of the centre of flotation
Centre of gravity of No. 4 hold is 45 m abaft of the centre of flotation
Centre of gravity of No. 4 DB tank is 5 m abaft of the centre of flotation

Total cargo to be discharged from 4 holds	3800 tonnes
Total cargo to be discharged from Nos. 2 and 3	1800 tonnes
Total cargo to be discharged from Nos. 1 and 4	<u>2000 tonnes</u>

Let 'x' tonnes of cargo be discharged from No. 1 hold
Let (2000 − x) tonnes of cargo be discharged from No. 4 hold

Take moments about the centre of flotation, or as shown in Figure 15.10.

$$\text{Original trim} = 25 \text{ cm by the stern, i.e.} + 25 \text{ cm}$$
$$\text{Required trim} = 0$$
$$\text{Change of trim required} = 25 \text{ cm by the head, i.e.} - 25 \text{ cm}$$

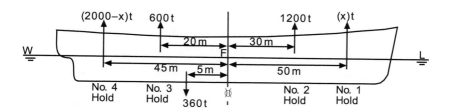

Fig. 15.10

Weight	Distance from C.F.	Moments	
		−ve	+ve
−x	−50	−	+50x
−1200	−30	−	+36 000
−600	+20	−12 000	−
−(2000 − x)	+45	−(90 000 − 45x)	−
+360	+5	−	+1800
		−102 000 + 45x	+37 800 + 50x

Trimming moment required = Change of trim × MCT 1 cm

$$= -25 \times 100 = -2500$$

Trimming moment required = 2500 tonnes m by the head

Resultant moment = Moment to change trim by head − MCT by stern

$$\therefore \ -2500 = -102\,000 + 45x + 37\,800 + 50x$$

$$= -102\,000 + 45x + 37\,800 + 50\,x$$

$$= 64\,200 - 95x$$

or

$$95x = 61\,700$$

$$\underline{x = 649.5 \text{ tonnes}}$$

and

$$\underline{2000 - x = 1350.5 \text{ tonnes}}$$

Ans. Discharge 649.5 tonnes from No. 1 hold and 1350.5 tonnes from No. 4 hold.

Using trim to find the position of the centre of flotation

Example

A ship arrives in port floating at drafts of 4.50 m A and 3.80 m F. The following cargo is then loaded:

> 100 tonnes in a position 24 m aft of amidships
> 30 tonnes in a position 30 m forward of amidships
> 60 tonnes in a position 15 m forward of amidships

The drafts are then found to be 5.10 m A and 4.40 m F. Find the position of the longitudinal centre of flotation aft of amidships.

Original drafts 4.50 m A 3.80 m F give 0.70 m trim by the stern, i.e. +70 cm.
New drafts 5.10 m A 4.40 m F give 0.70 m trim by the stern, i.e. +70 cm.
Therefore there has been no change in trim, which means that

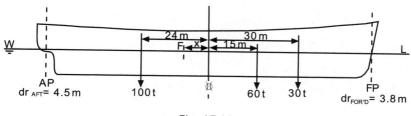

Fig. 15.11

The moment to change trim by the head = The moment to change trim by the stern.

Let the centre of flotation be 'x' metres aft of amidships. Taking moments, then,

$$100(24 - x) = 30(30 + x) + 60(15 + x)$$
$$2400 - 100x = 900 + 30x + 900 + 60x$$
$$190x = 600$$
$$x = 3.16\,m$$

Ans. Centre of flotation is 3.16 metres aft of amidships.

Note. In this type of question it is usual to assume that the centre of flotation is aft of amidships, but this may not be the case. Had it been assumed that the centre of flotation was aft of amidships when in actual fact it was forward, then the answer obtained would have been minus.

Remember. Levers, moments and trim by the stern all have a +ve sign. Levers, moments and trim by the head all have a −ve sign.

Loading a weight to keep the after draft constant

When a ship is being loaded it is usually the aim of those in charge of the operation to complete loading with the ship trimmed by the stern. Should the ship's draft on sailing be restricted by the depth of water over a dock-sill or by the depth of water in a channel, then the ship will be loaded in such a manner as to produce this draft aft and be trimmed by the stern.

Assume now that a ship loaded in this way is ready to sail. It is then found that the ship has to load an extra weight. The weight must be loaded in such a position that the draft aft is not increased and also that the maximum trim is maintained.

If the weight is loaded at the centre of flotation, the ship's drafts will increase uniformly and the draft aft will increase by a number of centimetres equal to w/TPC. The draft aft must now be decreased by this amount.

Now let the weight be shifted through a distance of 'd' metres forward. The ship will change trim by the head, causing a reduction in the draft aft by a number of centimetres equal to $l/L \times$ Change of trim.

Therefore, if the same draft is to be maintained aft, the above two quantities must be equal. i.e.

$$\frac{l}{L} \times \text{Change of trim} = \frac{w}{\text{TPC}}$$

So,

$$\text{Change of trim} = \frac{w}{\text{TPC}} \times \frac{L}{l} \qquad \text{(I)}$$

But,

$$\text{Change of trim} = \frac{w \times d}{\text{MCT 1 cm}} \qquad \text{(II)}$$

Equate (I) and (II)

$$\therefore \ \frac{w \times d}{\text{MCT 1 cm}} = \frac{w}{\text{TPC}} \times \frac{L}{l}$$

or

$$d = \frac{L \times \text{MCT 1 cm}}{l \times \text{TPC}}$$

where   d = the distance forward of the centre of flotation to load a weight
to keep the draft aft constant,
L = the ship's length, LBP and
l = the distance of the centre of flotation to the stern.

Example

A box-shaped vessel 60 m long, 10 m beam, and 6 m deep, is floating in salt water at drafts 4 m F and 4.4 m A. Find how far forward of amidships a weight of 30 tonnes must be loaded if the draft aft is to remain at 4.4 m.

$$\text{TPC}_{SW} = \frac{\text{WPA}}{97.56}$$

$$= \frac{60 \times 10}{97.56}$$

$$\text{TPC}_{SW} = 6.15 \text{ tonnes}$$

$$W = L \times B \times d \times \rho_{SW} \text{ tonnes}$$

$$= 60 \times 10 \times 4.2 \times 1.025$$

$$W = 2583 \text{ tonnes}$$

$$\text{BM}_L = \frac{L^2}{12d}$$

$$= \frac{60 \times 60}{12 \times 4.2}$$

$$\text{BM}_L = 71.42 \text{ metres}$$

$$\text{MCT 1 cm} \simeq \frac{W \times \text{BM}_L}{100L} \text{ because GM}_L \simeq \text{BM}_L$$

$$MCT\ 1\ cm = \frac{2583 \times 71.42}{100 \times 60}$$

$$MCT\ 1\ cm = 30.75\ t\,m/cm$$

$$d = \frac{L \times MCT\ 1\ cm}{l \times TPC_{SW}}$$

$$= \frac{60}{30} \times 30.75 \times \frac{1}{6.15}$$

$$d = 10\ \text{metres from LCF}$$

LCF is at amidships.

Ans. Load the weight 10 metres forward of amidships.

Loading a weight to produce a required draft

Example

A ship 150 metres long arrives at the mouth of a river with drafts 5.5 m F and 6.3 m A. MCT 1 cm 200 tonnes m. TPC 15 tonnes. Centre of flotation is 1.5 m aft of amidships. The ship has then to proceed up the river where the maximum draft permissible is 6.2 m. It is decided that SW ballast will be run into the forepeak tank to reduce the draft aft to 6.2 m. If the centre of gravity of the forepeak tank is 60 metres forward of the centre of flotation, find the minimum amount of water which must be run in and also find the final draft forward.

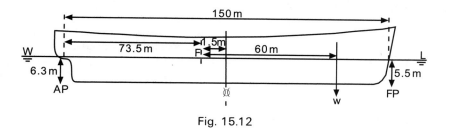

Fig. 15.12

(a) *Load 'w' tonnes at the centre of flotation.*

$$\text{Bodily sinkage} = \frac{w}{TPC}$$

$$= \frac{w}{15}\ cm$$

$$\text{New draft aft} = 6.3\ m + \frac{w}{15}\ cm \tag{I}$$

$$\text{Required draft aft} = 6.2\,\text{m} \tag{II}$$

$$\text{Equations (I)–(II)} = \underline{\text{Reduction required}} = 0.1\,\text{m} + \frac{w}{15}\,\text{cm}$$

$$= 10\,\text{cm} + \frac{w}{15}\,\text{cm}$$

$$= \left(10 + \frac{w}{15}\right)\,\text{cm} \tag{III}$$

(b) *Shift 'w' tonnes from the centre of flotation to the forepeak tank*

$$\text{Change of trim} = \frac{w \times d}{\text{MCT 1 cm}}$$

$$= \frac{60w}{200}$$

$$\text{Change of trim} = \frac{3w}{10}\,\text{cm by the head}$$

$$\text{Change of draft aft due to trim} = \frac{l}{L} \times \text{Change of trim}$$

$$= \frac{73.5}{150} \times \frac{3w}{10}$$

$$\text{Change of draft aft due to trim} = 0.147w\,\text{cm} \tag{IV}$$

$$\text{But change of draft required aft} = \left(10 + \frac{w}{15}\right)\,\text{cm as per equation (III)}$$

$$0.147w = 10 + \frac{w}{15}, \text{ i.e. equation (IV)} = \text{equation (III)}.$$

$$2.205w = 150 + w$$

$$1.205w = 150$$

$$w = 124.5\,\text{tonnes}$$

Therefore by loading 124.5 tonnes in the forepeak tank the draft aft will be reduced to 6.2 metres.

(c) *To find the new draft forward*

$$\text{Bodily sinkage} = \frac{w}{\text{TPC}}$$

$$= \frac{124.5}{15}$$

Bodily sinkage = 8.3 cm

$$\text{Change of trim} = \frac{w \times d}{\text{MCT 1 cm}}$$

$$= \frac{124.5 \times 60}{200}$$

Change of trim = 37.35 cm by the head

$$\text{Change of draft aft due trim} = \frac{l}{L} \times \text{Change of trim}$$

$$\text{Change of draft aft due trim} = \frac{73.5}{150} \times 37.35$$

$$= 18.3 \text{ cm}$$

Change of draft forward due trim = Change of trim − Change of draft aft

$$= 37.35 - 18.3 \text{ cm} = 19.05 \text{ cm, or}$$

$$\text{Change of draft forward due trim} = \frac{76.5 \times 37.35}{150} = 19.05 \text{ cm}$$

Original drafts	6.300 m A	5.500 m F
Bodily sinkage	+0.080 m	+0.080 m
	6.380 m	5.580 m
Change due trim	−0.180 m	+0.190 m
New drafts	6.200 m A	5.770 m F

Ans. Load 124.5 tonnes in forepeak tank. Final draft forward is 5.770 metres.

Using change of trim to find the longitudinal metacentric height (GM$_L$)

Earlier it was shown in this chapter that, when a weight is shifted longitudinally within a ship, it will cause a change of trim. It will now be shown how this effect may be used to determine the longitudinal metacentric height.

Consider Figure 15.13(a) which represents a ship of length 'L' at the waterline, floating upright on an even keel with a weight on deck forward. The centre of gravity is at G, the centre of buoyancy at B, and the longitudinal metacentre at M$_L$. The longitudinal metacentric height is therefore GM$_L$.

Now let the weight be shifted aft horizontally as shown in Figure 15.13(b). The ship's centre of gravity will also shift horizontally, from G to G$_1$, producing a trimming moment of W × GG$_1$ by the stern.

The ship will now trim to bring G$_1$ under M$_L$ as shown in Figure 15.13(c).

In Figure 15.13(c) W$_1$L$_1$ represents the new waterline, F the new draft forward, and A the new draft aft. It was shown in Figure 15.4(b) and by the

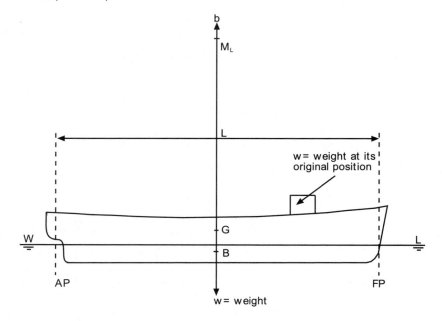

Fig. 15.13(a)

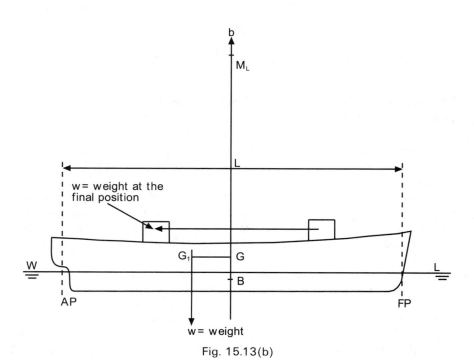

Fig. 15.13(b)

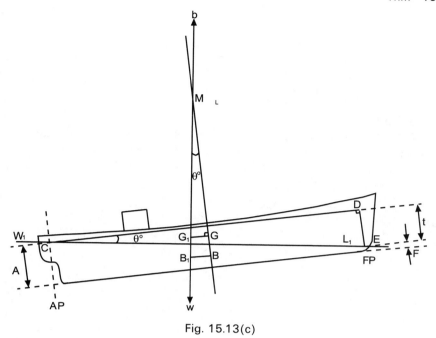

Fig. 15.13(c)

associated notes, that $F - A$ is equal to the new trim (t) and since the ship was originally on an even keel, then 't' must also be equal to the change of trim.

If the angle between the new and old verticals is equal to θ, then the angle between the new and old horizontals must also be equal to θ (the angle between two straight lines being equal to the angle between their normals).

It will also be seen in Figure 15.13(c) that the triangles GG_1M_L and CDE are similar triangles.

$$\therefore \frac{GM_L}{GG_1} = \frac{L}{t}$$

or

$$GM_L = \frac{L}{t} \times GG_1$$

(All measurements are in metres.)

Example 1

When a weight is shifted aft in a ship 120 metres long, it causes the ship's centre of gravity to move 0.2 metres horizontally and the trim to change by 0.15 metres. Find the longitudinal metacentric height.

$$\therefore \frac{GM_L}{GG_1} = \frac{L}{t}$$

$$\therefore \ GM_L = \frac{L}{t} \times GG_1$$

$$= \frac{120 \times 0.2}{0.15}$$

Ans. $\underline{GM_L = 160 \ metres}$

Example 2

A ship 150 metres long has a displacement of 7200 tonnes, and is floating upright on an even keel. When a weight of 60 tonnes, already on board, is shifted 24 metres forward, the trim is changed by 0.15 metres. Find the longitudinal metacentric height.

$$\frac{GM_L}{GG_1} = \frac{L}{t}$$

$$GM_L = GG_1 \times \frac{L}{t}$$

$$= \frac{w \times d}{W} \times \frac{L}{t}$$

$$= \frac{60 \times 24}{7200} \times \frac{150}{0.15}$$

Ans. $\underline{GM_L = 200 \ metres}$

Summary

1 Make a sketch from the given information.
2 Estimate the mean bodily sinkage.
3 Calculate the change of trim using levers measured from LCF.
4 Evaluate the trim ratio forward and aft at FP and AP, from the LCF position.
5 Collect the above calculated values to estimate the final end drafts.
6 In the solutions shown in the text, these final end drafts have been calculated to three decimal figures. In practice, naval architects and ship-officers round off the drafts to two decimal places only. This gives acceptable accuracy.
7 Note how the formulae were written in *letters* first and then put the *figures* in. In the event of a mathematical error, marks will be given for a correct formula and for a correct sketch.

EXERCISE 15

1   A ship of 8500 tonnes displacement has TPC 10 tonnes, MCT 1 cm = 100 tonnes m and the centre of flotation is amidships. She is completing loading under coal tips. Nos. 2 and 3 holds are full, but space is available in No. 1 hold (centre of gravity 50 m forward of amidships), and in No. 4 hold (centre of gravity 45 m aft of amidships). The present drafts are 6.5 m F and 7 m A, and the load draft is 7.1 m. Find how much cargo is to be loaded in each of the end holds so as to put the ship down to the load draft and complete loading on an even keel.

2   An oil tanker 150 m long, displacement 12 500 tonnes, MCT 1 cm 200 tonnes m, leaves port with drafts 7.2 m F and 7.4 m A. There is 550 tonnes of fuel oil in the foward deep tank (centre of gravity 70 m forward of the centre of flotation) and 600 tonnes in the after deep tank (centre of gravity 60 m aft of centre of flotation). The centre of flotation is 1 m aft of amidships. During the sea passage 450 tonnes of oil is consumed from aft. Find how much oil must be transferred from the forward tank to the after tank if the ship is to arrive on an even keel.

3   A ship 100 m long, and with a displacement of 2200 tonnes, has longitudinal metacentric height 150 m. The present drafts are 5.2 m F and 5.3 m A. Centre of flotation is 3 m aft of amidships. Find the new drafts if a weight of 5 tonnes already on board is shifted aft through a distance of 60 metres.

4   A ship is floating at drafts of 6.1 metres F and 6.7 metres A. The following cargo is then loaded:

> 20 tonnes in a position whose centre of gravity is 30 metres forward of amidships.
> 45 tonnes in a position whose centre of gravity is 25 metres forward of amidships.
> 60 tonnes in a position whose centre of gravity is 15 metres aft of amidships.
> 30 tonnes in a position whose centre of gravity is 3 metres aft of amidships.

The centre of flotation is amidships, MCT 1 cm = 200 tonnes m, and TPC = 35 tonnes. Find the new drafts forward and aft.

5   A ship arrives in port trimmed 0.3 m by the stern and is to discharge 4600 tonnes of cargo from 4 holds. 1800 tonnes of the cargo is to be discharged from No. 2 and 800 tonnes from No. 3 hold. Centre of flotation is amidships, MCT 1 cm = 250 tonnes m.

The centre of gravity of No. 1 hold is 45 m forward of amidships.
The centre of gravity of No. 2 hold is 25 m forward of amidships.
The centre of gravity of No. 3 hold is 20 m aft of amidships.
The centre of gravity of No. 4 hold is 50 m aft of amidships.

Find the amount of cargo which must be discharged from Nos. 1 and 4 holds if the ship is to sail on an even keel.

6   A ship is 150 m long, displacement 12 000 tonnes, and is floating at drafts of 7 m F and 8 m A. The ship is to enter port from an anchorage with a maximum draft of 7.6 m. Find the minimum amount of cargo to discharge from a hold whose centre of gravity is 50 m aft of the centre of flotation (which is amidships), TPC 15 tonnes, and MCT 1 cm = 300 tonnes m.

7   A ship 150 m × 20 m floats on an even keel at 10 m draft and has a block coefficient of fineness 0.8 and LGM of 200 metres. If 250 tonnes of cargo is discharged from a position 32 m from the centre of flotation, find the resulting change of trim.

8   A ship is floating in salt water at drafts of 6.7 m F and 7.3 m A. MCT 1 cm = 250 tonnes m. TPC 10 tonnes. Length of ship 120 metres. The centre of flotation is amidships. 220 tonnes of cargo is then discharged from a position 24 m forward of the centre of flotation. Find the weight of cargo which must now be shifted from 5 m aft of the centre of flotation to a position 20 m forward of the centre of flotation, to bring the draft aft to 7 metres. Find also the final draft forward.

9   A ship floats in salt water on an even keel displacing 6200 tonnes. KG = 5.5 m, KM = 6.3 m, and there is 500 tonnes of cargo yet to load. Space is available in No. 1 'tween deck (KG 7.6 m, centre of gravity 40 m forward of the centre of flotation) and in No. 4 lower hold (KG 5.5 m, centre of gravity 30 m aft of the centre of flotation). Find how much cargo to load in each space to complete loading trimmed 0.6 m by the stern, and find also the final GM. MCT 1 cm = 200 tonnes m.

10 A ship, floating at drafts of 7.7 m F and 7.9 m. A sustains damage in an end-on collision and has to lift the bow to reduce the draft forward to 6.7 m. The ship is about to enter a port in which the maximum permissible draft is 8.3 m. To do this it is decided to discharge cargo from No. 1 hold (centre of gravity 75 m forward of amidships) and No. 4 hold (centre of gravity 45 m aft of amidships). MCT 1 cm 200 tonnes m, TPC 15 tonnes. Centre of flotation is amidships. Find the minimum amount of cargo to discharge from each hold.

11 A ship 100 m long has centre of flotation 3 m aft of amidships and is floating at drafts 3.2 m F and 4.4 m A. TPC 10 tonnes. MCT 1 cm = 150 tonnes m. 30 tonnes of cargo is then discharged from 20 m forward of amidships and 40 tonnes is discharged from 12 m aft of amidships. Find the final drafts.

12 A ship 84 metres long is floating on an even keel at a draft of 5.5 metres. 45 tonnes of cargo is then loaded in a position 30 m aft of amidships. The centre of flotation is 1 m aft of amidships. TPC 15 tonnes. MCT 1 cm = 200 tonnes m. Find the final drafts.

13 A ship arrives in port with drafts 6.8 m. F and 7.2 m A. 500 tonnes of cargo is then discharged from each of 4 holds.

The centre of gravity of No. 1 hold is 40 m forward of amidships
The centre of gravity of No. 2 hold is 25 m forward of amidships
The centre of gravity of No. 3 hold is 20 m aft of amidships
The centre of gravity of No. 4 hold is 50 m aft of amidships

Also 50 tonnes of cargo is loaded in a position whose centre of gravity is 15 m aft of amidships, and 135 tonnes of cargo centre of gravity 40 m forward of amidships. TPC = 15 tonnes. MCT 1 cm = 400 tonnes m. The centre of flotation is amidships. Find the final drafts.

Using trim to find the position of the centre of flotation

14   A ship is floating at drafts 5.5 m F and 6.0 m A. The following cargo is then loaded:

   97 tonnes centre of gravity 8 m forward of amidships
   20 tonnes centre of gravity 40 m aft of amidships
   28 tonnes centre of gravity 20 m aft of amidships

The draft is now 5.6 metres F and 6.1 metres A. Find the position of the centre of flotation relative to amidships.

15   Find the position of the centre of flotation of a ship if the trim remains unchanged after loading the following cargo:

   100 tonnes centre of gravity 8 metres forward of amidships
   20 tonnes centre of gravity 40 metres aft of amidships
   28 tonnes centre of gravity 20 metres aft of amidships

16   A ship arrives in port with drafts 6.8 m F and 7.5 m A. The following cargo is discharged:

   90 tonnes centre of gravity 30 m forward of amidships
   40 tonnes centre of gravity 25 m aft of amidships
   50 tonnes centre of gravity 50 m aft of amidships

The drafts are now 6.7 m F and 7.4 m A. Find the position of the centre of flotation relative to amidships.

Loading a weight to keep a constant draft aft

17   A ship is 150 m long, MCT 1 cm 400 tonnes m, TPC 15 tonnes. The centre of flotation is 3 m aft of amidships. Find the position in which to load a mass of 30 tonnes, with reference to the centre of flotation, so as to maintain a constant draft aft.

18   A ship 120 metres long, with maximum beam 15 m, is floating in salt water at drafts 6.6 m F and 7 m A. The block coefficient and coefficient of fineness of the water-plane is 0.75. Longitudinal metacentric height 120 m. Centre of flotation is amidships. Find how much more cargo can be loaded and in what position relative to amidships if the ship is to cross a bar with a maximum draft of 7 m F and A.

Loading a weight to produce a required draft

19   A ship 120 m long floats in salt water at drafts 5.8 m F and 6.6 m A. TPC 15 tonnes. MCT 1 cm = 300 tonnes m. Centre of flotation is amidships.

What is the minimum amount of water ballast required to be taken into the forepeak tank (centre of gravity 60 m forward of the centre of flotation) to reduce the draft aft to 6.5 metres? Find also the final draft forward.

20   A ship leaves port with drafts 7.6 m F and 7.9 m A. 400 tonnes of bunkers are burned from a space whose centre of gravity is 15 m forward of the centre of flotation, which is amidships. TPC 20 tonnes. MCT 1 cm = 300 tonnes m. Find the minimum amount of water which must be run into the forepeak tank (centre of gravity 60 m forward of the centre of flotation) in order to bring the draft aft to the maximum of 7.7 m. Find also the final draft forward.

21   A ship 100 m long has MCT 1 cm 300 tonnes-m requires 1200 tonnes of cargo to complete loading and is at present floating at drafts of 5.7 m F and 6.4 m A. She loads 600 tonnes of cargo in a space whose centre of gravity is 3 m forward of amidships. The drafts are then 6.03 m F and 6.67 m A. The remainder of the cargo is to be loaded in No. 1 hold (centre of gravity 43 m forward of amidships) and in No. 4 hold (centre of gravity 37 m aft of amidships). Find the amount which must be loaded in each hold to ensure that the draft aft will not exceed 6.8 metres. LCF is at amidships.

22   A ship 100 metres long is floating in salt water at drafts 5.7 m F and 8 m A. The centre of flotation is 2 m aft of amidships. Find the amount of water to run into the forepeak tank (centre of gravity 48 m forward of amidships) to bring the draft aft to 7.9 m. TPC 30 tonnes. MCT 1 cm = 300 tonnes m.

23   A ship 140 m long arrives off a port with drafts 5.7 m F and 6.3 m A. The centre of flotation is 3 m aft of amidships. TPC 30 tonnes. MCT 1 cm = 420 tonnes m. It is required to reduce the draft aft to 6.2 m by running water into the forepeak tank (centre of gravity 67 m forward of amidships). Find the minimum amount of water to load and also give the final draft forward.

Using change of trim to find GM$_L$

24   A ship 150 m long is floating upright on an even keel. When a weight already on board is shifted aft, it causes the ship's centre of gravity to shift 0.2 m horizontally and the trim to change by 0.15 m. Find the longitudinal metacentric height.

25   A ship of 5000 tonnes displacement is 120 m long and floats upright on an even keel. When a mass of 40 tonnes, already on board, is shifted 25 m forward horizontally, it causes the trim to change by 0.1 m. Find the longitudinal metacentric height.

26   A ship is 130 m LBP and is loaded ready for departure as shown in the table below. From her Hydrostatic Curves at 8 m even-keel draft in salt water it is found that: MCTC is 150 tm/cm. LCF is 2.5 m forward ⟨⟩, W is 12 795 tonnes and LCB is 2 m for'd ⟨⟩. Calculate the final end drafts for

this vessel. What is the final value for the trim? What is the Dwt value for this loaded condition?

Item	Weight in tonnes	LCG from amidships
Lightweight	3600	2.0 m aft
Cargo	8200	4.2 m forward
Oil Fuel	780	7.1 m aft
Stores	20	13.3 m forward
Fresh Water	100	20.0 m aft
Feed Water	85	12.0 m aft
Crew and Effects	10	at amidships

Chapter 16
Stability and hydrostatic curves

1. Cross Curves of Stability

(a) GZ Cross Curves of Stability
These are a set of curves from which the righting lever about an assumed centre of gravity for any angle of heel at any particular displacement may be found by inspection. The curves are plotted for an assumed KG and, if the actual KG of the ship differs from this, a correction must be applied to the righting levers taken from the curves.

Figure 16.1 shows a set of Stability Cross Curves plotted for an imaginary ship called M.V. 'Tanker', assuming the KG to be 9 metres. A scale of displacements is shown along the bottom margin and a scale of righting levers (GZs) in metres on the left-hand margin. The GZ scale extends from +4.5 m through 0 to −1 metre. The curves are plotted at 15 degree intervals of heel between 15 degrees and 90 degrees.

To find the GZs for any particular displacement locate the displacement concerned on the bottom scale and, through this point erect a perpendicular to cut all the curves. Translate the intersections with the curves horizontally to the left-hand scale and read off the GZs for each angle of heel.

Example 1
Using the Stability Cross Curves for M.V. 'Tanker' find the GZs at 15-degree intervals between 0 degrees and 90 degrees heel when the displacement is 35 000 tonnes, and KG = 9 metres.

Erect a perpendicular through 35 000 tonnes on the displacement scale and read off the GZs from the left-hand scale as follows:

Angle of heel	0°	15°	30°	45°	60°	75°	90°
GZ in metres	0	0.86	2.07	2.45	1.85	0.76	−0.5

Should the KG of the ship be other than 9 metres, a correction must be applied to the GZs taken from the curves to obtain the correct GZs. The corrections are tabulated in the block at the top right-hand side of Figure 16.1

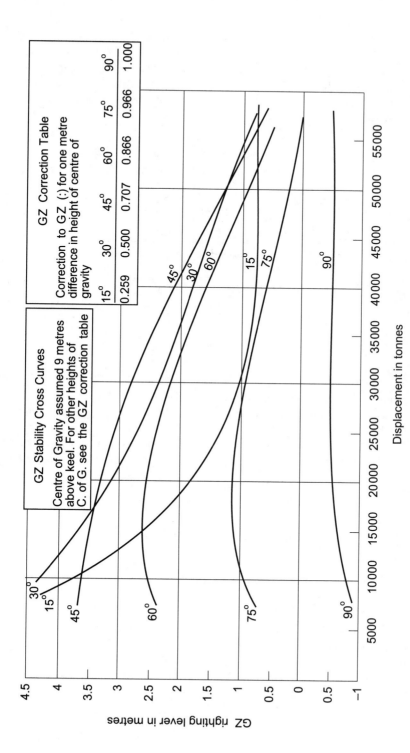

Fig. 16.1

and are given for each one metre difference between 9 metres and the ship's actual KG. To find the correction to the GZ, multiply the correction taken from the table for the angle of heel concerned, by the difference in KGs. To apply the correction: when the ship's KG is *greater* than 9 metres the ship is less stable and the correction must be *subtracted*, but when the KG is *less* than 9 metres the ship is more stable and the correction is to be *added*.

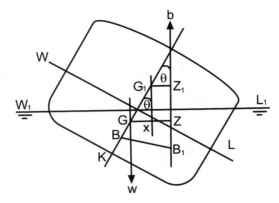

Fig. 16.2(a)

The derivation of the table is as follows:

In Figure 16.2(a), KG is 9 m, this being the KG for which this set of curves is plotted, and GZ represents the righting lever, as taken from the curves for this particular angle of heel.

Consider the case when the KG is greater than 9 m (KG_1 in Figure 16.2(a)). The righting lever is reduced to G_1Z_1. Let G_1X be perpendicular to GZ. Then

$$G_1Z_1 = XZ$$

$$= GZ - GX$$

or

$$\text{Corrected GZ} = \text{Tabulated GZ} - \text{Correction}$$

Also, in triangle GXG_1:

$$GX = GG_1 \sin \theta°$$

or

$$\text{Correction} = GG_1 \sin \theta° \text{ where } \theta° \text{ is the angle of heel.}$$

But GG_1 is the difference between 9 m and the ship's actual KG. Therefore, the corrections shown in the table on the Cross Curves for each one metre difference of KG are simply the Sines of the angle of heel.

Now consider the case where KG is less than 9 m (KG_2 in Figure 16.2(b)). The length of the righting lever will be increased to G_2Z_2.

Let GY be perpendicular to G_2Z_2 then

$$G_2Z_2 = YZ_2 + G_2Y$$

but

$$YZ_2 = GZ$$

therefore

$$G_2Z_2 = GZ + G_2Y$$

or

$$\text{Corrected } GZ = \text{Tabulated } GZ + \text{Correction}$$

Also, in triangle GG_2Y:

$$G_2Y = GG_2 \sin \theta°$$

or

$$\text{Correction} = GG_2 \sin \text{heel}$$

It will be seen that this is similar to the previous result except that in this case the correction is to be *added* to the tabulated GZ.

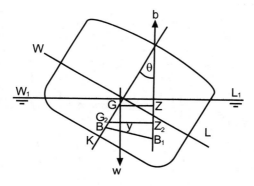

Fig. 16.2(b)

Example 2

Using the Stability Cross Curves for M.V. 'Tanker', find the GZs at 15-degree intervals between 0 degrees and 90 degrees when the displacement is 38 000 tonnes and the KG is 8.5 metres.

Heel	Tabulated GZ (KG 9 m)	Correction $(GG_1 \sin \theta°)$		Correct GZ (KG 8.5 m)		
0°	0	0.5×0	$= 0$	0	$+0$	$= 0$
15°	0.81	0.5×0.259	$= 0.129$	0.81	$+0.13$	$= 0.94$
30°	1.90	0.5×0.5	$= 0.250$	1.90	$+0.25$	$= 2.15$
45°	2.24	0.5×0.707	$= 0.353$	2.24	$+0.35$	$= 2.59$
60°	1.70	0.5×0.866	$= 0.433$	1.70	$+0.43$	$= 2.13$
75°	0.68	0.5×0.966	$= 0.483$	0.68	$+0.48$	$= 1.16$
90°	-0.49	0.5×1.000	$= 0.500$	-0.49	$+0.50$	$= 0.01$

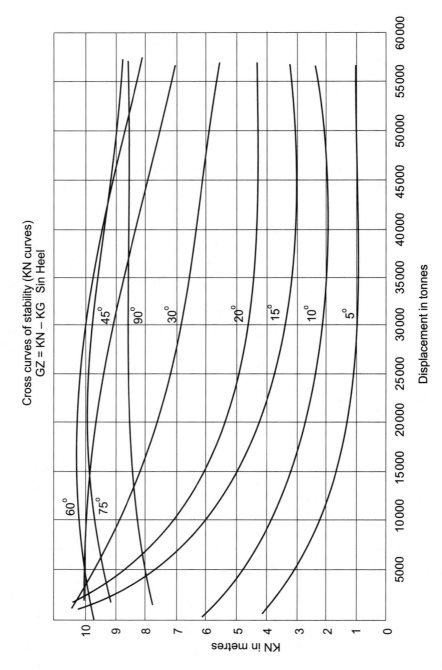

Cross curves of stability (KN curves)
GZ = KN – KG Sin Heel

Fig. 16.3(a).   M.V. 'Cargo-Carrier'

Displacement in tonnes

KN in metres

KN Cross Curves of Stability

It has already been shown that the Stability Cross Curves for a ship are constructed by plotting the righting levers for an assumed height of the centre of gravity above the keel. In some cases the curves are constructed for an assumed KG of zero. The curves are then referred to as KN curves, KN being the righting lever measured from the keel. Figure 16.3(a) shows the KN curves for an imaginary ship called the M.V. 'Cargo-Carrier'.

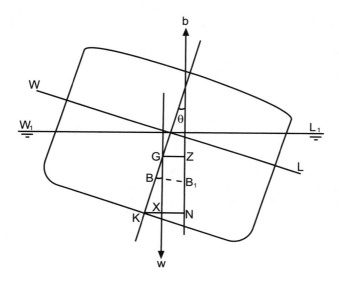

Fig. 16.3(b)

To obtain the righting levers for a particular displacement and KG the values of KN are first obtained from the curves by inspection at the displacement concerned. The correct righting levers are then obtained by subtracting from the KN values a correction equal to the product of the KG and sin Heel.

In Figure 16.3(b), let KN represent the ordinate obtained from the curves. Also, let the ship's centre of gravity be at G so that KG represents the actual height of the centre of gravity above the keel and GZ represents the length of the righting lever.

Now

$$GZ = XN$$

$$= KN - KX$$

or

$$GZ = KN - KG \sin \theta$$

Thus, the righting lever is found by *always* subtracting from the KN ordinate a correction equal to KG sin heel.

Example 3

Find the righting levers for M.V. 'Cargo-Carrier' when the displacement is
40 000 tonnes and the KG is 10 metres.

Heel (θ)	KN	$\sin \theta$	$KG \sin \theta$	$GZ = KN - KG \sin \theta$
5°	0.90	0.087	0.87	0.03
10°	1.92	0.174	1.74	0.18
15°	3.11	0.259	2.59	0.52
20°	4.25	0.342	3.42	0.83
30°	6.30	0.500	5.00	1.30
45°	8.44	0.707	7.07	1.37
60°	9.39	0.866	8.66	0.73
75°	9.29	0.966	9.66	− 0.37
90°	8.50	1.000	10.00	− 1.50

2. Statical Stability curves

The curve of statical stability for a ship in any particular condition of
loading is obtained by plotting the righting levers against angle of heel as
shown in Figures 16.4 and 16.5.

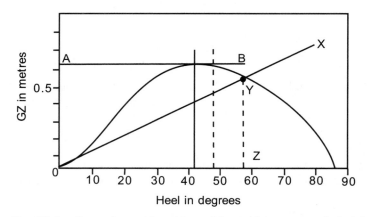

Fig. 16.4.   Curve for a ship with positive initial metacentric height.

From this type of graph a considerable amount of stability information
may be found by inspection:

The range of stability. This is the range over which the ship has positive
righting levers. In Figure 16.4 the range is from 0 degrees to 86 degrees.

The angle of vanishing stability. This is the angle of heel at which the
righting lever returns to zero, or is the angle of heel at which the sign of the

righting levers changes from positive to negative. The angle of vanishing stability in Figure 16.4 is 86 degrees.

The maximum GZ is obtained by drawing a tangent to the highest point in the curve. In Figure 16.4, AB is the tangent and this indicates a maximum GZ of 0.63 metres. If a perpendicular is dropped from the point of tangency, it cuts the heel scale at the angle of heel at which the maximum GZ occurs. In the present case the maximum GZ occurs at 42 degrees heel.

The initial metacentric height (GM) is found by drawing a tangent to the curve through the origin (OX in Figure 16.4), and then erecting a perpendicular through an angle of heel of 57.3 degrees. Let the two lines intersect at Y. Then the height of the intersection above the base (YZ), when measured on the GZ scale, will give the initial metacentric height. In the present example the GM is 0.54 metres.

Figure 16.5 shows the stability curve for a ship having a negative initial metacentric height. At angles of heel of less than 18 degrees the righting levers are negative, whilst at angles of heel between 18 degrees and 90 degrees the levers are positive. The angle of loll in this case is 18 degrees, the range of stability is 18 degrees to 90 degrees, and the angle of vanishing stability is 90 degrees. (For an explanation of angle of loll see Chapter 6, page 48.) Note how the −ve GM is plotted at 57.3°.

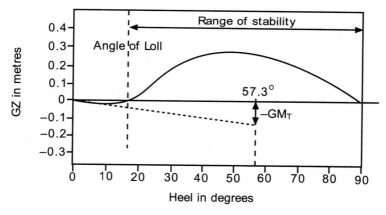

Fig. 16.5.   Curve for a ship with negative initial metacentric height.

Example 1

Using the stability cross curves for M.V. 'Tanker', plot the curve of statical stability when the displacement is 33 500 tonnes and KG = 9.3 metres. From the curve find the following:

(a) The range of stability.
(b) The angle of vanishing stability.
(c) The maximum righting lever and the angle of heel at which it occurs.

Heel	Tabulated GZ (KG 9 m)	Correction to GZ (GG₁ sin heel)	Required GZ (KG 9.3 m)
0°	0	$0 \times 0 \quad = 0$	$= \quad 0$
15°	0.90	$0.3 \times 0.259 = 0.08$	$0.90 - 0.08 = \quad 0.82$
30°	2.15	$0.3 \times 0.500 = 0.15$	$2.15 - 0.15 = \quad 2.00$
45°	2.55	$0.3 \times 0.707 = 0.21$	$2.55 - 0.21 = \quad 2.34$
60°	1.91	$0.3 \times 0.866 = 0.26$	$1.91 - 0.26 = \quad 1.65$
75°	0.80	$0.3 \times 0.966 = 0.29$	$0.80 - 0.29 = \quad 0.51$
90°	− 0.50	$0.3 \times 1.000 = 0.30$	$-0.50 - 0.30 = -0.80$

(d) The initial metacentric height.

(e) The moment of statical stability at 25 degrees heel.

For the graph see Figure 16.6(a),

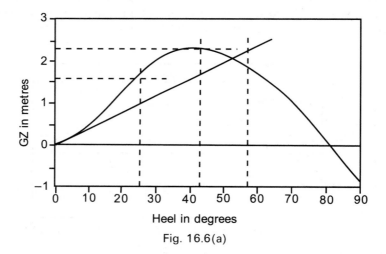

Fig. 16.6(a)

Answers from the curve:

(a) Range of Stability 0 degrees to 81 degrees.

(b) Angle of vanishing stability 81 degrees.

(c) Maximum GZ = 2.35 m occurring at 43 degrees heel.

(d) GM is 2.30 m.

(e) GZ at 25 degrees heel = 1.64 m.

$$\text{Moment of statical stability} = W \times GZ$$

$$= 33\,500 \times 1.64$$

$$= 54\,940 \text{ tonnes m}$$

Example 2

Construct the curve of statical stability for the M.V. 'Cargo-Carrier' when the displacement is 35 000 tonnes and KG is 9 metres. From the curve you have constructed find the following:

(a) The range of stability,
(b) The angle of vanishing stability,
(c) The maximum righting lever and the angle of the heel at which it occurs, and
(d) The approximate initial metacentric height.

From the Stability Cross Curves:

Heel (θ)	KN	$\sin \theta$	$KG \sin \theta$	$GZ = KN - KG \sin \theta$
5°	0.9	0.087	0.783	0.12
10°	2.0	0.174	1.566	0.43
15°	3.2	0.259	2.331	0.87
20°	4.4	0.342	3.078	1.32
30°	6.5	0.500	4.500	2.00
45°	8.75	0.707	6.363	2.39
60°	9.7	0.866	7.794	1.91
75°	9.4	0.966	8.694	0.71
90°	8.4	1.000	9.000	− 0.60

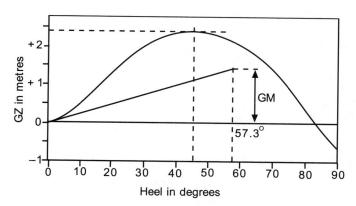

Fig. 16.6(b).   This is the curve of statical stability

Answers from the curve:
(a) Range of stability 0° to $83\frac{3}{4}°$,
(b) Angle of vanishing stability $83\frac{3}{4}°$,
(c) Maximum GZ = 2.39 m occurring at 45° heel,
(d) Approximate GM = 1.4 m.

3. Hydrostatic curves

Hydrostatic information is usually supplied to the ship's officer in the form of a table or a graph. Figure 16.7 shows the hydrostatic curves for the imaginary ship M.V. 'Tanker'. The various items of hydrostatic information are plotted against draft.

When information is required for a specific draft, first locate the draft on the scale on the left-hand margin of the figure. Then draw a horizontal line through the draft to cut all of the curves on the figure. Next draw a perpendicular through the intersections of this line with each of the curves in turn and read off the information from the appropriate scale.

Example 1

Using the hydrostatic curves for M.V. 'Tanker', take off all of the information possible for the ship when the mean draft is 7.6 metres.

(1) TPC = 39.3 tonnes
(2) MCT 1 cm = 475 tonnes-metres
(3) Displacement = 33 000 tonnes
(4) Longitudinal centre of flotation is 2.2 m forward of amidships
(5) Longitudinal centre of buoyancy is 4.0 m forward of amidships.

When information is required for a specific displacement, locate the displacement on the scale along the top margin of the figure and drop a perpendicular to cut the curve marked 'Displacement'. Through the intersection draw a horizontal line to cut all of the other curves and the draft scale. The various quantities can then be obtained as before.

Example 2

From the hydrostatic curves take off the information for M.V. 'Tanker' when the displacement is 37 500 tonnes.

(1) Draft = 8.55 m
(2) TPC = 40 tonnes
(3) MCT 1 cm = 500 tonnes m
(4) Longitudinal centre of flotation is 1.2 m forward of amidships.
(5) Longitudinal centre of buoyancy is 3.7 m forward of amidships.

The curves themselves are produced from calculations involving Simpson's Rules. These involve half-ordinates, areas, moments and moments of inertia for each water line under consideration.

Using the hydrostatic curves

After the end drafts have been taken it is necessary to interpolate to find the 'mean draft'. This is the draft immediately *below the LCF* which may be aft, forward or even at amidships. This draft can be labelled d_H.

If d_H is taken as being simply the average of the two end drafts then in large full-form vessels (supertankers) and fine-form vessels (container ships) an appreciable error in the displacement can occur. (See Fig. 16.8.)

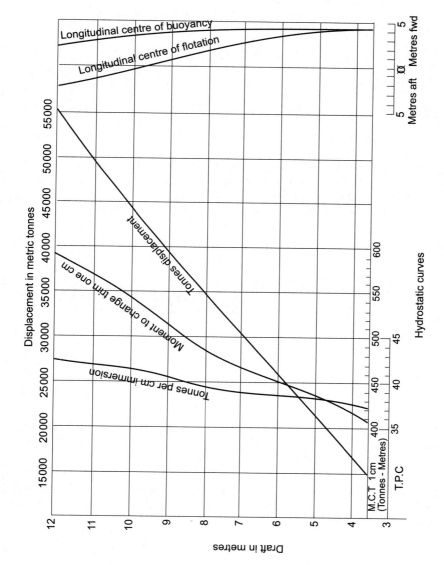

Fig. 16.7. M.V. 'Tanker'

Let us assume the true mean draft 'd_H' is 6 m. The Navel Architect or mate on board ship draws a horizontal line parallel to the SLWL at 6 m on the vertical axis right across all of the hydrostatic curves.

At each intersection with a curve and this 6 m line, he projects downwards and reads off on the appropriate scale on the 'x' axis.

For our hydrostatic curves, at a mean draft of 6 m, for example, we would obtain the following:

$$\text{TPC} = 19.70\,\text{t} \qquad\qquad \text{Displace}^{MT} = 10\,293\,\text{t}$$

$$\text{MCTC} = 152.5\,\text{tm/cm} \qquad\qquad \text{LCF}_{\text{⋈}} = 0.05\,\text{m forward } \text{⋈}$$

$$\text{LCB}_{\text{⋈}} = 0.80\,\text{m forward } \text{⋈} \qquad\qquad \text{KML} = 207.4\,\text{m}$$

$$\text{KM}_T = 7.46\,\text{m}$$

These values can then be used to calculate *the new end drafts* and *transverse stability*, if weights are *added* to the ship, *discharged* from the ship or simply *moved* longitudinally or transversely within the ship.

$\text{LCF}_{\text{⋈}}$ and $\text{LCB}_{\text{⋈}}$ are distances measured from amidships (⋈).

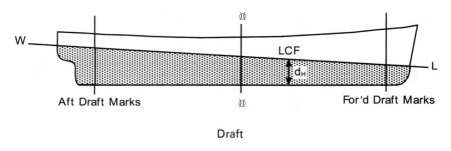

Fig. 16.8

Nowadays these values can be put on a spreadsheet in a computer package. When the hydrostatic draft d_H is keyed, the hydrostatic values appertaining to this draft are then displayed, ready for use.

A set of hydrostatic values has been calculated for a 135 m General Cargo Ship of about 10 000 tonnes deadweight. These are shown overpage. From those values a set of hydrostatic curves were drawn. These are shown in Fig. 16.9.

Hydrostatic values for Fig. 16.9 (overpage). These are for a 135 m LBP General Cargo Ship

Draft d_H (see below) m	TPC tonnes	KB m	Displace^{MT} tonnes	KM_L m	MCTC tm/cm	KM_T m	$LCF_⌀$ m	$LCB_⌀$ m
9 m	20.64	4.80	16 276	146.5	167.4	7.71	2.10 aft	0.45 aft
8 m	20.36	4.27	14 253	161.8	162.9	7.54	1.20 aft	⌀
7 m	20.06	3.74	12 258	181.5	158.1	7.44	0.50 aft	0.45 forward
6 m	19.70	3.21	10 293	207.4	152.5	7.46	0.05 forward	0.80 forward
5 m	19.27	2.68	8361	243.2	145.9	7.70	0.42 forward	1.05 forward
4 m	18.76	2.15	6486	296.0	138.3	8.28	0.70 forward	1.25 forward
3 m	18.12	1.61	4674	382.3	129.1	9.56	0.83 forward	1.30 forward
$2\frac{1}{2}$ m	17.69	1.35	3785	449.0	123.0	10.75	0.85 forward	1.30 forward

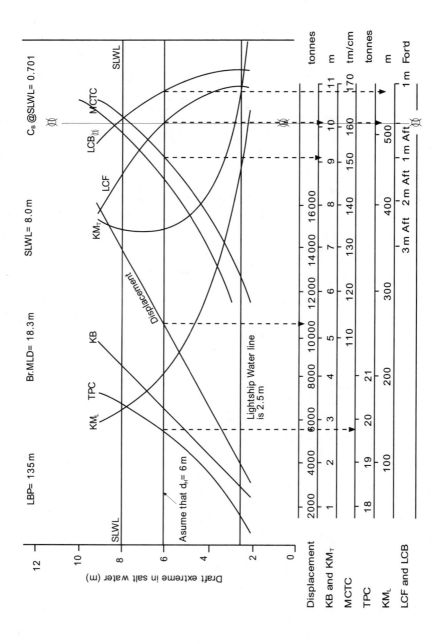

Fig. 16.9. Hydrostatic curves: based on values tabulated on previous page. These are for a 135 m LBP General Cargo Ship

EXERCISE 16

1   Plot the curve of stability for M.V. 'Tanker' when the displacement is 34 500 tonnes and KG = 9 m. From this curve find the approximate GM, the range of stability, the maximum GZ and the angle of heel at which it occurs.

2   Plot the curve of statical stability for M.V. 'Tanker' when the displacement is 23 400 tonnes and KG = 9.4 m. From this curve find the approximate GM, the maximum moment of statical stability and the angle of heel at which it occurs. Find also the range of stability.

3   The displacement of M.V. 'Tanker' is 24 700 tonnes and KG = 10 m. Construct a curve of statical stability and state what information may be derived from it. Find also the moments of statical stability at 10 degrees and 40 degrees heel.

4   Using the cross curves of stability for M.V. 'Tanker':
    (a) Draw a curve of statical stability when the displacement is 35 000 tonnes, KG = 9.2 metres, and KM = 11.2 m, and
    (b) From this curve determine the moment of statical stability at 10 degrees heel and state what other information may be obtained from the curve.

5   Plot the stability curve for M.V. 'Tanker' when the displacement is 46 800 tonnes and KG = 8.5 metres. From this curve find the approximate GM, the range of stability, the maximum GZ and the angle of heel at which it occurs.

6   From the hydrostatic curves for M.V. 'Tanker' find the mean draft when entering a dock where the density of the water is 1009 kg per cu. m, if the mean draft in salt water is 6.5 m.

7   Find the mean draft of M.V. 'Tanker' in dock water of density 1009 kg per cu. m when the displacement is 35 400 tonnes.

8   M.V. 'Tanker' is 200 m long and is floating at the maximum permissible draft aft. There is one more parcel of heavy cargo to load on deck to put her down to her marks at the load displacement of 51 300 tonnes. Find the position, relative to amidships, to load the parcel so as to maintain the maximum possible trim by the stern.

9   Using the hydrostatic curves for M.V. 'Tanker' find the displacement, MCT 1 cm and the TPC, when the ship is floating in salt water at a mean draft of 9 metres.
     Also find the new mean draft if she now enters a dock where the density of the water is 1010 kg per cu. m.

10   M.V. 'Tanker' is 200 m long and has a light displacement of 16 000 tonnes. She has on board 100 tonnes of cargo, 300 tonnes of bunkers, and 100 tonnes of fresh water and stores. The ship is trimmed 1.5 m by the stern. Find the new drafts if the 100 tonnes of cargo already on board is now shifted 50 m forward.

11   Construct the curve of statical stability for M.V. 'Cargo-Carrier' when

the displacement is 35 000 tonnes and KG is 8 metres. From this curve find

(a) the range of stability,
(b) the angle of vanishing stability and,
(c) the maximum GZ and the heel at which it occurs.

12   Construct the curve of statical stability for M.V. 'Cargo-Carrier' when the displacement is 28 000 tonnes and the KG is 10 metres. From the curve find

(a) the range of stability,
(b) the angle of vanishing stability, and
(c) the maximum GZ and the heel at which it occurs.

13   A vessel is loaded up ready for departure. KM is 11.9 m. KG is 9.52 m with a displacement of 20 550 tonnes. From the ship's Cross Curves of Stability, the GZ ordinates for a displacement of 20 550 tonnes and a VCG of 8 m above base are as follows

Angle of heel (θ)	0	15	30	45	60	75	90
GZ ordinate (m)	0	1.10	2.22	2.60	2.21	1.25	0.36

Using this information, construct the ship's Statical Stability curve for this condition of loading and determine the following:

(a) Maximum righting lever GZ.
(b) Angle of heel at which this maximum GZ occurs.
(c) Angle of heel at which the deck edge just becomes immersed.
(d) Range of stability.

14   Using the table of KN ordinates below calculate the righting levers for a ship when her displacement is 40 000 tonnes and her actual KG is 10 m. Draw the resulting Statical Stability curve and from it determine:

(a) Maximum GZ value.
(b) Approximate GM value.
(c) Righting moment at the angle of heel of 25°.
(d) Range of Stability.

Angle of heel (θ)	0	5	10	15	20	30	45	60
KN ordinates (m)	0	0.90	1.92	3.11	4.25	6.30	8.44	9.39

Angle of heel (θ)	75	90
KN ordinates (m)	9.29	8.50

Chapter 17
Increase in draft due to list

1. Box-shaped vessels

The draft of a vessel is the depth of the lowest point below the waterline. When a box-shaped vessel is floating upright on an even keel as in Figure 17.1(a) the draft is the same to port as to starboard. Let the draft be 'd' and let the vessel's beam be 'b'.

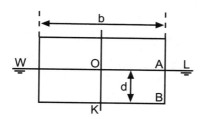

Fig. 17.1(a)

Now consider the same vessel when listed θ degrees as shown in Figure 17.1(b). The depth of the lowest point or draft is now increased to 'D' (XY).

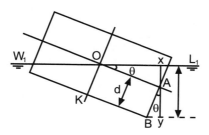

Fig. 17.1(b)

In triangle OXA:

$$OA = \tfrac{1}{2} b \text{ and angle } AXO = 90° \quad \therefore AX = \tfrac{1}{2} b \sin \theta°$$

In triangle ABY:

$$AB = d \text{ and angle } AYB = 90° \quad \therefore AY = d \cos \theta°$$

$$D = XY$$

$$= AX + AY$$

$$D = \tfrac{1}{2} b \sin \theta + d \cos \theta$$

or

$$\text{New draft} = \tfrac{1}{2} \text{ beam sin list} + \text{Old draft cos list}$$

Note. It will usually be found convenient to calculate the draft when listed by using the triangles AOX and ABY.

Example 1
A box-shaped ship with 12 m beam is floating upright at a draft of 6.7 m. Find the increase in draft if the vessel is now listed 18 degrees.

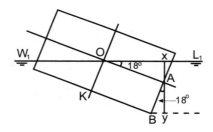

Fig. 17.2(a)

In triangle OAX:

$$\text{Angle } AOX = 18°$$

Therefore use course 18°

$$OA \text{ (Dist.)} = 6.0 \, m$$

$$AX \text{ (Dep.)} = 1.85 \, m$$

In triangle ABY:

$$\text{Angle } BAY = 18°$$

Therefore use course 18°

$$AB \text{ (Dist.)} = 6.7 \, m$$

$$AY \text{ (D. Lat.)} = 6.37 \, m$$

$$AX = 1.85\,m$$
$$AY = +6.37\,m$$
$$New\ draft = \overline{8.22\,m}$$
$$Old\ draft = +6.70\,m$$
$$\overline{1.52\,m}$$

Ans. Increase = 1.52 m

Example 2

Using the dimensions of the ship given in example 1, proceed to calculate the increase in draft at 3° intervals from 0° to 18°. Plot a graph of draft increase ∝ θ.

$$\tfrac{1}{2}\ \text{beam}\ \sin\theta = \tfrac{1}{2} \times 12 \times \sin\theta = 6\sin\theta \qquad (I)$$
$$\text{Old draft}\ \cos\theta = 6.7\cos\theta \qquad (II)$$

Increase in draft = (I) + (II) − Old draft in metres.

Angle of list	6 sin θ	6.7 cos θ	Old draft	Increase in draft (m)
0°	0	6.70	6.70	0
3°	0.31	6.69	6.70	0.30
6°	0.63	6.66	6.70	0.59
9°	0.94	6.62	6.70	0.86
12°	1.25	6.55	6.70	1.10
15°	1.55	6.47	6.70	1.32
18°	1.85	6.37	6.70	1.52

The above results clearly show the increase in draft or loss of underkeel clearance when a vessel lists.

Ships in the late 1990s are being designed with shorter lengths and wider breadths mainly to reduce first cost and hogging/sagging characteristics.

These wider ships are creating problems sometimes when initial underkeel clearance is only 10 per cent of the ship's static draft. It only requires a small angle of list for them to go aground in way of the bilge strakes.

One ship, for example, is the supertanker *Esso Japan*. She has an LBP of 350 m and a width of 70 m at amidships. Consequently extra care is required should possibilities of list occur.

Figure 17.2(b) (on page 182) shows the requested graph of draft increase ∝ θ.

2.   Vessels having a rise of floor

Example 3

A ship has 20 m beam at the waterline and is floating upright at 6 m draft. If the rise of floor is 0.25 m, calculate the new draft if the ship is now listed 15 degrees (See Figure 17.3)

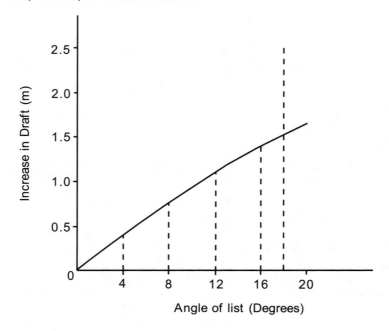

Fig. 17.2(b).   Draft increase ∝ angle of list θ

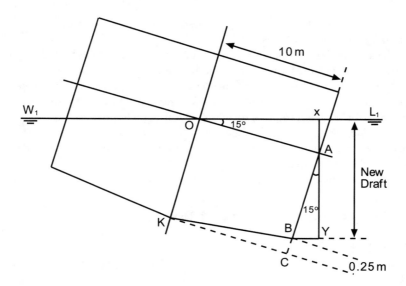

Fig. 17.3

In triangle OAX:

$$\text{Angle O} = 15°$$

Therefore use course 15°

$$\text{AO (Dist.)} = 10\,\text{m}$$
$$\text{AX (Dep.)} = 2.59\,\text{m}$$

In triangle ABY:

$$\text{Angle A} = 15°$$

Therefore use course 15°

$$\text{AB (Dist.)} = \text{AC} - \text{BC}$$
$$= \text{Old draft} - \text{Rise of floor}$$
$$= 6\,\text{m} - 0.25\,\text{m}$$
$$\text{AB (Dist.)} = 5.75\,\text{m}$$
$$\text{AY (D. Lat.)} = 5.55\,\text{m}$$

$$
\begin{array}{rcl}
\text{AX} & = & 2.59\,\text{m} \\
\text{AY} & = & +5.55\,\text{m} \\
\hline
\text{XY} & = & 8.14\,\text{m}
\end{array}
$$

Ans. New draft = 8.14 metres

If the formula is to be used to find the new draft it must now be amended to allow for the rise of floor as follows:

$$\text{New draft} = \tfrac{1}{2}\ \text{beam sin list} + (\text{Old draft} - \text{Rise})\cos \text{list.}$$

Note. In practise, the shipbuilder's naval architect usually calculates the increase in draft for the ship at various angles of list and suppliers the information to the ship's officer by means of a table on the plans of the ship.

The rise of floor, similar to tumblehome on merchant ships, has almost become obsolute on merchant ships of today.

Exercise 17

1   A box-shaped vessel with 10 m beam, and 7.5 m deep, floats upright at a draft of 3 m. Find the increase of draft when listed 15 degrees to starboard.

2   A ship 90 m long, 15 m beam at the waterline, is floating upright at a draft of 6 m. Find the increase of draft when the ship is listed 10 degrees, allowing 0.15 m rise of floor.

3   A box-shaped vessel 60 m × 6 m × 4 m draft is floating upright. Find the increase in the draft if the vessel is now listed 15 degrees to port.

4   A box-shaped vessel increases her draft by 0.61 m when listed 12 degrees to starboard. Find the vessel's beam if the draft, when upright, was 5.5 m.

5   A box-shaped vessel with 10 m beam is listed 10 degrees to starboard and the maximum draft is 5 m. A weight already on board is shifted transversely across the deck, causing the vessel to list to port. If the final list is 5 degrees to port, find the new draft.

Chapter 18
Water pressure

The water pressure at any depth is due to the weight of water above the point in question and increases uniformly with depth below the surface. From this it can be seen that the pressure at any depth will vary with the depth below the surface and the density of the water.

Pressure at any depth

Consider an area of 1 sq m at the water level as shown by ABCD in Figure 18.1. The water pressure on this area is zero as there is no water above it.

Now consider the area EFGH which is submerged to a depth of 1 m below the surface. There is 1 cu. m of water above it. Let the density of the water be 'w' tonnes per cu. m. Then the pressure on this area is 'w' tonnes per sq m, and the total pressure or thrust on an area of 'A' sq m whose centre of gravity is 1 m below the surface, will be wA tonnes.

Next consider the area IJKL whose centre of gravity is 2 m below the surface. The pressure is now due to 2 cu. m of water and will be 2 w tonnes per sq m. Also, the total pressure or thrust on any area whose centre of gravity is 2 m below the surface, is 2 wA tonnes.

Similarly, the pressure on the area MNOP will be 3 w tonnes per sq metre, and the total pressure or thrust on any area whose centre of gravity is 3 m below the surface will be 3 wA tonnes.

The following formulae may now be deduced:

$$\textit{Total pressure or thrust} = w \times A \times h \text{ tonnes}$$

where

h = the depth of the centre of gravity below the surface

w = the density of the water in tonnes/m^3, and

A = the area in sq m.

Example 1

Find the water pressure and the total thrust on the flat plate keel of a ship which is floating on an even keel at 4 metres mean draft in water of density 1.024 t/m³ per cu. m. The keel plate is 35 m long and 1.5 m wide.

$$\text{Pressure} = 4 \times 1.024 = 4.1 \text{ tonnes/m}^2$$

$$\text{Total Thrust} = w \times A \times h$$

$$= 1.024 \times 35 \times 1.5 \times 4$$

$$\text{Total Thrust} = 215.04 \text{ tonnes}$$

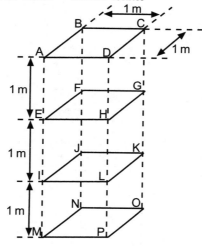

Fig. 18.1

Example 2

A lock gate which is 15 m wide has salt water on one side to a depth of 8 m and fresh water on the other side to a depth of 9 m. Find the resultant thrust on the lock gate and state on which side of the gate it acts.

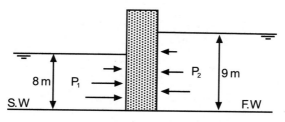

Fig. 18.2

Let P_1 = thrust on the SW side, and P_2 = thrust on the FW side

$$\therefore P_1 = \text{Pressure on the SW side}$$

$$P_1 = \rho_{SW} \times A \times h_1$$

$$= 1.025 \times 15 \times 8 \times \tfrac{8}{2}$$

$$P_1 = 492 \text{ tonnes}$$

$$\therefore P_2 = \text{Pressure on the FW side}$$

$$P_2 = \rho_{FW} \times A \times h_2$$

$$= 1.000 \times 15 \times 9 \times \tfrac{9}{2}$$

$$P_2 = 607.5 \text{ tonnes}$$

$$\text{Resultant thrust} = P_2 - P_1$$

$$= 607.5 - 492$$

Ans. Resultant thrust = 115.5 tonnes on the FW side

Example 3

Find the pressure and total thrust on two deep tank lids, each 4 m × 2.5 m, resting on coamings 30 cm high, when the tank is filled with salt water to a head of 9.3 m above the crown of the tank.

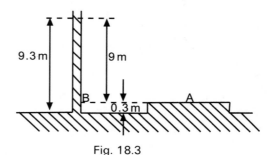

Fig. 18.3

$$\text{Pressure at A} = \text{Pressure at B (see Figure 18.3)}$$

$$= w \times A \times h$$

$$= 1.025 \times 1.0 \, m^2 \times 9.0$$

$$\text{Pressure on lids} = 9.225 \text{ tonnes per sq m}$$

$$\text{Total thrust} = 2 \times \text{thrust on one lid}$$

$$= 2 \times (P \times A)$$

$$= 2 \times 9.225 \times 4 \times 2.5 \text{ tonnes}$$

$$\text{Total thrust} = 184.5 \text{ tonnes}$$

Ans. Pressure = 9.225 tonnes per sq m. Total thrust = 184.5 tonnes.

Exercise 18

1   A sealed box is made of metal and is capable of withstanding a pressure of 15.54 kN per sq m. Find to what depth the box may be submerged in salt water before it collapses.

2   Find the water pressure, in kilo-newtons per sq m, on the keel of a ship which is floating upright on an even keel in salt water at a draft of 6 metres.

3   A ship is floating on an even keel in salt water at a draft of 7 metres. She has a flat plate keel which is 100 m long and 2 m wide. Find the water pressure and the total thrust on the keel due to the water.

4   Find the water pressure and thrust on a flat plate keel 6 m long and 1.5 m wide when the ship is floating on an even keel at 6 m draft in salt water.

5   Find the water pressure and thrust on the inner bottom plating of a double bottom tank (10 m × 10 m) when the tank is filled with fresh water to a head of 9 m above the crown of the tank.

6   A deep tank has two lids, each 4 m × 3 m, resting on coamings which are 30 cm high. Find the water pressure on each of the two lids and the total thrust on both lids when the tank is filled with salt water to a head of 6.3 m above the crown of the tank.

7   A rectangular plate 2 m × 1 m is held vertically in fresh water with the 2 m edge on the waterline. Find the thrust on one side of the plate.

8   A lock gate 12 m wide has water of density 1010 kg per cu. m to a depth of 10 m on one side and water of density 1015 kg per cu. m to a depth of 6 m on the other side. Find the resultant thrust on the lock gate and state on which side it acts.

9   A lock gate is 20 m wide and has water of density 1016 kg per cu. m on one side to a depth of 10 m and salt water on the other side to a depth of 7.5 m. Find the resultant thrust and state on which side of the gate it will act.

10 Find the total water pressure acting on a box-shaped barge keel plating which is 60 m long 10 m wide, and is floating upright in salt water on an even keel at 5 m draft.

11 A box-shaped barge has a rectangular collision bulkhead 10 m wide and 6 m deep. Find the total water pressure on this bulkhead if the forepeak is flooded to a depth of 5 m with salt water.

Chapter 19
Combined list and trim

When a problem involves a change of both list and trim, the two parts must be treated quite separately. It is usually more convenient to tackle the trim part of the problem first and then the list, but no hard and fast rule can be made on this point.

Example 1
A ship of 6000 tonnes displacement has KM = 7 m, KG = 6.4 m, and MCT 1 cm = 120 tonnes m. The ship is listed 5 degrees to starboard and trimmed 0.15 m by the head. The ship is to be brought upright and trimmed 0.3 m by the stern by transferring oil from No. 2 double bottom tank to No. 5 double bottom tank. Both tanks are divided at the centre line and their centres of gravity are 6 m out from the centre line. No. 2 holds 200 tonnes of oil on each side and is full. No. 5 holds 120 tonnes on each side and is empty. The centre of gravity of No. 2 is 23.5 m forward of amidships and No. 5 is 21.5 m aft of amidships. Find what transfer of oil must take place and give the final distribution of the oil. (Neglect the effect of free surface on the GM.) Assume that LCF is at amidships.

(a) To bring the ship to the required trim

$$\text{Present trim} = 0.15\,\text{m by the head} \rightleftharpoons$$

$$\text{Required trim} = \underline{0.30}\,\text{m by the stern} \leftarrow$$

$$\text{Change of trim} = 0.45\,\text{m by the stern} \leftarrow$$

$$= 45\,\text{cm by the stern} \leftarrow$$

$$\text{Trim moment} = \text{Change of trim} \times \text{MCT 1 cm}$$

$$= 45 \times 120$$

$$\text{Trim moment} = 5400\,\text{tonnes m by the stern} \leftarrow$$

Let 'w' tonnes of oil be transferred aft to produce the required trim.

$$\therefore \text{ Trim moment} = w \times d$$

$$= 45w \text{ tonnes m}$$

$$\therefore 45w = 5400$$

$$w = 120 \text{ tonnes}$$

From this it will be seen that, if 120 tonnes of oil is transferred aft, the ship will then be trimmed 0.30 m by the stern.

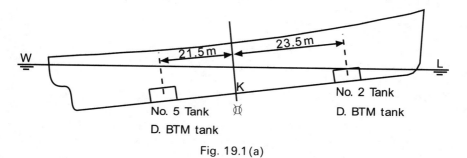

Fig. 19.1 (a)

(b) To bring the ship upright

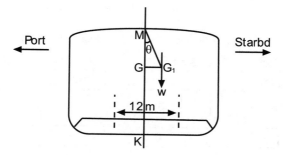

Fig. 19.1 (b).   Looking forward

$$KM = \quad 7.0 \text{ m}$$

$$KG = -6.4 \text{ m}$$

$$GM = \quad 0.6 \text{ m}$$

In triangle GG_1M,

$$GG_1 = GM \times \tan \theta$$

$$= 0.6 \times \tan 5°$$

$$GG_1 = 0.0525 \text{ m}$$

Let 'x' tonnes of oil be transferred from starboard to port.

$$\text{Moment to port} = x \times d$$

$$= 12x \text{ tonnes m}$$

$$\text{Initial moment to starboard} = W \times GG_1$$

$$= 6000 \times 0.0525$$

$$= 315 \text{ tonnes m}$$

But if the ship is to complete the operation upright:

$$\text{Moment to starboard} = \text{Moment to port}$$

or

$$315 = 12x$$

$$x = 26.25 \text{ tonnes}$$

The ship will therefore be brought upright by transferring 26.25 tonnes from starboard to port.

From this it can be seen that, to bring the ship to the required trim and upright, 120 tonnes of oil must be transferred from forward to aft and 26.25 tonnes from starboard to port. This result can be obtained by taking 120 tonnes from No. 2 starboard and by putting 93.75 tonnes of this oil in No. 5 starboard and the remaining 26.25 tonnes in No. 5 Port tank.

The distributions would then be as follows:

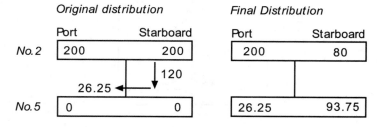

Note. There are, of course, alternative methods by which this result could have been obtained, but in each case a total of *120 tonnes* of oil must be transferred aft and *26.25 tonnes* must be transferred from starboard to port.

Exercise 19

1   A tanker has displacement of 10 000 tonnes, KM = 7 m, KG = 6.4 m and MCT 1 cm = 150 tonnes m. There is a centre line bulkhead in both No. 3 and No. 8 tanks. Centre of gravity of No. 3 tank is 20 m forward of the centre of flotation and the centre of gravity of No. 8 tank is 30 m aft of the centre of flotation. The centre of gravity of all tanks is 5 m out from the centre line. At present the ship is listed 4 degrees to starboard and trimmed 0.15 m by the head. Find what transfer of oil must take place if the ship is to complete upright and trimmed 0.3 m by the stern.

2   A ship of 10 000 tonnes displacement is listed 5 degrees to port and trimmed 0.2 m by the head. KM = 7.5 m, KG 6.8 m, and MCT 1 cm = 150 tonnes m. Centre of flotation is amidships. No.1 double bottom tank is divided at the centre line, each side holds 200 tonnes of oil and the tank is full. No. 4 double bottom tank is similarly divided each side having a capacity of 150 tonnes, but the tank is empty. The centre of gravity of No. 1 tank is 45 m forward of amidships and the centre of gravity of No. 4 tank is 15 m aft of amidships. The centre of gravity of all tanks is 5 m out from the centre line. It is desired to bring the ship upright and trimmed 0.3 m by the stern by transferring oil. If the free surface effect on GM be neglected, find what transfer of oil must take place and also the final distribution of the oil.

3   A ship of 6000 tonnes displacement, KG = 6.8 m., is floating upright in salt water, and the draft is 4 m F and 4.3 m A. KM = 7.7 m TPC = 10 tonnes. MCT 1 cm = 150 tonnes m. There is a locomotive to discharge from No. 2 lower hold (KG = 3 m, and centre of gravity 30 m forward of the centre of flotation which is amidships). If the weight of the locomotive is 60 tonnes and the height of the derrick head is 18 m above the keel and 20 m out from the centre line when plumbing overside, find the maximum list during the operation and the drafts after the locomotive has been discharged. Assume KM is constant.

4   A ship displaces 12 500 tonnes, is trimmed 0.6 m by the stern and listed 6 degrees to starboard. MCT 1 cm 120 tonnes m, KG 7.2 m, KM 7.3 m No. 2 and No. 5 double bottom tanks are divided at the centre line. Centre of gravity of No. 2 is 15 m forward of the centre of flotation and centre of gravity of No. 5 is 12 m abaft centre of flotation. Centre of gravity of all tanks is 4 m out from the centre line. The ship is to be brought upright and on to an even keel by transferring oil from aft to forward, taking equal quantities from each side of No. 5. Find the amounts of oil to transfer.

Chapter 20
Calculating the effect of free surface of liquids (FSE)

The effect of free surface of liquids on stability was discussed in general terms in Chapter 7, but the problem will now be studied more closely and the calculations involved will be explained.

When a tank is partially filled with a liquid, the ship suffers a virtual loss in metacentric height which can be calculated by using the formula:

$$\text{FSE} = \text{Virtual loss of GM} = \frac{i}{W} \times \rho \times \frac{1}{n^2} \text{ metres} \qquad (I)$$

where

i	=	the second moment of the free surface about the centre line, in m^4
w	=	the ship's displacement, in tonnes
ρ	=	the density of the liquid in the tank, in tonnes/cu. m
n	=	the number of the longitudinal compartments into which the tank is subdivided
$i \times p$	=	free surface moment, in tonnes m.

The derivation of this formula is as follows:

The ship shown in Figure 20.1(a) has an undivided tank which is partially filled with a liquid.

When the ship is inclined, a wedge of the liquid in the tank will shift from the high side to the low side such that its centre of gravity shifts from g to g_1. This will cause the centre of gravity of the ship to shift from G to G_1, where

$$GG_1 = \frac{w \times gg_1}{W}$$

Let

$$\rho_1 = \text{density of the liquid in the tank}$$

and

$$\rho_2 = \text{density of the water in which the ship floats}$$

then

$$GG_1 = \frac{v \times \rho_1 \times gg_1}{V \times \rho_2}$$

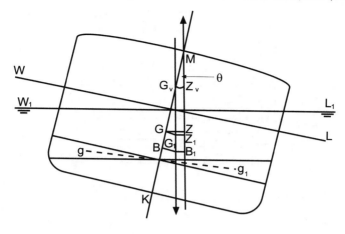

Fig. 20.1 (a)

Had there been no free surface when the ship inclined, the righting lever would have been GZ. But, due to the liquid shifting, the righting lever is reduced to G_1Z_1 or G_vZ_v. The virtual reduction of GM is therefore GG_v.

For a small angle of heel:

$$GG_1 = GG_v \times \theta$$

$$\therefore GG_v \times \theta = \frac{v \times gg_1 \times \rho_1}{V \times \rho_2}$$

or

$$GG_v = \frac{v \times gg_1 \times \rho_1}{V \times \theta \times \rho_2}$$

From the proof of $BM = I/V$, $I \times \theta = v \times gg_1$

Let i = the second moment of the free surface about the centre line.

Then

$$GG_v = \frac{i \times \rho_1}{V \times \rho_2}$$

This is the formula to find the virtual loss of GM due to the free surface effect in an undivided tank.

Now assume that the tank is subdivided longitudinally into 'n' compartments of equal width as shown in Figure 20.1(b).

Let

$$l = \text{length of the tank, and}$$

$$b = \text{breadth of the tank.}$$

The breadth of the free surface in each compartment is thus b/n, and the second moment of each free surface is given by $\dfrac{l \times (b/n)^3}{12}$

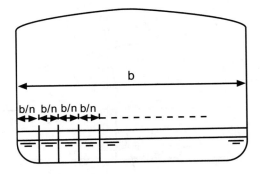

Fig. 20.1(b)

GG_v = virtual loss of GM for one compartment multiplied by the number of compartments.

$$= \frac{i \times \rho_1}{V \times \rho_2} \times n$$

where

i = the second moment of the water-plane area in one compartment about the centre line.

$$= \frac{l \times (b/n)^3 \times \rho_1}{12 \times V \times \rho_2} \times n$$

$$= \frac{l \times b^3 \times \rho_1}{12 \times V \times n^3 \times \rho_2} \times n$$

or

$$GG_v = \frac{i}{V} \times \frac{\rho_1}{\rho_2} \times \frac{1}{n^2}$$

where

i = the second moment of the water-plane area of the whole tank about the centre line.

But

$$W = V \times \rho_2$$

so

$$GG_v = \frac{i}{W} \times \rho_1 \times \frac{1}{n^2}$$

as shown in equation (I).

This is the formula to find the virtual loss of GM due to the free surface effect in a tank which is subdivided longitudinally.

From this formula it can be seen that, when a tank is subdivided longitudinally, the virtual loss of GM for the undivided tank is divided by the square of the number of compartments into which the tank is divided. Also note that the actual weight of the liquid in the tank will have no effect whatsoever on the virtual loss of GM due to the free surface.

For a rectangular area of free surface, the second moment to be used in the above formula can be found as follows:

$$i = \frac{LB^3}{12}$$

where

L = the length of the free surface, and

B = the total breadth of the free surface, ignoring divisions.

Note. Transverse subdivisions in partially filled tanks (slack tanks) *do not* have any influence on reducing free surface effects.

However, fitting longitudinal bulkheads *do* have a very effective influence in reducing this virtual loss in GM.

Example 1

A ship of 8153.75 tonnes displacement has KM = 8 m, KG = 7.5 m, and has a double bottom tank 15 m × 10 m × 2 m which is full of salt water ballast. Find the new GM if this tank is now pumped out till half empty.

Note. The mass of the water pumped out will cause an actual rise in the position of the ship's centre of gravity and the free surface created will cause a virtual loss in GM. There are therefore two shifts in the position of the centre of gravity to consider.

In Figure 20.2 the shaded portion represents the water to be pumped out with its centre of gravity at position g. The original position of the ship's centre of gravity is at G.

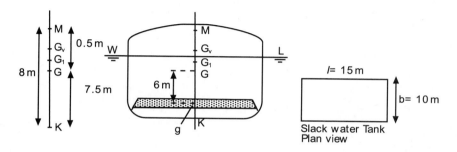

Fig. 20.2

Let GG_1 represent the actual rise of G due to the mass discharged.

The mass of water discharged (w) $= 15 \times 10 \times 1 \times 1.025$ tonnes

$$w = 153.75 \text{ tonnes}$$

$$W_2 = W_1 - w = 8153.75 - 153.75$$

$$= 8000 \text{ tonnes}$$

$$GG_1 = \frac{w \times d}{W_2}$$

$$= \frac{153.75 \times 6}{8000}$$

$$\underline{GG_1 = 0.115 \text{ m}}$$

Let G_1G_v represent the virtual loss of GM due to free surface or rise in G_1. Then:

$$G_1G_v = \frac{i}{W} \times \rho_1 \times \frac{1}{n^2}$$

as per equation (I)

$$n = 1$$

$$\therefore G_1G_v = \frac{i}{W_2} \times \rho_{SW}$$

or

$$G_1G_v = \frac{lb^3}{12} \times \frac{\rho_{SW}}{W_2} \times \frac{1}{n^2}$$

Loss in GM $=$ FSE

or

$$G_1G_v = \frac{15 \times 10^3 \times 1.025}{12 \times 8000}$$

$$\underline{G_1G_v = 0.160 \text{ m} \uparrow}$$

Old KM $= \underline{8.000 \text{ m}}$

Old KG $= \underline{7.500 \text{ m}}$

Old GM $= \underline{0.500 \text{ m}}$

Actual rise of G $= \underline{0.115 \text{ m}}$

$0.385 \text{ m} = GM_{solid}$

$G_1G_v =$ Virtual rise of G $= \underline{0.160 \text{ m} \uparrow}$

$$= \underline{0.225 \text{ m}}$$

Ans. New GM $= \underline{0.225 \text{ m} = GM_{fluid}}$

Hence G_1 has risen due to the discharge of the ballast water (loading change) and has also risen due to Free Surface Effects.

Be aware that in some cases these two rises of G do not take G above M thereby making the ship unstable.

Example 2

A ship of 6000 tonnes displacement, floating in salt water, has a double bottom tank 20 m × 12 m × 2 m which is divided at the centre line and is partially filled with oil of relative density 0.82. Find the virtual loss of GM due to the free surface of the oil.

$$\text{Virtual loss of GM} = \frac{i}{W} \times \rho_{oil} \times \frac{1}{n^2}$$

$$= \frac{lb^3}{12} \times \rho_{oil} \times \frac{1}{W} \times \frac{1}{n^2}$$

$$= \frac{20 \times 12^3}{12 \times 6000} \times 0.820 \times \frac{1}{2^2}$$

Ans. Virtual loss of GM = 0.098 metres

Example 3

A ship of 8000 tonnes displacement has KM 7.5 m, and KG 7.0 m. A double bottom tank is 12 m long, 15 m wide and 1 m deep. The tank is divided longitudinally at the centre line and both sides are full of salt water. Calculate the list if one side is pumped out until it is half empty. (See Fig. 20.3.)

$$\text{Mass of water discharge} = l_{DB} \times b_{DB} \times \frac{d_{DB}}{2} \times \rho_{SW}$$

$$\text{Mass of water discharged} = 12 \times 7.5 \times 0.5 \times 1.025$$

$$w = 46.125 \text{ tonnes}$$

$$\text{Vertical shift of G(GG}_1) = \frac{w \times d}{W_2}$$

$$= \frac{46.125 \times 6.25}{8000 - 46.125} = \frac{46.125 \times 6.25}{7953.875}$$

$$= 0.036 \text{ metres}$$

$$\text{Horizontal shift of G(G}_v\text{G}_2) = \frac{w \times d}{W - w}$$

$$= \frac{46.125 \times 3.75}{7953.875}$$

$$= \underline{0.022 \text{ metres}}$$

$$\text{Virtual loss of GM(G}_1\text{G}_v) = \frac{l \times b_2^3}{12} \times \frac{\rho_{SW}}{W_2} \times \frac{1}{n^2}$$

$$= \frac{12 \times 7.5^3}{12} \times \frac{1.025}{7953.875} \times \frac{1}{1^2}$$

$$= 0.054 \text{ metres}$$

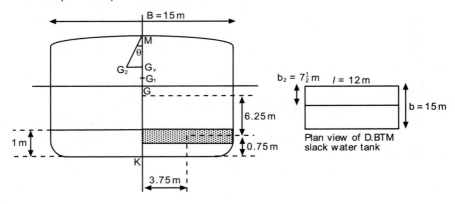

Fig. 20.3

$$KM = 7.500 \text{ metres}$$

$$\text{Original } KG = 7.000 \text{ metres}$$

$$\text{Original } GM = 0.500 \text{ metres} = GM_{solid}$$

$$\text{Vertical rise of } G(GG_1) = 0.036 \text{ metres } \uparrow$$

$$G_1M = 0.464 \text{ metres} = G_1M_{solid}$$

$$\text{Virtual loss of } GM(G_1G_v) = 0.054 \text{ metres}$$

$$\text{New } GM(G_vM) = 0.410 \text{ metres} = GM_{fluid}$$

In triangle G_vG_2M:

$$\tan \theta = \frac{G_2G_v}{G_vM}$$

$$= \frac{0.022}{0.410} = 0.0536$$

Ans. <u>List = 3° 04′</u>

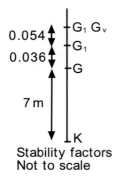

Stability factors
Not to scale

So again G has risen due to discharging water ballast. It has also risen due to free-surface effects. A further movement has caused G to move off the centreline and has produced this angle of list of 3° 04′.

The following worked example shows the effect of subdivisions in slack tanks in relation to free surface effects (FSE):

Question: A ship has a displacement of 3000 tonnes. On the vessel is a rectangular double-bottom tank 15 m long and 8 m wide. This tank is partially filled with ballast water having a density of $1.025 \, \text{t/m}^3$.

If the GM_T without free surface effects is 0.18 m calculate the virtual loss in GM_T and the final GM_T when the double bottom tank has:

(a) no divisional bulkheads fitted;
(b) one transverse bulkhead fitted at mid-length;
(c) one longitudinal bulkhead fitted on ₵ of the tank;
(d) two longitudinal bulkheads fitted giving three equal divisions.

Answer

$l_1 = 15 \, \text{m}$

$b_1 = 8 \, \text{m}$

Fig. 20.4(a)

$$\text{FSE} = \text{virtual loss in } GM_T \text{ or rise in } G = \frac{I \times \rho_{SW}}{W}$$

$$= \frac{l \times b_1^3 \times \rho_{SW}}{12 \times W} \quad (\text{see Fig. 20.4(a)})$$

$$\therefore \underline{\text{virtual loss in } GM_T} = \frac{15 \times 8^3 \times 1.025}{3000 \times 12}$$

$$= \underline{0.02187 \, \text{m}} \uparrow$$

$$\therefore \ GM_T \text{ finally} = 0.1800 - 0.2187$$

$$= \underline{-0.0387 \, \text{m}} \uparrow$$

i.e. unstable ship!!

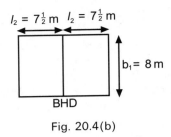

Fig. 20.4(b)

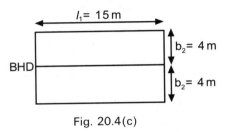

Fig. 20.4(c)

$$\text{FSE} = \text{virtual loss in } GM_T \text{ or rise in } G = \frac{2 @ l_2 \times b_1^3}{12 \times W} \times \rho_{SW} \quad (\text{see Fig. 20.4(b)})$$

$$\therefore \text{ virtual loss} = \frac{2 \times 7.5 \times 8^3 \times 1.025}{12 \times 3000}$$

$$= 0.2187 \, m \uparrow$$

This is same answer as for part (a). Consequently it can be concluded that fitting transverse divisional bulkheads in tanks does not reduce the free surface effects. Ship is still unstable!!

$$\text{FSE} = \text{vertical loss in } GM_T \text{ or rise in } G = \frac{2 @ l_1 b_2^3}{12 \times W} \rho_{SW}$$

$$\therefore \text{ virtual loss in } GM_T = \frac{2 \times 15 \times 4^3 \times 1.025}{12 \times 3000} \quad (\text{see Fig. 20.4(c)})$$

$$= 0.0547 \, m \uparrow \text{ i.e. } \tfrac{1}{4} \text{ of answer to part (a)}$$

Hence

$$\text{final } GM_T = 0.1800 - 0.0547 \, m = +0.1253 \, m \text{ Ship is stable.}$$

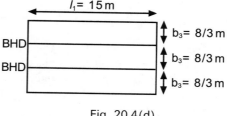

Fig. 20.4(d)

GM$_T$ is now +ve, but below the minimum GM$_T$ of 0.15 m that is allowable by D.Tp. regulations.

$$FSE = \text{virtual loss in } GM_T \text{ or rise in } G = \frac{3 @ l_1 \times b_3^3}{12 \times W} \times \rho_{SW} \qquad \text{(see Fig. 20.4(d))}$$

$$\therefore \text{ Virtual loss in } GM_T = \frac{3 \times 15 \times \left(\frac{8}{3}\right)^3 \times 1.025}{12 \times W}$$

$$= 0.0243 \text{ m} \uparrow \quad \text{i.e. } \tfrac{1}{9} \text{ of answer to part (a)}$$

Hence

$$\text{final } GM_T = 0.1800 - 0.0243 = +0.1557 \text{ m ship is stable.}$$

Ship is stable and above D.Tp. minimum GM$_T$ value of 0.15 m.

So longitudinal divisional bulkheads (watertight or wash-bulkheads) are effective. They cut down rapidly the loss in GM$_T$. Note the $1/n^2$ law where n is the number of equal divisions made by the longitudinal bulkheads.

Free surface effects therefore depend on:

   (I)   density of slack liquid in the tank;
   (II) ship's displacement in tonnes;
   (III) dimensions and shape of the slack tanks;
   (IV) bulkhead subdivision within the slack tanks.

The longitudinal divisional bulkheads referred to in examples in this chapter need not be absolutely watertight; they could have openings in them. Examples on board ship are the centreline wash bulkhead in the Fore Peak tank and in Aft Peak tank.

Exercise 20

1   A ship of 10 000 tonnes displacement is floating in dock water of density 1024 kg per cu. m, and is carrying oil of relative density 0.84 in a double-bottom tank. The tank is 25 m long, 15 m wide, and is divided at the centre line. Find the virtual loss of GM due to this tank being slack.

2   A ship of 6000 tonnes displacement is floating in fresh water and has a deep tank (10 m × 15 m × 6 m) which is undivided and is partly filled with nut oil of relative density 0.92. Find the virtual loss of GM due to the free surface.

3   A ship of 8000 tonnes displacement has KG = 3.75 m, and KM = 5.5 m. A double-bottom tank 16 m × 16 m × 1 m is subdivided at the centre line and is full of salt water ballast. Find the new GM if this tank is pumped out until it is half empty.

4   A ship of 10 000 tonnes displacement, KM 6 m, KG 5.5 m, is floating upright in dock water of density 1024 kg per cu. m. She has a double bottom tank 20 m × 15 m which is subdivided at the centre line and is partially filled with oil of relative density 0.96. Find the list if a mass of 30 tonnes is now shifted 15 m transversely across the deck.

5   A ship is at the light displacement of 3000 tonnes and has KG 5.5 m, and KM 7.0 m. The following weights are then loaded:

> 5000 tonnes of cargo KG 5 m
> 2000 tonnes of cargo KG 10 m
> 700 tonnes of fuel oil of relative density 0.96.

The fuel oil is taken into Nos. 2, 3 and 5 double bottom tanks, filling Nos. 3 and 5, and leaving No. 2 slack.

   The ship then sails on a 20-day passage consuming 30 tonnes of fuel oil per day. On arrival at her destination Nos. 2 and 3 tanks are empty, and the remaining fuel oil is in No. 5 tank. Find the ship's GM's for the departure and arrival conditions.

Dimensions of the tanks:

> No. 2   15 × 15 m × 1 m
> No. 3   22 m × 15 m × 1 m
> No. 5   12 m × 15 m × 1 m

Assume that the KM is constant and that the KG of the fuel oil in every case is half of the depth of the tank.

6   A ship's displacement is 5100 tonnes, KG = 4 m, and KM = 4.8 m. A double-bottom tank on the starboard side is 20 m long, 6 m wide and 1 m deep and is full of fresh water. Calculate the list after 60 tonnes of this water has been consumed.

7   A ship of 6000 tonnes displacement has KG 4 m and KM 4.5 m. A double-bottom tank in the ship 20 m long and 10 m wide is partly full of salt-water

ballast. Find the moment of statical stability when the ship is heeled 5 degrees.

8   A box-shaped vessel has the following data.

Length is 80 m, breadth is 12 m, draft even keel is 6 m, KG is 4.62 m.

A double bottom tank 10 m long, of full width and 2.4 m depth is then half-filled with water ballast having a density of 1.025 t/m³. The tank is located at amidships.

Calculate the new even keel draft and the new transverse GM after this water ballast has been put in the double bottom tank.

Chapter 21
Bilging and permeability

Bilging amidships compartments

When a vessel floats in still water it displaces its own weight of water. Figure 21.1(a) shows a box-shaped vessel floating at the waterline WL. The weight of the vessel (W) is considered to act downwards through G, the centre of gravity. The force of buoyancy is also equal to W and acts upwards through B, the centre of buoyancy. b = W.

Now let an empty compartment amidships be holed below the waterline to such an extent that the water may flow freely into and out of the compartment. A vessel holed in this way is said to be 'bilged'.

Figure 21.1(b) shows the vessel in the bilged condition. The buoyancy provided by the bilged compartment is lost. The draft has increased and the vessel now floats at the waterline W_1L_1, where it is again displacing its own

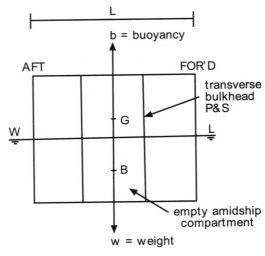

Fig. 21.1 (a)

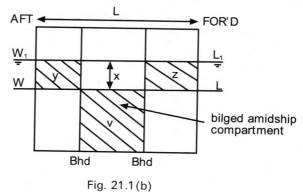

Fig. 21.1(b)

weight of water. 'X' represents the increase in draft due to bilging. The volume of lost buoyancy (v) is made good by the volumes 'y' and 'z'.

$$\therefore v = y + z$$

Let 'A' be the area of the water-plane before bilging, and let 'a' be the area of the bilged compartment. Then:

$$y + z = Ax - ax$$

or

$$v = x(A - a)$$

$$\text{Increase in draft} = x = \frac{v}{A - a}$$

i.e.

$$\text{Increase in draft} = \frac{\text{Volume of lost buoyancy}}{\text{Area of intact waterplane}}$$

Note. Since the distribution of weight within the vessel has not been altered the KG after bilging will be the same as the KG before bilging.

Example 1

A box-shaped vessel is 50 metres long and is floating on an even keel at 4 metres draft. A compartment amidships is 10 metres long and is empty. Find the increase in draft if this compartment is bilged. See Fig. 21.1(c).

$$x = \frac{v}{A - a} = \frac{l \times B \times B}{(L - l)B}$$

let

$$B = \text{Breadth of the vessel}$$

then

$$x = \frac{10 \times B \times 4}{50 \times B - 10 \times B}$$

$$= \frac{40B}{40B}$$

$$\underline{\text{Increase in draft} = 1 \text{ metre}}$$

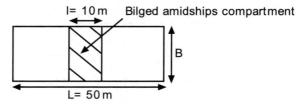

Fig. 21.1 (c)

Example 2

A box-shaped vessel is 150 metres long × 24 metres wide × 12 metres deep and is floating on an even keel at 5 metres draft. GM = 0.9 metres. A compartment amidships is 20 metres long and is empty. Find the new GM if this compartment is bilged.

$$\text{Old KB} = \tfrac{1}{2} \text{ Old draft}$$

$$= 2.5 \text{ m}$$

$$\text{Old BM} = B^2/12d$$

$$= \frac{24 \times 24}{12 \times 5}$$

$$= 9.6 \text{ m}$$

$$\text{Old KB} = +2.5 \text{ m}$$

$$\overline{\text{Old KM} = 12.1 \text{ m}}$$

$$\text{Old GM} = -0.9 \text{ m}$$

$$\overline{\text{KG} = 11.2 \text{ m}}$$

This KG will not change after bilging has taken place.

$$x = \frac{v}{A - a}$$

$$= \frac{20 \times 24 \times 5}{150 \times 24 - 20 \times 24}$$

$$= \frac{2400}{130 \times 24}$$

$$\text{Increase in draft} = 0.77 \text{ m}$$

$$\text{Old draft} = 5.00 \text{ m}$$

$$\overline{\text{New draft} = 5.77 \text{ m}} = \text{say draft } d_2$$

$$\text{New KB} = \frac{1}{2} \text{ New draft} = \frac{d_2}{2}$$

$$= 2.89 \text{ m}$$

$$\text{New BM} = B^2/12d_2$$

$$= \frac{24 \times 24}{12 \times 5.77}$$

$$= 8.32 \text{ m}$$

$$\text{New KB} = {}^+2.89 \text{ m}$$

$$\text{New KM} = {}_{-}11.21 \text{ m}$$

$$\text{As before, KG} = {}^-11.20 \text{ m}$$

Ans. New GM = 0.01 m
This is +ve but dangerously low in value!!

Permeability μ

Permeability is the amount of water that can enter a compartment or tank after it has been bilged. When an empty compartment is bilged, the whole of the bouyancy provided by that compartment is lost. Typical values for permeability μ are as follows:

Empty compartment	$\mu = 100\%$
Engine room	$\mu = 80\%$ to 85%
Grain filled cargo hold	$\mu = 60\%$ to 65%
Coal filled compartment	$\mu = 36\%$ approx
Filled water ballast tank (when ship is in salt water)	$\mu = 0\%$

Consequently, the higher the value of the permeability for a bilged compartment, the greater will be a ship's loss of bouyancy when the ship is bilged.

The permeability of a compartment can be found from the formula:

$$\mu = \text{Permeability} = \frac{\text{Broken Stowage}}{\text{Stowage Factor}} \times 100 \text{ per cent}$$

The broken stowage to be used in this formula is the broken stowage per tonne of stow.

When a bilged compartment contains cargo, the formula for finding the increase in draft must be amended to allow for the permeability. If 'μ' represents the permeability, expressed as a fraction, then the volume of lost buoyancy will be 'μv' and the area of the intact waterplane will be 'A − μv' square metres. The formula then reads:

$$x = \frac{\mu v}{A - \mu a}$$

Example 3

A box-shaped vessel is 64 metres long and is floating on an even keel at 3 metres draft. A compartment amidships is 12 m long and contains cargo having a permeability of 25 per cent. Calculate the increase in the draft if this compartment be bilged.

$$x = \frac{\mu v}{A - \mu a}$$

$$= \frac{\frac{1}{4} \times 12 \times B \times 3}{64 \times B - \frac{1}{4} \times 12 \times B}$$

$$= \frac{9B}{61B}$$

Ans. Increase in draft = 0.15 m

Example 4

A box-shaped vessel 150 m × 20 m × 12 m is floating on an even keel at 5 metres draft. A compartment amidships is 15 metres long and contains timber of relative density 0.8, and stowage factor 1.5 cubic metres per tonne. Calculate the new draft if this compartment is now bilged.

The permeability 'μ' must first be found by using the formula given above. i.e.

$$\text{Permeability} = \frac{BS}{SF} \times 100 \text{ per cent} = \text{'}\mu\text{'}$$

The stowage factor is given in the question. The broken stowage per tonne of stow is now found by subtracting the space which would be occupied by one tonne of solid timber from that actually occupied by one tonne of timber in the hold. One tonne of fresh water occupies one cubic metre and the relative density of the timber is 0.8.

$$\therefore \text{ Space occupied by one tonne of solid timber} = \frac{1}{0.8}$$

$$= 1.25 \text{ cubic metres}$$

$$\text{Stowage Factor} = 1.50 \text{ cubic metres}$$

$$\therefore \text{ Broken Stowage} = 0.25 \text{ cubic metres}$$

$$\text{Permeability '}\mu\text{'} = \frac{BS}{SF} \times 100 \text{ per cent}$$

$$= \frac{0.25}{1.50} \times 100 \text{ per cent}$$

$$= 100/6 \text{ per cent}$$

$$\therefore \text{ '}\mu\text{'} = 1/6 \text{ or } 16.67 \text{ per cent}$$

$$\text{Increase in draft} = x = \frac{\mu v}{A - \mu a}$$

$$= \frac{1/6 \times 15 \times 20 \times 5}{150 \times 20 - 1/6 \times 15 \times 20}$$

$$= 250/2950 = 0.085 \text{ m}$$

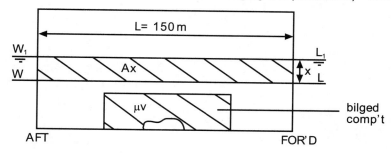

Fig. 21.2

$$\text{Increase in draft} = 0.085 \text{ metres}$$

$$\text{Old draft} = \underline{5.000 \text{ metres}} = \text{draft } d_1$$

Ans. New draft $= 5.085$ metres $=$ draft d_2

When the bilged compartment does not extend above the waterline, the area of the intact waterplane remains constant as shown in Figure 21.2.

In this figure:

$$\mu v = Ax$$

Let

$$d = \text{Density of the water, then}$$

$$\mu v \times d = Ax \times d$$

but

$$\mu v \times d = \text{Mass of water entering the bilged compartment, and}$$

$$Ax \times d = \text{Mass of the extra layer of water displaced.}$$

Therefore, when the compartment is bilged, the extra mass of water displaced is equal to the buoyancy lost in the bilged compartment. It should be carefully noted, however, that although the effect on draft is similar to that of loading a mass in the bilged compartment equal to the lost buoyancy, no mass has in fact been loaded. The *displacement* after bilging is *the same* as the displacement before bilging and there is *no alteration* in the position of the vessel's *centre of gravity*. The increase in the draft is due solely to lost buoyancy.

Example 5

A ship is floating in salt water on an even keel at 6 metres draft. TPC is 20 tonnes. A rectangular-shaped compartment amidships is 20 metres long, 10 metres wide, and 4 metres deep. The compartment contains cargo with permeability 25 per cent. Find the new draft if this compartment is bilged.

$$\text{Buoyancy lost} = \frac{25}{100} \times 20 \times 10 \times 4 \times 1.025 \text{ tonnes}$$

$$= 205 \text{ tonnes}$$

$$\text{Extra mass of water displaced} = TPC \times X \text{ tonnes}$$

$$\therefore X = w/TPC$$

$$= 205/20$$

$$\text{Increase in draft} = 10.25 \text{ cm}$$

$$= 0.1025 \text{ m}$$

$$\text{plus the old draft} = \underline{6.0000 \text{ m}}$$

Ans. New draft = 6.1025 m

Note: The *lower* the permeability is the *less* will be the changes in end drafts after bilging has taken place.

Bilging end compartments

When the bilged compartment is situated in a position away from amidships, the vessel's mean draft will increase to make good the lost buoyancy but the trim will also change.

Consider the box-shaped vessel shown in Figure 21.3(a). The vessel is floating upright on an even keel, WL representing the waterline. The centre of buoyancy (B) is at the centre of the displaced water and the vessel's centre of gravity (G) is vertically above B. There is no trimming moment.

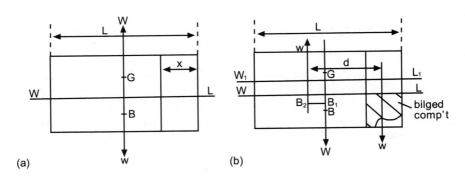

Fig. 21.3

Now let the forward compartment which is X metres long be bilged. To make good the loss in buoyancy, the vessel's mean draft will increase as shown in Figure 21.3(b), where W_1L_1 represents the new waterline. Since there has been no change in the distribution of mass within the vessel, the centre of gravity will remain at G. It has already been shown that the effect on mean draft will be similar to that of loading a mass in the compartment equal to the mass of water entering the bilged space to the original waterline.

The vertical component of the shift of the centre of buoyancy (B to B_1) is due to the increase in the mean draft. KB_1 is equal to half of the new draft. The horizontal component of the shift of the centre of buoyancy (B_1B_2) is equal to X/2.

A trimming moment of $W \times B_1B_2$ by the head is produced and the vessel will trim about the centre of flotation (F), which is the centre of gravity of the new water-plane area.

$$B_1B_2 = \frac{w \times d}{W}$$

or

$$W \times B_1B_2 = w \times d$$

but

$$W \times B_1B_2 = \text{Trimming moment,}$$

$$\therefore w \times d = \text{Trimming moment}$$

It can therefore be seen that the effect on trim is similar to that which would be produced if a mass equal to the lost buoyancy were loaded in the bilged compartment.

Note. When calculating the TPC, MCTC, etc., it must be remembered that the information is required for the vessel in the bilged condition, using draft d_2 and intact length l_2.

Example 6

A box-shaped vessel 75 metres long × 10 metres wide × 6 metres deep is floating in salt water on an even keel at a draft of 4.5 metres. Find the new drafts if a forward compartment 5 metres long is bilged.

(a) First let the vessel sink bodily.

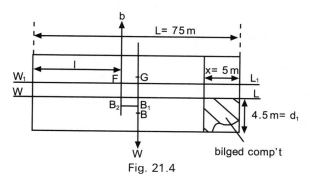

Fig. 21.4

$w = x \times B \times d_1 \times 1.025$ tonnes

$\quad = 5 \times 10 \times 4.5 \times 1.025$

$w = 230.63$ tonnes

$\text{TPC} = \dfrac{\text{WPA}}{97.56} = \dfrac{L_2 \times B}{97.56}$

$\quad = \dfrac{70 \times 10}{97.56}$

$\text{TPC} = 7.175$

$$\text{Increase in draft} = w/\text{TPC}$$
$$= 230.63/7.175$$
$$= 32.14 \, \text{cm}$$
$$= 0.321 \, \text{m}$$
$$+$$

$$\text{Old draft} = 4.500 \, \text{m} = \text{draft } d_1$$
$$\text{New mean draft} = 4.821 \, \text{m} = \text{draft } d_2$$

(b) *Now consider the trim.*

$$W = L \times B \times d_1 \times 1.025 \text{ tonnes} \qquad BM_L = I_L/V$$

$$= 75 \times 10 \times 4.5 \times 1.025 \qquad\qquad = \frac{BL_2^3}{12V}$$

$$W = 3459 \text{ tonnes}$$

$$= \frac{10 \times 70^3}{12 \times 75 \times 10 \times 4.5}$$

$$BM_L = 84.7 \text{ metres}$$

$$MCTC \simeq \frac{W \times BM_L}{100L}$$

$$= \frac{3459 \times 84.7}{100 \times 75}$$

$$= 39.05 \text{ tonnes m per cm}$$

$$\text{Change of trim} = \frac{\text{Moment changing trim}}{MCTC}$$

where

$$d = \frac{LBP}{2} = \frac{75}{2} = 37.5 \, \text{m} = \text{lever from new LCF}$$

$$= \frac{230.6 \times 37.5}{39.05}$$

$$= 221.4 \text{ cm by the head}$$

After bilging, LCF has moved to F, i.e. $(L - x)/2$ from the stern

$$\text{Change of draft aft} = \frac{l}{L} \times \text{Change of trim}$$

$$= \frac{35}{75} \times 221.4$$

$$= 103.3 \text{ cm} = 1.033 \, \text{m}$$

$$\text{Change of draft forward} = \frac{40}{75} \times 221.4$$

$$= 118.1 \text{ cm} = 1.181 \, \text{m}$$

(c) Now find new drafts.

Drafts before trimming	A 4.821 m	F 4.821 m
Change due to trim	−1.033 m	+1.181 m
Ans. New Drafts	A 3.788 m	F 6.002 m

Example 7

A box-shaped vessel 100 metres long × 20 metres wide × 12 metres deep is floating in salt water on an even keel at 6 metres draft. A forward compartment is 10 metres long, 12 metres wide and extends from the outer bottom to a watertight flat, 4 metres above the keel. The compartment contains cargo of permeability 25 per cent. Find the new drafts if this compartment is bilged.

$$\text{Mass of water entering the bilged compartment} = \frac{25}{100} \times 10 \times 12 \times 4 \times 1.025$$
$$= 123 \text{ tonnes}$$

$$TPC_{SW} = \frac{WPA}{97.56}$$

$$= \frac{100 \times 20}{97.56}$$

$$\underline{TPC = 20.5 \text{ tonnes}}$$

Increase in draft $= w/TPC$

$$= 123/20.5$$

$$= 6 \text{ cm}$$

$$\underline{\text{Increase in draft} = 0.06 \text{ m}}$$

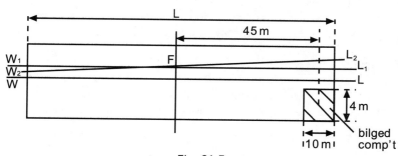

Fig. 21.5

$$W = L \times B \times d_1 \times 1.025$$
$$= 100 \times 20 \times 6 \times 1.025$$
$$\underline{W = 12\,300 \text{ tonnes}}$$

$$BM_L = \frac{I_L}{V} = \frac{BL^3}{12V} = \frac{B \times L^3}{12 \times L \times B \times d} = \frac{L^2}{12 \times d_1}$$

$$BM_L = \frac{100 \times 100}{12 \times 6}$$

$$\underline{BM_L = 139 \text{ metres}}$$

$$MCTC \simeq \frac{W \times BM_L}{100 \times L} = \frac{12\,300 \times 139}{100 \times 100}$$

$$MCTC = 171 \text{ tonnes m per cm}$$

$$\text{Trimming moment} = W \times B_1 B_2$$

$$= w \times d$$

$$\text{Trimming moment} = 123 \times 45 \text{ tonnes m}$$

$$\text{Change of trim} = \frac{\text{Trimming moment}}{\text{MCTC}} = \frac{123 \times 45}{171}$$

$$\text{Change of trim} = 32.4 \text{ cm by the head,}$$

i.e. 0.32 m by the head

Note. The centre of flotation, being the centroid of the water-plane area, remains amidships.

Old drafts	A	6.00 m	F	6.00 m
Bodily increase		+0.06 m		+0.06 m
		6.06 m		6.06 m
Change due to trim		−0.16 m		+0.16 m
Ans. New Drafts	A	5.90 m	F	6.22 m

Effect of bilging on stability

It has already been shown that when a compartment in a ship is bilged the mean draft is increased. The change in mean draft causes a change in the positions of the centre of buoyancy and the initial metacentre. Hence KM is changed and, since KG is constant, the GM will be changed.

Example 8

A box-shaped vessel 40 metres long, 8 metres wide and 6 metres deep, floats in salt water on an even keel at 3 metres draft. GM = 1 metre. Find the new GM if an empty compartment 4 metres long and situated amidships is bilged.

(a) Original condition before bilging.

Find the KG

$$KB = \frac{d_1}{2} \qquad\qquad BM = \frac{I}{V}$$

$$= 1.5 \text{ metres} \qquad = \frac{LB^3}{12V} = \frac{B^2}{12 \times d_1}$$

$$= \frac{8 \times 8}{12 \times 3}$$

$$
\begin{aligned}
BM &= \quad 1.78 \text{ m} \\
KB &= +1.50 \text{ m} \\
KM &= \quad 3.28 \text{ m} \\
GM &= -1.00 \text{ m} \\
KG &= \quad 2.28 \text{ m}
\end{aligned}
$$

(b) Vessel's condition after bilging.

Find the New Draft

$$\text{Lost buoyancy} = 4 \times 8 \times 3 \times 1.025 \text{ tonnes}$$

$$\text{TPC}_{SW} = \frac{\text{WPA}}{97.56} = \frac{36 \times 8}{97.56}$$

$$\text{Increase in draft} = \frac{\text{Lost buoyancy}}{\text{TPC}}$$

$$= 4 \times 8 \times 3 \times 1.025 \times \frac{100}{36 \times 8 \times 1.025} \text{ cm}$$

$$= 33.3 \text{ cm or } 0.33 \text{ m}$$

It should be noted that the increase in draft can also be found as follows:

$$\text{Increase in draft} = \frac{\text{Volume of lost buoyancy}}{\text{Area of intact water-plane}} = \frac{4 \times 8 \times 3}{36 \times 8}$$

$$= 1/3 \text{ metres.}$$

$$\text{Original draft} = 3.000 \text{ m} = \text{draft } d_1$$

$$\text{New draft} = 3.333 \text{ m} = \text{draft } d_2$$

(c) Find the New GM

$$\text{KB} = \frac{d_2}{2} = 1.67 \text{ m}$$

$\text{BM} = \text{I/V}$ (Note: 'I' represents the second moment
of the intact water-plane about the centre line)

$$= \frac{(\text{L} - 1)\text{B}^3}{12 \times \text{V}} = \frac{36 \times 8^3}{12 \times 40 \times 8 \times 3}$$

$$\begin{aligned}
\text{BM}_2 &= \quad 1.60 \text{ m} \\
&\quad\quad + \\
\text{KB}_2 &= \quad 1.67 \text{ m} \\
\hline
\text{KM}_2 &= \quad 3.27 \text{ m} \\
&\quad\quad - \\
\text{KG} &= \quad 2.28 \text{ m as before bilging occurred} \\
\hline
\text{Final GM}_2 &= \quad 0.99 \text{ m}
\end{aligned}$$

GM_2 is +ve so vessel is in stable equilibrium.

Summary

When solving problems involving bilging and permeability it is suggested
that:

1 Make a sketch from given information.
2 Calculate mean bodily sinkage using w and TPC.
3 Calculate change of trim using GM_L or BM_L.
4 Collect calculated data to evaluate the final requested end drafts.

Exercise 21

Bilging amidships compartments

1   (a) Define permeability, 'μ'.
    (b) A box-shaped vessel 100 m long, 15 m beam floating in salt water, at a
        mean draft of 5 m, has an amidships compartment 10 m long which is
        loaded with a general cargo. Find the new mean draft if this
        compartment is bilged, assuming the permeability to be 25 per cent.

2   A box-shaped vessel 30 m long, 6 m beam, 5 m deep, has a mean draft of
    2.5 m. An amidships compartment 8 m long is filled with coal stowing at
    1.2 cu. m per tonne. 1 cu. m of solid coal weighs 1.2 tonnes. Find the
    increase in the draft if the compartment is holed below the waterline.

3   A box-shaped vessel 60 m long, 15 m beam, floats on an even keel at 3 m
    draft. An amidships compartment is 12 m long and contains coal
    (SF = 1.2 cu. m per tonne and relative density = 1.28). Find the increase
    in the draft if this compartment is bilged.

4   A box-shaped vessel 40 m long, 6 m beam, is floating at a draft of 2 m F
    and A. She has an amidships compartment 10 m long which is empty. If
    the original GM was 0.6 m, find the new GM if this compartment is
    bilged.

5   If the vessel in Question 4 had cargo stowed in the central compartment
    such that the permeability was 20 per cent, find the new increase in the
    draft when the vessel is bilged.

6   A box-shaped vessel 60 m × 10 m × 6 m floats on an even keel at a draft
    of 5 m F and A. An amidships compartment 12 m long contains timber of
    relative density 0.8 and stowage factor 1.4 cu. m per tonne. Find the
    increase in the draft if this compartment is holed below the waterline.

7   A box-shaped vessel 80 m × 10 m × 6 m is floating upright in salt water
    on an even keel at 4 m draft. She has an amidships compartment 15 m long
    which is filled with timber (SF = 1.5 cu. m per tonne). 1 tonne of solid
    timber would occupy 1.25 cu. m of space. What would be the increase in
    the draft if this compartment is now bilged?

Bilging end compartments

8   A box-shaped vessel 75 m × 12 m is floating upright in salt water on an
    even keel at 2.5 m draft F and A. The forepeak tank which is 6 m long is
    empty. Find the final drafts if the vessel is now holed forward of the
    collision bulkhead.

9   A box-shaped vessel 150 m long, 20 m beam, is floating upright in salt
    water at drafts of 6 m F and A. The collision bulkhead is situated 8 m from
    forward. Find the new drafts if the vessel is now bilged forward of the
    collision bulkhead.

10   A box-shaped vessel 60 m long, 10 m beam, is floating upright in salt
    water on even keel at 4 m draft F and A. The collision bulkhead is 6 m

from forward. Find the new drafts if she is now bilged forward of the collision bulkhead.

11   A box-shaped vessel 65 m × 10 m × 6 m is floating on an even keel in salt water at 4 m draft F and A. She has a forepeak compartment 5 m long which is empty. Find the new drafts if this compartment is now bilged.

12   A box-shaped vessel 64 m × 10 m × 6 m floats in salt water on an even keel at 5 m draft. A forward compartment 6 metres long and 10 metres wide, extends from the outer bottom to a height of 3.5 m, and is full of cargo of permeability 25 per cent. Find the new drafts if this compartment is now bilged.

Chapter 22
Dynamical stability

Dynamical stability is defined as the work done in inclining a ship.

Consider the ship shown in Figure 22.1. When the ship is upright the force 'W' acts upwards through B and downwards through G. These forces act throughout the inclination. b = w.

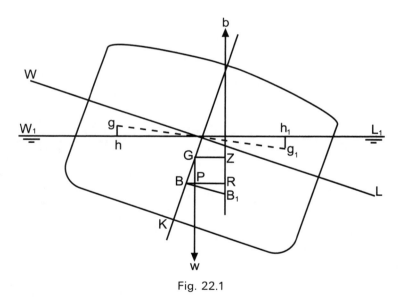

Fig. 22.1

Work done = Weight × vertical separation of G and B

or

$$\text{Dynamical stability} = W \times (B_1Z - BG)$$

$$= W \times (B_1R + RZ - BG)$$

$$= W \times \left[\frac{v(gh + g_1h_1)}{V} + PG - BG\right]$$

$$= W \times \left[\frac{v(gh + g_1h_1)}{V} + BG \cos \theta - BG\right]$$

$$\text{Dynamical stability} = W \left[\frac{v(gh + g_1h_1)}{V} - BG(1 - \cos \theta)\right]$$

This is known as *Moseley's formula* for dynamical stability.

If the curve of statical stability for a ship has been constructed the dynamical stability to any angle of heel may be found by multiplying the area under the curve to the angle concerned by the vessel's displacement. i.e.

Dynamical stability = W × Area under the stability curve

The derivation of this formula is as follows:

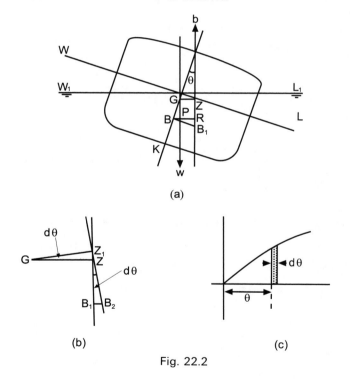

Fig. 22.2

Consider Figure 22.2(a) which shows a ship heeled to an angle θ. Now let the ship be heeled through a further very small angle dθ. The centre of buoyancy B_1 will move parallel to W_1L_1 to the new position B_2 as shown in Figure 22.2(b).

B_2Z_1 is the new vertical through the centre of buoyancy and GZ_1 is the new righting arm. The vertical separation of Z and Z_1 is therefore $GZ \times d\theta$. But this is also the vertical separation of B and G. Therefore the dynamical stability from θ to $(\theta + d\theta)$ is $W \times (GZ \times d\theta)$.

Refer now to Figure 22.2(c) which is the curve of statical stability for the ship. At θ the ordinate is GZ. The area of the strip is $GZ \times d\theta$. But $W \times (GZ \times d\theta)$ gives the dynamical stability from θ to $(\theta+d\theta)$, and this must be true for all small additions of inclination.

$$\therefore \text{ Dynamical stability} = \int_O^\theta W \times GZ \times d\theta$$

$$= W \int_O^\theta GZ\, d\theta$$

Therefore the dynamical stability to any angle of heel is found by multiplying the area under the stability curve to that angle by the displacement.

It should be noted that in finding the area under the stability curve by the use of Simpson's Rules, the common interval must be expressed in *radians*.

$$57.3° = 1 \text{ radian}$$

$$1° = \frac{1}{57.3} \text{ radians}$$

or

$$x° = \frac{x}{57.3} \text{ radians}$$

Therefore to convert degrees to radians simply divide the number of degrees by 57.3.

Example 1

A ship of 5000 tonnes displacement has righting levers as follows:

Angle of heel	10°	20°	30°	40°
GZ (metres)	0.21	0.33	0.40	0.43

Calculate the dynamical stability to 40 degrees heel.

GZ	SM	Functions of area
0	1	0
0.21	4	0.84
0.33	2	0.66
0.40	4	1.60
0.43	1	0.43
		$3.53 = \Sigma_1$

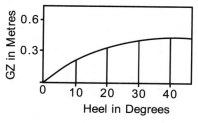

Fig. 22.3

$$h = 10°$$

$$h = \frac{10}{57.3} \text{ radians} = \text{common interval CI}$$

The area under the stability curve $= \frac{1}{3} \times CI \times \Sigma_1$

$$= \frac{1}{3} \times \frac{10}{57.3} \times 3.53$$

$$= 0.2053 \text{ metre-radians}$$

Dynamical stability $= W \times$ Area under the stability curve

$$= 5000 \times 0.2053$$

Ans. Dynamical stability $= 1026.5$ metre tonnes

Example 2

A box-shaped vessel 45 m × 10 m × 6 m is floating in salt water at a draft of 4 m F and A. GM $= 0.6$ m. Calculate the dynamical stability to 20 degrees heel.

$$BM = \frac{B^2}{12d} \qquad \text{Displacement} = 45 \times 10 \times 4 \times 1.025 \text{ tonnes}$$

$$= \frac{10 \times 10}{12 \times 4} \qquad \text{Displacement} = 1845 \text{ tonnes}$$

$$BM = 2.08 \text{ m}$$

Note. When calculating the GZ's 10 degrees may be considered a small angle of heel, but 20 degrees is a large angle of heel, and therefore, the wall-sided formula must be used to find the GZ.

GZ	SM	Products for area
0	1	0
0.104	4	0.416
0.252	1	0.252
		$0.668 = \Sigma_1$

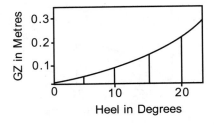

Fig. 22.4

At 10° heel:

$$GZ = GM \times \sin \theta$$

$$= 0.6 \times \sin 10°$$

$$GZ = 0.104 \, m$$

At 20° heel:

$$GZ = (GM + \tfrac{1}{2} BM \tan^2 \theta) \sin \theta$$

$$= (0.6 + \tfrac{1}{2} \times 2.08 \times \tan^2 20°) \sin 20°$$

$$= (0.6 + 0.138) \sin 20°$$

$$= 0.738 \sin 20°$$

$$GZ = 0.252 \, m$$

$$\text{Area under the curve} = \frac{1}{3} \times CI \times \Sigma_1$$

$$= \frac{1}{3} \times \frac{10}{57.3} \times 0.668$$

$$\text{Area under the curve} = 0.0389 \text{ metre radians}$$

$$\text{Dynamical stability} = W \times \text{Area under the curve}$$

$$= 1845 \times 0.0389$$

Ans. Dynamical stability = 71.77 m tonnes

Exercise 22

1   A ship of 10 000 tonnes displacement has righting levers as follows:

Heel	10°	20°	30°	40°
GZ (m)	0.09	0.21	0.30	0.33

   Calculate the dynamical stability to 40 degrees heel.

2   When inclined, a ship of 8000 tonnes displacement has the following righting levers:

Heel	15°	30°	45°	60°
GZ (m)	0.20	0.30	0.32	0.24

   Calculate the dynamical stability to 60 degrees heel.

3   A ship of 10 000 tonnes displacement has the following righting levers when inclined:

Heel	0°	10°	20°	30°	40°	50°
GZ (m)	0.0	0.02	0.12	0.21	0.30	0.33

   Calculate the dynamical stability to 50 degrees heel.

4   A box-shaped vessel 42 m × 6 m × 5 m, is floating in salt water on an even keel at 3 m draft and has KG = 2 m. Assuming that the KM is constant, calculate the dynamical stability to 15 degrees heel.

5   A box-shaped vessel 65 m × 10 m × 6 m is floating upright on an even keel at 4 m draft in salt water. GM = 0.6 m. Calculate the dynamical stability to 20 degrees heel.

Chapter 23
Effect of beam and freeboard on stability

To investigate the effect of beam and freeboard on stability, it will be necessary to assume the stability curve for a particular vessel in a particular condition of loading. Let Curve A in Figure 23.1 represent the curve of stability for a certain box-shaped vessel whose deck edge becomes immersed at about 17 degrees heel.

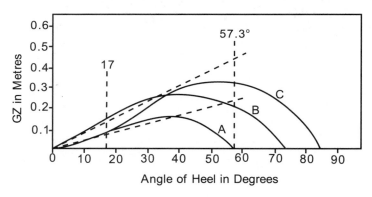

Fig. 23.1

The effect of increasing the beam

Let the draft, freeboard and KG remain unchanged, but increase the beam and consider the effect this will have on the stability curve.

For a ship-shaped vessel BM = I/V, and for a box-shaped vessel BM = B²/12d. Therefore an increase in beam will produce an increase in BM. Hence the GM will also be increased, as will the righting levers at all angles of heel. The range of stability is also increased. The new curve of stability would appear as curve B in Figure 23.1.

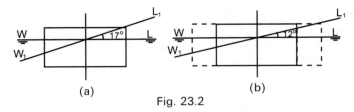

Fig. 23.2

It will be noticed that the curve, at small angles of heel, is much steeper than the original curve, indicating the increase in GM. Also, the maximum GZ and the range of stability have been increased whilst the angle of heel at which the deck edge becomes immersed, has been reduced. The reason for the latter change is shown in Figure 23.2. Angle θ reduces from $17°$ to $12°$.

Figure 23.2(a) represents the vessel in her original condition with the deck edge becoming immersed at about 17 degrees. The increase in the beam, as shown in Figure 23.2(b), will result in the deck edge becoming immersed at a smaller angle of heel. When the deck edge becomes immersed, the breadth of the water-plane will decrease and this will manifest itself in the curve by a reduction in the rate of increase of the GZs with increase in heel.

The effect of increasing the freeboard

Now return to the original vessel. Let the draft, KG, and the beam, remain unchanged, but let the freeboard be increased from f_1 to f_2. The effect of this is shown by Curve C in Figure 23.1.

There will be no effect on the stability curve from the origin up to the angle of heel at which the original deck edge was immersed. When the vessel is now inclined beyond this angle of heel, the increase in the freeboard will cause an increase in the water-plane area and, thus, the righting levers will also be increased. This is shown in Figure 23.2(c), where WL represents the original breadth of the water-plane when heeled x degrees, and WL_1 represents the breadth of the water-plane area for the

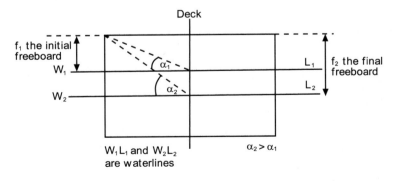

Fig. 23.2(c)

same angle of heel but with the increased freeboard. Thus, the vessel can heel further over before her deck edge is immersed, because $\alpha_2 > \alpha_1$.

From the above it may be concluded that an increase in freeboard has no effect on the stability of the vessel up to the angle of heel at which the original deck edge became immersed, but beyond this angle of heel all of the righting levers will be increased in length. The maximum GZ and the angle at which it occurs will be increased as also will be the range of stability.

Summary

With increased Beam
GM_T and GZ increase.
Range of stability increases.
Deck edge immerses earlier.
KB remains similar.

With increased Freeboard
GM_T and GZ increase.
Range of stability increases.
Deck edge immerses later at greater θ.
KB decreases.

Chapter 24
Angle of loll

When a ship with negative initial metacentric height is inclined to a small angle, the righting lever is negative, resulting in a capsizing moment. This effect is shown in Figure 24.1(a) and it can be seen that the ship will tend to heel still further.

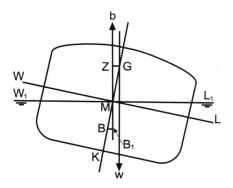

Fig. 24.1(a)

At a large angle of heel the centre of buoyancy will have moved further out the low side and the force of buoyancy can no longer be considered to act vertically upwards though M, the initial metacentre. If, by heeling still further, the centre of buoyancy can move out far enough to lie vertically under G the centre of gravity, as in Figure 24.1(b), the righting lever and thus the righting moment, will be zero.

The angle of heel at which this occurs is referred to as the *angle of loll* and may be defined as the angle to which a ship with negative initial metacentric height will lie at rest in still water.

If the ship should now be inclined to an angle greater than the angle of loll, as shown in Figure 24.1(c), the righting lever will be positive, giving a moment to return the ship to the angle of loll.

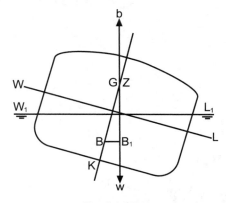

Fig. 24.1(b)

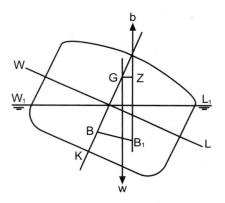

Fig. 24.1(c)

From this it can be seen that the ship will oscillate about the angle of loll instead of the upright.

The curve of statical stability for a ship in this condition of loading is illustrated in Figure 24.2. Note from the figure that the GZ at the angle of loll is zero. At angles of heel less than the angle of loll the righting levers are negative, whilst beyond the angle of loll the righting levers are positive up to the angle of vanishing stability.

Note how the range of stability in this case is measured from the angle of loll and not from the 'o–o' axis.

To calculate the angle of loll

When the vessel is 'wall-sided' between the upright and inclined waterlines, the GZ may be found using the formula:

$$GZ = \sin \theta (GM + \tfrac{1}{2} BM \tan^2 \theta)$$

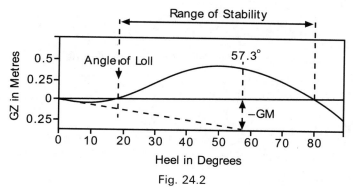

Fig. 24.2

At the angle of loll:

$$GZ = 0$$

$$\therefore \text{ either } \sin\theta = 0$$

or

$$(GM + \tfrac{1}{2} BM \tan^2\theta) = 0$$

If

$$\sin\theta = 0$$

then

$$\theta = 0$$

But then angle of loll cannot be zero, therefore:

$$(GM + \tfrac{1}{2} BM \tan^2\theta) = 0$$

$$\tfrac{1}{2} BM \tan^2\theta = -GM$$

$$BM \tan^2\theta = -2\,GM$$

$$\tan^2\theta = \frac{-2\,GM}{BM}$$

$$\tan\theta = \sqrt{\frac{-2\,GM}{BM}}$$

The angle of loll is caused by a negative GM, therefore:

$$\tan\theta = \sqrt{\frac{-2(-GM)}{BM}}$$

or

$$\tan\theta = \sqrt{\frac{2\,GM}{BM}}$$

where

$$\theta = \text{the angle of loll,}$$

$$GM = \text{a negative initial metacentric height, and}$$

$$BM = \text{the BM when upright.}$$

Example

Will a homogeneous log 6 m × 3 m × 3 m and relative density 0.4 float in fresh water with a side perpendicular to the waterline? If not, what will be the angle of loll?

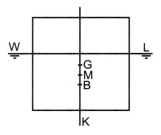

Fig. 24.3

Since the log is homogeneous the centre of gravity must be at half-depth, i.e. KG = 1.5 m.

$$\frac{\text{Draft of log}}{\text{Depth of log}} = \frac{\text{SG of log}}{\text{SG of water}}$$

$$\text{Draft of log} = \frac{3 \times 0.4}{1}$$

$$d = 1.2 \, \text{m}$$

$$KB = \frac{1}{2} \, \text{draft}$$

$$KB = 0.6 \, \text{m}$$

$$BM = B^2/12d$$

$$= \frac{3 \times 3}{12 \times 1.2}$$

$$BM = \quad 0.625 \, \text{m}$$

$$+$$

$$KB = \quad 0.600 \, \text{m}$$

$$KM = \quad 1.225 \, \text{m}$$

$$KG = \quad 1.500 \, \text{m}$$

$$GM = -0.275 \, \text{m}$$

Therefore the log is unstable and will take up an angle of loll.

$$\tan \theta = \sqrt{\frac{2\,GM}{BM}}$$

$$= \sqrt{\frac{0.55}{0.625}} = 0.9381$$

$$\theta = 43° \, 10'$$

Ans. The angle of loll = 43° 10'

Question: What exactly is angle of list and angle of loll? List the differences/characteristics.

Angle of list

'G', the centroid of the loaded weight, has *moved off the centre line* due to a shift of cargo or bilging effects, say to the port side.

GM *is positive*, i.e. 'G' is below 'M'. In fact GM will *increase* at the angle of list compared to GM when the ship is upright. The ship is in *stable equilibrium*.

In still water conditions the ship will remain at this *fixed* angle of heel. She will list to one side only, that is the same side as movement of weight.

In heavy weather conditions the ship will roll about this angle of list, say 3° P, but will not stop at 3° S. See comment below.

To bring the ship back to upright, load weight on the other side of the ship, for example if she lists 3° P add weight onto starboard side of ship.

Angle of loll

KG = KM so GM *is zero*. 'G' remains *on the centre line* of the ship.

The ship is in *neutral equilibrium*. She is in a *more dangerous situation* than a ship with an angle of list, because once 'G' goes above 'M' she will capsize.

Angle of loll may be *3° P or 3° S* depending upon external forces such as wind and waves acting on her structure. She may suddenly flop over from 3° P to 3° S and then back again to 3° P.

To improve this condition 'G' must be brought below 'M'. This can be done by moving weight downwards towards the keel, adding water ballast in double-bottom tanks or removing weight above the ship's 'G'. Beware of free surface effects when moving, loading, and discharging liquids.

With an angle of list or an angle of loll the calculations must be carefully made *prior* to any changes in loading being made.

Exercise 24

1   Will a homogeneous log of square cross-section and relative density 0.7 be stable when floating in fresh water with two opposite sides parallel to the waterline? If not, what will be the angle of loll?

2   A box-shaped vessel 30 m × 6 m × 4 m floats in salt water on an even keel at 2 m, draft F and A. KG = 3 m. Calculate the angle of loll.

3   A ship is upright and is loaded with a full cargo of timber with timber on deck. During the voyage the ship develops a list, even though stores, fresh water and bunkers have been consumed evenly from each side of the centre line. Discuss the probable cause of the list and the method which should be used to bring the ship to the upright.

4   A ship loaded with a full cargo of timber and timber on deck is alongside a quay and has taken up an angle of loll away from the quay. Describe the correct method of discharging the deck cargo and the precautions which must be taken during this process.

Chapter 25
True mean draft

In previous chapters it has been shown that a ship trims about the centre of flotation. It will now be shown that, for this reason, a ship's true mean draft is measured at the centre of flotation and may not be equal to the average of the drafts forward and aft. It only does when LCF is at average $\textcircled{\#}$.

Consider the ship shown in Figure 25.1(a) which is floating on an even keel and whose centre of flotation is FY aft of amidships. The true mean draft is KY, which is also equal to ZF, the draft at the centre of flotation.

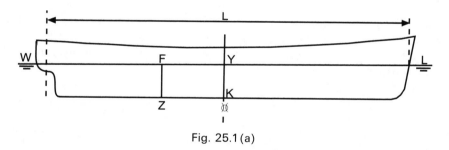

Fig. 25.1 (a)

Now let a weight be shifted aft within the ship so that she trims about F as shown in Figure 25.1(b).

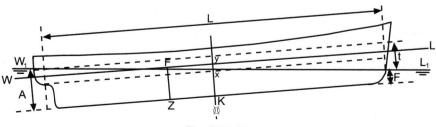

Fig. 25.1 (b)

The draft at the centre of flotation (ZF) remains unchanged.

Let the new draft forward be F and the new draft aft be A, so that the trim (A − F) is equal to 't'.

Since no weights have been loaded or discharged, the ship's displacement will not have changed and the true mean draft must still be equal to KY. It can be seen from Figure 25.1(b) that the average of the drafts forward and aft is equal to KX, the draft amidships.

Also

$$ZF = KY = KX + XY$$

or

$$\text{True mean draft} = \text{Draft amidships} + \text{correction}$$

Referring to Figure 25.1(b) and using the property of similar triangles:

$$\frac{XY}{FY} = \frac{t}{L} \qquad XY = \frac{t \times FY}{L}$$

or

$$Correction\ FY = \frac{Trim \times FY}{Length}$$

where FY is the distance of the centre of flotation from amidships.

It can also be seen from the figure that, when a ship is trimmed by the stern and the centre of flotation is aft of amidships, the correction is to be added to the mean of the drafts forward and aft. Also by substituting forward for aft and aft for forward in Figure 25.1(b), it can be seen that the correction is again to be added to the mean of the drafts forward and aft when the ship is trimmed by the head and the centre of flotation is forward of amidships.

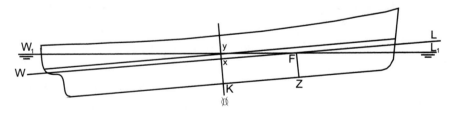

Fig. 25.1 (c)

Now consider the ship shown in Figure 25.1(c), which is trimmed by the stern and has the centre of flotation forward of amidships.

In this case

$$ZF = KY = KX - XY$$

or

$$\text{True mean draft} = \text{Draft amidships} - \text{correction}$$

The actual correction itself can again be found by using the above formula, but in this case the correction is to be subtracted from the mean of the drafts forward and aft. Similarly, by substituting forward for aft and aft for forward in this figure, it can be seen that the correction is again to be subtracted from the average of the drafts forward and aft when the ship is trimmed by the head and the centre of flotation is aft of amidships.

A general rule may now be derived for the application of the correction to the draft amidships in order to find the true mean draft.

Rule

When the centre of flotation is in the *same direction* from amidships as the maximum draft, the correction is to be *added* to the mean of the drafts. When the centre of flotation is in the *opposite direction* from amidships to the maximum draft, the correction is to be *subtracted*.

Example 1

A ship's minimum permissible freeboard is at a true mean draft of 8.5 m. The ship's length is 120 m, centre of flotation being 3 m aft of amidships. TPC = 50 tonnes. The present drafts are 7.36 m F and 9.00 m A. Find how much more cargo can be loaded.

$$\text{Draft forward} = 7.36\,\text{m}$$

$$\text{Draft aft} = 9.00\,\text{m}$$

$$\text{Trim} = 1.64\,\text{m by the stern}$$

$$\text{Correction} = \frac{t \times FY}{L} = \frac{1.64 \times 3}{120}$$

$$\text{Correction} = 0.04\,\text{m}$$

$$\text{Draft forward} = 7.36\,\text{m}$$

$$\text{Draft aft} = 9.00\,\text{m}$$

$$\text{Sum} = 16.36\,\text{m}$$

$$\text{Average} = \text{Draft amidships} = 8.18\,\text{m}$$

$$\text{Correction} = +0.04\,\text{m}$$

$$\text{True mean draft} = 8.22\,\text{m}$$

$$\text{Load mean draft} = 8.50\,\text{m}$$

$$\text{Increase in draft} = 0.28\,\text{m or 28 cm}$$

$$\text{Cargo to load} = \text{Increase in draft required} \times \text{TPC}$$

$$= 28 \times 50$$

Ans. Cargo to load = 1400 tonnes

Effect of hog and sag on draft amidships

When a ship is neither hogged nor sagged the draft amidships is equal to the mean of the drafts forward and aft. In Figure 25.1(d) the vessel is shown in hard outline floating without being hogged or sagged. The draft forward is F, the draft aft is A, and the draft amidships (KX) is equal to the average of the drafts forward and aft.

Now let the vessel be sagged as shown in Figure 25.1(d) by the broken outline. The draft amidships is now K_1X, which is equal to the mean of the drafts forward and aft (KX), plus the sag (KK_1). The amount of hog or sag must therefore be taken into account in calculations involving the draft amidships. The depth of the vessel amidships from the keel to the deck line (KY or K_1Y_1) is constant being equal to the draft amidships plus the freeboard.

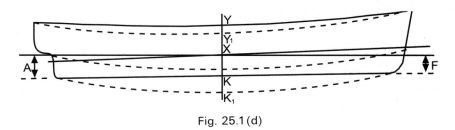

Fig. 25.1 (d)

Example

A ship is floating in water of relative density 1.015. The present displacement is 12 000 tonnes, KG 7.7 m, KM 8.6 m. The present drafts are F 8.25 m, A 8.65 m, and the present freeboard amidships is 1.06 m. The Summer draft is 8.53 m and the Summer freeboard is 1.02 m FWA 160 mm TPC 20. Assuming that the KM is constant, find the amount of cargo (Kg 10.0 m) which can be loaded for the ship to proceed to sea at the loaded Summer draft. Also find the amount of the hog or sag and the initial GM on departure.

Summer freeboard	1.02 m	Present mean freeboard	1.06 m
Summer draft	+ 8.53 m	Depth Mld	9.55 m
Depth Mld =	9.55 m	Present draft amidships	8.49 m
		Average of drafts F and A	8.45 m
		Ship is sagged by	0.04 m

$$\text{Dock water allowance (DWA)} = \frac{(1025 - \rho_{DW})}{25} \times \text{FWA} = \frac{10}{25} \times 160 = 64\,\text{mm}$$

$$= 0.064\,\text{m}$$

$$\text{TPC in dock water} = \frac{RD_{DW}}{RD_{SW}} \times TPC_{SW} = \frac{1.015}{1.025} \times 20$$

$$= 19.8\,\text{tonnes}$$

$$\text{Summer freeboard} = 1.020\,\text{m}$$

$$\text{DWA} = 0.064\,\text{m}$$

$$\text{Min. permissible freeboard} = \underline{0.956\,\text{m}}$$

$$\text{Present freeboard} = 1.060\,\text{m}$$

$$\text{Mean sinkage} = \underline{0.104\,\text{m} \text{ or } 10.4\,\text{cm}}$$

$$\text{Cargo to load} = \text{Sinkage} \times \text{TPC}_{\text{dw}} = 10.4 \times 19.8$$

$$\text{Cargo to load} = \underline{205.92\,\text{tonnes}}$$

$$GG_1 = \frac{w \times d}{W + w} = \frac{205.92 \times (10 - 7.7)}{12\,000 + 205.92} = \frac{473.62}{12\,205.92}$$

$$\therefore \text{ Rise of G} = 0.039\,\text{m}$$

$$\text{Present GM } (8.6 - 7.7) = 0.900\,\text{m}$$

$$\text{GM on departure} = \underline{0.861\,\text{m}}$$

and ship has a sag of 0.04 m.

Exercise 25

1   The minimum permissible freeboard for a ship is at a true mean draft of 7.3 m. The present draft is 6.2 m F and 8.2 m A. TPC = 10. The centre of flotation is 3 m aft of amidships. Length of the ship 90 m. Find how much more cargo may be loaded.

2   A ship has a load salt water displacement of 12 000 tonnes, load draft in salt water 8.5 m, length 120 m, TPC 15 tonnes, and centre of flotation 2 m aft of amidships. The ship is at present floating in dock water of density 1015 kg per cu. m at drafts of 7.2 m F and 9.2 m A. Find the cargo which must yet be loaded to bring the ship to the maximum permissible draft.

3   Find the weight of the cargo the ship in Question 2 could have loaded had the centre of flotation been 3 m forward of amidships instead of 2 m aft.

4   A ship is floating in dock water of relative density 1.020. The present displacement is 10 000 tonnes, KG 6.02 m, KM 6.92 m. Present drafts are F 12.65 m, A 13.25 m. Present freeboard 1.05 m. Summer draft 13.10 m and Summer freeboard is 1.01 m. FWA 150 mm. TPC 21. Assuming that the KM is constant find the amount of cargo (KG 10.0 m) which can be loaded for the ship to sail at the load Summer draft. Find also the amount of the hog or sag and the initial metacentric height on departure.

Chapter 26
The inclining experiment

It has been shown in previous chapters that, before the stability of a ship in any particular condition of loading can be determined, the initial conditions must be known. This means knowing the ship's lightweight, the VCG or KG at this lightweight, plus the LCG for this lightweight measured from amidships. For example, when dealing with the height of the centre of gravity above the keel, the initial position of the centre of gravity must be known before the final KG can be found. It is in order to find the KG for the light condition that the Inclining Experiment is performed.

The experiment is carried out by the builders when the ship is as near to completion as possible; that is, as near to the light condition as possible. The ship is forcibly inclined by shifting weights a fixed distance across the deck. The weights used are usually concrete blocks, and the inclination is measured by the movement of plumb lines across specially constructed battens which lie perfectly horizontal when the ship is upright. Usually two or three plumb lines are used and each is attached at the centre line of the ship at a height of about 10 m above the batten. If two lines are used then one is placed forward and the other aft. If a third line is used it is usually placed amidships. For simplicity, in the following explanation only one weight and one plumb line is considered.

The following conditions are necessary to ensure that the KG obtained is as accurate as possible:

1 There should be little or no wind, as this may influence the inclination of the ship. If there is any wind the ship should be head on or stern on to it.
2 The ship should be floating freely. This means that nothing outside the ship should prevent her from listing freely. There should be no barges or lighters alongside; mooring ropes should be slacked right down, and there should be plenty of water under the ship to ensure that at no time during the experiment will she touch the bottom.
3 Any loose weights within the ship should be removed or secured in place.

4 There must be no free surfaces within the ship. Bilges should be dry. Boilers and tanks should be completely full or empty.

5 Any persons not directly concerned with the experiment should be sent ashore.

6 The ship must be upright at the commencement of the experiment.

7 A note of 'weights on' and 'weights off' to complete the ship each with a VCG and LCG₥.

When all is ready and the ship is upright, a weight is shifted across the deck transversely, causing the ship to list. A little time is allowed for the ship to settle and then the deflection of the plumb line along the batten is noted. If the weight is now returned to its original position the ship will return to the upright. She may now be listed in the opposite direction. From the deflections the GM is obtained as follows.

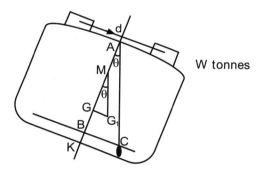

Fig. 26.1

In Figure 26.1 let a mass of 'w' tonnes be shifted across the deck through a distance 'd' metres. This will cause the centre of gravity of the ship to move from G to G_1 parallel to the shift of the centre of gravity of the weight. The ship will then list to bring G_1 vertically under M, i.e. to θ degrees list. The plumb line will thus be deflected along the batten from B to C. Since AC is the new vertical, angle BAC must also be θ degrees.

In triangle ABC,

$$\cot \theta = \frac{AB}{BC}$$

In triangle GG_1M,

$$\tan \theta = \frac{GG_1}{GM}$$

$$\therefore \frac{GM}{GG_1} = \frac{AB}{BC}$$

Or

$$GM = GG_1 \times \frac{AB}{BC}$$

But

$$GG_1 = \frac{w \times d}{W}$$

$$\therefore GM = \frac{w \times d}{W} \times \frac{AB}{BC}$$

Hence

$$GM = \frac{w \times d}{W \tan \theta}$$

In this formula AB, the length of the plumb line and BC, the deflection along the batten can be measured. 'w' the mass shifted, 'd' the distance through which it was shifted, and 'W' the ship's displacement, will all be known. The GM can therefore be calculated using the formula.

The naval architects will already have calculated the KM for this draft and hence the present KG is found. By taking moments about the keel, allowance can now be made for weights which must be loaded or discharged to bring the ship to the light condition. In this way the light KG is found.

Example 1

When a mass of 25 tonnes is shifted 15 m transversely across the deck of a ship of 8000 tonnes displacement, it causes a deflection of 20 cm in a plumb line 4 m long. If the KM = 7 m, calculate the KG.

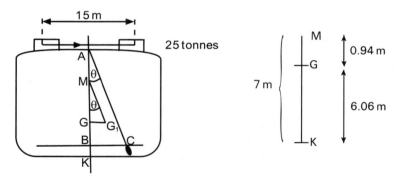

Fig. 26.2

$$\frac{GM}{GG_1} = \frac{AB}{BC} = \frac{1}{\tan \theta}$$

$$\therefore \tan \theta \, GM = GG_1$$

$$GM = \frac{w \times d}{W} \times \frac{1}{\tan \theta}$$

$$= \frac{25 \times 15}{8000} \times \frac{4}{0.2}$$

$$GM = 0.94\,m$$

$$KM = 7.00\,m$$

Ans. KG = 6.06 m as shown in sketch on page 240.

Example 2

When a mass of 10 tonnes is shifted 12 m, transversely across the deck of a ship with a GM of 0.6 m it causes 0.25 m deflection in a 10 m plumb line. Calculate the ship's displacement.

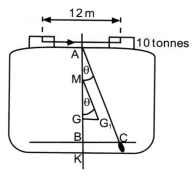

Fig. 26.3

$$GM = \frac{w \times d}{W} \times \frac{1}{\tan\theta}$$

$$W = \frac{w \times d}{GM} \times \frac{1}{\tan\theta}$$

$$= \frac{10 \times 12 \times 10}{0.6 \times 0.25}$$

$$W = 8000.$$

Ans. Displacement = 8000 tonnes

Summary

Every new ship should have an Inclining Experiment. However, some shipowners do not request one if their ship is a sister-ship to one or more in the company's fleet.

If a ship has undergone major repair or refit, she should then have an Inclining Experiment to obtain her modified Lightweight and centre of gravity (VCG and LCG).

Exercise 26

1   A ship of 8000 tonnes displacement has KM = 7.3 m and KG = 6.1 m. A mass of 25 tonnes is moved transversely across the deck through a distance of 15 m. Find the deflection of a plumb line which is 4 m long.

2   As a result of performing the inclining experiment it was found that a ship had an initial metacentric height of 1 m. A mass of 10 tonnes, when shifted 12 m transversely, had listed the ship $3\frac{1}{2}$ degrees and produced a deflection of 0.25 m in the plumb line. Find the ship's displacement and the length of the plumb line.

3   A ship has KM = 6.1 m and displacement of 3150 tonnes. When a mass of 15 tonnes, already on board, is moved horizontally across the deck through a distance of 10 m it causes 0.25 m deflection in an 8 m long plumb line. Calculate the ship's KG.

4   A ship has an initial GM = 0.5 m. When a mass of 25 tonnes is shifted transversely a distance of 10 m across the deck, it causes a deflection of 0.4 m in a 4 m plumb line. Find the ship's displacement.

5   A ship of 2304 tonnes displacement has an initial metacentric height of 1.2 m. Find the deflection in a plumb line which is suspended from a point 7.2 m above a batten when a mass of 15 tonnes, already on board, is shifted 10 m transversely across the deck.

6   During the course of an inclining experiment in a ship of 4000 tonnes displacement, it was found that, when a mass of 12 tonnes was moved transversely across the deck, it caused a deflection of 75 mm in a plumb line which was suspended from a point 7.5 m above the batten. KM = 10.2 m. KG = 7 m. Find the distance through which the mass was moved.

7   A box-shaped vessel 60 m × 10 m × 3 m is floating upright in fresh water on an even keel at 2 m draft. When a mass of 15 tonnes is moved 6 m transversely across the deck a 6 m plumb line is deflected 20 cm. Find the ship's KG.

8   The transverse section of a barge is in the form of a triangle, apex downwards. The ship's length is 65 m, breadth at the waterline 8 m, and the vessel is floating upright in salt water on an even keel at 4 m draft. When a mass of 13 tonnes is shifted 6 m transversely it causes 20 cm deflection in a 3 m plumb line. Find the vessel's KG,

9   A ship of 8000 tonnes displacement is inclined by moving 4 tonnes transversely through a distance of 19 m. The average deflections of two pendulums, each 6 m long, was 12 cm 'Weights on' to complete this ship were 75 t centred at Kg of 7.65 m 'Weights off' amounted to 25 t centred at Kg of 8.16 m.

   (a) Calculate the GM and angle of heel relating to this information, for the ship as inclined.

   (b) From Hydrostatic Curves for this ship as inclined, the KM was 9 m. Calculate the ship's final Lightweight and VCG at this weight.

Chapter 27
Effect of trim on tank soundings

A tank sounding pipe is usually situated at the after end of the tank and will therefore only indicate the depth of the liquid at that end of the tank. If a ship is trimmed by the stern, the sounding obtained will indicate a greater depth of liquid than is actually contained in the tank. For this reason it is desirable to find the head of liquid required in the sounding pipe which will indicate that the tank is full.

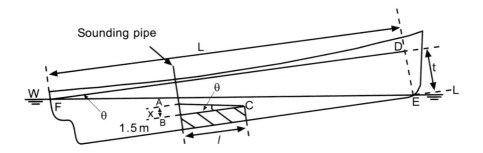

Fig. 27.1

In Figure 27.1, 't' represents the trim of the ship, 'L' the length of the ship, 'l' the length of a double bottom tank, and 'x' the head of liquid when the tank is full.

In triangles ABC and DEF, using the property of similar triangles:

$$\frac{x}{l} = \frac{t}{L}$$

or

$$\frac{Head\ when\ full}{Length\ of\ tank} = \frac{Trim}{Length\ of\ ship}$$

Example 1

A ship 100 m long is trimmed 1.5 m by the stern. A double bottom tank 12 m × 10 m × 1.5 m has the sounding pipe at the after end. Find the sounding which will indicate that the tank is full.

$$\frac{\text{Head}}{l} = \frac{\text{Trim}}{L}$$

$$\therefore \text{ Head when full} = \frac{1.5 \times 12}{100}$$

$$\text{X or AB} = 0.18 \, \text{m}$$

$$\text{Depth of tank} = 1.50 \, \text{m}$$

Ans. Sounding when full = 1.68 m

Example 2

A ship 100 m long is trimmed 2 m by the stern. A double bottom tank 15 m × 20 m × 1.5 m, which has the sounding pipe situated at the after end, is being filled with fuel oil of relative density 0.8. The present tank sounding is 1.6 m. Find the sounding when the tank is full, and also how much more oil is required to fill the tank.

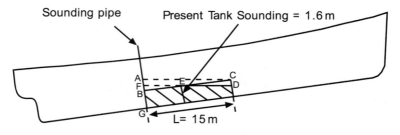

Fig. 27.2

In Figure 27.2 the right-angled triangles ABC, CDE, and BEF are similar. BG = 1.5 m. FG = the present sounding (1.6 m).

$$\frac{\text{Head}}{l} = \frac{\text{Trim}}{L}$$

$$\text{Head} = \frac{2 \times 15}{100}$$

$$\text{Head of oil full} = 0.30 \, \text{m}$$

$$\therefore \text{ The sounding when full} = 1.80 \, \text{m (AG)}$$

Also:

$$\text{CD} = \text{Head of oil full} - \text{present tank sounding}$$

$$= 1.80 \, \text{m} - 1.60 \, \text{m}$$

$$\text{CD} = 0.20 \, \text{m}$$

In triangles CED and ABC:

$$\frac{CE}{CD} = \frac{BC}{AB}$$

$$CE = \frac{CD \times BC}{AB}$$

$$= \frac{0.20}{0.30} \times 15$$

$$CE = 10 \text{ metres}$$

Volume of oil yet required = Area triangle CED × Breadth of tank

$$= \tfrac{1}{2} \times CE \times CD \times 20$$

$$= \tfrac{1}{2} \times 10 \times 0.20 \times 20$$

$$= 20 \text{ cu. m}$$

Mass of oil required = Volume × density

$$= 20 \times 0.8$$

$$= 16 \text{ tonnes}$$

Ans. Sounding when full 1.8 m. Oil yet required 16 tonnes

Exercise 27

1   A ship 120 m long is trimmed 1.5 m by the stern. A double bottom tank is 15 m × 20 m × 1 m and has the sounding pipe situated at the after end of the tank. Find the sounding which will indicate that the tank is full.

2   A ship 120 m long is trimmed 2 m by the stern. A double bottom tank 36 m × 15 m × 1 m is being filled with fuel oil of relative density 0.96. The sounding pipe is at the after end of the tank and the present sounding is 1.2 m. Find how many tonnes of oil are yet required to fill this tank and also find the sounding when the tank is full.

Chapter 28
Drydocking and grounding

When a ship enters a drydock she must have a positive initial GM, be upright, and trimmed slightly, usually by the stern. On entering the drydock the ship is lined up with her centre line vertically over the centre line of the keel blocks and the shores are placed loosely in position. The dock gates are then closed and pumping out commences. The rate of pumping is reduced as the ship's stern post nears the blocks. When the stern lands on the blocks the shores are hardened up commencing from aft and gradually working forward so that all of the shores will be hardened up in position by the time the ship takes the blocks overall. The rate of pumping is then increased to quickly empty the dock.

As the water level falls in the drydock there is no effect on the ship's stability so long as the ship is completely waterborne, but after the stern lands on the blocks the draft aft will decrease and the trim will change by the head. This will continue until the ship takes the blocks overall throughout her length, when the draft will then decrease uniformly forward and aft.

The interval of time between the stern post landing on the blocks and the ship taking the blocks overall is referred to as the *critical period*. During this period part of the weight of the ship is being borne by the blocks, and this creates an upthrust at the stern which increases as the water level falls in the drydock. The upthrust causes a virtual loss in metacentric height and it is essential that positive effective metacentric height be maintained throughout the critical period, or the ship will heel over and perhaps slip off the blocks with disastrous results.

The purpose of this chapter is to show the methods by which the effective metacentric height may be calculated for any instant during the drydocking process.

Figure 28.1 shows the longitudinal section of a ship during the critical period. 'P' is the upthrust at the stern and '*l*' is the distance of the centre of flotation from aft. The trimming moment is given by P × *l*. But the trimming moment is also equal to MCTC × Change of trim.

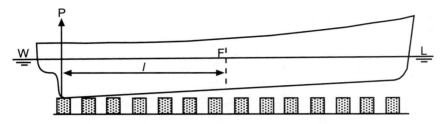

Fig. 28.1

Therefore,

$$P \times l = \text{MCTC} \times t$$

or,

$$P = \frac{\text{MCTC} \times t}{l}$$

where

P = the upthrust at the stern in tonnes,

t = the change of trim since entering the drydock in centimetres, and

l = the distance of the centre of flotation from aft in metres.

Now consider Figure 28.2 which shows a transverse section of the ship during the critical period after she has been inclined to a small angle (θ degrees) by a force external to the ship. For the sake of clarity the angle of heel has been magnified. The weight of the ship (W) acts downwards through the centre of gravity (G). The force P acts upwards through the keel (K) and is equal to the weight being borne by the blocks. For equilibrium the force of buoyancy must now be (W − P) and will act upwards through the initial metacentre (M).

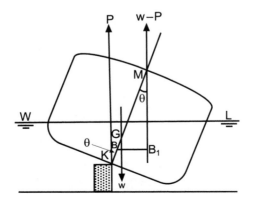

Fig. 28.2

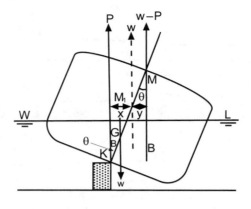

Fig. 28.3

There are, thus, three parallel forces to consider when calculating the effect of the force P on the ship's stability. Two of these forces may be replaced by their resultant (see page 4) in order to find the effective metacentric height and the moment of statical stability.

Method (a)

In Figure 28.3 consider the two parallel forces P and $(W - P)$. Their resultant W will act upwards through M_1 such that:

$$(W - P) \times y = P \times X$$

or

$$(W - P) \times MM_1 \times \sin \theta = P \times KM_1 \times \sin \theta$$

$$(W - P) \times MM_1 = P \times KM_1$$

$$W \times MM_1 - P \times MM_1 = P \times KM_1$$

$$W \times MM_1 = P \times KM_1 + P \times MM_1$$

$$= P\left(KM_1 + MM_1\right)$$

$$= P \times KM$$

$$MM_1 = \frac{P \times KM}{W}$$

There are now two forces to consider: W acting upwards through M_1 and W acting downwards through G. These produce a righting moment of $W \times GM_1 \times \sin \theta$.

Note also that the original metacentric height was GM but has now been reduced to GM_1. Therefore MM_1 is the virtual loss of metacentric height due to drydocking.

Or

$$Virtual\ loss\ of\ GM\ (MM_1) = \frac{P \times KM}{W}$$

Method (b)
Now consider the two parallel forces W and P in Figure 28.4. Their resultant (W − P) acts downwards through G_1 such that:

$$W \times y = P \times X$$

or

$$W \times GG_1 \times \sin\theta = P \times KG_1 \times \sin\theta$$

$$W \times GG_1 = P \times KG_1$$

$$= P\,(KG + GG_1)$$

$$= P \times KG + P \times GG_1$$

$$W \times GG_1 - P \times GG_1 = P \times KG$$

$$GG_1\,(W - P) = P \times KG$$

$$GG_1 = \frac{P \times KG}{W - P}$$

There are now two forces to consider: (W − P) acting upwards through M, and (W − P) acting downwards through G_1. These produce a righting moment of (W − P) $\times G_1M \times \sin\theta$.

The original metacentric height was GM but has now been reduced to G_1M. Therefore GG_1 is the virtual loss of metacentric height due to drydocking.

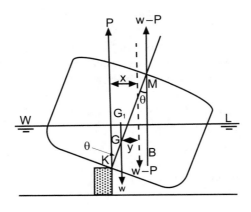

Fig. 28.4

Or

$$Virtual\ loss\ of\ GM\ (GG_1) = \frac{P \times KG}{W - P}$$

Example 1

A ship of 6000 tonnes displacement enters a drydock trimmed 0.3 m by the stern. KM = 7.5 m, KG = 6 m. MCTC = 90 tonnes m. The centre of flotation is 45 m from aft. Find the effective metacentric height at the critical instant before the ship takes the blocks overall.

Note. Assume that the trim at the critical instant is zero.

$$P = \frac{MCTC \times t}{l}$$

$$= \frac{90 \times 30}{45}$$

$$P = 60\ tonnes$$

Method (a)

$$Virtual\ loss\ of\ GM\ (MM_1) = \frac{P \times KM}{W}$$

$$= \frac{60 \times 7.5}{6000}$$

$$= 0.075\ m$$

$$Original\ GM = 7.5 - 6.0 = 1.500\ m$$

Ans. New GM = 1.425 m

Method (b)

$$Virtual\ loss\ of\ GM = \frac{P \times KG}{W - P}$$

$$GG_1 = \frac{60 \times 6}{5940}$$

$$= 0.061\ m$$

$$Original\ GM = 1.500\ m$$

Ans. New GM = 1.439 m

From these results it would appear that there are two possible answers to the same problem, but this is not the case. The ship's ability to return to the upright is indicated by the righting moment and not by the effective metacentric height alone.

To illustrate this point, calculate the righting moments given by each method when the ship is heeled to a small angle ($\theta°$)

Method (a)

$$Righting\ moment = W \times GM_1 \times \sin\theta$$

$$= 6000 \times 1.425 \times \sin\theta°$$

$$= (8550 \times \sin\theta°)\ tonnes\ m.$$

Method (b)

$$\text{Righting moment} = (W - P) \times G_1M \times \sin\theta$$

$$= 5940 \times 1.439 \times \sin\theta°$$

$$= (8549 \times \sin\theta) \text{ tonnes metres.}$$

Thus each of the two methods used gives a correct indication of the ship's stability during the critical period.

Example 2

A ship of 3000 tonnes displacement is 100 m long, has KM = 6 m, KG = 5.5 m. The centre of flotation is 2 m aft of amidships. MCTC = 40 tonnes m. Find the maximum trim for the ship to enter a drydock if the metacentric height at the critical instant before the ship takes the blocks forward and aft is to be not less than 0.3 m.

$$KM = 6.0\,\text{m}$$

$$KG = 5.5\,\text{m}$$

$$\overline{\text{Original GM} = 0.5\,\text{m}}$$

$$\text{Virtual GM} = 0.3\,\text{m}$$

$$\overline{\text{Virtual loss} = 0.2\,\text{m}}$$

Method (a)

$$\text{Virtual loss of GM (MM}_1) = \frac{P \times KM}{W}$$

or

$$P = \frac{\text{Virtual loss} \times W}{KM}$$

$$= \frac{0.2 \times 3000}{6}$$

$$\underline{\text{Maximum P} = 100 \text{ tonnes}}$$

But

$$P = \frac{MCTC \times t}{l}$$

or

$$\text{Maximum } t = \frac{P \times l}{MCTC}$$

$$= \frac{100 \times 48}{40}$$

Ans. $\underline{\text{Maximum trim} = 120\,\text{cm by the stern}}$

Method (b)

$$\text{Virtual loss of GM} \, (GG_1) = \frac{P \times KG}{W - P}$$

$$0.2 = \frac{P \times 5.5}{3000 - P}$$

$$600 - 0.2\,P = 5.5\,P$$

$$5.7\,P = 600$$

$$\text{Maximum P} = \frac{600}{5.7} = 105.26 \text{ tonnes}$$

But

$$P = \frac{MCTC \times t}{l}$$

or

$$\text{Maximum } t = \frac{P \times l}{MCTC}$$

$$= \frac{105.26 \times 48}{40}$$

Ans. Maximum trim = 126.3 cm by the stern

There are therefore two possible answers to this question, depending upon the method of solution used. The reason for this is that although the effective metacentric height at the critical instant in each case will be the same, the righting moments at equal angles of heel will not be the same.

Example 3

A ship of 5000 tonnes displacement enters a drydock trimmed 0.45 m by the stern. KM = 7.5 m, KG = 6.0 m. MCTC = 120 tonnes m. The centre of flotation is 60 m from aft. Find the effective metacentric height at the critical instant before the ship takes the blocks overall, assuming that the transverse metacentre rises 0.075 m.

$$P = \frac{MCTC \times t}{l}$$

$$= \frac{120 \times 45}{60}$$

$$P = 90 \text{ tonnes}$$

Method (a)

$$\text{Virtual loss } (MM_1) = \frac{P \times KM}{W}$$

$$= \frac{90 \times 7.575}{5000}$$

$$= 0.136 \text{ m}$$

$$\text{Original KM} = 7.500\,\text{m}$$

$$\text{Rise of M} = 0.075\,\text{m}$$

$$\text{New KM} = 7.575\,\text{m}$$

$$\text{KG} = 6.000\,\text{m}$$

$$\text{GM} = 1.575\,\text{m}$$

$$\text{Virtual loss } (\text{MM}_1) = 0.136\,\text{m}$$

Ans. New GM = 1.439 m

Method (b)

$$\text{Virtual loss } (\text{GG}_1) = \frac{P \times KG}{W - P}$$

$$= \frac{90 \times 6.0}{4910}$$

$$= 0.110\,\text{m}$$

$$\text{Old KG} = 6.000\,\text{m}$$

$$\text{Virtual loss } (\text{GG}_1) = 0.110\,\text{m}$$

$$\text{New KG} = 6.110\,\text{m}$$

$$\text{New KM} = 7.575\,\text{m}$$

Ans. New GM = 1.465 m

The virtual loss of GM after taking the blocks overall

When a ship takes the blocks overall, the water level will then fall uniformly about the ship, and for each centimetre fallen by the water level P will be increased by a number of tonnes equal to the TPC. Also, the force P at any time during the operation will be equal to the difference between the weight of the ship and the weight of water she is displacing at that time.

Example 4

A ship of 5000 tonnes displacement enters a drydock on an even keel. $KM = 6\,\text{m}$. $KG = 5.5\,\text{m}$, and $TPC = 50$ tonnes. Find the virtual loss of metacentric height after the ship has taken the blocks and the water has fallen another 0.24 m.

$$P = \text{TPC} \times \text{reduction in draft in cm}$$

$$= 50 \times 24$$

$$P = 1200 \text{ tonnes}$$

Method (a)

$$\text{Virtual loss}(MM_1) = \frac{P \times KM}{W}$$

$$= \frac{1200 \times 6}{5000}$$

Ans. Virtual loss $= 1.44\,\text{m}$

Method (b)

$$\text{Virtual loss }(GG_1) = \frac{P \times KG}{W - P}$$

$$= \frac{1200 \times 5.5}{3800}$$

Ans. Virtual loss $= 1.74\,\text{m}$

Note to Students

In the D.Tp. examinations, when sufficient information is given in a question, either method of solution may be used. It has been shown in this chapter that both are equally correct. In some questions, however, there is no choice, as the information given is sufficient for only one of the methods to be used. It is therefore advisable for students to learn both of the methods.

Example 5

A ship of 8000 tonnes displacement takes the ground on a sand bank on a falling tide at an even keel draft of 5.2 metres. KG 4.0 metres. The predicted depth of water over the sand bank at the following low water is 3.2 metres. Calculate the GM at this time assuming that the KM will then be 5.0 metres and that the mean TPC is 15 tonnes.

$$P = TPC \times \text{Fall in water level (cm)} = 15 \times (520 - 320)$$

$$= 15 \times 200$$

$$P = 3000 \text{ tonnes}$$

Method (a)

$$\text{Virtual loss of GM }(MM_1) = \frac{P \times KM}{W}$$

$$= \frac{3000 \times 5}{8000}$$

$$= 1.88\,\text{m}$$

$$\text{Actual KM} = 5.00\,\text{m}$$

$$\text{Virtual KM} = 3.12\,\text{m}$$

$$\text{KG} = 4.00\,\text{m}$$

Ans. New GM $= -0.88\,\text{m}$

Method (b)

$$\text{Virtual loss of GM}\,(GG_1) = \frac{P \times KG}{W - P}$$

$$= \frac{3000 \times 4}{5000}$$

$$= 2.40\,\text{m}$$

$$KG = 4.00\,\text{m}$$

$$\text{Virtual KG} = 6.40\,\text{m}$$

$$KM = 5.00\,\text{m}$$

Ans. New GM $= -1.40\,\text{m}$

Note that in Example 5, this vessel has developed a negative GM. Consequently she is *unstable*. She would capsize if transverse external forces such as wind or waves were to remove her from zero angle of heel. Suggest a change of loading to reduce KG and make GM a positive value greater that D.Tp. minimum of 0.15 m.

EXERCISE 28

1 A ship being drydocked has a displacement of 1500 tonnes. TPC $= 5$ tonnes, KM $= 3.5$ m, GM $= 0.5$ m, and has taken the blocks fore and aft at 3 m draft. Find the GM when the water level has fallen another 0.6 m.

2 A ship of 4200 tonnes displacement has GM 0.75 m and present drafts 2.7 m F and 3.7 m A. She is to enter a drydock. MCTC $= 120$ tonnes m. The after keel block is 60 m aft of the centre of flotation. At 3.2 m mean draft KM $= 8$ m. Find the GM on taking the blocks forward and aft.

3 A box-shaped vessel 150 m long, 10 m beam, and 5 m deep, has a mean draft in salt water of 3 m and is trimmed 1 m by the stern, KG $= 3.5$ m. State whether it is safe to drydock this vessel in this condition or not, and give reasons for your answer.

4 A ship of 6000 tonnes displacement is 120 m long and is trimmed 1 m by the stern. KG $= 5.3$ m, GM $= 0.7$ m. MCTC $= 90$ tonnes m. Is it safe to drydock the ship in this condition? (Assume that the centre of flotation is amidships.)

5 A ship of 4000 tonnes displacement, 126 m long, has KM $= 6.7$ m. KG $= 6.1$ m. The centre of flotation is 3 m aft of amidships. MCTC $= 120$ tonnes m. Find the maximum trim at which the ship may enter a drydock if the minimum GM at the critical instant is to be 0.3 m.

Chapter 29
Second moments of areas

The second moment of an element of an area about an axis is equal to the product of the area and the square of its distance from the axis. Let dA in Figure 29.1 represent an element of an area and let y be its distance from the axis AB.

The second moment of the element about AB is equal to $dA \times y^2$.

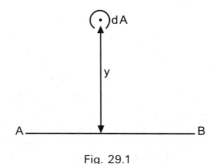

Fig. 29.1

To find the second moment of a rectangle about an axis parallel to one of its sides and passing through the centroid.

In Figure 29.2, l represents the length of the rectangle and b represents the breadth. Let G be the centroid and let AB, an axis parallel to one of the sides, pass through the centroid.

Consider the elementary strip which is shown shaded in the figure. The second moment (i) of the strip about the axis AB is given by the equation:

$$i = l \cdot dx \times x^2$$

Let I_{AB} be the second moment of the whole rectangle about the axis AB then:

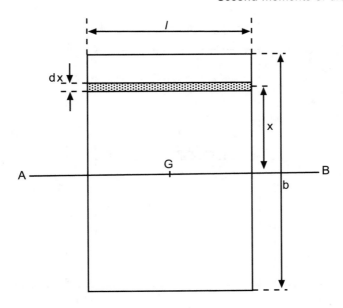

Fig. 29.2

$$I_{AB} = \int_{-b/2}^{+b/2} lx^2\, dx$$

$$I_{AB} = l \int_{-b/2}^{+b/2} x^2\, dx$$

$$= l \left[\frac{x^3}{3} \right]_{-b/2}^{+b/2}$$

$$I_{AB} = \frac{lb^3}{12}$$

To find the second moment of a rectangle about one of its sides.

Consider the second moment (i) of the elementary strip shown in Figure 29.3 about the axis AB.

$$i = l \cdot dx \times x^2$$

Let I_{AB} be the second moment of the rectangle about the axis AB, then:

$$I_{AB} = \int_{O}^{b} lx^2\, dx$$

$$= l \left[\frac{x^3}{3} \right]_{O}^{b}$$

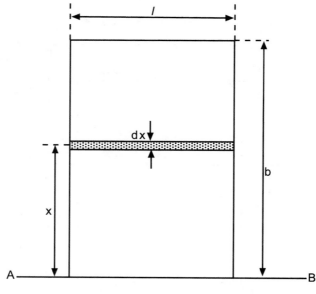

Fig. 29.3

or

$$I_{AB} = \frac{lb^3}{3}$$

The Theorem of Parallel Axes

The second moment of an area about an axis through the centroid is equal to the second moment about any other axis parallel to the first reduced by the product of the area and the square of the perpendicular distance between the two axes. Thus, in Figure 29.4, if G represents the centroid of the area (A) and the axis OZ is parallel to AB, then:

$$I_{OZ} = I_{AB} - Ay^2 = \text{parallel axis theorem equation}$$

To find the second moment of a ship's waterplane area about the centre line.

In Figure 29.5:

$$\text{Area of elementary strip} = y \cdot dx$$

$$\text{Area of waterplane} = \int_{O}^{L} y \cdot dx$$

It has been shown in chapter 10 that the area under the curve can be found by Simpson's Rules, using the values of y, the half-breadths, as ordinates.

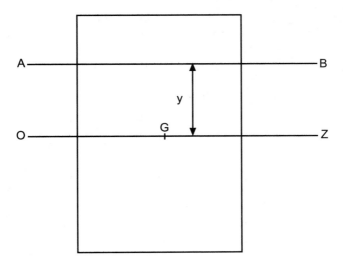

Fig. 29.4

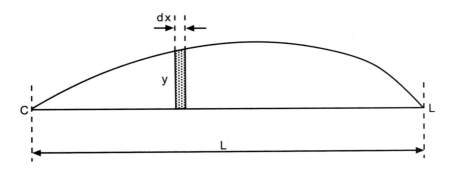

Fig. 29.5

The second moment of a rectangle about one end is given by $\dfrac{lb^3}{3}$, and therefore the second moment of the elementary strip about the centre line is given by $\dfrac{y^3 \, dx}{3}$ and the second moment of the half waterplane about the centre line is given by

$$\int_O^L \frac{y^3}{3} \, dx$$

Therefore, if I_{CL} is the second moment of the whole waterplane area about the centre line, then:

$$I_{CL} = \frac{2}{3} \int_O^L y^3 \, dx$$

The integral part of this expression can be evaluated by Simpson's Rules using the values of y^3 (i.e. the half-breadths cubed), as ordinates, and I_{CL} is found by multiplying the result by $\frac{2}{3}$.

Example 1

A ship's waterplane is 18 metres long. The half-ordinates at equal distances from forward are as follows:

$$0,\ 1.2,\ 1.5,\ 1.8,\ 1.8,\ 1.5,\ \text{and}\ 1.2\ \text{metres},$$

respectively. Find the second moment of the waterplane area about the centre line.

$\frac{1}{2}$ ord.	$\frac{1}{2}$ ord.^{3}	S.M.	Products for I_{CL}
0	0	1	0
1.2	1.728	4	6.912
1.5	3.375	2	6.750
1.8	5.832	4	23.328
1.8	5.832	2	11.664
1.5	3.375	4	13.500
1.2	1.728	1	1.728
			$63.882 = \Sigma_1$

$$I_{CL} = \frac{2}{9} \times CI \times \Sigma_1$$

$$I_{CL} = \frac{2}{9} \times \frac{18}{6} \times 63.882$$

$$= \underline{42.588\,m^4}$$

To find the second moment of the waterplane area about a transverse axis through the centre of flotation.

$$\text{Area of elementary strip} = y\,dx$$

$$I_{AB}\ \text{of the elementary strip} = x^2\,y\,dx$$

$$I_{AB}\ \text{of the waterplane area} = 2\int_{O}^{L} x^2\,y\,dx$$

Once again the integral part of this expression can be evaluated by Simpson's Rules using the values of $x^2\,y$ as ordinates and the second moment about AB is found by multiplying the result by two.

Let OZ be a transverse axis through the centre of flotation. The second moment about OZ can then be found by the theorem of parallel axes. i.e.

$$I_{OZ} = I_{AB} - A\bar{X}^2$$

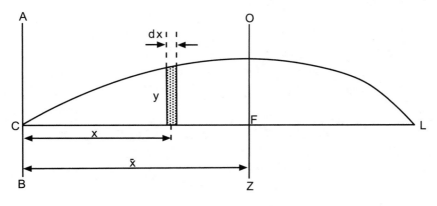

Fig. 29.6

Example 2

A ship's waterplane is 18 metres long. The half-ordinates at equal distances from forward are as follows:

0, 1.2, 1.5, 1.8, 1.8, 1.5, 1.2 metres, respectively.

Find the second moment of the waterplane area about a transverse axis through the centre of flotation.

$\frac{1}{2}$ ord.	SM	Area func	Lever	Moment func	Lever	Inertia func.
0	1	0	0	0	0	0
1.2	4	4.8	1	4.8	1	4.8
1.5	2	3.0	2	6.0	2	12.0
1.8	4	7.2	3	21.6	3	64.8
1.8	2	3.6	4	14.4	4	57.6
1.5	4	6.0	5	30.0	5	150.0
1.2	1	1.2	6	7.2	6	43.2
		$25.8 = \Sigma_1$		$84.0 = \Sigma_2$		$332.4 = \Sigma_3$

$$\text{Area of waterplane} = \frac{1}{3} \times \text{CI} \times \Sigma_1 \times 2$$

$$\text{Area of waterplane} = \frac{1}{3} \times \frac{18}{6} \times 25.8 \times 2$$

$$= 51.6 \, \text{sq. m}$$

$$\text{Distance of the Centre of Flotation from forward} = \frac{\Sigma_2}{\Sigma_1} \times \text{CI}$$

$$= \frac{84}{25.8} \times \frac{18}{6}$$

$$= 9.77 \, \text{m}$$

$$= 0.77 \, \text{m aft of amidships}$$

$$I_{AB} = \frac{1}{3} \times (CI)^3 \times \Sigma_3 \times 2$$

$$= \frac{1}{3} \times \left(\frac{18}{6}\right)^3 \times 332.4 \times 2 = 5983 \, \text{m}^4$$

$$I_{OZ} = I_{AB} - A\bar{X}^2$$

$$= 5983 - 51.6 \times 9.77^2$$

$$= 5983 - 4925$$

Ans. $\underline{I_{OZ} = 1058 \, \text{metres}^4}$

There is a quicker and more efficient method of obtaining the solution to the above problem. Instead of using the foremost ordinate at the datum, use the midship ordinate. Proceed as follows:

$\frac{1}{2}$ord.	SM	Area func.	Lever⊗	Moment func.	Lever⊗	Inertia func.
0	1	0	−3	0	−3	0
1.2	4	4.8	−2	−9.6	−2	+19.2
1.5	2	3.0	−1	−3.0	−1	+3.0
1.8	4	7.2	0	0	0	0
1.8	2	3.6	+1	+3.6	+1	+3.6
1.5	4	6.0	+2	+12.0	+2	+24.0
1.2	1	1.2	+3	+3.6	+3	+10.8
		$25.8 = \Sigma_1$		$+6.6 = \Sigma_2$		$60.6 = \Sigma_3$

$$\text{Area of waterplane} = \frac{1}{3} \times \Sigma_1 \times h \times 2 \qquad h = \frac{18}{6} = 3 \, \text{m}$$

$$= \frac{1}{3} \times 25.8 \times 3 \times 2$$

$$= 51.6 \, \text{m}^2 \text{ (as before)}$$

$$\Sigma_2 = +6.6$$

The +ve sign shows Centre of Flotation is in aft body

$$\text{Centre of Flotation from } ⊗ = \frac{\Sigma_2}{\Sigma_1} \times h$$

$$= + \frac{6.6}{25.8} \times 3$$

$\therefore$ Centre of Flotation $= +0.77$ m or 0.77 m aft amidships (as before)

$$I_{\cancel{\oplus}} = \tfrac{1}{3} \times \Sigma_3 \times h^3 \times 2 = \tfrac{1}{3} \times 60.6 \times 3^3 \times 2$$

$$\therefore I_{\cancel{\oplus}} = 1090.8 \, \text{m}^4$$

But

$$I_{\text{LCF}} = I_{\cancel{\oplus}} - A\bar{y} = 1090.8 - \left(51.6 \times 0.77^2\right)$$

$$= 1090.8 - 30.6$$

$$= \underline{1060 \, \text{m}^4}$$

i.e. very close to previous answer.

With this improved method the levers are much less in value. Consequently the error is decreased when predicting $LCF_{\cancel{\oplus}}$ and I_{LCF}.

Summary

When using Simpson Rules for second moments of area the procedure should be as follows:

1 Make a sketch from the given information.
2 Use a moment Table and insert values.
3 Using summations obtained in the Table proceed to calculate area, LCF, $I_{\cancel{\oplus}}$, I_{LCF}, $I_{\text{\textcent}}$, etc.
4 Remember: sketch, table, calculation

Exercise 29

1   A large square has a smaller square cut out of its centre such that the second moment of the smaller square about an axis parallel to one side and passing through the centroid is the same as that of the portion remaining about the same axis. Find what proportion of the area of the original square is cut out.

2   Find the second moment of a square of side 2a about its diagonals.

3   Compare the second moment of a rectangle 40 cm × 30 cm about an axis through the centroid and parallel to the 40 cm side with the second moment about an axis passing through the centroid and parallel to the 30 cm side.

4   An H-girder is built from 5 cm thick steel plate. The central web is 25 cm high and the overall width of each of the horizontal flanges is 25 cm. Find the second moment of the end section about an axis through the centroid and parallel to the horizontal flanges.

5   A ship's waterplane is 36 m long. The half-ordinates, at equidistant intervals, commencing from forward, are as follows:

0, 4, 5, 6, 6, 5 and 4 m respectively.

Calculate the second moment of the waterplane area about the centre line and also about a transverse axis through the centre of flotation.

6   A ship's waterplane is 120 metres long. The half-ordinates at equidistant intervals from forward are as follows:

0, 3.7, 7.6, 7.6, 7.5, 4.6 and 0.1 m respectively.

Calculate the second moment of the waterplane area about the centre line and about a transverse axis through the centre of flotation.

7   A ship of 12 000 tonnes displacement is 150 metres long at the waterline. The half-ordinates of the waterplane at equidistant intervals from forward are as follows:

0, 4, 8.5. 11.6, 12.2, 12.5, 12.5, 11.6, 5.2, 2.4 and 0.3 m respectively.

Calculate the longitudinal and transverse BM's.

8   The half-ordinates of a ship's waterplane at equidistant intervals from forward are as follows:

0, 1.3, 5.2, 8.3, 9.7, 9.8, 8.3, 5.3, and 1.9 m respectively.

If the common interval is 15.9 metres, find the second moment of the waterplane area about the centre line and a transverse axis through the centre of flotation.

9   A ship's waterplane is 120 metres long. The half-ordinates commencing from aft are as follows:

0, 1.3, 3.7, 7.6, 7.6, 7.5, 4.6, 1.8 and 0.1 m respectively.

The spacing between the first three and the last three half-ordinates is half of that between the other half-ordinates. Calculate the second moment of the waterplane area about the centre line and about a transverse axis through the centre of flotation.

10 A ship's waterplane is 90 metres long between perpendiculars. The half-ordinates at this waterplane are as follows:

Station	AP	$\frac{1}{2}$	1	2	3	4	5	$5\frac{1}{2}$	FP
$\frac{1}{2}$ Ords. (m)	0	2	4.88	6.71	7.31	7.01	6.40	2	0.9

Calculate the second moment of the waterplane area about the centre line and also about a transverse axis through the centre of flotation.

Chapter 30
Liquid pressure and thrust. Centres of pressure

Pressure in liquids

When a fluid is in equilibrium the stress across any surface in it is normal to the surface and the pressure intensity at any point of a fluid at rest is the same in all directions. The pressure intensity in a homogeneous liquid at rest under gravity increases uniformly with depth. i.e.

$$P = w \times g \times D$$

where

P = Pressure intensity

w = Density of the liquid,

g = Acceleration due to gravity,

and

D = Depth below the surface.

Total Thrust and Resultant Thrust

If the thrust on each element of area of a surface immersed in a fluid is found, the scalar sum of all such thrusts is called the 'Total Thrust' whilst their vector sum is called the 'Resultant Thrust'. When the surface is plane then the Total Thrust is equal to the Resultant Thrust.

To find the Resultant Thrust

In Figure 30.1, G represents the centroid of an area which is immersed, though not necessarily vertical, in a liquid, and Z represents the depth of the centroid of the area below the surface. Let w be the mass density of the liquid. If an element (dA) of the area, whose centroid is Z_1 below the surface, is considered, then:

Thrust on the element dA = Pressure intensity × Area

$$= w \times g \times Z_1 \times dA$$

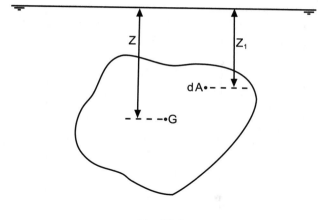

Fig. 30.1

Resultant thrust on the whole area are $= \int w \times g \times Z_1 \, dA$

$$= wg \times \int Z_1 \, dA$$

but

$$\int Z_1 \, dA = Z \cdot A \cdot$$

and

$$w \times g \int Z_1 \, dA = w \times g \cdot Z \cdot A \cdot$$

∴ Resultant thrust = Density × g × Depth of centroid × Area

It should be noted that this formula gives only the magnitude of the resultant thrust. It does not indicate the point at which the resultant thrust may be considered to act.

The centre of pressure

The centre of pressure is the point at which the resultant thrust on an immersed surface may be considered to act. Its position may be found as follows:

(i) For a rectangular lamina immersed with one side in the surface of the liquid. In Figure 30.2, each particle of the strip GH is approximately at the same depth and therefore, the pressure intensity is nearly the same on each particle. Hence the resultant thrust on each strip will act at its mid-point. The resultant of the thrusts on all of the strips in the lamina will act at a point on EF.

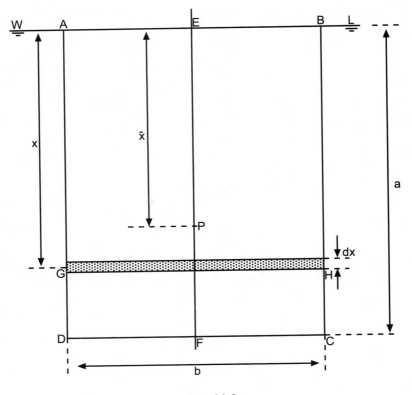

Fig. 30.2

Let w = Mass density of the liquid

The area of the elementary strip = b dx

The depth of the centroid of the strip below the surface is x if the plane of the rectangle is vertical, or x sin θ if the plane is inclined at an angle θ to the horizontal.

The thrust on the strip = $w \cdot g \cdot b \cdot x \cdot \sin \theta \cdot dx$

The resultant thrust on the lamina = $\int_{O}^{a} w \cdot g \cdot b \cdot x \cdot \sin \theta \cdot dx$

$$= \frac{w \cdot g \cdot b \cdot a^2}{2} \sin \theta$$

$$= a \cdot b \cdot \times \tfrac{1}{2} \cdot a \cdot \sin \theta \times w \times g$$

$$= \text{Area} \times \text{Depth of centroid}$$

$$\times g \times \text{Density}$$

The moment of the thrust $= w \cdot g \cdot b \cdot x^2 \cdot \sin \theta \cdot dx$
on the strip about AB

The moment of the total thrust about AB $= \displaystyle\int_O^a w \cdot g \cdot b \cdot x^2 \cdot \sin \theta$

$$= w \cdot g \cdot b \cdot \frac{a^3}{3} \cdot \sin \theta$$

Let $\bar{X}$ be the distance of the centre of pressure (P) from AB, then:

$$\bar{X} \times \text{Total thrust} = \text{Total moment about AB}$$

$$\bar{X} \times w \cdot g \cdot b \cdot \frac{a^2}{2} \cdot \sin \theta = w \cdot g \cdot b \frac{a^3}{3} \cdot \sin \theta$$

or

$$\bar{X} = \tfrac{2}{3} a \text{ (unless } \sin \theta = 0)$$

(ii) For any Plane Area immersed in a liquid.

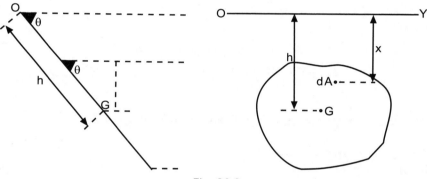

Fig. 30.3

In Figure 30.3, let OY be the line in which the plane cuts the surface of the liquid. Let the plane be inclined at an angle θ to the horizontal.

Let h = the x co-ordinate of the centroid (G), and

let w = the mass density of the liquid.

Depth of the element $dA = x \cdot \sin \theta$

Thrust on $dA = w \cdot g \cdot x \cdot \sin \theta \cdot dA$

Moment of thrust about OY $= w \cdot g \cdot x^2 \cdot \sin \theta \cdot dA$

Moment of total thrust about OY $= \displaystyle\int w \cdot g \cdot x^2 \cdot \sin \theta \cdot dA$

$$= w \cdot g \cdot \sin \theta \cdot \int x^2 \cdot dA$$

$$\text{Total thrust on } A = w \cdot g \cdot A \cdot \text{Depth of centroid}$$

$$= w \cdot g \cdot A \cdot h \cdot \sin \theta$$

$$\text{Moment of total thrust about } OY = w \cdot g \cdot A \cdot h \cdot \sin \theta \cdot \bar{X}$$

$$\therefore \; w \cdot g \cdot A \cdot h \cdot \sin \theta \cdot \bar{X} = w \cdot g \cdot \sin \theta \cdot \int x^2 \cdot dA$$

or

$$\bar{X} = \frac{\int x^2 \cdot dA}{hA} \quad (\text{Unless } \sin \theta = 0)$$

Let I_{OY} be the second moment of the area about OY, then

$$I_{OY} = \int x^2 \cdot dA$$

and

$$\bar{X} = \frac{I_{OY}}{hA}$$

or

$$\bar{X} = \frac{\text{Second moment of area about the waterline}}{\text{First moment of area about the waterline}}$$

Centres of pressure by Simpson's Rules

Using Horizontal Ordinates
Referring to Figure 30.4:

$$\text{Thrust on the element} = w \cdot g \cdot x \cdot y \cdot dx$$

$$\text{Moment of the thrust about } OY = w \cdot g \cdot x^2 \cdot y \cdot dx$$

$$\text{Moment of total thrust about } OY = \int w \cdot g \cdot x^2 \cdot y \cdot dx$$

$$= w \cdot g \int x^2 \cdot y \cdot dx$$

$$\text{Total Thrust} = w \cdot g \cdot A \cdot \text{Depth of centroid}$$

$$= w \cdot g \cdot \int y \cdot dx \cdot \frac{\int x \cdot y \cdot dx}{\int y \cdot dx}$$

$$= w \cdot g \cdot \int x \cdot y \cdot dx$$

$$\text{Moment of total thrust about } OY = \text{Total Thrust} \times \bar{X}$$

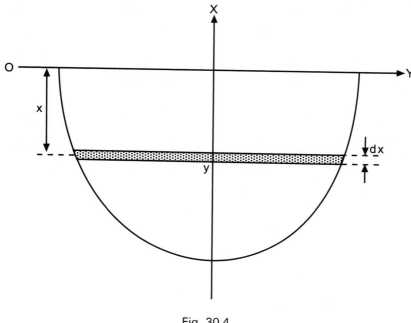

Fig. 30.4

where

$$\bar{X} = \text{Depth of centre of pressure below the surface}$$

$$\therefore \text{ Moment of total thrust about OY} = w \cdot g \cdot \int x \cdot y \cdot dx \times \bar{X}$$

or

$$w \cdot g \cdot \int x \cdot y \cdot dx \times \bar{X} = w \cdot g \cdot \int x^2 \cdot y \cdot dx$$

and

$$\bar{X} = \frac{\int x^2 \cdot y \cdot dx}{\int x \cdot y \cdot dx}$$

The value of the expression $\int x^2 \cdot y \cdot dx$ can be found by Simpson's Rules using values of the product $x^2 y$ as ordinates, and the value of the expression $\int x \cdot y \cdot dx$ can be found in a similar manner using values of the product xy as ordinates.

Example 1

A lower hold bulkhead is 12 metres deep. The transverse widths of the bulkhead, commencing at the upper edge and spaced at 3 m intervals, are as follows:

15.4, 15.4, 15.4, 15.3 and 15 m respectively.

Find the depth of the centre of pressure below the waterplane when the hold is flooded to a depth of 2 metres above the top of the bulkhead.

Ord.	SM	Area func.	Lever	Moment func.	Lever	Inertia func.
15.4	1	15.4	0	0	0	0
15.4	4	61.6	1	61.6	1	61.6
15.4	2	30.8	2	61.6	2	123.2
15.3	4	61.2	3	183.6	3	550.8
15.0	1	15.0	4	60.0	4	240.0
		$184.0 = \Sigma_1$		$366.8 = \Sigma_2$		$975.6 = \Sigma_3$

$$\text{Area} = \tfrac{1}{3} \times h \times \Sigma_1 = \tfrac{3}{3} \times 184.0$$
$$= 184 \, \text{sq m}$$

Referring to Figure 30.5:

$$CG = \frac{\Sigma_2}{\Sigma_1} \times h$$
$$= \frac{366.8}{184} \times 3$$
$$= 5.98 \, \text{m}$$
$$+CD = 2.00 \, \text{m}$$
$$\bar{z} = 7.98 \, \text{m}$$
$$I_{OZ} = \tfrac{1}{3} \times h^3 \times \Sigma_3 = \tfrac{1}{3} \times 3^3 \times 975.6$$
$$= 8780 \, \text{m}^4$$
$$I_{CG} = I_{OZ} - A(CG)^2, \text{ i.e. parallel axis theorem}$$
$$I_{WL} = I_{CG} + A\bar{z}^2$$
$$= I_{OZ} - A(CG^2 - \bar{z}^2)$$
$$I_{WL} = 8780 - 184(5.98^2 - 7.98^2)$$
$$= 13\,928 \, \text{m}^4$$
$$\bar{y} = \frac{I_{WL}}{A\bar{z}}$$
$$= \frac{13\,928}{184 \times 7.98}$$
$$\bar{y} = 9.5 \, \text{m}.$$

Ans. The Centre of Pressure is 9.5 m below the waterline.

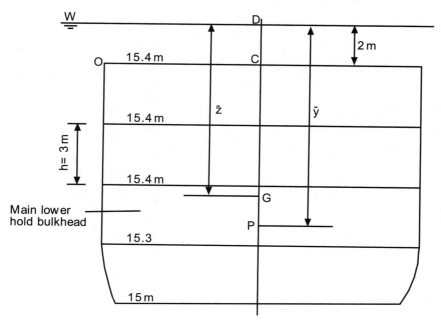

Fig. 30.5

Using vertical ordinates

Referring to Figure 30.6.

$$\text{Thrust on the element} = w \cdot g \cdot \frac{y}{2} \cdot y \cdot dx$$

$$= \frac{w \cdot g \cdot y^2}{2} \cdot dx$$

$$\text{Moment of the thrust about OX} = \frac{w \cdot g \cdot y^2}{2} \cdot dx \cdot \frac{2}{3} y$$

$$= \frac{w \cdot g \cdot y^3}{3} \cdot dx$$

$$\text{Moment of total thrust about OX} = \frac{w}{3} \cdot g \cdot \int y^3 \cdot dx$$

$$\text{Total Thrust} = w \cdot g \cdot A \cdot \text{Depth at centre of gravity}$$

$$= w \cdot g \cdot \int y \cdot dx \cdot \frac{\frac{1}{2} \int y^2 \cdot dx}{\int y \cdot dx}$$

$$= \frac{w}{2} \cdot g \cdot \int y^2 \cdot dx$$

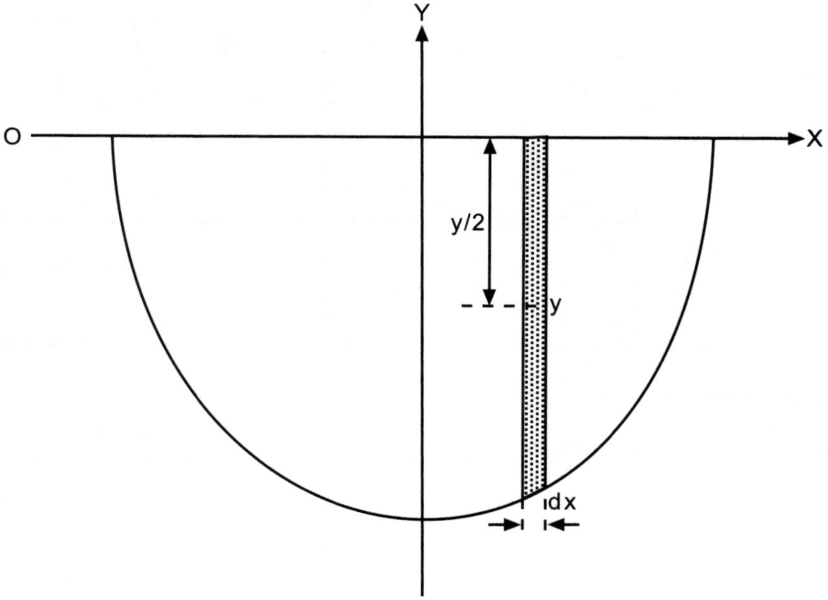

Fig. 30.6

Let $\bar{Y}$ be the depth of the centre of pressure below the surface, then:

Moment of total thrust about OX = Total Thrust $\times \bar{Y}$

$$\frac{wg}{3}\int y^3 \cdot dx = \frac{wg}{2}\int y^2 \cdot dx \cdot \bar{Y}$$

or

$$\bar{Y} = \frac{\frac{1}{3}\int y^3 \cdot dx}{\frac{1}{2}\int y^2 \cdot dx}$$

The values of the two integrals can again be found using Simpson's Rules.

Example 2
The breadth of the upper edge of a deep tank bulkhead is 12 m. The vertical heights of the bulkhead at equidistant intervals across it are 0, 3, 5, 6, 5, 3 and 0 m respectively. Find the depth of the centre of pressure below the waterline when the tank is filled to a head of 2 m above the top of the tank.

$$\text{Area} = \tfrac{1}{3} \times CI \times \Sigma_1$$

$$\text{Area} = \tfrac{1}{3} \times 2 \times 68$$

$$= 45\tfrac{1}{3} \text{ sq m}$$

Ord,	SM	Area func.	Ord.	Moment func.	Ord.	Inertia func.
0	1	0	0	0	0	0
3	4	12	3	36	3	108
5	2	10	5	50	5	250
6	4	24	6	144	6	864
5	2	10	5	50	5	250
3	4	12	3	36	3	108
0	1	0	0	0	0	0
		$68 = \Sigma_1$		$316 = \Sigma_2$		$1580 = \Sigma_3$

Referring to Figure 30.7:

$$CG = \frac{\Sigma_2}{\Sigma_1} \times \frac{1}{2}$$

$$= \frac{316}{68} \times \frac{1}{2}$$

$$= 2.324\,\text{m}$$

$$CD = 2.000\,\text{m}$$

$$DG = 4.324\,\text{m} = \bar{z}$$

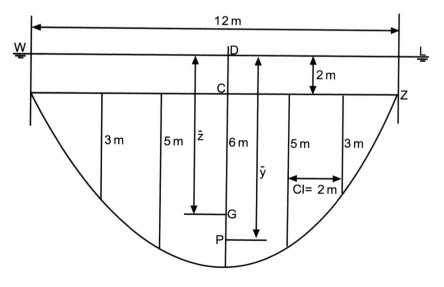

Fig. 30.7

$$I_{OZ} = \tfrac{1}{9} \times CI \times \Sigma_3$$

$$= \tfrac{1}{9} \times 2 \times 1580 = 351\,\text{m}^4$$

$$I_{CG} = I_{OZ} - A\,(CG)^2$$

$$I_{WL} = I_{CG} + A\bar{z}^2$$

$$= I_{OZ} - A\,(CG)^2 + A\bar{z}^2$$

$$= I_{OZ} - A\,(CG^2 - \bar{z}^2)$$

$$= 351 - 45.33\,(2.324^2 - 4.324^2)$$

$$I_{WL} = 953.75\,\text{m}^4$$

$$\bar{y} = \frac{I_{WL}}{A\bar{z}}$$

$$= \frac{953.75}{45.33 \times 4.324}$$

$$\bar{y} = 4.87\,\text{m}$$

Ans. The Centre of Pressure is 4.87 m below the waterline.

Summary

When using Simpson's Rules to estimate the area of a bulkhead under liquid pressure together with the VCG and centre of pressure the procedure should be as follows:

1 Make a sketch from the given information.
2 Make a table and insert the relevant ordinates and multipliers.
3 Calculate the area of bulkhead's plating.
4 Estimate the ship's VCG below the stipulated datum level.
5 Using the parallel axis theorem, calculate the requested centre of pressure.
6 Remember: sketch, table, calculation.

Exercise 30

1   A fore-peak tank bulkhead is 7.8 m deep. The widths at equidistant intervals from its upper edge to the bottom are as follows:

   16, 16.6, 17, 17.3, 16.3, 15.3 and 12 m respectively.

Find the load on the bulkhead and the depth of the centre of pressure below the top of the bulkhead when the fore peak is filled with salt water to a head of 1.3 m above the crown of the tank.

2   A deep tank transverse bulkhead is 30 m deep. Its width at equidistant intervals from the top to the bottom is:

   20, 20.3, 20.5, 20.7, 18, 14 and 6 m respectively.

Find the depth of the centre of pressure below the top of the bulkhead when the tank is filled to a head of 4 m above the top of the tank.

3   The transverse end bulkhead of a deep tank is 18 m wide at its upper edge. The vertical depths of the bulkhead at equidistant intervals across it are as follows:

   0, 3.3, 5, 6, 5, 3.3 and 0 m respectively.

Find the depth of the centre of pressure below the top of the bulkhead when the tank is filled with salt water to a head of 2 m above the top of the bulkhead. Find also the load on the bulkhead.

4   A fore-peak bulkhead is 18 m wide at its upper edge. Its vertical depth at the centre line is 3.8 m. The vertical depths on each side of the centre line at 3 m intervals are 3.5, 2.5 and 0.2 m respectively. Calculate the load on the bulkhead and the depth of the centre of pressure below the top of the bulkhead when the fore-peak tank is filled with salt water to a head of 4.5 m above the top of the bulkhead.

5   The vertical ordinates across the end of a deep tank transverse bulkhead measured downwards from the top at equidistant intervals, are:

   4, 6, 8, 9.5, 8, 6 and 4 m respectively.

Find the distance of the centre of pressure below the top of the bulkhead when the tank is filled with salt water.

6   A square plate of side 'a' is vertical and is immersed in water with an edge of its length in the free surface. Prove that the distance between the centres of pressure of the two triangles into which the plate is divided by a diagonal, is $\dfrac{a\sqrt{13}}{8}$

Chapter 31
Ship squat

What exactly is ship squat?

When a ship proceeds through water, she pushes water ahead of her. In order not to have a 'hole' in the water, this volume of water must return down the sides and under the bottom of the ship. The streamlines of return flow are speeded up under the ship. This causes a drop in pressure, resulting in the ship dropping vertically in the water.

As well as dropping vertically, the ship generally trims forward or aft. The overall decrease in the static underkeel clearance, forward or aft, is called ship squat. It is *not* the difference between the draughts when stationary and the draughts when the ship is moving ahead.

If the ship moves forward at too great a speed when she is in shallow water, say where this static even-keel underkeel clearance is 1.0 to 1.5 m, then grounding due to excessive squat could occur at the bow or at the stern.

For full-form ships such as supertankers or OBO vessels, grounding will occur generally at the *bow*. For fine-form vessels such as passenger liners or container ships the grounding will generally occur at the stern. This is assuming that they are on even keel when stationary. It must be *generally*, because in the last two decades, several ship types have tended to be shorter in LBP and wider in Breadth Moulded. This has led to reported groundings due to ship squat at the bilge strakes at or near to amidships when slight rolling motions have been present.

Why has ship squat become so important in the last thirty years? Ship squat has always existed on smaller and slower vessels when underway. These squats have only been a matter of centimetres and thus have been inconsequential.

However, from the mid-1960s to the late 1990s, ship size has steadily grown until we have supertankers of the order of 350 000 tonnes dwt and above. These supertankers have almost outgrown the ports they visit, resulting in small static even-keel underkeel clearances of 1.0 to 1.5 m. Alongside this development in ship size has been an increase in service speed on several ships, for example container ships, where speeds have gradually increased from 16 knots up to about 25 knots.

Ship design has seen tremendous changes in the 1980s and 1990s. In oil tanker design we have the *Jahre Viking* with a dwt of 564 739 tonnes and an LBP of 440 m. This is equivalent to the length of 9 football pitches. In 1997, the biggest container ship to date, namely the NYK *Antares* came into service. She has a dwt of 72 097 tonnes, a service speed of 23 kts., an LBP of 283.8 m; Br. Moulded of 40 m; Draft Moulded of 13 m; TEU of 5700, and a fuel consumption of 190 tonnes/day.

As the static underkeel clearances have decreased and as the service speeds have increased, ship squats have gradually increased. They can now be of the order of 1.50 to 1.75 m, which are of course by no means inconsequential.

To help focus the mind on the dangers of excessive squat one only has to recall the recent grounding of four vessels:

Herald of Free Enterprise	Ro-Ro vessel	06/03/87
QEII	Passenger liner	07/08/92
Sea Empress	Supertanker	15/02/96
Diamond Grace	260 000 t. dwt VLCC at Tokyo Harbour	02/07/97

In the United Kingdom, over the last 20 years the D.Tp. have shown their concern by issuing four 'M' notices concerning the problems of ship squat and accompanying problems in shallow water. These alert all mariners to the associated dangers.

Signs that a ship has entered shallow water conditions can be one or more of the following:

1. Wave-making increases, especially at the forward end of the ship.
2. Ship becomes more sluggish to manoeuvre. A pilot's quote, 'almost like being in porridge'.
3. Draught indicators on the bridge or echo-sounders will indicate changes in the end draughts.
4. Propeller rpm indicator will show a decrease. If the ship is in 'open water' conditions, i.e. without breadth restrictions, this decrease may be up to 15 per cent of the service rpm in deep water. If the ship is in a confined channel, this decrease in rpm can be up to 20 per cent of the service rpm.
5. There will be a drop in speed. If the ship is in open water conditions this decrease may be up to 30 per cent. If the ship is in a confined channel such as a river or a canal then this decrease can be up to 60 per cent.
6. The ship may start to vibrate suddenly. This is because of the entrained water effects causing the natural hull frequency to become resonant with another frequency associated with the vessel.

7. Any rolling, pitching and heaving motions will all be reduced as the ship moves from deep water to shallow water conditions. This is because of the cushioning effects produced by the narrow layer of water under the bottom shell of the vessel.

8. The appearance of mud could suddenly show in the water around the ship's hull say in the event of passing over a raised shelf or a submerged wreck.

9. Turning circle diameter (TCD) increases. TCD in shallow water could increase 100 per cent.

10. Stopping distances and stopping times increase, compared to when a vessel is in deep waters.

What are the factors governing ship squat?

The main factor is ship speed V_k. Squat varies approximately with the speed squared. In other words, we can take as an example that if we halve the speed we quarter the squat. In this context, speed V_k is the ship's speed relative to the water; in other words, effect of current/tide speed with or against the ship must be taken into account.

Another important factor is the block coefficient C_b. Squat varies directly with C_b. Oil tankers will therefore have comparatively more squat than passenger liners.

The blockage factor 'S' is another factor to consider. This is the immersed cross-section of the ship's midship section divided by the cross-section of water within the canal or river. If the ship is in open water the width of influence of water can be calculated. This ranges from about 8.25b for supertankers, to about 9.50b for general cargo ships, to about 11.75 ship-breadths for container ships.

The presence of another ship in a narrow river will also affect squat, so much so, that squats can *double in value* as they pass/cross the other vessel.

Formulae have been developed that will be satisfactory for estimating maximum ship squats for vessels operating in confined channels and in open water conditions. These formulae are the results of analysing about 600 results some measured on ships and some on ship models. Some of the emperical formulae developed are as follows:

Let

b = breadth of ship.

B = breadth of river or canal.

H = depth of water.

T = ship's even-keel static draft.

C_b = block co-efficient.

V_k = ship speed relative to the water or current.

CSA = Cross Sectional Area.   (See Fig. 31.3.)

Let
$$S = \text{blockage factor} = \text{CSA of ship/CSA of river or canal.}$$

If ship is in open water conditions, then the formula for B becomes

$$B = \{7.7 + 20(1 - C_B)^2\}.\ b, \text{ known as the 'width of influence'.}$$

$$\text{Blockage factor} = S = \frac{b \times T}{B \times H}$$

$$\text{Maximum squat} = \delta_{max}$$

$$= \frac{C_B \times S^{0.81} \times V_k^{2.08}}{20} \quad \text{metres, for } \textit{open water} \\ \text{and } \textit{confined channels}$$

Two short-cut formulae relative to the previous equation are:

$$\text{Maximum squat} = \frac{C_b \times V_k^2}{100} \text{ metres for } \textit{open water} \text{ conditions } \textit{only,}$$

with H/T of 1.1 to 1.4.

$$\text{Maximum squat} = \frac{C_b \times V_k^2}{50} \text{ metres for } \textit{confined channels,}$$

where $S = 0.100$ to 0.265.

A worked example, showing how to predict maximum squat and how to determine the remaining underkeel clearance is shown at the end of this chapter. It shows the use of the more detailed formula and then compares the answer with the short-cut method.

These formulae have produced several graphs of maximum squat against ship's speed V_k. One example of this in Figure 31.2, for a 250 000 t. dwt supertanker. Another example is in Figure 31.3, for a container vessel having shallow water speeds up to 18 knots.

Figure 31.4 shows the maximum squats for merchant ships having C_b values from 0.500 up to 0.900, in open water and in confined channels. Three items of information are thus needed to use this diagram. First, an idea of the ship's C_b value, secondly the speed V_k and thirdly to decide if the ship is in open water or in confined river/canal conditions. A quick graphical prediction of the maximum squat can then be made.

In conclusion, it can be stated that if we can predict the maximum ship squat for a given situation then the following advantages can be gained:

1. The ship operator will know which speed to reduce to in order to ensure the safety of his/her vessel. This could save the cost of a very large repair bill. It has been reported in the technical press that the repair bill for the *QEII* was *$13 million*, plus an estimation for lost passenger booking of *$50 million!!*

    In Lloyd's Lists, the repair bill for the *Sea Empress* had been estimated to be in the region of *$28 million*. In May 1997, the repairs to the *Sea*

Empress were completed at Harland & Wolff Ltd of Belfast, for a reported cost of *£20 million*. Rate of exchange in May 1997 was the order of £1 = $1.55. She was then renamed the *Sea Spirit*.

2. The ship officers could load the ship up an extra few centimetres (except of course where load-line limits would be exceeded). If a 100 000 tonne dwt tanker is loaded by an extra 30 cm or an SD14 general cargo ship is loaded by an extra 20 cm, the effect is an extra 3 per cent onto their dwt. This gives these ships extra earning capacity.

3. If the ship grounds due to excessive squatting in shallow water, then apart from the large repair bill, there is the time the ship is 'out of service'. Being 'out of service' is indeed very costly because loss of earnings can be as high as *£100 000* per *day*.

4. When a vessel goes aground their is always a possibility of leakage of oil resulting in compensation claims for oil pollution and fees for clean-up operations following the incident. These costs eventually may have to be paid for by the shipowner.

These last four paragraphs illustrate very clearly that not knowing about ship squat can prove to be very costly indeed. Remember, in a marine court hearing, ignorance is not acceptable as a legitimate excuse!!

Summarizing, it can be stated that because maximum ship squat can now be predicted, it has removed the 'grey area' surrounding the phenomenon. In the past ship pilots have used 'trial and error', 'rule of thumb' and years of experience to bring their vessels safely in and out of port.

Empirical formulae quoted in this study, modified and refined over a period of 25 years' research on the topic, give *firm guidelines*. By maintaining the ship's trading availability a shipowner's profit margins are not decreased. More important still, this research can help prevent loss of life as occurred with the *Herald of Free Enterprise* grounding.

It should be remembered that the quickest method for reducing the danger of grounding due to ship squat is to *reduce the ship's speed*. 'Prevention is better than cure' and *much cheaper*.

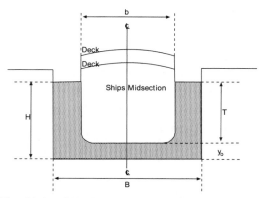

Fig. 31.1.   Ship in a canal in static condition.

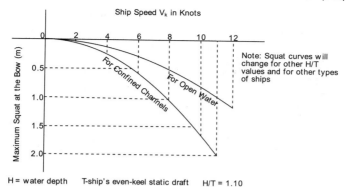

H = water depth   T-ship's even-keel static draft   H/T = 1.10

Fig. 31.2.   Maximum squats against ship speed for 250 000 t. dwt supertanker.

A_S = cross-section of ship at amidships = $b \times T$.

A_C = cross-section of canal = $B \times H$.

Blockage factor = $S = \dfrac{A_S}{A_C} = \dfrac{b \times T}{B \times H}$.

y_o = static underkeel clearance.

$\dfrac{H}{T}$ range is 1.10 to 1.40.

Blockage factor range is 0.100 to 0.265.

Width of influence = $F_B = \dfrac{\text{Equivalent 'B'}}{b}$ in open water.

V_k = speed of ship relative to the water, in knots.

$A_w = A_c - A_S$

'B' = $7.7 + 20(1 - C_B)^2$ ship breadths

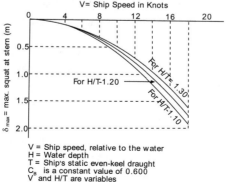

V = Ship speed, relative to the water
H = Water depth
T = Ship's static even-keel draught
C_B is a constant value of 0.600
V and H/T are variables

Fig. 31.3

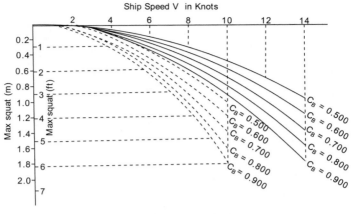

--- Denotes ship is in a confined channel where S= 0.100 to 0.265
— Denotes ship is in open water, where H/T= 1.10 to 1.40

Ship type	Typical C_B, fully loaded	Ship type	Typical C_B, fully loaded
ULCC	0.850	General cargo	0.700
Supertanker	0.825	Passenger liner	0.625
Oil tanker	0.800	Container ship	0.575
Bulk carrier	0.750	Coastal tug	0.500

Fig. 31.4.   Maximum ship squats in confined channels and in open water conditions.

Worked example – ship squat for a supertanker

Question:

A supertanker operating in open water conditions is proceeding at a speed of 11 knots. Her $C_B = 0.830$, static even-keel draft = 13.5 m with a static underkeel clearance of 2.5 m. Her breadth moulded is 55 m with LBP of 320 m.

Calculate the maximum squat for this vessel at the given speed via *two* methods, and her remaining ukc (underkeel clearance) at V_k of 11 kts.

Answer:

$$\text{Width of influence} = \{7.7 + 20[1 - C_B]^2\} \times b = \text{'B'}$$

$$\therefore \text{'B'} = \{7.7 + 20[1 - 0.830]^2\} \times 55$$

$$\therefore \underline{\text{'B'} = 455\,\text{m},}$$

i.e. artificial boundaries in open water or wide rivers

$$\text{Blockage factor, } S = \frac{b \times T}{'B' \times H} = \frac{55 \times 13.5}{455 \times [13.5 + 2.5]} = \underline{0.102}$$

(water depth)

Method 1:

$$\text{Maximum squat} = \frac{C_B \times S^{0.81} \times V_k^{2.08}}{20} = \delta_{max}$$

$$\therefore \delta_{max} = 0.830 \times 0.102^{0.81} \times 11^{2.08} \times \frac{1}{20}$$

$$\therefore \underline{\delta_{max} = 0.96\,m,}$$

at the bow, because $C_B > 0.700$.

Method 2:

Simplified approx. formula

$$\delta_{max} = \frac{C_B \times V_k^2}{100} \text{ metres}$$

$$\therefore \delta_{max} = \frac{0.830 \times 11^2}{100} = 1.00\,m;$$

i.e. slightly above previous answer, so overpredicting on the *safe side*.

$$\text{Average } \delta_{max} = \frac{0.96 + 100}{2} = 0.98\,m \quad y_o = 2.50\,m$$

Hence, remaining underkeel clearance at bow $= y_o - \delta_{max} = y_2$.

$$\therefore y_2 = 2.500 - 0.98 = \underline{1.52\,m} \ @ \ V_k \text{ of } 11\,kts.$$

Exercise 31

1   A container ship is operating in open water river conditions at a forward speed of 12.07 kts. Her C_B is 0.572 with a static even-keel draft of 13 m. Breadth moulded is 32.25 m. If the depth of water is 14.5 m; calculate the following:
(a) Width of influence for this wide river.
(b) Blockage factor.
(c) Maximum squat, stating with reasoning where it occurs.
(d) Dynamical underkeel clearance corresponding to this maximum squat.

2   A vessel has the following particulars:
Br.Mld is 50 m. Depth of water in river is 15.50 m. C_B is 0.817. Width of water in river is 350 m. Static even-keel draft is 13.75 m.
(a) Prove this ship is operating in a 'confined channel' situation.
(b) Draw a graph of maximum squat against ship speed for a range of speeds up to 10 kts.
(c) The pilot decides that the dynamical underkeel clearance is not to be less than 1.00 m.
Determine graphically and mathematically the maximum speed of transit that this pilot must have in order to adhere to this prerequisite.

3   A 75 000 tonne dwt oil tanker has the following particulars:
Br.Mld is 37.25 m. Static even-keel draft is 13.5 m. C_B is 0.800. Depth of water is 14.85 m. Width of river is 186 m. Calculate the forward speed at which, due to ship squat, this vessel would just go aground at the bow.

Chapter 32
Heel due to turning

When a body moves in a circular path there is an acceleration towards the centre equal to v^2/r where v represents the velocity of the body and r represents the radius of the circular path. The force required to produce this acceleration, called a 'Centripetal' force, is equal to $\dfrac{Mv^2}{r}$, where M is the mass of the body.

In the case of a ship turning in a circle, the centripetal force is produced by the water acting on the side of the ship away from the centre of the turn. The force is considered to act at the centre of lateral resistance which, in this case, is the centroid of the underwater area of the ship's side away from the centre of the turn. The centroid of this area is considered to be at the level of the centre of buoyancy. For equilibrium there must be an equal and opposite force, called the 'Centrifugal' force, and this force is considered to act at the centre of mass (G).

When a ship's rudder is put over to port, the forces on the rudder itself will cause the ship to develop a small angle of heel initially to port, say α_1°.

However, the underwater form of the ship and centrifugal force on it cause the ship to heel to starboard, say α_2°.

In this situation α_2° is always greater than α_1°. Consequently for port rudder helm, the final angle of heel due to turning will be to starboard and vice versa.

It can be seen from Figure 32.1 that these two forces produce a couple which tends to heel the ship away from the centre of the turn. i.e.

$$\text{Heeling couple} = \frac{Mv^2}{r} \times B_1 Z$$

Equilibrium is produced by a righting couple equal to $W \times GZ$, where W is equal to the weight of the ship, the weight being a unit of force, i.e. $W = Mg$.

$$\therefore M \cdot g \times GZ = \frac{M \cdot v^2}{r} \times B_1 Z$$

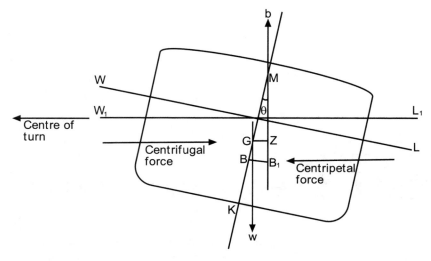

Fig. 32.1

or

$$GZ = \frac{v^2}{g \cdot r} \times B_1Z$$

but at a small angle

$$GZ = GM \cdot \sin \theta$$

and

$$B_1Z = BG \cdot \cos \theta$$

$$\therefore \ GM \sin \theta = \frac{v^2}{g \cdot r} BG \cdot \cos \theta$$

and

$$\tan \theta = \frac{v^2 \times BG}{g \cdot r \cdot GM}$$

Example
A ship turns to port in a circle of radius 100 m at a speed of 15 knots. The GM is 0.67 m and BG is 1 m. If $g = 981 \text{ cm/sec}^2$ and 1 knot is equal to 1852 km/hour, find the heel due to turning.

$$\text{Ship speed in m/sec} = 15 \times \frac{1852}{3600}$$

$$v = 7.72 \text{ m/sec}$$

$$\tan \theta = \frac{v^2 \times BG}{g \cdot r \cdot GM}$$

$$= \frac{7.72^2 \times 1.0}{9.81 \times 100 \times 0.67}$$

$$\tan \theta = 0.0907$$

Ans. Heel $= 5° 11'$ to starboard, due to Contrifugal forces only

In practice, this angle of heel will be slightly smaller. Forces on the rudder will have produced an angle of heel, say $1° 17'$ to port. Consequently the overall angle of heel due to turning will be:

$$\text{Heel} = 5° 11' - 1° 17' = 3° 54' \text{ or } 3.9° \text{ to starboard}$$

Exercise 32

1   A ship's speed is 12 knots. The helm is put hard over and the ship turns in a circle of radius 488 m. GM $= 0.3$ m and BG $= 3$ m. Assuming that 1 knot is equal to 1852 km/hour, find the heel due to turning.
2   A ship steaming at 10 knots turns in a circle of radius 366 m. GM $= 0.24$ m. BM $= 3.7$ m. Calculate the heel produced.
3   A ship turns in a circle of radius 100 m at a speed of 15 knots. BG $= 1$ m. Find the heel if the GM $= 0.6$ m.
4   A ship with a transverse metacentric height of 0.40 m has a speed of 21 kts. The centre of gravity is 6.2 m above keel whilst the centre of lateral resistance is 4.0 m above keel. The rudder is put hard over to port and the vessel turns in a circle of 550 m radius.

Considering only the centrifugal forces involved, calculate the angle of heel as this ship turns at the given speed.

Chapter 33
Unresisted rolling in still water

A ship will not normally roll in still water but if a study be made of such rolling some important conclusions may be reached. For this study it is assumed that the amplitude of the roll is small and that the ship has positive initial metacentric height. Under the conditions rolling is considered to be simple harmonic motion so it will be necessary to consider briefly the principle of such motion.

Let XOY in Figure 33.1 be a diameter of the circle whose radius is 'r' and let OA be a radius vector which rotates about O from position OY at a constant angular velocity of 'w' radians per second. Let P be the projection of the point A on to the diameter XOY. Then, as the radius vector rotates, the point P will oscillate backwards and forwards between Y and X. The motion of the point P is called 'Simple Harmonic'.

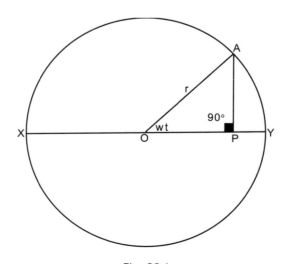

Fig. 33.1

Let the radius vector rotate from OY to OA in 't' seconds, then angle AOY is equal to 'wt'. Let the time taken for the radius vector to rotate through one complete revolution (2π radians) be equal to 'T' seconds, then:

$$2\pi = wT$$

or

$$T = 2\pi/w$$

Let

$$OP = x$$

then

$$x = r\cos wt$$

$$\frac{dx}{dt} = -rw\sin wt$$

$$\frac{d^2x}{dt^2} = -rw^2\cos wt$$

but

$$r\cos wt = x$$

$$\therefore \frac{d^2x}{dt^2} = -w^2x$$

or

$$\frac{d^2x}{dt^2} + w^2x = 0$$

The latter equation is the type of differential equation for simple harmonic motion and since $T = 2\pi/w$ and 'w' is the square root of the coefficient of x in the above equation, then

$$T = \frac{2\pi}{\sqrt{\text{coeff. of } x}}$$

When a ship rolls, the axis about which the oscillation takes place cannot be accurately determined but it would appear to be near to the longitudinal axis through the ship's centre of gravity. Hence the ship rotates or rolls about her 'G'.

The mass moment of inertia (I) of the ship about this axis is given by:

$$I = M \cdot K^2$$

where

$$M = \text{The ship's mass, and}$$

$$K = \text{The radius of gyration about this axis.}$$

But

$$M = \frac{W}{g}$$

where

$$W = \text{the ship's weight, and}$$
$$g = \text{the acceleration due to gravity.}$$

$$\therefore I = \frac{W}{g} K^2$$

When a ship is inclined to a small angle (θ) the righting moment is given by:

$$\text{Righting moment} = W \times GZ$$

where

$$W = \text{the ship's Weight, and}$$
$$GZ = \text{the righting lever.}$$

But

$$GZ = GM \cdot \sin \theta$$

$$\therefore \text{Righting moment} = W \times GM \times \sin \theta$$

And since θ is a small angle, then:

$$\text{Righting moment} = W \times GM \times \theta$$

$$\text{The angular acceleration} = \frac{d^2 \theta}{dt^2}$$

$$\therefore I \times \frac{d^2 \theta}{dt^2} = -W \times GZ$$

or

$$\frac{W}{g} \cdot K^2 \times \frac{d^2 \theta}{dt^2} = -W \times GM \times \theta$$

$$\frac{W}{g} \cdot K^2 \times \frac{d^2 \theta}{dt^2} + W \times GM \times \theta = 0$$

$$\frac{d^2 \theta}{dt^2} + \frac{g \cdot GM \cdot \theta}{K^2} = 0$$

This is the equation for a simple harmonic motion having a period 'T' given by the equation:

$$T = \frac{2\pi}{\sqrt{\text{Coeff. of } \theta}}$$

or

$$T = \frac{2\pi K}{\sqrt{g \cdot GM}} = \frac{2\pi}{\sqrt{g}} \times \frac{K}{\sqrt{GM}} = \frac{2K}{\sqrt{GM}} \text{ approx.}$$

From the above it can be seen that:

1 The time period of roll is completely independent of the actual amplitude of the roll so long as it is a small angle.
2 The time period of roll varies directly as K, the radius of gyration. Hence if the radius of gyration is increased, then the time period is also increased. K may be increased by moving weights away from the axis of oscillation. Average K value is about $0.35 \times$ Br.Mld.
3 The time period of roll varies inversely as the square root of the initial metacentric height. Therefore ships with a large GM will have a short period and those with a small GM will have a long period.
4 The time period of roll will change when weights are loaded, discharged, or shifted within a ship, as this usually affects both the radius of gyration and the initial metacentric height.

Example 1

Find the still water period of roll for a ship when the radius of gyration is 6 m and the metacentric height is 0.5 m.

$$T = \frac{2\pi K}{\sqrt{g \cdot GM}} = \frac{2K}{\sqrt{GM_T}} \text{ approx.}$$

$$T = \frac{2\pi K}{\sqrt{9.81 \times 0.5}} = \frac{2 \times 6}{\sqrt{0.5}} \text{ approx.}$$

$$= 16.97 \text{ s.} \quad \text{Average} = 17 \text{ s.}$$

(99.71 per cent correct giving only 0.29 per cent error!!)

Ans. $\underline{T = 17.02 \text{ s}}$

Note. In the S.I. system of units the value of g to be used in problems is 9.81 m per second per second, unless another specific value is given.

Example 2

A ship of 10 000 tonnes displacement has GM = 0.5 m. The period of roll in still water is 20 seconds. Find the new period of roll if a mass of 50 tonnes is discharged from a position 14 m above the centre of gravity. Assume

$$g = 9.81 \text{ m/sec}^2$$

$$W_2 = W_0 - w = 10\,000 - 50 = 9950 \text{ tonnes}$$

$$T = \frac{2\pi K}{\sqrt{g \cdot GM}} \qquad\qquad GG_1 = \frac{w \times d}{W_2}$$

$$20 = \frac{2\pi K}{\sqrt{9.81 \times 0.5}} \qquad\qquad = \frac{50 \times 14}{9950}$$

$$400 = \frac{4 \cdot \pi^2 \cdot K^2}{9.81 \times 0.5} \qquad\qquad GG_1 = 0.07 \text{ m}$$

$$GM = 0.50 \text{ m}$$

$$\text{New GM} = 0.57 \text{ m}$$

or

$$K^2 = \frac{400 \times 9.81 \times 0.5}{4 \times \pi^2}$$

$$= 49.69$$

$$\therefore K = 7.05$$

$$I \ (Originally) = M \cdot K^2$$

$$I_o = 10\,000 \times 49.69$$

$$I_o = 496\,900 \ tonnes \cdot m^2$$

I of discharged mass about $G = 50 \times 14^2$

$$= 9800 \ tonnes \cdot m^2$$

New I of ship about the original C of G = Original I − I of discharged mass

$$= 496\,900 - 9800$$

$$= 487\,100 \ tonnes \cdot m^2$$

By the Theorem of parallel axes:
  Let

$$I_2 = \frac{\text{New I of ship about}}{\text{the new C of G}} = \frac{\text{New I of ship about}}{\text{the original C of G}} - W \times GG_1^2$$

$$I_2 = 487\,100 - 9950 \times 0.07^2$$

$$I_2 = 487\,100 - 49$$

$$I_2 = 487\,051 \ tonnes \cdot m^2$$

$$I_2 = M_2 \cdot K_2^2$$

$$\therefore \ New \ K^2 = \frac{I_2}{M_2}$$

$$\therefore \ K_2^2 = \frac{487\,051}{9950}$$

Let

$$K_2 = New \ K = \sqrt{\frac{487\,051}{9950}}$$

$$K_2 = 7 \ m$$

Let

$$T_2 = New \ T = \frac{2\pi K_2}{\sqrt{g \cdot GM_2}}$$

$$T_2 = \frac{2\pi 7}{\sqrt{9.81 \times 0.57}}$$

Ans. $\underline{T_2 = 18.6 \ s}$

Procedure steps for Example 2

1 Calculate the new displacement in tonnes (W_2).
2 Estimate the original radius of gyration (K).
3 Evaluate the new displacement and new GM (W_2 and GM_2).
4 Calculate the new mass moment of inertia (I_2).
5 Calculate the new radius of gyration (K_2).
6 Finally evaluate the new period of roll (T_2).

For 'stiff ships' the period of roll could be as low as 8 seconds due to a large GM. For 'tender ships' the period of roll will be, say, 30 to 35 seconds, due to a small GM. A good comfortable period of roll for those on board ship will be 20 to 25 seconds.

Exercise 33

1 Find the still water period of roll for a ship when the radius of gyration is 5 m and the initial metacentric height is 0.25 m.
2 A ship of 5000 tonnes displacement has GM = 0.5 m. The still water period of roll is 20 seconds. Find the new period of roll when a mass of 100 tonnes is discharged from a position 14 m above the centre of gravity.
3 A ship of 9900 tonnes displacement has GM = 1 m, and a still water rolling period of 15 seconds. Calculate the new rolling period when a mass of 100 tonnes is loaded at a position 10 m above the ship's centre of gravity.
4 A vessel has the following particulars:
   Displacement is 9000 tonnes, natural rolling period is T_R of 15 seconds, GM is 1.20 m. Determine the new natural rolling period after the following changes in loading have taken place:

   2000 tonnes added at 4.0 m above ship's VCG.
   500 tonnes discharged at 3.0 m below ship's VCG.

   Assume that KM remains at the same value before and after changes of loading have been completed. Discuss if this final condition results in a 'stiff ship' or a 'tender ship'.

Chapter 34
List due to bilging side compartments

When a compartment in a ship is bilged the buoyancy provided by that compartment is lost. This causes the centre of buoyancy of the ship to move directly away from the centre of the lost buoyancy and, unless the centre of gravity of the compartment is on the ship's centre line, a listing moment will be created, b = w.

Let the ship in Figure 34.1 float upright at the waterline WL. G represents the position of the ship's centre of gravity and B the centre of buoyancy.

Now let a compartment which is divided at the centre line be bilged on the starboard side as shown in the figure. To make good the lost buoyancy

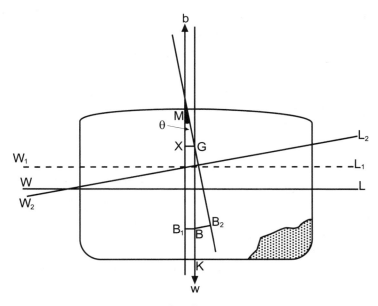

Fig. 34.1

the ship will sink to the waterline W_1L_1. That is, the lost buoyancy is made good by the layer between WL and W_1L_1.

The centre of buouancy will move from B to B_1, directly away from the centre of gravity of the lost buoyancy, and the distance BB_1 is equal to $\dfrac{w \times d}{W}$, where w represents the lost buoyancy and d represents the distance between the ship's centre of buoyancy and the centre of the lost buoyancy.

The shift in the centre of buoyancy produces a listing moment.

Let θ be the resultant list.

Then

$$\tan \theta = GX/XM$$

$$= BB_1/XM$$

where XM represents the initial metacentric height for the bilged condition.

Example 1

A box-shaped vessel of length 100 m and breadth 18 m, floats in salt water on an even keel at 7.5 m draft. KG = 4 m. The ship has a continuous centre line bulkhead which is watertight. Find the list if a compartment amidships, which is 15 m long and is empty, is bilged on one side.

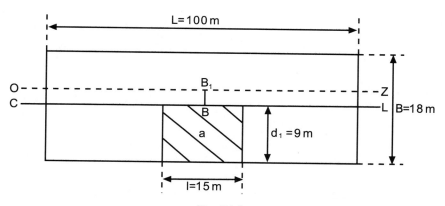

Fig. 34.2

(a) *Find the New Mean Draft*

$$\text{Bodily increase in draft} = \frac{\text{Volume of lost buoyancy}}{\text{Area of intact W.P.}}$$

$$= \frac{15 \times 9 \times 7.5}{100 \times 18 - 15 \times 9} = 0.61$$

$$\text{New draft} = 7.50 + 0.61$$

$$\therefore \text{New draft} = 8.11 \, \text{m} = \text{draft } d_2$$

(b) Find the Shift of the Centre of Buoyancy

$$BB_1 = \frac{a \times B/4}{LB - a}$$

$$= \frac{15 \times 9 \times 18/4}{100 \times 18 - 15 \times 9} = \frac{607.5}{1665}$$

$$= 0.37\,m$$

(c) To Find I_{OZ}

$$I_{CL} = \left(\frac{B}{2}\right)^3 \cdot \frac{L}{3} + \left(\frac{B}{2}\right)^3 \cdot \frac{(L-1)}{3}$$

$$I_{CL} = \frac{9^3 \times 100}{3} + \frac{9^3 \times 85}{3} = 24\,300 + 20\,655$$

$$= 44\,955\,m^4$$

$$I_{OZ} = I_{CL} - A \cdot BB_1^2$$

$$= 44\,955 - (100 \times 18 - 15 \times 9) \times 0.365^2$$

$$= 44\,955 - 222$$

$$= 44\,733\,m^4$$

(d) To Find GM

$$BM = \frac{I_{OZ}}{V}$$

$$= \frac{44\,733}{100 \times 18 \times 7.5}$$

$$= 3.31\,m$$

$$+$$

$$KB = \frac{d_2}{2} \quad \therefore KB = \quad 4.06\,m$$

$$KM = \quad 7.37\,m$$

$$-$$

$$KG = \quad 4.00\,m \text{ as before bilging}$$

$$\text{After bilging, } GM = \quad 3.37\,m$$

(e) To Find the List

$$\tan List = \frac{BB_1}{GM}$$

$$= \frac{0.37}{3.37} = 0.1098$$

Ans. List = 6° 16′

Example 2

A box-shaped vessel, 50 m long × 10 m wide, floats in salt water on an even keel at a draft of 4 m. A centre line longitudinal watertight bulkhead extends from end to end and for the full depth of the vessel. A compartment amidships on the starboard side is 15 m long and contains cargo with permeability 'μ' of 30 per cent. Calculate the list if this compartment is bilged. KG = 3 m.

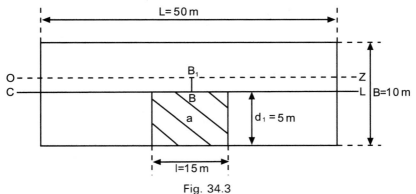

Fig. 34.3

(a) Find the New Mean Draft

$$\text{Bodily increase in draft} = \frac{\text{Volume of lost buoyancy}}{\text{Area of intact W.P.}}$$

$$= \frac{\dfrac{30}{100} \times 15 \times 5 \times 4}{50 \times 10 - \dfrac{30}{100} \times 15 \times 5} = \frac{90}{477.5}$$

$$= 0.19\,\text{m}$$

$$\therefore \text{ New draft} = 4.00 + 0.19 = 4.19\,\text{m say draft } d_2$$

(b) Find the Shift of the Centre of Buoyancy

$$BB_1 = \frac{\mu a \times \dfrac{B}{4}}{LB - \mu a}$$

$$= \frac{\dfrac{30}{100} \times 15 \times 5 \times \dfrac{10}{4}}{50 \times 10 - \dfrac{30}{100} \times 15 \times 5} = \frac{56.25}{477.5}$$

$$= 0.12\,\text{m}$$

(c) To Find I_{OZ}

$$I_{CL} = \frac{LB^3}{12} - \frac{\mu l b^3}{3}$$

$$= \frac{50 \times 10^3}{12} - \frac{30}{100} \times \frac{15 \times 5^3}{3}$$

$$= 4166.7 - 187.5$$

$$= 3979\,\text{m}^4$$

$$I_{OZ} = I_{CL} - A \cdot BB_1^2$$

$$= 3979 - 477.5 \times 0.12^2$$

$$= 3979 - 7$$

$$= 3972\,m^4$$

(d) To Find GM

$$BM_2 = \frac{I_{OZ}}{V}$$

$$BM_2 = \frac{3972}{50 \times 10 \times 4}$$

$$\therefore BM_2 = \quad 1.99\,m$$

$$+$$

$$KB_2 = \quad 2.10\,m$$

$$KM_2 = \quad \overline{4.09\,m}$$

$$-$$

$$\text{as before bilging, } KG = \quad 3.00\,m$$

$$GM_2 = \quad \overline{1.09\,m}$$

(e) To Find the List

$$\tan \text{List} = BB_1/GM$$

$$= \frac{0.12}{1.09} = 0.1101$$

Ans. List = 6° 17′ to starboard

Note: When $\mu = 100$ per cent then:

$$I_{CL} = \left(\frac{B}{2}\right)^3 \cdot \frac{L}{3} + \left(\frac{B}{2}\right)^3 \left(\frac{L-l}{3}\right)\,m^4$$

or

$$I_{CL} = \frac{LB^3}{12} - \frac{lb^3}{3}\,m^4$$

Both formulae give the same answer

Summary

1 Make a sketch from the given information.
2 Calculate the mean bodily increase in draft.
3 Calculate the ship in the centre of buoyancy.
4 Estimate the second moment of area in the bilged condition with the use of the parallel axis theorem.
5 Evaluate the new KB, BM, KM and GM.
6 Finally calculate the requested angle of list.

Exercise 34

1   A box-shaped tanker barge is 100 m long, 15 m wide and floats in salt water on an even keel at 5 m draft. KG = 3 m. The barge is divided longitudinally by a centre line watertight bulkhead. An empty compartment amidships on the starboard side is 10 m long. Find the list if this compartment is bilged.

2   A box-shaped vessel, 80 m long and 10 m wide, is floating on an even keel at 5 m draft. Find the list if a compartment amidships, 15 m long is bilged on one side of the centre line bulkhead. KG = 3 m.

3   A box-shaped vessel, 120 m long and 24 m wide, floats on an even keel in salt water at a draft of 7 m. KG = 7 m. A compartment amidships is 12 m long and is divided at the centre line by a full depth watertight bulkhead. Calculate the list if this compartment is bilged.

4   A box-shaped vessel is 50 m long, 10 m wide and is divided longitudinally at the centre line by a watertight bulkhead. The vessel floats on an even keel in salt water at a draft of 4 m. KG = 3 m. A compartment amidships is 12 m long and contains cargo of permeability 30 per cent. Find the list if this compartment is bilged.

5   A box-shaped vessel 68 m long and 14 m wide has KG = 4.7 m, and floats on an even keel in salt water at a draft of 5 m. A compartment amidships 18 m long is divided longitudinally at the centre line and contains cargo of permeability 30 per cent. Calculate the list if this compartment is bilged.

Chapter 35
The Deadweight Scale

The Deadweight Scale provides a method for estimating the additional draft or for determining the extra load that could be taken onboard when a vessel is being loaded in water of density less than that of salt water. For example, the vessel may be loading in a port where the water density is that of fresh water at 1.000 t/cu.m.

This Deadweight Scale (see Figure 35.1) displays columns of scale readings for:

Freeboard (f).
Dwt in salt water and in fresh water.
Draft of ship (mean).
Displacement in tonnes in salt water and in fresh water.
Tonnes per cm (TPC) in salt water and in fresh water.
Moment to Change Trim 1 cm (MCTC).

On every dwt scale the following constants must exist:

$$\text{Any Freeboard (f)} + \text{Any draft (d)} = \text{Depth of ship (D)}$$

hence $f + d = C1$.

$$\text{Any Displacement (W)} - \text{Any Dwt} = \text{Lightweight (L wt)}$$

hence $W - \text{Dwt} = C2$.

The main use of the Dwt Scale is to observe Dwt against Draft. Weight in tonnes remains the same but the volume of displacement will change with a change in density of the water in which the ship floats. The salt water and fresh water scales relate to these changes.

On many ships this Dwt Scale has been replaced by the data being presented in tabular form. The officer onboard only needs to interpolate to obtain the information that is required. Also the Dwt Scale can be part of a computer package supplied to the ship. In this case the officer only needs to key in the variables and the printout supplies the required data.

The following worked example shows the use of the Dwt Scale:

Question:

Determine the TPC at the fully loaded draft from the Dwt Scale shown in Figure 35.1 (on page 304) and show the final displacement in tonnes remains similar for fresh and salt water.

From Figure 35.1 TPC is 31.44 and the permitted fresh water sinkage as shown on the freeboard marks is 19 cm with displacement in salt water being almost 23 900 t.

Consequently, the approximate load displacement in fresh water is given by:

$$\text{FW sinkage} = W/\text{TPC} \times 40 \, \text{cm}$$

So

$$W = \text{TPC} \times \text{FW sinkage} \times 40 = 31.44 \times 19 \times 40 = 23\,894 \text{ tonnes}$$

Hence this vessel has loaded up an extra 19 cm of draft in fresh water whilst keeping her displacement at 23 894 t (equivalent to salt water draft of 9.17 m).

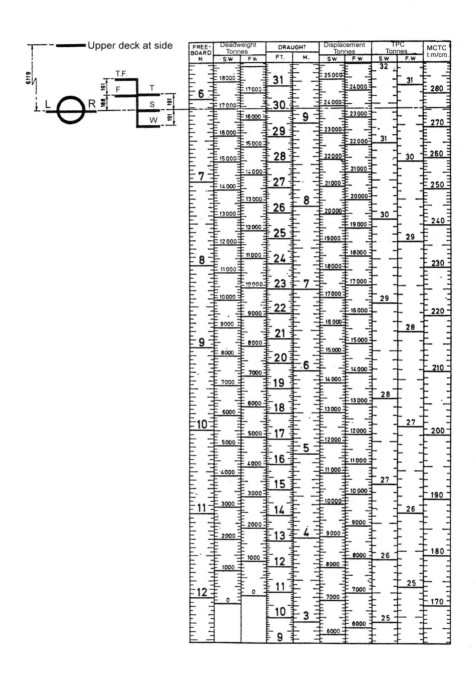

Fig. 35.1.   Deadweight Scale

Chapter 36
Interaction

What exactly is interaction?

Interaction occurs when a ship comes too close to another ship or too close to, say, a river or canal bank. As ships have increased in size (especially in Breadth Moulded), Interaction has become very important to consider. In February 1998, the Marine Safety Agency (MSA) issued a Marine Guidance note 'Dangers of Interaction', alerting Owners, Masters, Pilots, and Tug-Masters on this topic.

Interaction can result in one or more of the following characteristics:

1 If two ships are on a passing or overtaking situation in a river the squats of both vessels could be doubled when their amidships are directly in line.
2 When they are directly in line each ship will develop an angle of heel and the smaller ship will be drawn bodily towards the larger vessel.
3 Both ships could lose steerage efficiency and alter course without change in rudder helm.
4 The smaller ship may suddenly veer off course and head into the adjacent river bank.
5 The smaller ship could veer into the side of the larger ship or worse still be drawn across the bows of the larger vessel, bowled over and capsized.

In other words there is:

(a) a ship to ground interaction;
(b) a ship to ship interaction;
(c) a ship to shore interaction.

What causes these effects of interaction? The answer lies in the pressure bulbs that exist around the hull form of a moving ship model or a moving ship. See Figure 36.1. As soon as a vessel moves from rest, hydrodynamics produce the shown positive and negative pressure bulbs. For ships with greater parallel body such as tankers these negative bulbs will be comparatively longer in length. When a ship is stationary in water of zero current speed these bulbs disappear.

Note the elliptical Domain that encloses the vessel and these pressure bulbs. This Domain is very important. When the Domain of one vessel interfaces with the Domain of another vessel then interaction effects will occur. Effects of interaction are increased when ships are operating in shallow waters.

Ship to ground (squat) interaction

In a report on measured ship squats in the St Lawrence seaway, A. D. Watt stated: 'meeting and passing in a channel also has an effect on squat. It was found that when two ships were moving at the low speed of five knots that squat increased up to double the normal value. At higher speeds the squat when passing was in the region of one and a half times the normal value.' Unfortunately, no data relating to ship types, gaps between ships, blockage factors etc. accompanied this statement.

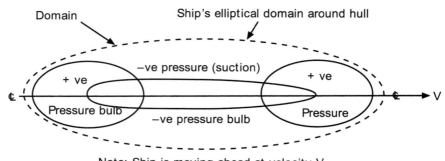

Note: Ship is moving ahead at velocity V

Fig. 36.1.   Pressure distribution around ship's hull (not drawn to scale).

Thus, at speeds of the order of five knots the squat increase is $+100$ per cent whilst at higher speeds, say ten knots, this increase is $+50$ per cent. Figure 36.2 illustrates this passing manoeuvre. Figure 36.3 interprets the percentages given in the previous paragraph.

How may these squat increases be explained? It has been shown in the chapter on Ship Squat that its value depends on the ratio of the ship's cross-section to the cross-section of the river. This is the blockage factor 'S'. The presence of a second ship meeting and crossing will of course increase the blockage factor. Consequently the squat on each ship will increase.

Maximum squat is calculated by using the equation:

$$\delta_{max} = \frac{C_b \times S^{0.81} \times V_k^{2.08}}{20} \text{ metres}$$

Consider the following example.

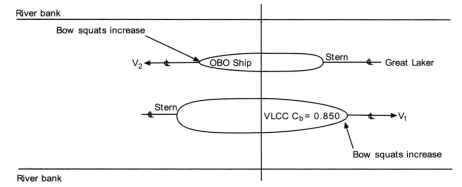

Fig. 36.2.   Amidships (⌗) of VLCC directly in line with amidships of OBO ship in St Lawrence seaway.

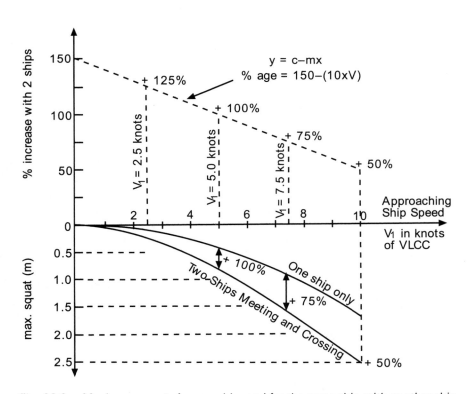

Fig. 36.3.   Maximum squats for one ship, and for the same ship with another ship present.

Example 1

A supertanker has a breadth of 50 m with a static even-keel draft of 12.75 m. She is proceeding along a river of 250 m and 16 m depth rectangular cross-section. If her speed is 5 kts and her C_B is 0.825, calculate her maximum squat when she is on the centre line of this river.

$$S = \frac{b \times T}{B \times H} = \frac{50 \times 12.75}{250 \times 16} = 0.159$$

$$\delta_{max} = \frac{0.825 \times 0.159^{0.81} \times 5^{2.08}}{20} = \underline{0.26\,m}$$

Example 2

Assume now that this supertanker meets an oncoming container ship also travelling at 5 kts. See Figure 36.4. If this container ship has a breadth of 32 m a C_b of 0.580, and a static even-keel draft of 11.58 m calculate the maximum squats of both vessels when they are transversely in line as shown.

$$S = \frac{(b_1 \times T_1) + (b_2 \times T_2)}{B \times H}$$

$$S = \frac{(50 \times 12.75) + (32 \times 11.58)}{250 \times 16} = 0.252$$

Supertanker:

$$\delta_{max} = \frac{0.825 \times 0.252^{0.81} \times 5^{2.08}}{20}$$

$$= \underline{0.38\,m\ at\ the\ bow}$$

Container ship:

$$\delta_{max} = \frac{0.580 \times 0.252^{0.81} \times 5^{2.08}}{20}$$

$$= \underline{0.27\,m\ at\ the\ stern}$$

The maximum squat of 0.38 m for the supertanker will be at the bow because her C_b is greater than 0.700. Maximum squat for the container ship will be at the stern, because her C_b is less than 0.700. As shown this will be 0.27 m.

If this container ship had travelled alone on the centre line of the river then her maximum squat at the stern would have only been 0.12 m. Thus the presence of the other vessel has more than doubled her squat.

Clearly, these results show that the presence of a second ship does increase ship squat. Passing a moored vessel would also make blockage effect and squat greater. These values are not qualitative but only illustrative of this phenomenon of interaction in a ship to ground (squat) situation. Nevertheless, they are supportive of A. D. Watt's statement.

Ship to ship Interaction

Consider Figure 36.5 where a tug is overtaking a large ship in a narrow river. Three cases have been considered:

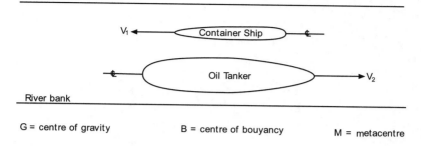

V₁ and V₂ are ship velocities

G = centre of gravity   B = centre of bouyancy   M = metacentre

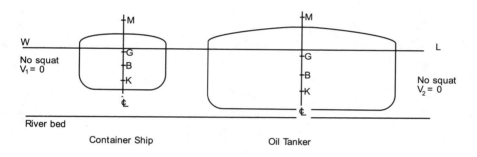

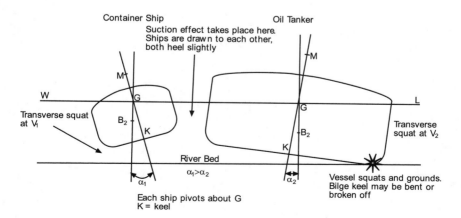

Fig. 36.4.   Transverse squat caused by ships crossing in a confined channel.

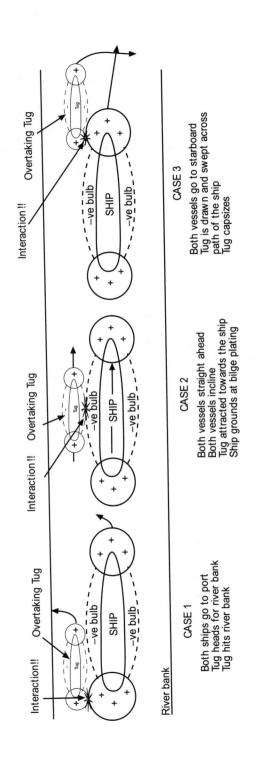

Fig. 36.5. Ship to ship interaction in a narrow river during an overtaking manoeuvre.

Case 1. The tug has just come up to aft port quarter of the ship. The Domains have become in contact. Interaction occurs. The positive bulb of the ship reacts with the positive bulb of the tug. Both vessels veer to port side. Rate of turn is greater on the tug. There is a possibility of the tug veering off into the adjacent river bank as shown in Figure 36.5.

Case 2. The tug is in danger of being drawn bodily towards the ship because the negative pressure (suction) bulbs have interfaced. The bigger the differences between the two deadweights of these ships the greater will be this transverse attraction. Each ship develops an angle of heel as shown. There is a danger of the ship losing a bilge keel or indeed fracture of the bilge strakes occurring. This is 'transverse squat', the loss of underkeel clearance at forward speed. Figure 36.4 shows this happening with the tanker and the container ship.

Case 3. The tug is positioned at the ship's forward port quarter. The Domains have become in contact via the positive pressure bulbs. Both vessels veer to the starboard side. Rate of turn is greater on the tug. There is great danger of the tug being drawn across the path of the ship's heading and bowled over. This has actually occurred with resulting loss of life.

Note how in these three cases that it is the smaller vessel, be it a tug, a pleasure craft or a local ferry involved, that ends up being the casualty!!

Figures 36.6 and 36.7 give further examples of ship to ship Interaction effects in a river.

Methods for reducing the effects of Interaction in Cases 1 to 5

Reduce speed of both ships and then if safe increase speeds after the meeting crossing manoeuvre time slot has passed. Resist the temptation to go for the order 'increase revs' This is because the forces involved with Interaction vary as the *speed squared*. However, too much a reduction in speed produces a loss of steerage because rudder effectiveness is decreased. This is even more so in shallow waters, where the propeller rpm decrease for similar input of deep water power. Care and vigilance are required.

Keep the distance between the vessels as large as practicable bearing in mind the remaining gaps between each ship side and nearby river bank.

Keep the vessels from entering another ship's Domain, for example crossing in wider parts of the river.

Cross in deeper parts of the river rather than in shallow waters, bearing in mind those increases in squat.

Make use of rudder helm. In Case 1, starboard rudder helm could be requested to counteract loss of steerage. In Case 3, port rudder helm would conteract loss of steerage.

Ship to shore interaction

Figures 36.8 and 36.9 show the ship to shore Interaction effects. Figure 36.8 shows the forward positive pressure bulb being used as a pivot to bring a ship alongside a river bank.

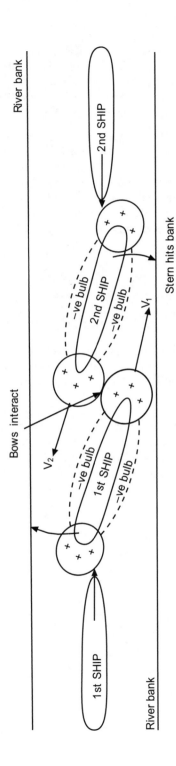

Fig. 36.6. Case 4. Ship to ship interaction. Both sterns swing towards river banks. The approach situation.

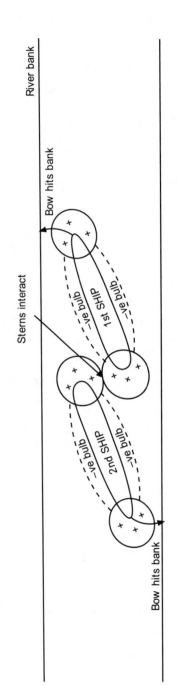

Fig. 36.7. Case 5. Ship to ship interaction. Both bows swing towards river banks. The leaving situation.

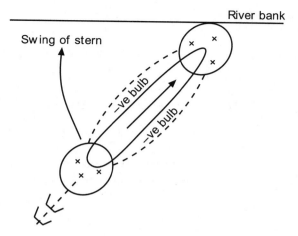

Fig. 36.8.   Ship to bank interaction. Ship approaches slowly and pivots on forward positive pressure bulb.

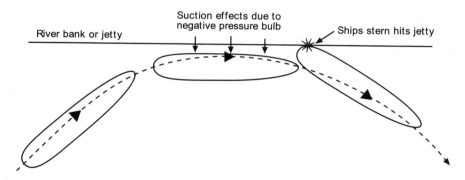

Fig. 36.9.   Ship to bank interaction. Ship comes in at too fast a speed. Interaction
causes stern to swing towards river bank and then hits it.

Figure 36.9 shows how the positive and negative pressure bulbs have caused the ship to come alongside and then to veer away from the jetty. Interaction could in this case cause the stern to swing and collide with the wall of this jetty.

Summary

An understanding of the phenomenon of Interaction can avert a possible marine accident. Generally a reduction in speed is the best preventive procedure. This could prevent on incident leading to loss of sea worthiness, loss of income for the shipowner, cost of repairs, compensation claims and maybe loss of life.

Exercise 36

1   A river is 150 m wide and has 12 m depth of water. A passenger liner having a breadth of 30 m a static even-keel draft of 10 m and a C_b of 0.625 is proceeding along this river at 8 kts. She meets an approaching general cargo vessel having a breadth of 20 m, a static even-keel draft of 8 m and a C_b of 0.700 moving at 7 kts.

   Estimate the maximum squats of each vessel when their amidships are transversely in line.

2   With the aid of sketches, define Interaction and list how its effects may be limited. Show clearly how Interaction and transverse squat are inter-related.

Chapter 37
Effect of change of density on draft and trim

When a ship passes from water of one density to water of another density the mean draft is changed and if the ship is heavily trimmed, the change in the position of the centre of buoyancy will cause the trim to change.

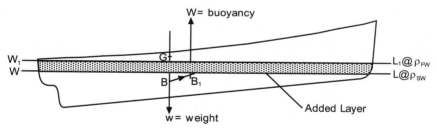

Fig. 37.1

Let the ship in Figure 37.1 float in salt water at the waterline WL. B represents the position of the centre of buoyancy and G the centre of gravity. For equilibrium, B and G must lie in the same vertical line.

If the ship now passes into fresh water, the mean draft will increase. Let W_1L_1 represent the new waterline and b the centre of gravity of the extra volume of the water displaced. The centre of buoyancy of the ship, being the centre of gravity of the displaced water, will move from B to B_1 in a direction directly towards b. The force of buoyancy now acts vertically upwards through B_1 and the ship's weight acts vertically downwards through G, giving a trimming moment equal to the product of the displacement and the longitudinal distance between the centres of gravity and buoyancy. The ship will then change trim to bring the centres of gravity and buoyancy back in to the same vertical line.

Example

A box-shaped pontoon is 36 m long, 4 m wide and floats in salt water at drafts F 2.00 m. A 4.00 m. Find the new drafts if the pontoon now passes into fresh

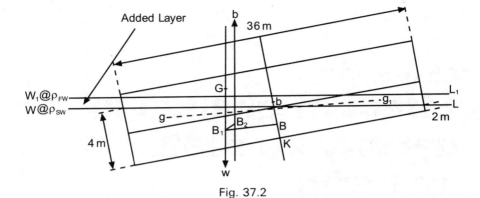

Fig. 37.2

water. Assume salt water density is $1.025 \, \text{t/m}^3$. Assume fresh water density $= 1.000 \, \text{t/m}^3$.

(a) To Find the Position of B_1

$$BB_1 = \frac{v \times gg_1}{V}$$

$$v = \frac{1}{2} \times 1 \times \frac{36}{2} \times 4 \qquad gg_1 = \frac{2}{3} \times 36 \qquad V = 36 \times 4 \times 3$$

$$= 36 \, \text{cu. m} \qquad\qquad gg_1 = 24 \, \text{m} \qquad\quad = 432 \, \text{cu. m}$$

$$\therefore \; BB_1 = \frac{36 \times 24}{432}$$

$$= 2 \, \text{m}$$

Because the angle of trim is small, BB_1 is considered to be the horizontal component of the shift of the centre of buoyancy.

Now let the pontoon enter fresh water, i.e. from ρ_{SW} into ρ_{FW}. Pontoon will develop mean bodily sinkage.

(b) To Find the New Draft
In Salt Water

$$Mass = Volume \times Density$$

$$= 36 \times 4 \times 3 \times 1.025$$

In Fresh Water.

$$Mass = Volume \times Density$$

$$\therefore \; Volume = \frac{Mass}{Density}$$

$$= \frac{36 \times 4 \times 3 \times 1.025}{1.000} \, \text{cu. m}$$

(Mass in Salt water = Mass in Fresh Water)

Let

$$MBS = \text{Mean Bodily Sinkage} \quad \rho_{SW} = \text{higher density}, \rho_{FW} = \text{lower density}$$

$$MBS = \frac{W}{TPC_{SW}} \times \frac{(\rho_{SW} - \rho_{FW})}{\rho_{FW}}$$

$$MBS = \frac{\cancel{L} \cancel{B} d\cancel{\rho_{SW}}}{\dfrac{\cancel{L} \times \cancel{B}}{100} \times \cancel{\rho_{SW}}} \left\{ \frac{\rho_{SW} - \rho_{FW}}{\rho_{FW}} \right\}$$

$$\therefore MBS = \frac{d(\rho_{SW} - \rho_{FW})}{\rho_{FW}} \times 100$$

$$MBS = \frac{3 \times 0.025}{1.000} \times 100 = \underline{0.075\,m}$$

$$\therefore MBS = 0.075\,m$$

Original mean draft $= 3.000\,m$

New mean draft $= 3.075\,m$ say draft d_2

(c) Find the Change of Trim

Let $B_1 B_2$ be the horizontal component of the shift of the centre of buoyancy.
Then

$$B_1 B_2 = \frac{v \times d}{V} \qquad\qquad W = LBd_{SW} \times \rho_{SW}$$

$$= \frac{10.8 \times 2}{442.8} \qquad\qquad = 36 \times 4 \times 3 \times 1.025$$

$$\therefore B_1 B_2 = 0.0487\,m \qquad\qquad \therefore W = 442.8\text{ tonnes}$$

$$\text{Trimming Moment} = W \times B_1 B_2$$

$$= 36 \times 4 \times 3 \times \frac{1.025}{1.000}\,t \times 0.0487\,m = 21.56\,t\,m$$

$$BM_{L(2)} = \frac{L^2}{12d_{(2)}}$$

$$= \frac{36^2}{12 \times 3.075}$$

$$= \frac{36}{1.025}\,m = 35.12\,m$$

$$MCTC \simeq \frac{W \times BM_L}{100 \times L}$$

$$= \frac{442.8 \times 35.12}{100 \times 36}$$

$$= 4.32\text{ tonnes metres}$$

$$\text{Change of Trim} = \frac{\text{Trimming Moment}}{MCTC}$$

$$= \frac{21.56}{4.32} = 5\,cm$$

$$\text{Change of Trim} = 5 \text{ cm by the stern}$$

$$= 0.05 \text{ m by the stern}$$

Drafts before Trimming	A	4.075 m	F	2.075 m
Change due to trim		+0.025 m		−0.025 m
New Drafts	A	4.100 m	F	2.050 m

In practice the trimming effects are so small that they are often ignored by shipboard personnel. Note in the above example the trim ratio forward and aft was only $2\frac{1}{2}$ cm.

However, for D.Tp. examinations, they must be studied and fully understood.

Exercise 37

1   A box-shaped vessel is 72 m long, 8 m wide and floats in salt water at drafts F 4.00 m. A 8.00 m. Find the new drafts if the vessel now passes into fresh water.

2   A box-shaped vessel is 36 m long, 5 m wide and floats in fresh water at drafts F 2.50 m. A 4.50 m. Find the new drafts if the vessel now passes into salt water.

3   A ship has a displacement of 9100 tonnes, LBP of 120 m, even-keel draft of 7 m in fresh water of density of 1.000 t/m^3.

   From her Hydrostatic Curves it was found that:

$$\text{MCTC}_{SW} \text{ is } 130 \text{ t m/cm}$$
$$\text{TPC}_{SW} \text{ is } 17.3 \text{ t}$$
$$\text{LCB is } 2 \text{ m forward } \text{\textcircled{Φ}} \text{ and}$$
$$\text{LCF is } 1.0 \text{ aft } \text{\textcircled{Φ}}.$$

Calculate the new end drafts when this vessel moves into water having a density of 1.02 t/m^3 without any change in the ship's displacement of 9100 tonnes.

Chapter 38
List with zero metacentric height

When a weight is shifted transversely in a ship with zero initial metacentric height, the resulting list can be found using the 'Wall sided' formula.

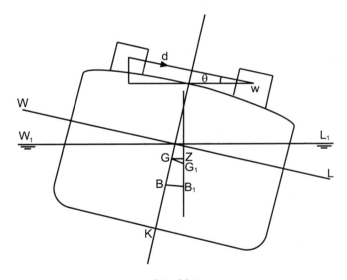

Fig. 38.1

The ship shown in Figure 38.1 has zero initial metacentric height. When a weight of mass 'w' is shifted transversely through a distance 'd', the ship's centre of gravity shifts from G to G_1 where the direction GG_1 is parallel to the shift of the centre of gravity of the weight shifted. The ship will then incline to bring the centres of gravity and buoyancy in the same vertical line.

The horizontal component of the shift of the ship's centre of gravity is equal to GZ and the horizontal component of the shift of the centre of gravity of the weight is equal to $d\cos\theta$.

$$\therefore\ w\times d\cdot\cos\theta = W\times GZ$$

The length GZ, although not a righting lever in this case can be found using the 'Wall-sided' formula.
  i.e.

$$GZ = (GM + \tfrac{1}{2}\cdot BM\cdot\tan^2\theta)\sin\theta$$

$$\therefore\ w\times d\cdot\cos\theta = W\cdot\sin\theta\,(GM + \tfrac{1}{2}\cdot BM\cdot\tan^2\theta)$$

If

$$GM = 0$$

Then

$$w\times d\cdot\cos\theta = W\cdot\sin\theta\cdot\tfrac{1}{2}\,BM\cdot\tan^2\theta$$

$$\frac{w\times d}{W} = \frac{\sin\theta}{\cos\theta}\cdot\tfrac{1}{2}\cdot BM\cdot\tan^2\theta$$

$$\frac{2\cdot w\cdot d}{BM\cdot W} = \tan^3\theta$$

or

$$\tan\theta = \sqrt[3]{\frac{2\cdot w\cdot d}{BM\cdot W}}$$

Example
A ship of 12 250 tonnes displacement, has KM = 8 m, KB = 3.8 m, KG = 8 m and is floating upright. Find the list if a weight of 2 tonnes, already on board, is shifted transversely through a horizontal distance of 12 m, assuming that the ship is wall-sided.

$$KM = \quad 8.0\,\text{m}$$
$$-$$
$$KB = \quad 3.8\,\text{m}$$
$$BM = \quad 4.2\,\text{m}$$

The ship has zero GM

$$\therefore\ \tan\text{list} = \sqrt[3]{\frac{2\cdot w\cdot d}{W\cdot BM}}$$

$$\tan\text{list} = \sqrt[3]{\frac{2\cdot 2\cdot 12}{12\,250\times 4.2}} = 0.0977$$

Ans. List = 5° 34′

Exercise 38

1 Find the list when a mass of 10 tonnes is shifted transversely through a horizontal distance of 14 m in a ship of 8000 tonnes displacement which has zero initial metacentric height. BM = 2 m.

2 A ship of 8000 tonnes displacement has zero initial metacentric height. BM = 4 m. Find the list if a weight of 20 tonnes is shifted transversely across the deck through a horizontal distance of 10 m.

3 A ship of 10 000 tonnes displacement is floating in water of density 1.025 kg/cu. m and has a zero initial metacentric height. Calculate the list when a mass of 15 tonnes is moved transversely across the deck through a horizontal distance of 18 m. The second moment of the waterplane area about the centre line is 10^5 m^4.

4 A ship of 12 250 tonnes displacement is floating upright. KB = 3.8 m, KM = 8 m and KG = 8 m. Assuming that the ship is wall-sided, find the list if a mass of 2 tonnes, already on board, is shifted transversely through a horizontal distance of 12 m.

Chapter 39
The Trim and Stability book

When a new ship is nearing completion, a Trim and Stability book is produced by the shipbuilder and presented to the shipowner. Shipboard officers will use this for the day to day operation of the vessel. In the Trim and Stability book is the following technical data:

1 General particulars of the ship.
2 Inclining experiment report and its results.
3 Capacity, VCG, LCG particulars for all holds, compartments, tanks etc.
4 Cross curves of stability. These may be GZ curves or KN curves.
5 Deadweight scale data. May be in diagram form or in tabular form.
6 Hydrostatic curves. May be in graphical form or in tabular form.
7 Example conditions of loading such as:

    Lightweight (empty vessel) condition.
    Full-loaded Departure and Arrival conditions.
    Heavy-ballast Departure and Arrival conditions.
    Medium-ballast Departure and Arrival conditions.
    Light-ballast Departure and Arrival conditions.

On each condition of loading there is a profile and plan view (at upper deck level usually). A colour scheme is adopted for each item of deadweight. Examples could be red for cargo, blue for fresh water, green for water ballast, brown for oil. Hatched lines for this Dwt distribution signify wing tanks P and S.

For each loaded condition, in the interests of safety, it is necessary to show:

Deadweight.
End draughts, thereby signifying a satisfactory and safe trim situation.
KG with no Free Surface Effects (FSE), and KG with FSE taken into account.

Final transverse metacentric height (GM). This informs the officer if the ship is in stable, unstable or neutral equilibrium. It can also indicate if the ship's stability is approaching a dangerous state.

Total Free Surface Effects of all slack tanks in this condition of loading.

A statical stability curve relevant to the actual loaded condition with the important characteristics clearly indicated. For each S/S curve it is important to observe the following:

Maximum GZ and the angle of heel at which it occurs.

Range of stability.

Area enclosed from zero degrees to thirty degrees (A1) and the area enclosed from thirty degrees to forty degrees (A2) as shown in Figure 39.1.

Shear force and bending moment curves, with upper limit lines clearly superimposed as shown in Figure 39.2.

8 Metric equivalents. For example, TPI″ to TPC, MCTI″ to MCTC, or tons to tonnes.

All of this information is sent to a D.Tp. surveyor for appraisal. On many ships today this data is part of a computer package. The deadweight items are keyed in by the officer prior to any weights actually being moved. The computer screen will then indicate if the prescribed condition of loading is indeed safe from the point of view of stability and strength.

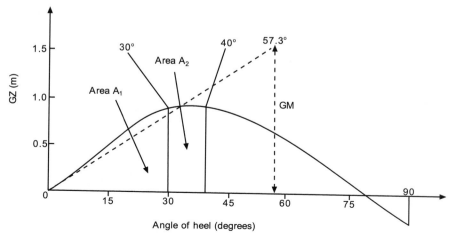

Fig. 39.1.   Enclosed areas on a statical stability curve.

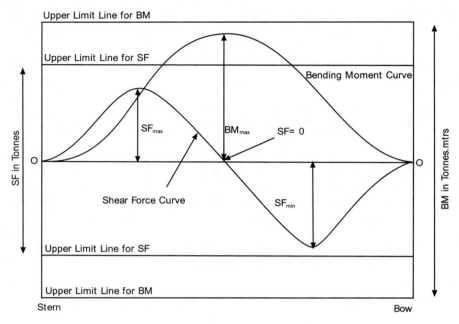

Fig. 39.2.   SF and BM curves with upper limit lines.

Chapter 40
Bending of beams

Beam theory

The bending of ships can be likened to the bending of beams in many cases. This chapter shows the procedures employed with beam theory.

The problem of calculating the necessary strength of ships is made difficult by the many and varied forces to which the ship structure is subjected during its lifetime. These forces may be divided into two groups, namely statical forces and dynamical forces.

The statical forces are due to:

1 The weight of the structure which varies throughout the length of the ship.
2 Buoyancy forces, which vary over each unit length of the ship and are constantly varying in a seaway.
3 Direct hydrostatic pressure.
4 Concentrated local weights such as machinery, masts, derricks, winches, etc.

The dynamical forces are due to:

1 Pitching, heaving and rolling,
2 Wind and waves.

These forces cause bending in several planes and local strains are set up due to concentrated loads. The effects are aggravated by structural discontinuities.

The purpose of the present chapter is to consider the cause of longitudinal bending and its effect upon structures.

Stresses

A stress is the mutual actual between the parts of a material to preserve their relative positions when external loads are applied to the material.

Thus, whenever external loads are applied to a material stresses are created within the material.

Tensile and compressive stresses
When an external load is applied to a material in such a way as to cause an extension of the material it is called a 'tensile' load, whilst an external load tending to cause compression of the material is a 'compressive' load.

Figure 40.1 shows a piece of solid material of cylindrical section to which an external load W is applied. In the first case the load tends to cause an extension of the material and is therefore a tensile load. The applied load creates stresses within the material and these stresses are called 'tensile' stresses. In the second case the load applied is one of compression and the consequent stresses within the material are called 'compressive' stresses.

When a tensile or compressive external load is applied to a material the material will remain in equilibrium only so long as the internal forces can resist the stresses created.

Shearing stresses
A shearing stress is a stress within a material which tends to break or shear the material across.

Figure 40.2(a) and 40.2(b) illustrate shearing stresses which act normally to the axis of the material.

In the following text when the direction of a shearing stress is such that

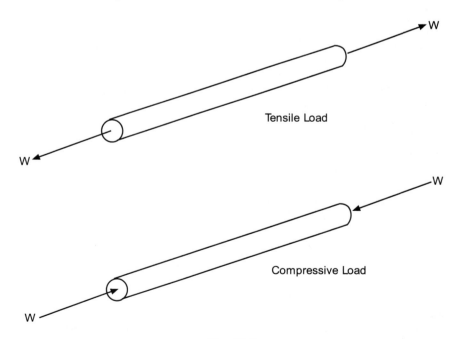

Fig. 40.1

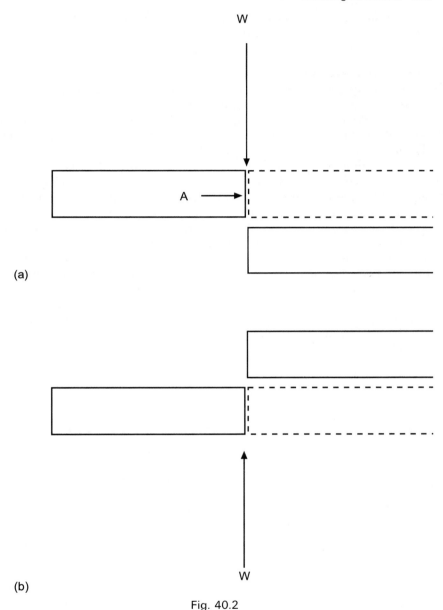

Fig. 40.2

the section on the right-hand side of the material tends to move downwards, as shown in Figure 40.2(a), the stress is considered to be positive, and when the direction of a stress is such that the section on the right-hand side tends to move upwards as shown in Figure 40.2(b), the shearing stress is considered to be negative.

Shearing stresses are resisted by the material but shearing will take place when the shear stress reaches the ultimate shear stress of the material.

Complementary stress

It has already been stated that when a direct load is applied to a material stresses are created within the material and that the material will remain in equilibrium only so long as the internal forces can resist the stresses created.

Let the bar in Figure 40.3(a) be subjected to tensile load W and imagine the bar to be divided into two parts at section AB.

For equilibrium, the force W on the left-hand side of the bar is balanced by an equal force acting to the right at section AB. The balancing force is supplied by the individual molecular forces which represent the action of the molecules on the right-hand side of the section on those of the left-hand section. Similarly, the force W on the right-hand side of the bar is balanced by the individual molecular forces to the left of the section. Therefore, when an external load W is applied to the bar, at any section normal to the axis of the bar, there are equal and opposite internal forces acting, each of which balances the external force W. The magnitude of the internal forces per unit area of cross-section is called the stress. When the section is well removed from the point of application of the external load then the stress may be considered constant at all parts of the section and may be found by the formula:

$$\text{Stress (f)} = \frac{\text{Load (W)}}{\text{Area (A)}} \quad \therefore f = \frac{W}{A}$$

Let us now consider the stresses created by the external load W in a section which is inclined to the axis of the bar. For example, let section CD in Figure 40.3(b) be inclined at an angle θ to the normal to the axis of the bar and let the section be sufficiently removed from the point of application of the load to give uniform stress across the section.

The load transmitted by the section CD, for equilibrium, is equal to the external force W. This load can be resolved into two components, one of which is $W \cdot \cos \theta$ and acts normal to the section, and the other is $W \cdot \sin \theta$ and acts tangential to the section. This shows that for direct tensile or compressive loading of the bar stresses other than normal stresses may be created.

Now let us consider the small block of material abcd in the section on the left-hand side of the plane, as shown in Figure 40.3(c). Let the face ab be coincident with the plane CD and let F_N be the internal force normal to this face and F_T the internal force tangential to the face. For the block to be in equilibrium the left-hand side of the section must provide two stresses on the face cd. These are F_N and F_T. Thus the stress F_N normal to the face ab is balanced by the stress F_N normal to the face cd whilst the two tangential stresses (F_T) on these faces tend to produce clockwise rotation in the block. Rotation can only be prevented if an equal and opposite couple is produced

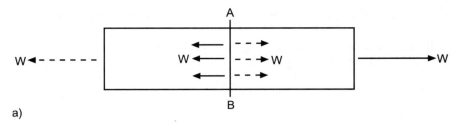

a)

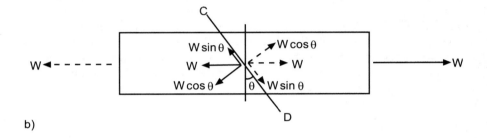

b)

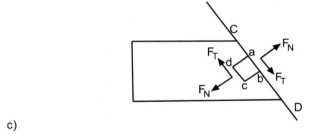

c)

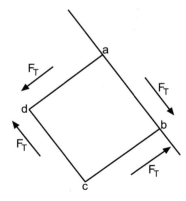

d)

Fig. 40.3

by opposing shearing stresses on the faces ad and bc as shown in Figure 40.3(d).

It can therefore be seen that when shear stresses occur at any plane within a material, equal shear stresses are produced on planes at right angles. These equal and opposing shearing stresses are called 'Complementary' shearing stresses.

Bending moments in beams

The shear forces and bending moments created within a beam depend upon both the way in which the beam is supported and the way in which it is loaded. The bending moment at any section within the beam is the total moment tending to alter the shape of the beam as shown in Figures 40.4 and 40.5 and is equal to the algebraic sum of the moments of all loads acting between the section concerned and either end of the beam.

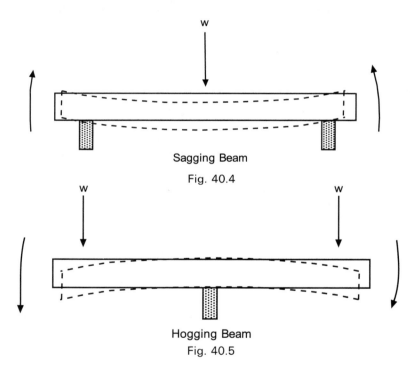

Sagging Beam

Fig. 40.4

Hogging Beam

Fig. 40.5

In the following text, when a bending moment tends to cause sagging or downwards bending of the beam as shown in Figure 40.4 it is considered to be a negative bending moment and when it tends to cause hogging or convex upwards bending of the beam, as shown in Figure 40.5, it is considered to be positive. Also, when bending moments are plotted on a graph, positive bending moments are measured below the beam and negative bending moments above.

Shear Force and Bending Moment Diagrams

The shear forces and bending moments created in a beam which is supported and loaded in a particular way can be illustrated graphically.

Consider first the case of cantilevers which are supported at one end only.

Case I

The beam AB in Figure 40.6 is fixed at one end only and carries a weight 'W' at the other end.

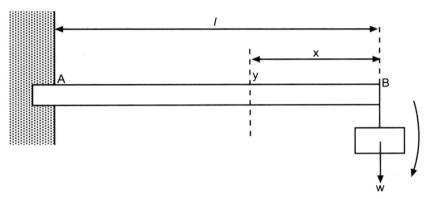

Fig. 40.6

If the weight of the beam is ignored then at any point Y in the beam, which is at distance X from the end B, there is a positive shearing force W and a positive bending moment W × X. There is thus a positive shearing force W at all sections throughout the length of the beam. This is shown graphically in Figure 40.7 where AB represents the length of the beam (*l*), and the ordinate AC, which represents the shearing force at A, is equal to the ordinate BD which represents the shearing force at B.

The bending moment at any section of the beam is the algebraic sum of the moments of forces acting on either side of the section. In the present case, the only force to consider is W which acts downwards through the end B. Thus the bending moment at B is zero and from B towards A the bending moment increases, varying directly as the distance from the end B. The maximum bending moment, which occurs at A, is equal to W × *l*. This is shown graphically in Figure 40.7 by the straight line BGE.

The shearing force and bending moment at any point in the length of the beam can be found from the graph by inspection. For example, at Y the shearing force is represented by the ordinate YF and the bending moment by the ordinate YG.

It should be noted that the bending moment at any point in the beam is equal to the area under the shearing force diagram from the end of the beam to that point. For example, in Figure 40.7, the bending moment at Y is

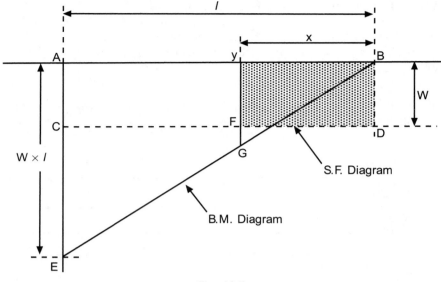

Fig. 40.7

equal to $W \times X$ and this, in turn, is equal to the area under the shearing force diagram between the ordinates BD and YF.

Case II
Now consider a solid beam of constant cross-section which is supported at one end as shown in Figure 40.8. Let w be the weight per unit length of the beam.

At any section Y in the beam, which is at distance 'X' from B, there is a positive shearing force wX where wX is the weight of the beam up to that section and, since the weight wX may be taken to act half-way along the length X, there is a bending moment $wX \times X/2$ or $\dfrac{wX^2}{2}$.

This is shown graphically in Figure 40.9, where AB represents the length of the beam (l).

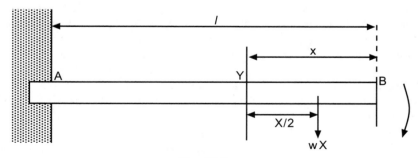

Fig. 40.8

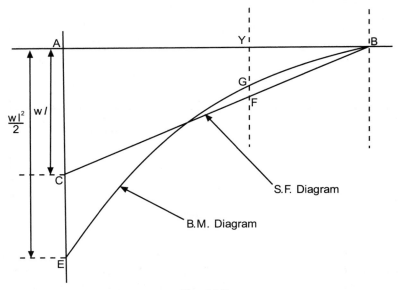

Fig. 40.9

The shearing force at B is zero and then increases towards A, varying directly as X, to reach its maximum value at A of wl. This is represented in Figure 40.9 by the straight line BFC.

The bending moment at any point in the beam is equal to $wX^2/2$. It is therefore zero at B and then increases towards A, varying directly as X^2, to reach its maximum value of $wl^2/2$ at A. The curve of bending moments is therefore a parabola and is shown in Figure 40.9 by the curve BGE.

Since the bending moment at any section is equal to the area under the shearing force diagram from the end of the beam to that section, it follows that the bending moment curve may be drawn by first calculating the area under the shearing force diagram from the end of the beam to various points along it and then plotting these values as ordinates of the curve. For example, at section Y in Figure 40.9 the ordinate YF represents the shearing force at this section (wX), and the area under the shearing force diagram between B and the ordinate FY is equal to $\frac{1}{2} \times wX \times X$ or $wX^2/2$. The ordinate YG could now be drawn to scale to represent this value.

Freely supported beams

Case I
Consider now a beam which is simply supported at its ends, and loaded in the middle as shown in Figure 40.10. In this figure AB represents the length of the beam (l), and W represents the load. If the weight of the beam is neglected then the reaction at each support is equal to $W/2$, denoted by R_A and R_B.

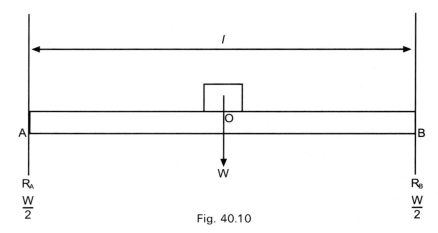

Fig. 40.10

To plot the shearing force diagram first draw two axes of reference as shown in Figure 40.11 with AB representing the length of the beam (l).

Now cover Figure 40.10 with the right hand, fingers pointing to the left, and slowly draw the hand to the right gradually uncovering the figure. At A there is a negative shearing force of $W/2$ and this is plotted to scale on the graph by the ordinate AC. The shearing force is then constant along the beam to its mid-point O. As the hand is drawn to the right, O is uncovered

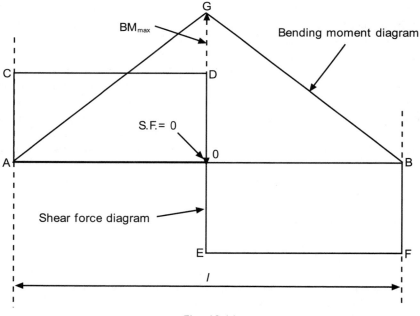

Fig. 40.11

and a force W downwards appears. This must be considered in addition to the force W/2 upwards at A. The resultant is a shearing force of W/2 downwards and this force is then constant from O to B as shown in Figure 40.11 by the straight line EF.

The bending moment diagram can now be drawn in the same way or by first calculating the area under the shearing force diagram between the ordinate AC and various points along the beam and then plotting these values as ordinates on the bending moment diagram. It will be seen that the bending moment is zero at the ends and attains its maximum value at the mid-point in the beam indicated by the ordinate OG. Note BM_{max} occurs when $SF = 0$.

Case II

Now consider a beam of constant cross-sectional area, of length l, and weight w per unit length. Let the beam be simply supported at its ends as shown in Figure 40.12, at reactions R_A and R_B.

The total weight of the beam is wl. The reaction at each end is equal to $wl/2$, half of the weight of the beam.

The shearing force and bending moment diagrams can now be drawn as in the previous example. In Figure 40.12, let AB represent the length of the beam (l) drawn to scale. At A the shearing force is $wl/2$ upwards and this is shown on the graph by the ordinate AC. Because the weight of the beam is evenly distributed throughout its length, the shearing force decreases uniformly from A towards B.

At the mid-point (O) of the beam there is a shearing force of $wl/2$ downwards (half the weight of the beam) and one of $wl/2$ upwards (the reaction at A) to consider. The resultant shearing force at O is therefore zero. Finally, at B, there is a shearing force of wl downwards (the weight of the beam) and $wl/2$ upwards (the reaction at A) to consider, giving a resultant shearing force of $wl/2$ downwards which is represented on the graph by the ordinate BD.

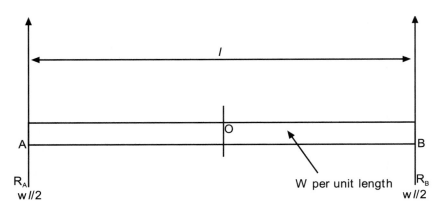

Fig. 40.12

The bending moment diagram can now be drawn in the same way or by first calculating the area under the shearing force diagram between the ordinate AC and other sections along the beam and then plotting these values as ordinates on the bending moment diagram. The bending moment diagram is represented in Figure 40.13 by the curve AEB.

It should be noted that the shearing force at any point Y which is at a distance X from the end A is given by the formula:

$$\text{Shearing force} = \frac{wl}{2} - wX$$

$$= w\left(\frac{l}{2} - X\right)$$

Also, the bending moment at Y is given by the formula:

$$\text{Bending moment} = \frac{wlX}{2} - \frac{wX^2}{2}$$

$$= \frac{wX}{2}(l - X)$$

The maximum bending moment occurs at the mid-point of the beam. Using the above formula:

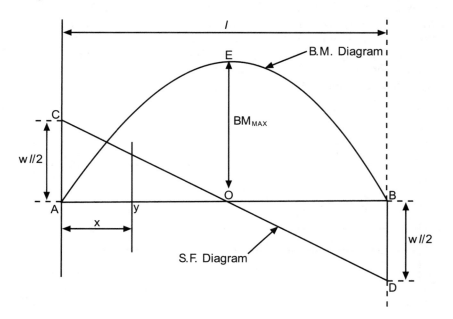

Fig. 40.13

$$\text{Bending moment} = \frac{wX}{2}(l - X)$$

$$\text{Maximum BM} = \frac{wl}{4}\left(l - \frac{1}{2}\right)$$

$$\therefore \text{BM}_{max} = \frac{wl^2}{8}$$

Also, the area of the shearing force diagram between the ordinate AC and O is equal to $\frac{1}{2} \times \frac{l}{2} \times \frac{wl}{2}$ or $\frac{wl^2}{8}$.

These principles can now be applied to find the shearing forces and bending moments for any simply supported beam.

Note again how BM_{max} occurs at point 'O', the point at which $\text{SF} = 0$. This must be so for equilibrium or balance of forces to exist.

Example

A uniform beam is 16 m long and has a mass of 10 kg per metre run. The beam is supported on two knife edges, each positioned 3 m from the end of the beam. Sketch the shearing force and bending moment diagrams and state where the bending moment is zero.

$$\text{Mass per metre run} = 10 \, \text{kg}$$

$$\text{Total Mass of beam} = 160 \, \text{kg}$$

$$\text{The Reaction at C} = \text{The Reaction at B}$$

$$= 80 \, \text{kg}$$

$$\text{The Shear force at A} = O$$

$$\text{The Shear force at L.H. side of B} = +30 \, \text{kg}$$

$$\text{The Shear force at R.H. side of B} = -50 \, \text{kg}$$

$$\text{The Shear force at O} = O$$

$$\text{Bending moment at A} = O$$

$$\text{Bending moment at 1 m from A} = 1 \times 10 \times \tfrac{1}{2}$$

$$= 5 \, \text{kg m (negative)}$$

$$\text{Bending moment at 2 m from A} = 2 \times 10 \times 1$$

$$= 20 \, \text{kg m (negative)}$$

$$\text{Bending moment at 3 m from A} = 3 \times 10 \times 1\tfrac{1}{2}$$

$$= 45 \, \text{kg m (negative)}$$

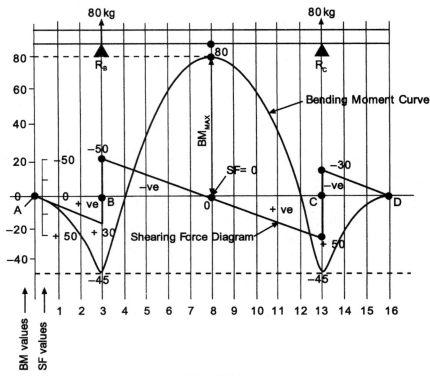

Fig. 40.14

Bending moment at 4 m from A = 4 × 10 × 2 − 80 × 1

$$= 0$$

Bending moment at 5 m from A = 5 × 10 × $\frac{5}{2}$ − 80 × 2

$$= 35 \text{ kg m (positive)}$$

Bending moment at 6 m from A = 6 × 10 × 3 − 80 × 3

$$= 60 \text{ kg m (positive)}$$

Bending moment at 7 m from A = 7 × 10 × $\frac{7}{2}$ − 80 × 4

$$= 75 \text{ kg m (positive)}$$

Bending moment at 8 m from A = 8 × 10 × 4 − 80 × 5

$$= 80 \text{ kg m (positive)}$$

Ans. Bending moment = 0 at 4 m from each end, and at each end of the beam

The results of the above investigation into the shearing forces and consequent bending moments in simply supported beams will now be applied to find the longitudinal shearing forces and bending moments in floating vessels. Sufficient accuracy of prediction can be obtained.

However, beam theory such as this cannot be used for supertankers and ULCCs. For these very large vessels it is better to use what is known as the finite element theory. This is beyond the remit of this book.

EXERCISE 40

1 A beam AB of length 10 m is supported at each end and carries a load which increases uniformly from zero at A to 0.75 tonnes per metre run at B. Find the position and magnitude of the maximum bending moment.

2 A beam 15 m long is supported at its ends and carries two point loads. One of 5 tonnes mass is situated 6 m from one end and the other of 7 tonnes mass is 4 m from the other end. If the mass of the beam is neglected, sketch the curves of shearing force and bending moments. Also find (a), The maximum bending moment and where it occurs, and (b), The bending moment and shearing force at $\frac{1}{3}$ of the length of the beam from each end.

Chapter 41
Bending of ships

Longitudinal stresses in still water

First consider the case of a homogeneous log of rectangular section floating freely at rest in still water as shown in Figure 41.1.

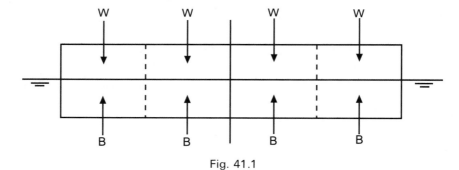

Fig. 41.1

The total weight of the log is balanced by the total force of buoyancy and the weight (W) of any section of the log is balanced by the force of buoyancy (B) provided by that section. There is therefore no bending moment longitudinally which would cause stresses to be set up in the log.

Now consider the case of a ship floating at rest in still water, on an even keel, at the light draft as shown in Figure 41.2

Although the total weight of the ship is balanced by the total force of buoyancy, neither is uniformly distributed throughout the ship's length. Imagine the ship to be cut as shown by a number of transverse sections. Imagine, too, that each section is watertight and is free to move in a vertical direction until it displaces its own weight of water. The weight of each of the end sections (1 and 5) exceeds the buoyancy which they provide and these sections will therefore sink deeper into the water until equilibrium is reached at which time each will be displacing its own weight of water. If

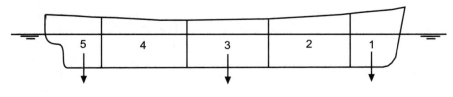

Fig. 41.2

sections 2 and 4 represent the hold sections, these are empty and they therefore provide an excess of buoyancy over weight and will rise to displace their own weight of water. If section 3 represents the engine room then, although a considerable amount of buoyancy is provided by the section, the weight of the engines and other apparatus in the engine room, may exceed the buoyancy and this section will sink deeper into the water. The nett result would be as shown in Figure 41.3 where each of the sections is displacing its own weight of water.

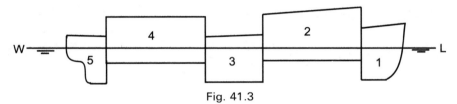

Fig. 41.3

Although the sections in the ship are not free to move in this way, bending moments, and consequently longitudinal stresses, are created by the variation in the longitudinal distribution of weight and buoyancy and these must be allowed for in the construction of the ship.

Longitudinal stresses in waves

When a ship encounters waves at sea the stresses created differ greatly from those created in still water. The maximum stresses are considered to exist when the wave length is equal to the ship's length and either a wave crest or trough is situated amidships.

Consider first the effect when the ship is supported by a wave having its crest amidships and its troughs at the bow and the stern, as shown in Figure 41.4.

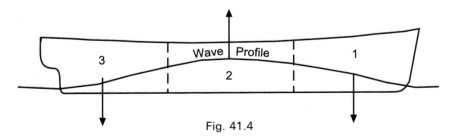

Fig. 41.4

In this case, although once more the total weight of the ship is balanced by the total buoyancy, there is an excess of buoyancy over the weight amidships and an excess of weight over buoyancy at the bow and the stern. This situation creates a tendency for the ends of the ship to move downwards and the section amidships to move upwards as shown in Figure 41.5.

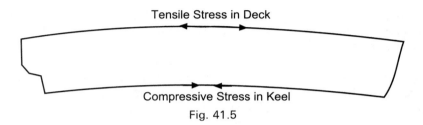

Fig. 41.5

Under these conditions the ship is said to be subjected to a 'Hogging' stress.

A similar stress can be produced in a beam by simply supporting it at its mid-point and loading each end as shown in Figure 41.6.

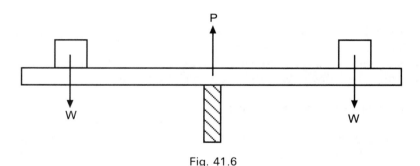

Fig. 41.6

Consider the effect after the wave crest has moved onwards and the ship is now supported by wave crests at the bow and the stern and a trough amidships as shown in Figure 41.7.

There is now an excess of buoyancy over weight at the ends and an excess of weight over buoyancy amidships. The situation creates a tendency for the bow and the stern to move upwards and the section amidships to move downwards as shown in Figure 41.8.

Under these conditions a ship is said to be subjected to a sagging stress. A stress similar to this can be produced in a beam when it is simply supported at its ends and is loaded at the mid-length as shown in Figure 41.9.

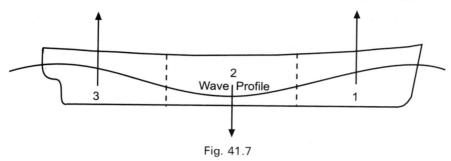

Fig. 41.7

Compressive Stress in Deck

Tensile Stress in Keel

Fig. 41.8

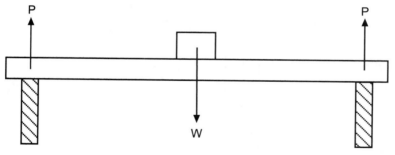

Fig. 41.9

Weight, buoyancy and load diagrams

It has already been shown that the total weight of a ship is balanced by the total buoyancy and that neither the weight nor the buoyancy is evenly distributed throughout the length of the ship.

In still water, the uneven loading which occurs throughout the length of a ship varies considerably with different conditions of loading and leads to longitudinal bending moments which may reach very high values. Care is therefore necessary when loading or ballasting a ship to keep these values within acceptable limits.

In waves, additional bending moments are created, these being brought about by the uneven distribution of buoyancy. The maximum bending moment due to this cause is considered to be created when the ship is moving head-on to waves whose length is the same as that of the ship, and when there is either a wave crest or trough situated amidships.

To calculate the bending moments and consequent shearing stresses created in a ship subjected to longitudinal bending it is first necessary to construct diagrams showing the longitudinal distribution of weight and buoyancy.

The weight diagram

A weight diagram shows the longitudinal distribution of weight. It can be constructed by first drawing a base line to represent the length of the ship, and then dividing the base line into a number of sections by equally spaced ordinates as shown in Figure 41.10. The weight of the ship between each pair of ordinates is then calculated and plotted on the diagram. In the case considered it is assumed that the weight is evenly distributed between successive ordinates but is of varying magnitude.

Let

$$CSA = Cross\ Sectional\ Area$$

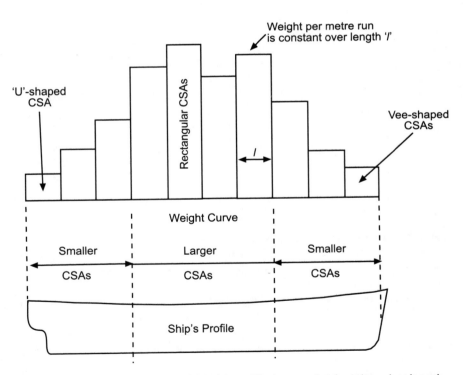

Fig. 41.10.   Shows the ship divided into 10 elemental strips along her length LOA. In practice the Naval Architect may split the ship into 40 elemental strips in order to obtain greater accuracy of prediction for the weight distribution.

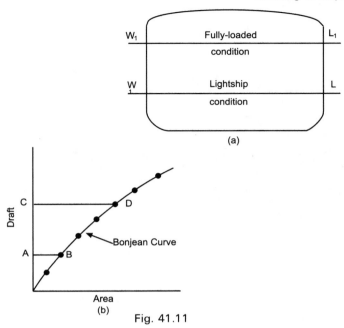

(a)

(b)

Fig. 41.11

Bonjean Curves

Bonjean Curves are drawn to give the immersed area of transverse sections to any draft and may be used to determine the longitudinal distribution of buoyancy. For example, Figure 41.11(a) shows a transverse section of a ship and Figure 41.11(b) shows the Bonjean Curve for the same section. The immersed area to the waterline WL is represented on the Bonjean Curve by ordinate AB, and the immersed area to waterline W_1L_1 is represented by ordinate CD.

In Figure 41.12 the Bonjean Curves are shown for each section throughout the length of the ship. If a wave formation is superimposed on the Bonjean Curves and adjusted until the total buoyancy is equal to the total weight of the ship, the immersed transverse area at each section can then be found by inspection and the buoyancy in tonnes per metre run is equal to the immersed area multiplied by 1.025.

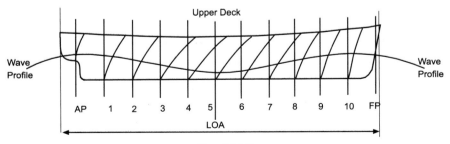

Fig. 41.12

Chapter 42
Strength curves for ships

Strength curves consist of five curves that are closely inter-related. The curves are:

1 Weight curve – tonnes/m run or kg/m run.
2 Buoyancy curve – either for hogging or sagging condition – tonnes/m or kg/m run.
3 Load curve – tonnes/m run or kg/m run.
4 Shear force curve – tonnes or kg.
5 Bending moment curve – tonnes m or kg m.

Some forms use units of MN/m run, MN and MN. m.

Buoyancy curves

A buoyancy curve shows the longitudinal distribution of buoyancy and can be constructed for any wave formation using the Bonjean Curves in the manner previously described in Chapter 41. In Figure 42.1 the buoyancy

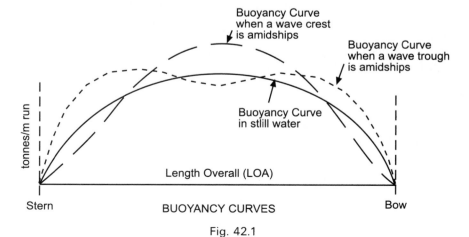

BUOYANCY CURVES

Fig. 42.1

curves for a ship are shown for the still water condition and for the conditions of maximum hogging and sagging. It should be noted that the total area under each curve is the same, i.e. the total buoyancy is the same. Units usually tonnes/m run along the length of the ship.

Load curves
A load curve shows the difference between the weight ordinate and buoyancy ordinate of each section throughout the length of the ship. The curve is drawn as a series of rectangles, the heights of which are obtained by drawing the buoyancy curve (as shown in Figure 42.1) parallel to the weight curve (as shown in Figure 41.10) at the mid-ordinate of a section and measuring the difference between the two curves. Thus the load is considered to be constant over the length of each section. An excess of weight over buoyancy is considered to produce a positive load whilst an excess of buoyancy over weight is considered to produce a negative load. Units are tonnes/m run longitudinally.

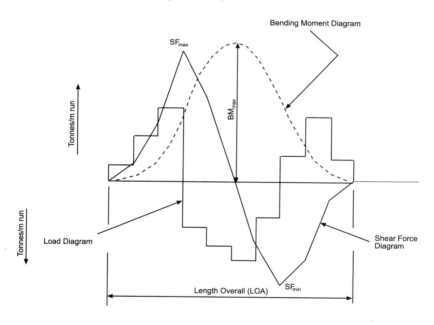

Fig. 42.2.   Showing three ship strength curves for a ship in still water conditions

Shear forces and bending moments of ships
The shear force and bending moment at any section in a ship may be determined from load curve. It has already been shown that the shearing force at any section in a girder is the algebraic sum of the loads acting on either side of the section and that the bending moment acting at any section of the girder is the algebraic sum of the moments acting on either

side of the section. It has also been shown that the shearing force at any section is equal to the area under the load curve from one end to the section concerned and that the bending moment at that section is equal to the area under the shearing force curve measured from the same end to that section.

Thus, for the mathematically minded, the shear force curve is the first-order integral curve of the load curve and the bending moment curve is the first-order integral curve of the shearing force curve. Therefore, the bending moment curve is the second-order integral curve of the load curve.

Figure 42.2 shows typical curves of load, shearing force and bending moments for a ship in still water.

After the still water curves have been drawn for a ship, the changes in the distribution of the buoyancy to allow for the conditions of hogging and sagging can be determined and so the resultant shearing force and bending moment curves may be found for the ship in waves.

Example

A box-shaped barge of uniform construction is 32 m long and displaces 352 tonnes when empty, is divided by transverse bulkheads into four equal compartments. Cargo is loaded into each compartment and level stowed as follows:

No. 1 hold − 192 tonnes   No. 2 hold − 224 tonnes

No. 3 hold − 272 tonnes   No. 4 hold − 176 tonnes

Construct load and shearing force diagrams, before calculating the bending moments at the bulkheads and at the position of maximum value; hence draw the bending moment diagram.

$$\text{Mass of barge per metre run} = \frac{\text{Mass of barge}}{\text{Length of barge}}$$

$$= \frac{352}{32}$$

$$= 11 \text{ tonnes per metre run}$$

$$\text{mass of barge when empty} = 352 \text{ tonnes}$$

$$\text{Cargo} = 192 + 224 + 272 + 176$$

$$= 864 \text{ tonnes}$$

$$\text{Total mass of barge and cargo} = 352 + 864$$

$$= 1216 \text{ tonnes}$$

$$\text{Buoyancy per metre run} = \frac{\text{Total buoyancy}}{\text{Length of barge}}$$

$$= \frac{1216}{32}$$

$$= 38 \text{ tonnes per metre run}$$

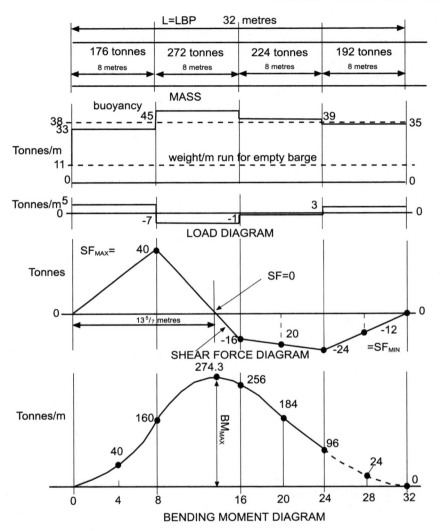

Fig. 42.3

From Figure 42.3.

Bending moments along the barge's length

$$BM_8 = \frac{8 \times 40}{2} = 160 \, t\,m$$

$$= \underline{160 \, tonnes\,m}$$

$$BM_0 = 0 \, t\,m$$

$$BM_4 = \frac{20 \times 4}{2} = 40 \, t\,m$$

$$BM_8 = \frac{8 \times 40}{2} = 160\,t\,m$$

$$BM_{13\frac{5}{7}} = \frac{13\frac{5}{7} \times 40}{2} = 274.3\,t\,m$$

$$BM_{16} = \left(\frac{13\frac{5}{7} \times 40}{2}\right) - \left(\frac{2\frac{2}{7} \times 16}{2}\right) = 256\,t\,m$$

$$BM_{20} = 256 - \left(\frac{16 + 20}{2}\right) \cdot 4 = 184\,t\,m$$

$$BM_{24} = 184 - \left(\frac{20 + 24}{2}\right) \cdot 4 = 96\,t\,m$$

$$BM_{28} = 96 - \left(\frac{24 + 12}{2}\right) \cdot 4 = 24\,t\,m$$

$$BM_{32} = 24 - \left(\frac{12 \times 4}{2}\right) = 0\,t\,m$$

Murray's Method

Murray's Method is used to find the total longitudinal bending moment amidships on a ship in waves and is based on the division of the total bending moment into two parts:

(a) the Still Water Bending Moment, and
(b) the wave bending moment.

The Still Water Bending Moment is the longitudinal bending moment amidships when the ship is floating in still water.

When using Murray's Method the wave bending moment amidships is that produced by the waves when the ship is supported on what is called a 'Standard Wave'. A Standard Wave is one whose length is equal to the length of the ship (L), and whose height is equal to $0.607 \sqrt{L}$, where L is measured in metres. See Figure 42.4.

The Wave Bending Moment is then found using the formula:

$$WBM = b \cdot B \cdot L^{2.5} \times 10^{-3}\ \text{tonnes metres}$$

where B is the beam of the ship in metres and b is a constant based on the ship's block coefficient (C_b) and on whether the ship is hogging or sagging. The value of b can be obtained from the table on page 351.

The Still Water Bending Moment (SWBM)

Let

W_F represent the moment of the weight forward of amidships,

B_F represent the moment of buoyancy forward of amidships,

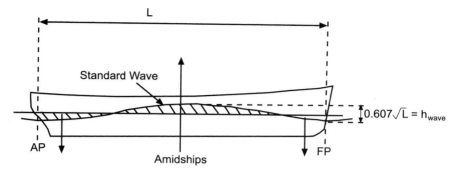

Fig. 42.4

Murray's coefficient 'b' values

C_b	Values of b	
	Hogging	Sagging
0.80	10.555	11.821
0.78	10.238	11.505
0.76	9.943	11.188
0.74	9.647	10.850
0.72	9.329	10.513
0.70	9.014	10.175
0.68	8.716	9.858
0.66	8.402	9.541
0.64	8.106	9.204
0.62	7.790	8.887
0.60	7.494	8.571

Let

W_A represent the moment of the weight aft of amidships,
B_A represent the moment of the buoyancy aft of amidships, and
W represent the ship's displacement,

then:

$$\text{Still Water Bending Moment (SWBM)} = W_F - B_F$$

$$= W_A - B_A$$

This equation can be accurately evaluated by resolving in detail the many constituent parts, but Murray's Method may be used to give an approximate solution with sufficient accuracy for practical purposes.

The following approximations are then used:

$$\text{Mean Weight Moment } (M_W) = \frac{W_F + W_A}{2}$$

This moment is calculated using the full particulars of the ship in its loaded condition.

$$\text{Mean Buoyancy Moment } (M_B) = \frac{W}{2} \times \text{Mean LCB of fore and aft bodies}$$

An analysis of a large number of ships has shown that the Mean LCB of the fore and aft bodies for a trim not exceeding 0.01 L can be found using the formula:

$$\text{Mean LCB} = L \times C$$

where L is the length of the ship in metres, and the value of C can be found from the following table in terms of the block coefficient (C_b) for the ship at a draft of 0.06 L.

Murray's coefficient 'C' values	
Draft	*C*
0.06 L	$0.179C_b + 0.063$
0.05 L	$0.189C_b + 0.052$
0.04 L	$0.199C_b + 0.041$
0.03 L	$0.209C_b + 0.030$

The Still Water Bending Moment Amidships (SWBM) is then given by the formula:

$$\text{SWBM} = \text{Mean Weight Moment } (M_W)$$

$$- \text{Mean Buoyancy Moment } (M_B)$$

or

$$\text{SWBM} = \frac{W_F + W_A}{2} - \frac{W}{2} \cdot L \cdot C$$

where the value of C is found from the table above.

If the Mean Weight Moment is greater than the Mean Buoyancy Moment then the ship will be hogged, but if the Mean Buoyancy Moment exceeds the Mean Weight Moment then the ship will sag. So

(i) If $M_W > M_B$ · · · · · · · · ship hogs. $\left.\begin{array}{l}\end{array}\right\} M_W \wr M_B$
(ii) If $M_B > M_W$ · · · · · · · · ship sags.

The Wave Bending Moment (WBM)

The actual wave bending moment depends upon the height and the length of the wave and the beam of the ship. If a ship is supported on a Standard

Wave, as defined above, then the Wave Bending Moment (WBM) can be calculated using the formula:

$$WBM = b \cdot B \cdot L^{2.5} \times 10^{-3} \text{ tonnes metres}$$

where B is the beam of the ship and where the value of b is found from the table on page 351.

Example

The length LBP of a ship is 200 m, the beam is 30 m and the block coefficient is 0.750. The hull weight is 5000 tonnes having LCG 25.5 m from amidships. The mean LCB of the fore and after bodies is 25 m from amidships. Values of the constant b are: hogging 9.795 and sagging 11.02.

Given the following data and using Murray's Method, calculate the longitudinal bending moments amidships for the ship on a standard wave with: (a) the crest amidships, and (b) the trough amidships. Use Figure 42.5 to obtain solution.

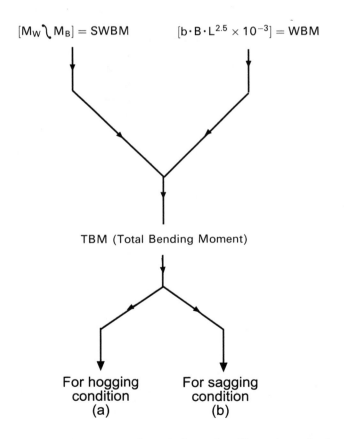

Fig. 42.5.   Line diagram for solution using Murray's method.

Data

Item	Weight	LCG from amidships
No. 1 hold	1800 t	55.0 m aft
No. 2 hold	3200 t	25.5 m forward
No. 3 hold	1200 t	5.5 m forward
No. 4 hold	2200 t	24.0 m aft
No. 5 hold	1500 t	50.0 m aft
Machinery	1500 t	7.5 m aft
Fuel oil	400 t	8.0 m aft
Fresh water	150 t	10.0 m forward

Item	Weight	LCG from amidships	Moment
No. 1 hold	1800	55.0 m forward	99 000
No. 2 hold	3200	25.5 m forward	81 600
No. 3 hold	1200	5.5 m forward	6 600
No. 4 hold	2200	24.0 m aft	52 800
No. 5 hold	1500	50.0 m aft	75 000
Machinery	1500	7.5 m aft	11 250
Fuel oil	400	8.0 m aft	3200
Fresh water	150	10.0 m forward	1500
Hull	5000	25.5 m	127 500
	16 950		458 450

To find the Still Water Bending Moment (SWBM)

$$\text{Mean Weight Moment } (M_W) = \frac{W_F + W_A}{2}$$

$$= \frac{458\,450}{2}$$

$$M_W = 229\,225\,\text{t m}$$

$$\text{Mean Buoyancy Moment } (M_B) = \frac{W}{2} \cdot \text{LCB} = \frac{16\,950}{2} \cdot 25$$

$$= 211\,875\,\text{t m}$$

$$\text{Still Water Bending Moment (SWBM)} = M_W - M_B$$

$$= 229\,225 - 211\,875$$

$$\text{SWBM} = 17\,330\,\text{t m (Hogging) because } M_W > M_B$$

(see page 352)

Wave Bending Moment (WBM)

$$\text{Wave Bending Moment (WBM)} = b \cdot B \cdot L^{2.5} \times 10^{-3} \, \text{t m}$$

$$\text{WBM Hogging} = 9.795 \times 30 \times 200^{2.5} \times 10^{-3} \, \text{t m}$$

$$= 166\,228 \, \text{t m}$$

$$\text{WBM Sagging} = 11.02 \times 30 \times 200^{2.5} \times 10^{-3} \, \text{t m}$$

$$= 187\,017 \, \text{t m}$$

Total Bending Moment (TBM)

$$\text{TBM Hogging} = \text{WBM hogging} + \text{SWBM hogging}$$

$$= 166\,228 + 17\,350$$

$$= 183\,578 \, \text{t m}$$

$$\text{TBM Sagging} = \text{WBM Sagging} - \text{SWBM hogging}$$

$$= 187\,017 - 17\,350$$

$$= 169\,667 \, \text{t m}$$

Answer (a) with crest amidships, the Total Bending Moment, *TBM is 183 578 tonnes metres.*

Answer (b) with trough amidships, the Total Bending Moment, *TBM is 169 667 tonnes metres.*

The *greatest* danger for a ship to break her back is when the wave crest is at amidships, or when the wave trough is at amidships with the crests at the stem and at the bow.

In the previous example the greatest BM occurs with the crest amidships. Consequently, this ship would fracture across the Upper Deck if the tensile stress due to hogging condition became too high.

Chapter 43
Bending and shear stresses

The shear forces and bending moments which act upon a ship's structure cause shear and bending stresses to be generated in the structure. We have seen earlier that the shearing forces and bending moments experienced by a ship are similar to those occurring in a simply supported beam. We shall therefore consider the shear and bending stresses created when an ordinary beam of rectangular section is simply supported.

Bending stresses
The beam in Figure 43.1(a) is rectangular in cross-section, is simply supported at each end and has a weight W suspended from its mid-point.

This distribution will tend to cause the beam to bend and sag as shown in Figure 43.1(b).

Consider first the bending stresses created in the beam. Let ab and cd in Figure 43.1(a) be two parallel sections whose planes are perpendicular to the plane AB. Let their distance apart be dx. When the beam bends the

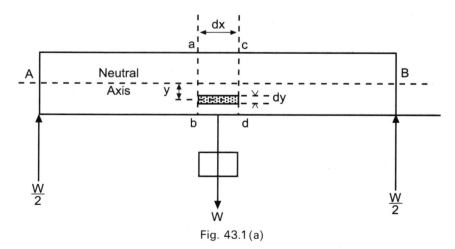

Fig. 43.1 (a)

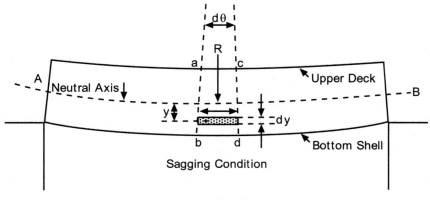

Fig. 43.1 (b)

planes of these two sections will remain perpendicular to the plane AB but will now be inclined at an angle dθ to each other. The parts of the beam above the layer AB are in compression and those below the layer AB are in tension. Thus the layer AB is neither in compression or tension and this layer is called the Neutral Axis.

Let the radius of curvature of the neutral axis layer be R.

Consider a layer of thickness dy which is situated at distance y from the plane of the Neutral Axis.

Original length of layer = dx

After bending, this length = R·dθ no stress or strain here

Length of layer after bending = (R + y) dθ at a distance y below A − B

But

$$\text{Strain} = \frac{\text{Elongation}}{\text{Orig. length}}$$

$$= \frac{(R + y)\, d\theta - Rd \cdot \theta}{Rd \cdot \theta}$$

$$\text{Strain} = y/R$$

This equation indicates that strain varies directly as the distance from the neutral axis. Also, if the modules of elasticity is constant throughout the beam, then:

$$E = \frac{\text{Stress}}{\text{Strain}}$$

or

$$\text{Stress} = E \times \text{Strain}$$

and

$$\text{Stress} = E \times \frac{y}{R}$$

So

$$f = E \times \frac{y}{R}$$

This equation indicates that stress is also directly proportional to distance from the neutral axis, stress being zero at the neutral axis and attaining its maximum value at top and bottom of the beam. The fibres at the top of the beam will be at maximum compressive stress whilst those at the bottom will be at maximum tensile stress. Since the beam does not move laterally, the sum of the tensile stresses must equal the sum of the compressive stresses. This is illustrated in Figure 43.2.

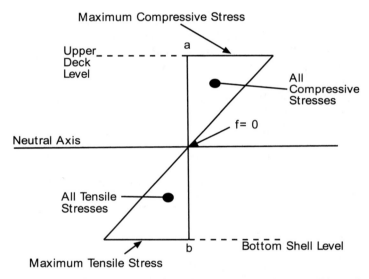

Fig. 43.2.   Bending Stress diagram for a Beam in a sagging condition of loading.

Figure 43.3 shows the cross-section of the beam at ab. NA is a section of the neutral surface at ab and is called the neutral axis at ab. At NA there is no compressive or tensile stress, so $f = 0$.

In Figure 43.3 bdy is an element of area at distance y from the Neutral Axis. Let bdy be equal to dA. The force on dA is equal to the product of the stress and the area. i.e.

$$\text{Force on dA} = \frac{Ey}{R} \times dA.$$

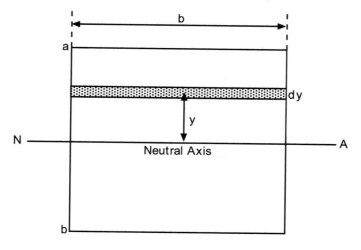

Fig. 43.3

The total or resultant force on the section is equal to the sum of the forces on the section. i.e.

$$\text{Total or Resultant force on the section} = \Sigma \frac{Ey}{R} \, dA$$

But the total or resultant force on the section is zero.

$$\therefore \Sigma \frac{Ey}{R} \, dA = 0$$

Since E and R are constant, then

$$\Sigma \, ydA = 0$$

But ΣydA is the first moment of the area about the neutral axis and if this is to be equal to zero then the neutral axis must pass through the centre of gravity of the section. In the case being considered, the neutral axis is at half-depth of the beam.

The sum of the moments of the internal stresses on the section is equal to M, the external bending moment at the section.

At a distance y from the neutral axis, the moment (m) of the stress acting on dA is given by the formula:

$$m = \frac{Ey}{R} \times y \times dA$$

Also,

$$M = \Sigma \frac{Ey}{R} \times y \times dA$$

$$= \Sigma \frac{E}{R} y^2 \, dA$$

Since E and R are constant, then:

$$M = \frac{E}{R} \Sigma y^2 dA$$

But $\Sigma y^2 dA$ is the second moment of the area of the section about the neutral axis. Let $\Sigma y^2 dA$ be equal to I.

$$\therefore M = \frac{E}{R} \times I$$

Now if f is the stress at a distance of y from the neutral axis, then:

$$f = \frac{Ey}{R}$$

or

$$\frac{E}{R} = \frac{f}{y}$$

But

$$\frac{M}{I} = \frac{E}{R}$$

$$\therefore \frac{f}{y} = \frac{M}{I}$$

and

$$f = \frac{M}{I/y}$$

The expression I/y is called the section modulus, designated Z, and attains its minimum value when y has its maximum value. The section modulus is the strength criterion for the beam so far as bending is concerned.

Example

A steel beam is 40 cm deep and 5 cm wide. The bending moment at the middle of its length is 15 tonnes metre. Find the maximum stress on the steel.

$$I = \frac{lb^3}{12} \qquad\qquad f = \frac{M}{I} \times y$$

$$= \frac{5 \times 40^3}{12} \qquad\quad y = \frac{d}{2} = \frac{40}{2} = 20\,cm$$

$$I = \frac{80\,000}{3}\ cm^4$$

So

$$f = \frac{1500 \times 3 \times 20}{80\,000} \quad \text{tonnes per sq cm}$$

$$f = 1.125 \text{ tonnes per sq cm}$$

Ans. Maximum Stress = 1.125 tonnes per sq cm or 1125 kg per sq cm

Example

A deck beam is in the form of an H-girder as shown in the accompanying Figure 43.4.

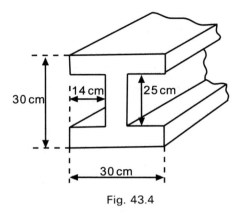

30 cm

14 cm

25 cm

30 cm

Fig. 43.4

If the bending moment at the middle of its length is 15 tonnes metres, find the maximum stress in the steel.

$$I = \frac{BH^3 - 2bh^3}{12}$$

$$I = \frac{30 \times 30^3 - 2.14.25^3}{12}$$

$$I = \frac{810\,000 - 437\,500}{12}$$

$$I = \frac{372\,500}{12} \text{ cm}^4$$

$$f = \frac{M}{I} \cdot y$$

$$y = \frac{H}{2} = \frac{30}{2} = 15 \text{ cm}$$

$$f = \frac{1500 \times 12}{372\,500} \times 15$$

$$f = 0.725 \text{ tonnes per sq cm}$$

Ans. Max. Stress = 0.725 tonnes per sq cm or 725 kg per sq cm

The above theory can now be used to find the section modulus of the ship. The external bending moment can be calculated, as can the stress at the transverse sections under the conditions of maximum bending moment. The neutral axis passes through the centre of gravity of the section and, because of this, its position can be found. The moments of inertia of all of the continuous longitudinal material about this axis can be found. Then the section modulus is equal to I/y.

Shearing Stresses

It has already been shown that a shearing stress across one plane within a material produces another shearing stress of equal intensity on a plane at right angles. (See **Complementary Stresses** in Chapter 40.)

The mean shearing stress in any section of a structure can be obtained by dividing the shearing force at that section by the cross-sectional area of the section. i.e.

$$\text{Mean shearing stress} = \frac{F}{A}$$

where

$$F = \text{Vertical shearing force and}$$

$$A = \text{Area of cross-section}$$

A more accurate estimation of shear stress distribution can be obtained from a consideration of the bending of beams.

Consider the short length of beam dx in Figure 43.5(a) which lies between the vertical planes ab and cd. Let dy be a layer on this short length of beam which is situated at distance y from the neutral plane.

From the formula for bending moments deduced earlier, the longitudinal stress 'f' on a small area b·dy of section ab can be found from the formula:

$$f = \frac{M_1}{I_1} \cdot y$$

where

$$M_1 = \text{the bending moment at this section,}$$

$$I_1 = \text{second moment of the section abut the neutral axis, and}$$

$$y = \text{the distance of the area from the neutral axis.}$$

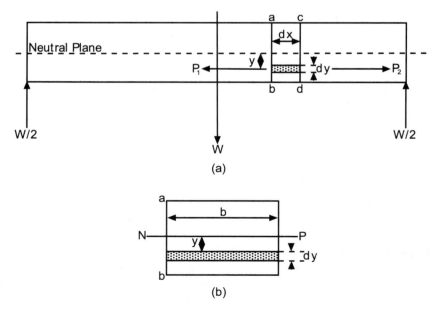

Fig. 43.5

Let

$$b \cdot dy = dA$$

The force acting on $dA = f \cdot dA$

$$= \frac{M_1}{I_1} y \cdot dA$$

Let A_1 be the cross-sectional area at ab, then the total force (P_1) acting on the area A_1 is given by:

$$P_1 = \frac{M_1}{I_1} \times \Sigma y \cdot dA$$

$$= \frac{M_1}{I_1} \times y \times A_1$$

Let P_2 be the force acting on the same area (A_2) at section cd.
   Then

$$P_2 = \frac{M_2}{I_2} \times y \times A_2$$

where

$$M_2 = \text{Bending moment at this section,}$$

and

$$I_2 = \text{Second moment of the section about the neutral axis.}$$

Since dx is small then $A_1 = A_2$ and $I_1 = I_2$. Therefore let $A =$ area and $I =$ second moment of the section about the neutral axis.

Shearing force at $A = P_1 - P_2$

$$= \frac{M_1 - M_2}{I} \times y \times A$$

$$= \frac{M_1 - M_2}{dx} \times \frac{dx \times y \times A}{I}$$

But $\dfrac{M_1 - M_2}{dx}$ is equal to the vertical shearing force at this section of the beam.

$$\therefore P_1 - P_2 = F \times \frac{y \times A \times dx}{I}$$

Now let 'q' be the shearing stress per unit area at A and let 't' be the thickness of the beam, then the shearing force is equal to $q \cdot t \cdot dx$.

$$\therefore q \cdot t \cdot dx = \frac{F \times y \times A \times dx}{I}$$

or

$$q = \frac{F \cdot A \cdot y}{I \cdot t}$$

Example

A solid beam of rectangular section has depth 'd' and thickness 't' and at a given section in its length is under a vertical force 'F'. Find where the maximum shearing stress occurs and also determine its magnitude in terms of 'd', 't' and 'F'.

Since the section is rectangular, the I and y about the neutral axis are given by:

$$I = \frac{td^3}{12}$$

and

$$y = \frac{d}{2} \times \frac{1}{2} = \frac{d}{4}$$

and

$$\text{Area } A = \frac{t \times d}{2}$$

In the case being considered, Ay attains its maximum value at the neutral axis and this is therefore where the maximum shearing stress (q) occurs.

$$q = \frac{F \cdot A \cdot y}{I \cdot t}$$

$$\therefore q_{max} = \frac{F \cdot \frac{td}{2} \cdot \frac{d}{4}}{\frac{td^3}{12} \times t}$$

Ans. $q_{max} = \dfrac{3F}{2td}$

Consider the worked example for the H-girder shown in Fig. 43.6.

When the shear stress distribution for an H-girder is calculated and plotted on a graph it appears similar to that shown in Figure 43.8. It can be seen from this figure that the vertical web of the beam takes the greatest amount of shear.

Example 1. A worked example showing distribution of shear Stress 'q' (with flanges). (See Figs. 43.6 and 43.7.)

Let

$$F = 30 \text{ tonnes.}$$

$$I_{NA} = \tfrac{1}{12}\left(6 \times 12^3 - 5.5 \times 11^3\right)$$

$$\therefore \underline{I_{NA} = 254 \text{ cm}^4}$$

At upper edge of top flange and lower edge of lower flange the stress 'q' = zero.

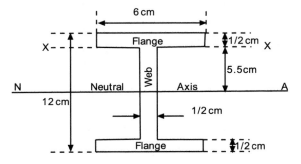

Fig. 43.6

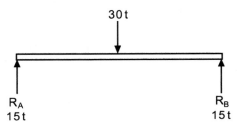

Fig. 43.7

(a) 'q'_a' value:

$$Ay = m = 6 \times \tfrac{1}{2} \times 5.75 = 17.25 \text{ cm}^3$$

$$b = 6 \text{ cm}$$

$$q = \frac{F \times A \times y}{I_{NA} \times b}$$

$$\therefore \; 'q'_a = \frac{30 \times 17.25}{254 \times 6} = \underline{0.34 \text{ t/cm}^2}$$

(b) Just below '$x - x$':

$$Ay = 17.25 \text{ cm}^2$$

$$b = \tfrac{1}{2} \text{ cm}$$

$$q_b = \frac{30 \times 17.25}{254 \times 0.5} = \underline{4.07 \text{ t/cm}^2}$$

(c) At 3 cm from Neutral Axis

$$m = 17.25 + (2.5 \times 0.5) \times 4.25$$

$$= 22.56 \text{ cm}^3 = Ay$$

$$b = \tfrac{1}{2} \text{ cm}$$

$$q_c = \frac{30 \times 22.56}{254 \times 0.5} = \underline{5.33 \text{ t/cm}^2}$$

(d) At Neutral Axis

$$m = 17.25 + \left(5.5 \times \tfrac{1}{2} \times 2.75\right)$$

$$= 24.81 \, \text{cm}^3 = Ay$$

$$b = \tfrac{1}{2} \, \text{cm}$$

$$q_d = \frac{30 \times 24.81}{254 \times 0.5} = \underline{5.86 \, \text{t/cm}^2}$$

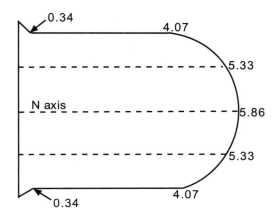

Fig. 43.8

q_{max} occurs at Neutral Axis.

Load carried by the Web is 28.9 t when Force F = 30 t. Web gives resistance to shearing stress. Flanges give resistance to Bending stress.

Example 2. Second worked example showing distribution of shear stress 'q' (with no flanges). (See Figs 43.9 and 43.10.)

Let

$$F = 30 \, \text{tonnes}$$

$$q = \frac{F \times A \times y}{I_{NA} \times b}$$

$$I_{NA} = \frac{td^3}{12} = \frac{0.5 \times 12^3}{12} = 72 \, \text{cm}^4$$

$$\therefore q = \frac{30 \times Ay}{72 \times 0.5} = \underline{0.833 \times A \times y}$$

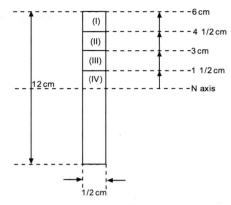

Fig. 43.9

$$q_{(I)} = 0.833 \times 1.5 \times 0.5 \times 5.25 = \underline{3.281\,t/cm^2}$$

$$q_{(I+II)} = 0.833 \times 3.0 \times 0.5 \times 4.5 = \underline{5.625\,t/cm^2}$$

$$q_{(I+II+III)} = 0.833 \times 4.5 \times 0.5 \times 3.75 = \underline{7.031\,t/cm^2}$$

$$q_{(I\ to\ IV)} = 0.833 \times 6.0 \times 0.5 \times 3 = \underline{7.500\,t/cm^2}$$

Check:

$$q_{max} = \frac{3 \times F}{2td} = \frac{3 \times 30}{2 \times 0.5 \times 12} = \underline{7.500\,t/cm^2}$$

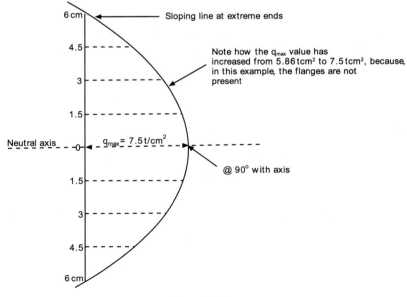

Fig. 43.10

Summary sketches for the two worked examples relating to shear stress

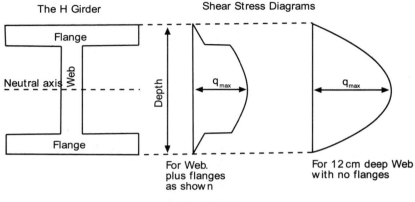

The H Girder   Shear Stress Diagrams

For Web.
plus flanges
as shown

For 12 cm deep Web
with no flanges

Fig. 43.11

In a loaded ship with a wave crest or trough amidships, the shearing force attains its maximum value in the vicinity of the neutral axis at about a quarter of the ship's length from each end. The minimum shearing force is exerted at the keel and the top deck.

Bending stresses in the hull girder

Example
The effective part of a transverse section of a ship amidships is represented by the steel material shown in Fig. 43.12 (also see note at the end of this chapter).

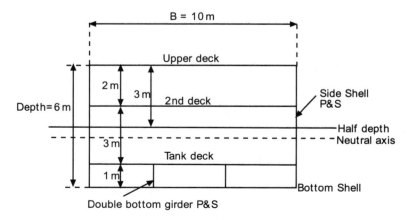

Fig. 43.12

The beam of the ship is 10 m and the depth is 6 m. All plating is 1.5 cm thick. Find the maximum tensile and compressive stresses when the ship is subjected to a sagging moment of 6000 tonnes metres.

Assume initially that Neutral Axis is at $\frac{1}{2}$ depth, i.e. 3 m above base.

Item	Area (sq m)	Lever	Moment	Lever	I
Upper Deck	$10 \times 0.015 = 0.15$	3	0.45	3	1.35
2nd Deck	$10 \times 0.015 = 0.15$	1	0.15	1	0.15
Tank Top	$10 \times 0.015 = 0.15$	-2	-0.30	-2	0.60
Bottom Shell	$10 \times 0.015 = 0.15$	-3	-0.45	-3	1.35
Sideshell P&S	$2 \times 6 \times 0.015 = 0.18$	0	0	0	0
Double Bottom Girders	$2 \times 1 \times 0.015 = 0.03$	-2.5	-0.075	-2.5	0.1875
	0.81		-0.225		3.6375

Item	Own inertia $= \frac{1}{12} Ah^2$
Upper Deck	$\frac{1}{12} \times 0.15 \times 0.015^2 = 2.8 \times 10^{-6}$ $\Big\}$
2nd Deck	$\frac{1}{12} \times 0.15 \times 0.015^2 = 2.8 \times 10^{-6}$
Tank Top	$\frac{1}{12} \times 0.15 \times 0.015^2 = 2.8 \times 10^{-6}$ *
Bottom Shell	$\frac{1}{12} \times 0.15 \times 0.015^2 = 2.8 \times 10^{-6}$
Sideshell P&S	$\frac{1}{12} \times 0.18 \times 36 \quad = 0.54$
Double Bottom Girders	$\frac{1}{12} \times 0.03 \times 1 \quad = 2500 \times 10^{-6}$
	0.5425

*It can be seen from this table that the second moment of area of *horizontal* members in the structure such as decks, tank tops and outer bottom, about their own neutral axes are small and in practice these values are ignored in the calculation.

$$\text{Depth of Neutral Axis below half depth} = \frac{-0.225}{0.81}$$

$$= -0.28 \, \text{m}$$

$$\text{Total second moment about half depth} = 3.6375 + 0.5425$$

$$= 4.18 \, \text{m}^4$$

$$\text{Total second moment about neutral axis} = 4.18 - 0.81 \times 0.28^2$$

$$I_{NA} = 4.18 - 0.06$$

$$= 4.12 \, \text{m}^4$$

The maximum compressive bending stress is at the Upper deck level.

$$\frac{f}{y} = \frac{M}{I}$$

$$\therefore f = \frac{6000}{4.12} \times 3.28$$

$$= 4777 \text{ tonnes per sq m}$$

The maximum tensile bending stress is at the bottom shell.

$$f = \frac{6000}{4.12} \times 2.72$$

$$= 3961 \text{ tonnes per sq m}$$

Ans. Maximum tensile bending stress = 3961 tonnes per sq m.
Maximum compressive bending stress = 4777 tonnes per sq m

Summary

The steel material shown in Fig. 43.12 is steel that is *continuous* in a longitudinal direction. Intercostal structures are not considered because they contribute very little resistance to longitudinal bending of the ship.

The calculation and table on page 369 is known as the 'Equivalent Girder Calculation'. It is the I_{NA} that helps resist hogging and sagging motions of a ship. In doing so, I_{NA} helps reduce the tensile and compressive bending stresses.

Lloyds suggest maximum value for these bending stresses in conjunction with a factor of safety of 4. If mild steel structure, f_{max} is about 110 MN/m^2 or about 11 000 tonnes/sq. m for medium-sized ships. If high tensile steel is used, f_{max} is about 150 MN/m^2 or about 15 000 tonnes/sq. m for medium-sized ships.

Take medium-sized ships as being 100 m to 150 m LBP. If there is any danger of these bending stresses being too high in value for a ship in service, a change in the loading arrangement could help make this loaded condition safer.

EXERCISE 43

1   The hull of a box-shaped vessel is 50 m long and has a mass of 600 tonnes. The mass of the hull is uniformly distributed over its length. Machinery of 200 tonnes mass extends uniformly over the quarter length amidships. Two holds extending over the fore and aft quarter length each have 140 tonnes of cargo stowed uniformly over their lengths. Draw the curves of shearing force and bending moments for this condition and state their maximum values.

2   A uniform box-shaped barge, 40 m × 12 m beam, is divided into four cargo compartments each 10 m long. The barge is loaded with 600 tonnes of iron ore, level stowed, as follows:

No. 1 hold − 135 tonnes,   No. 2 hold − 165 tonnes,
No. 3 hold − 165 tonnes,   No. 4 hold − 135 tonnes

The loaded barge floats in fresh water on an even keel at a draft of 1.75 m. Construct the curves of shearing force and bending moment for this condition and also find the position and value of the maximum bending moment for the still water condition.

3   A box-shaped vessel, 100 m long, floats on an even keel displacing 2000 tonnes. The mass of the vessel alone is 1000 tonnes evenly distributed and she is loaded at each end for a length of 25 m with 500 tonnes of cargo, also evenly distributed. Sketch the curve of loads, shearing force and bending moments. Also state the maximum shearing force and bending moment and state where these occur.

4   Describe in detail Murray's Method for ascertaining the longitudinal bending moments in a ship when she is supported on a standard wave with: (a) the crest amidships, and (b) the trough amidships. Include in your answer details of what is meant by a 'Standard Wave'.

5   A supertanker is 300 m LOA. Second moment of area (I_{NA}) is 752 m^4. Neutral axis above the keel is 9.30 m and 9.70 m below the upper deck. Using the information in the table below, proceed to draw the Shear Force and Bending Moment curves for this ship. From these two Strength curves determine:
(a) Maximum Shear Force in MN.
(b) Maximum Bending Moment in MNm.
(c) Position along the ship's length at which this maximum BM occurs.
(d) Bending stress f_{max} in MN/m^2 at the upper deck and at the keel.

Station	Stern	1	2	3	4	5
SF(MN)	0	26.25	73.77	115.14	114.84	21.12
BM(MNm)	0	390	1887	4717	8164	10199

	6	7	8	9	Bow
SF(MN)	−78.00	−128.74	−97.44	−45.78	0
BM(MNm)	9342	6238	2842	690	0

Chapter 44
Simplified stability information

DEPARTMENT OF TRADE   MERCHANT SHIPPING NOTICE NO. 1122

SIMPLIFIED STABILITY INFORMATION
Notice to Shipowners, Masters and Shipbuilders

1 It has become evident that the masters' task of ensuring that his ship complies with the minimum statutory standards of stability is in many instances not being adequately carried out. A feature of this is that undue traditional reliance is being placed on the value of GM alone, while other important criteria which govern the righting lever GZ curve are not being assessed as they should be. For this reason the Department, appreciating that the process of deriving and evaluating GZ curves is often difficult and time-consuming, strongly recommends that in future simplified stability information be incorporated into ships' stability booklets. In this way masters can more readily assure themselves that safe standards of stability are met.

2. Following the loss of the *Lairdsfield*, referred to in Notice M.627, the Court of Inquiry recommended that simplified stability information be provided. This simplified presentation of stability information has been adopted in a large number of small ships and is considered suitable for wider application in order to overcome the difficulties referred to in paragraph 1.

3. Simplified stability information eliminates the need to use cross curves of stability and develop righting lever GZ curves for varying loading conditions by enabling a ship's stability to be quickly assessed, to show whether or not all statutory criteria are complied with, by means of a single diagram or table. Considerable experience has now been gained and three methods of presentation are in common use. These are:

(a) The Maximum Deadweight Moment Diagram or Table,
(b) The Minimum Permissible GM Diagram or Table,
(c) The Maximum Permissible KG Diagram or Table.

In all three methods the limiting values are related to salt water displacement or draft. Free surface allowances for slack tanks are however applied slightly differently.

4 Consultation with the industry has revealed a general preference for the Maximum Permissible KG approach, and graphical presentation also appears to be preferred rather than a tabular format. The Department's view is that any of the methods may be adopted subject to:

(a) clear guidance notes for their use being provided and
(b) submission for approval being made in association with all other basic data and sample loading conditions.

In company fleets it is however recommended that a single method be utilized throughout.

5 It is further recommended that the use of a *Simplified Stability Diagram* as an adjunct to the *Deadweight Scale* be adopted to provide a direct means of comparing stability relative to other loading characteristics. Standard work forms for calculating loading conditions should also be provided.

6 It is essential for masters to be aware that the standards of stability obtainable in a vessel are wholly dependent on exposed openings such as hatches, doorways, air pipes and ventilators being securely closed weathertight; or in the case of automatic closing appliances such as airpipe ball valves that these are properly maintained in order to function as designed.

7 Shipowners bear the responsiblity to ensure that adequate, accurate and up-to-date stability information for the master's use is provided. It follows that it should be in a form which should enable it to be readily used in the trade in which the vessel is engaged.

Maximum Permissible Deadweight Moment Diagram

This is one form of simplified stability data diagram in which a curve of Maximum Permissible Deadweight Moments is plotted against Displacement in tonnes on the vertical axis and Deadweight Moment in Tonnes metres on the horizontal axis, the Deadweight Moment being the moment of the Deadweight about the keel.

The total Deadweight Moment at any Displacement must not, under any circumstances, exceed the Maximum Permissible Deadweight Moment at that Displacement.

Diagram 3 (Figure 44.1) illustrates this type of diagram. The ship's Displacement in tonnes is plotted on the vertical axis from 1500 to 4000 tonnes while the Deadweight Moments in tonnes metres are plotted on the horizontal axis. From this diagram it can be seen that, for example, the Maximum Deadweight Moment for this ship at a displacement of 3000 tonnes is 10 260 tonnes metres (Point 1). If the light displacement for this ship is 1000 tonnes then the Deadweight at this displacement is 2000 tonnes. The maximum kg for the Deadweight tonnage is given by:

$$\text{Maximum kg} = \frac{\text{Deadweight Moment}}{\text{Deadweight}}$$

$$= \frac{10\,260}{2000}$$

$$= 5.13\,\text{m}$$

Example 1

Using the Simplified Stability Data shown in Diagram 3 (Figure 44.1), estimate the amount of cargo (kg 3 m) which can be loaded so that after completion of loading the ship does not have deficient stability. Prior to loading the cargo the following weights were already on board:

250 t fuel oil	kg 0.5 m	Free Surface Moment	1400 t m
50 t fresh water	kg 5.0 m	Free Surface Moment	500 t m
2000 t cargo	kg 4.0 m		

The light displacement is 1000 t, and the loaded Summer displacement is 3500 t

Item	Weight	Kg	Deadweight Moment
Light disp.	1000 t	—	—
Fuel oil	250 t	0.5 m	125 t m
Free surface	—	—	1400 t m
Fresh water	50 t	5.0 m	250 t m
Free surface	—	—	500 t m
Cargo	2000 t	4.0 m	8000 t m
Present cond.	3300 t		10 275 t m − Point 2 (Satisfactory)
Maximum balance	200 t	3.0 m	600 t m
Summer displ.	3500		10 875 t m − Point 3 (Satisfactory)

Since 10 875 tonnes metres is less than the maximum permissible deadweight moment at a displacement of 3500 tonnes, the ship will not have deficient stability and may load 200 tonnes of cargo.

Ans. Load 200 tonnes.

Example 2

Using the Maximum Permissible Deadweight Moment diagram 3 (Figure 44.1) and the information given below, find the quantity of timber deck cargo (Kg 8.0 m) which can be loaded, allowing 15 per cent for water absorption during the voyage.

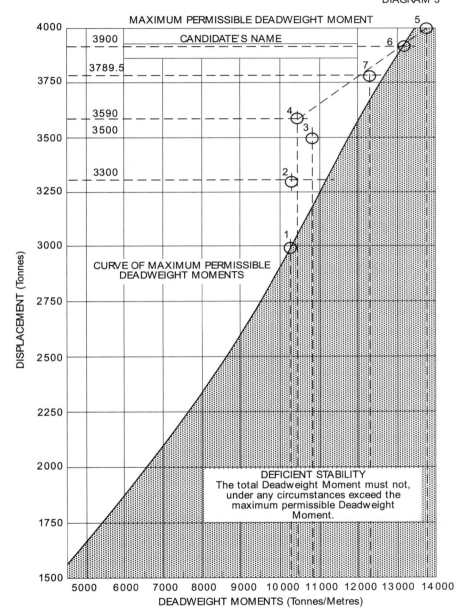

Fig. 44.1

Summer displacement 4000 tonnes, Light Displacement 1000 tonnes. Weights already on board:

Fuel oil	200 tonnes,	Kg 0.5 m, free surface moment 1400 t m
Fresh water	40 tonnes,	Kg 5.0 m, free surface moment 600 t m
Cargo	2000 tonnes,	Kg 4.0 m
Ballast	350 tonnes,	Kg 0.5 m

The following weights will be consumed during the voyage:

Fuel oil   150 tonnes, Kg 0.5 m. Free surface moment will be
reduced by 800 t m

Fresh water   30 tonnes, Kg 5.0 m. Free surface moment will be
by 200 t m

Departure Condition

Item	Weight	Kg	Deadweight Moment
Light ship	1000	—	—
Fuel oil	200	0.5	100
Free surface			1400
Fresh water	40	5.0	200
Free surface			600
Cargo	2000	4.0	8000
Ballast	350	0.5	175
Departure Disp. (without deck cargo)	3590		10 475 – Point 4 (Satisfactory)
Maximum deck cargo	410	8.0	3280
Summer disp.	4000		13 755 – Point 5 (Deficient Stability)

From diagram 3, where the line joining points 4 and 5 cuts the curve of Maximum Permissible Deadweight Moments (point 6), the displacement is 3920 tonnes.

Total departure displacement	3920 tonnes
Departure displacement without deck cargo	3590 tonnes
∴ Max deck cargo to load	330 tonnes

$$\text{Absorption during voyage} = \frac{15}{100} \times 330 = 49.5 \text{ tonnes}$$

Arrival Condition

Item	Weight	Kg	Deadweight Moment
Departure disp. without			
deck cargo	3590		10 475
Fuel oil	− 150	0.5	−75
Free Surface			−800
Fresh water	−30	5.0	−150
Free surface			−200
Arrival disp. without			
deck cargo	3410		9250
Deck cargo	330	8.0	2640
Absorption	49.5	8.0	396
Total arrival disp.	3789.5		12 286 − Point 7 (Satisfactory Stability)

Ans. Load 330 tonnes of deck cargo.

Exercise 44

1 Using the Maximum Permissible Deadweight Moment diagram 3, find the amount of deck cargo (kg 8.0 m) which can be loaded allowing 15 per cent for water absoption during the voyage given the following data:

Light displacement 1000 tonnes, Loaded displacement 4000 tonnes. Weights already on board:

Item	Weight	Kg	Free Surface Moment
Cargo	1800	4.0	−
Fuel oil	350	0.5	1200
Fresh water	50	5.0	600
Ballast	250	0.5	−

During the voyage the following will be consumed (tonnes and kg):

Fuel oil   250   0.5   Reduction in free surface moment 850 t m.
Fresh water 40   5.0   Reduction in free surface moment 400 t m.

Appendix I
Standard abbreviations and symbols

K	The keel.
B	The centre of buoyancy when the ship is upright.
B_1	The centre of buoyancy when the ship is inclined.
BM	The height of the transverse metacentre above the centre of buoyancy.
BM_L	The height of the longitudinal metacentre above the centre of buoyancy.
CB	Centre of buoyancy.
G	The original position of the centre of gravity.
G_1	The new position of the centre of gravity.
M	The original position of the transverse metacentre.
M_1	The new position of the transverse metacentre.
M_L	The longitudinal metacentre.
KB	The height of the centre of buoyancy above the keel.
KG	The height of the centre of gravity above the keel.
Kg	The height of the centre of gravity of an item above keel.
KM	The height of the transverse metacentre above the keel.
GM	Initial transverse metacentric height.
CF	Centre of Flotation.
GZ	The length of the righting lever about centre of gravity.
KN	The length of the righting lever about keel.
V or ▽	The ship's volume of displacement.
W or △	The ship's weight of displacement.
w	A weight to be loaded, discharged, or shifted.
⌀	Amidships. (The symbol ⌀ is shown on trim diagrams).
L	The ship's length.
D	The ship's depth.

B	The ship's maximum beam.
d	The ship's draft.
F	Forward, or centre of flotation.
A	Aft.
M or m	Metres.
C_w	The water-plane coefficient.
C_b	Block coefficient.
C_m	Coefficient of midships area.
C_p	Prismatic coefficient.
I or i	Second moment of an area.
l	The distance of the centre of flotation from aft.
P	The upthrust on the keel blocks when drydocking.
μ	The permeability of a compartment.
WL	The original waterline.
W_1L_1	The new waterline.
G_v	The virtual centre of gravity.
t	The trim.
MCTC or MCT 1 cm	The moment to change the trim by 1 cm.
TPC	The tonnes per centimetre immersion.
GM_L	The longitudinal metacentric height.
SG	Specific gravity.
θ	An angle of list or heel.
WPA	Area of a water-plane.
FWA	Fresh water allowance.
FW	Fresh water.
SW	Salt water.
CDB	Cellular double-bottom tank.
CI or h	The common interval used in Simpson's Rules.
E	Young's Modulus.
y	Depth from the neutral layer.
f	Stress.
q	Shearing stress.
ρ	Density in tonnes/m^3.
ρ_{FW}	Fresh water density @ 1.000 t/m^3.
ρ_{SW}	Salt water density @ 1.025 t/m^3.
ρ_{DW}	Dock water density as given in t/m^3.
δ_{max}	Maximum squat.
S	Blockage factor.
y	Static underkeel clearance.
y_2	Dynamical underkeel clearance.
H	Water depth relating to squat.
T	Ship's mean draft relating to squat.
V_k	Speed of ship relative to the water.

Appendix II
Summary of stability formulae*

Form Coefficients

$$\text{Area of waterplane} = L \times B \times C_w$$
$$\text{Area of amidships} = B \times d \times C_m$$
$$\text{Volume of displacement} = L \times B \times d \times C_b$$
$$C_b = C_m \times C_p$$

Drafts
When displacement is constant: (For box-shapes):

$$\frac{\text{New draft}}{\text{Old draft}} = \frac{\text{Old density}}{\text{New density}}$$

When draft is constant:

$$\frac{\text{New displacement}}{\text{Old displacement}} = \frac{\text{New density}}{\text{Old density}}$$

$$\text{TPC} = \frac{\text{WPA}}{97.56}$$

$$\text{FWA} = \frac{W}{4 \times \text{TPC}}$$

$$\begin{array}{l}\text{Change of draft or} \\ \text{Dock Water Allowance}\end{array} = \frac{\text{FWA}\,(1025 - \rho_{DW})}{25}$$

Homogeneous log:

$$\frac{\text{draft}}{\text{depth}} = \frac{\text{relative density of log}}{\text{relative density of water}}$$

*See note on page 386.

Variable immersion hydrometer:

$$\text{Density} = \frac{M_y}{M_y - x\left(\frac{M_y - M_x}{L}\right)}$$

Trim

$$MCTC = \frac{W \times GM_L}{100 \times L}$$

$$\text{Change of trim} = \frac{\text{Trimming moment}}{MCTC}$$

$$\text{Change of draft aft} = \frac{l}{L} \times \text{Change of trim}$$

$$\text{Change of draft forward} = \text{Change of trim}$$
$$- \text{Change of draft aft}$$

Effect of trim on tank soundings:

$$\frac{\text{Head when full}}{\text{Length of tank}} = \frac{\text{Trim}}{\text{Length of ship}}$$

True Mean Draft:

$$\frac{\text{Correction}}{FY} = \frac{\text{Trim}}{\text{Length}}$$

To Keep the Draft Aft Constant:

$$d = \frac{MCTC \times L}{TPC \times l}$$

To find GM_L:

$$\frac{GM_L}{GG_1} = \frac{L}{t}$$

Simpson's Rules

1st Rule:

Area = h/3 (a + 4b + 2c + 4d + e) or $\frac{1}{3} \times CI \times \Sigma_1$

2nd Rule:

Area = 3h/8 (a + 3b + 3c + 2d + 3e + 3f + g) or $\frac{3}{8} \times CI \times \Sigma_2$

3rd Rule:

Area = h/12 (5a + 8b − c) or $\frac{1}{12} \times CI \times \Sigma_3$

KB and BM

Transverse Stability

For rectangular waterplanes:

$$I = \frac{LB^3}{12}$$

$$BM = I/V$$

For box-shapes:

$$BM = B^2/12d$$

$$KB = d/2$$

$$KM_{min} = B/\sqrt{6}$$

For triangular prisms:

$$BM = B^2/6d$$

$$KB = 2d/3$$

Depth of centre of buoyancy below the waterline $= \dfrac{1}{3}\left(\dfrac{d}{2} + \dfrac{V}{A}\right)$

Longitudinal Stability

For rectangular waterplanes:

$$I_L = \frac{BL^3}{12}$$

$$BM_L = \frac{I_L}{V}$$

For box-shapes:

$$BM_L = L^2/12d$$

For triangular prisms:

$$BM_L = \frac{L^2}{6d}$$

Transverse Statical Stability

Moment of Statical Stability $= W \times GZ$

At Small Angles of Heel:

$$GZ = GM \times \sin\theta$$

By Wall-Sided Formula:

$$GZ = (GM + \tfrac{1}{2} BM \tan^2 \theta) \sin \theta$$

By Attwood's Formula:

$$GZ = \frac{v \times hh_1}{V} - BG \sin \theta$$

Stability Curves:

$$New\ GZ = Old\ GZ \pm GG_1 \sin Heel\ or$$

$$New\ GZ = KN - KG \sin Heel$$

Dynamical Stability = W × Area under stability curve

$$= W \left[\frac{v(gh + g_1 h_1)}{V} - BG(1 - \cos \theta) \right]$$

List

$$Final\ KG = \frac{Final\ Moment}{Final\ Displacement}$$

$$GG_1 = \frac{w \times d}{Final\ W}$$

$$\tan List = \frac{GG_1}{GM}$$

Increase in draft due to list:

$$New\ draft = \tfrac{1}{2} \cdot b \cdot \sin \theta + (d - r) \cos \theta$$

Inclining Experiment:

$$\frac{GM}{GG_1} = \frac{Length\ of\ plumbline}{Deflection}$$

Effect of Free Surface

$$Virtual\ loss\ of\ GM = \frac{lb^3}{12} \times \frac{\rho}{W} \times \frac{1}{n^2}$$

Drydocking and Grounding

Upthrust at Stern:

$$P = \frac{MCTC \times t}{l}$$

or P = Old − New displacement

$$\text{Virtual loss of GM} = \frac{P \times KM}{W}$$

$$\text{or} = \frac{P \times KG}{W - P}$$

Pressure of Liquids

$$\text{Pressure (P)} = Dwg$$

$$\text{Thrust} = P \times \text{Area}$$

$$\text{Depth of centre of pressure} = \frac{I_{WL}}{AZ}$$

Bilging and Permeability

$$\text{Permeability} = \frac{BS}{SF} \times 100 \text{ per cent}$$

$$\text{Increase in draft} = \frac{\mu v}{A - \mu a}$$

Strength of Ships

$$\text{Stress} = \frac{\text{Load}}{\text{Area}}$$

$$\text{Strain} = \frac{\text{Change in length}}{\text{Original length}} = \frac{y}{R}$$

Young's Modulus:

$$E = \frac{\text{Stress}}{\text{Strain}}$$

Bending Moment:

$$M = \frac{E}{R} \times I$$

$$\text{Section Modulus} = \frac{I}{Y}$$

Stress:

$$f = \frac{E}{R} \times y$$

Shearing Stress:

$$q = \frac{F \cdot A \cdot y}{I \cdot t}$$

Ship Squat

$$\text{Blockage factor} = \frac{b \times T}{B \times H}$$

$$\delta_{max} = \frac{C_B \times S^{0.81} \times V_k{}^{2.08}}{20}$$

$$y_o = H - T$$

$$y_2 = y_o - \delta_{max}$$

In open water:

$$\delta_{max} = \frac{C_B \times V_k^2}{100}$$

In confined channel:

$$\delta_{max} = \frac{C_B \times V_k^2}{50}$$

$$\text{Width of Influence} = 7.7 + 20\left(1 - C_B\right)^2$$

Miscellaneous

Angle of Loll:

$$\tan \text{loll} = \sqrt{\frac{2GM}{BM}}$$

$$GM = \frac{2 \times \text{Initial GM}}{\cos \text{loll}}$$

Heel Due to Turning:

$$\tan \text{Heel} = \frac{v^2 \times BG}{g \cdot r \cdot GM}$$

Rolling Period:

$$T = 2\pi \frac{k}{\sqrt{g \cdot GM}} = \frac{2k}{\sqrt{GM}} \quad \text{approx.}$$

Zero GM:

$$\tan \text{list} = \sqrt[3]{\frac{2 \cdot w \cdot d}{W \times BM}}$$

Theorem of Parallel Axes:

$$I_{CG} = I_{OZ} - Ay^2$$

$$\text{or } I_{NA} = I_{xx} - Ay^2$$

Summary
Always write your formula first in letters. If you then make a mathematical error you will at least obtain some marks for a correct formula.

Appendix III
Conversion tables

Metric-Imperial	Imperial-Metric

Metric-Imperial

$1\,m = 3.281\,ft$

$1\,m = 39.37\,ins$

$1\,m^2 = 10.764\,ft^2$

$1\,m^3 = 11.77\,ft^3$

$1\,litre = 61.02\,ins^3$

$1\,litre = 1.76\,pints$

$1\,litre = 0.22\,galls$

$1\,tonne = 0.985\,tons$

$1\,kg = 2.205\,lbs$

$1\,m^3/tonne = 35.88\,ft^3/ton$

$1\,litre/kg = 0.016\,ft^3/lb$

$1000\,kg/m^3 = 1000\,oz/ft^3$

$1025\,kg/m^3 = 1025\,oz/ft^3$

Imperial-Metric

$1\,ft = 0.3048\,m$

$1\,in = 25.4\,mm$

$1\,ft^2 = 0.0929\,m^2$

$1\,in^2 = 645.2\,mm^2$

$40\,ft^3 = 1.133\,m^3$

$100\,ft^3 = 2.832\,m^3$

$1\,ft^3 = 0.02832\,m^3$

$1\,gall = 4.5461\,litres$

$1\,t = 1.016\,tonne$

$1\,lb = 0.4536\,kg$

$1\,cwt = 50.80\,kg$

$1\,ft^3/t = 0.02787\,m^3/tonne$

$1\,ft^3/lb = 62.428\,litres/kg$

$1000\,oz/ft^3 = 1000\,kg/m^3$

$1025\,oz/ft^3 = 1025\,kg/m^3$

$$TPI'' \times 0.4 = TPC$$

$$MCTI'' \times 0.12 = MCTC$$

$$1\,ton/in^2 \times 15.444 = 1\,MN/m^2$$

$$1\,lbf = 4.448\,N$$

$$MN/m^2 \times 100 = tonnes/m^2$$

Appendix IV
Extracts from the M.S. (Load Lines) Rules, 1968

Information as to stability of ships

30.-(1) The owner of any ship to which freeboards are assigned under these Rules shall provide for the guidance of the master of the ship information relating to the stability of the ship in accordance with the following provisions of this Rule.

(2) Except as otherwise provided in paragraph (6) of this Rule, such information shall include particulars appropriate to the ship in respect of all matters specified in Schedule 7 to these Rules and shall be in the form required by that Schedule.

(3) Subject to the following paragraph, the information shall, when first supplied, be based on the determination of stability by means of an inclining test which shall unless the Board otherwise permits be carried out in the presence of a surveyor appointed by the Board. The information first supplied shall be replaced by fresh information whenever its accuracy is materially affected by alteration of the ship. Such fresh information shall if the Board so require be based on a further inclining test.

(4) The Board may:
  (a) in the case of any ship allow the information to be based on the determination, by means of an inclining test, of the stability of a sister ship;
  (b) in the case of a ship specially designed for the carriage of liquids or ore in bulk; or of any class of such ships, dispense with an inclining test if satisfied from the information available in respect of similar ships that the ship's proportions and arrangements are such as to ensure more than sufficient stability in all probable loading conditions.

(5) The information, and any fresh information to replace the same pursuant to paragraph (3) of this Rule, shall before issue to the master be submitted by or on behalf of the owner of the ship to the Board for their approval, together with a copy thereof for retention by the Board, and shall incorporate such additions and amendments as the Board may in any particular case require.

(6) (a) The owner of any ship which, by virtue of the Merchant Shipping (Load Lines) (Transitional Provisions) Regulations 1968, is to be treated as a ship to which freeboards have been assigned under these Rules shall provide for the information of the master such information relating to the stability of the ship as was required to be so provided under the law in force immediately prior to the coming into operation of these Rules (a).

   (b) The requirement in the preceding sub-paragraph shall have effect in relation to any ship to which it applies until the date on which the load line certificate currently in force in respect of the ship on the date these Rules come into operation ceases to be valid.

(7) Information provided pursuant to the foregoing provisions of this Rule shall be furnished by the owner of the ship to the master in the form of a book which shall be kept on the ship at all times in the custody of the master.

Information as to loading and ballasting of ships

31.-(1) The owner of any ship to which freeboards are assigned under these Rules, being a ship of more than 150 metres in length specially designed for the carriage of liquids or ore in bulk, shall provide for the information of the master information relating to the loading and ballasting of the ship in accordance with the following provisions of this Rule.

(2) Such information shall consist of working instructions specifying in detail the manner in which the ship is to be loaded and ballasted so as to avoid the creation of unacceptable stresses in her structure and shall indicate the maximum stresses permissible for the ship.

(3) The provisions of paragraph (5) of the preceding Rule shall have effect in respect of information required under this Rule, and the information duly approved in accordance with that paragraph shall be contained in the book to be furnished to the master of the ship pursuant to paragraph (7) of that Rule, so however that the information to be provided pursuant to each Rule is separately shown in the book under separate headings specifying the number and heading of each Rule.

Part 1

SHIPS IN GENERAL

Structural Strength and Stability

2.-(1) The construction of the ship shall be such that her general structural strength will be sufficient for the freeboards to be assigned to her.

  (a) See section 18 of the Merchant Shipping (Safety Convention) Act 1949 (12,13 & 14 Geo. 6 c 43.) and section 14 of the Merchant Shipping Act 1964 (1964 c 47).

(2) The design and construction of the ship shall be such as to ensure that her stability in all probable loading conditions will be sufficient for the freeboards to be assigned to her, and for this purpose regard shall be had, in addition to the intended service of the ship and to any relevant requirements of Rules made under the Merchant Shipping (Safety Convention) Act 1949(a) and the Merchant Shipping Act 1964(b), to the following criteria:

  (a) The Area under the curve of Righting Levers (GZ curve) shall not be less than:

      (i) 0.055 metre-radians up to an angle of 30 degrees;
      (ii) 0.09 metre-radians up to an angle of either 40 degrees or the angle at which the lower edges of any openings in the hull, superstructures or deckhouses, being openings which cannot be closed weathertight, are immersed if that angle be less;
      (iii) 0.03 metre-radians between the angles of heel of 30 degrees and 40 degrees or such lesser angle as is referred to in (ii).

  (b) The Righting Lever (GZ) shall be at least 0.20 metres at an angle of heel equal to or greater than 30 degrees.

  (c) The maximum Righting Lever (GZ) shall occur at an angle of heel not less than 30 degrees.

  (d) The initial transverse metacentric height shall not be less than 0.15 metres. In the case of a ship carrying a timber deck cargo which complies with sub-paragraph (a) by taking into account the volume of timber deck cargo the initial transverse metacentric height shall not be less than 0.05 metres.

(3) To determine whether the ship complies with the requirements of sub-paragraph (2) the ship shall, unless the Board otherwise permit, be subjected to an inclining test carried out in the presence of a surveyor appointed by the Board, and the Board shall notify the Assigning Authority whether or not they are satisfied that the ship complies with those requirements.

  (a) 1949 12, 13 & 14 Geo. 6 c. 43.
  (b) 1964 c. 47.

SCHEDULE 7

Information as to Stability of Ships
(Rule 30)

The information relating to the stability of a ship to be provided for the master pursuant to Rule 30 of these Rules shall include particulars appropriate to the ship of the matters specified below. Such particulars shall be in the form of a statement unless the contrary is indicated.

1. The ship's name, official number, port of registry, gross and register tonnages, principal dimensions, displacement, deadweight and draft to the Summer load line.

2. A profile view and, if the Board so require in a particular case, plan views of the ship drawn to scale showing with their names all compartments, tanks, storerooms and crew and passenger accommodation spaces, and also showing the mid-length position.

3. The capacity and the centre of gravity (longitudinally and vertically) of every compartment available for the carriage of cargo, fuel, stores, feed water domestic water or water ballast. In the case of a vehicle ferry, the vertical centre of gravity of compartments for the carriage of vehicles shall be based on the estimated centres of gravity of the vehicles and not on the volumetric centres of the compartments.

4. The estimated total weight of (a) passengers and their effects and (b) crew and their effects, and the centre of gravity (longitudinally and vertically) of each such total weight. In assessing such centres of gravity passengers and crew shall be assumed to be distributed about the ship in the spaces they will normally occupy, including the highest decks to which either or both have access.

5. The estimated weight and the disposition and centre of gravity of the maximum amount of deck cargo which the ship may reasonably be expected to carry on an exposed deck. The estimated weight shall include in the case of deck cargo likely to absorb water the estimated weight of water likely to be so absorbed and allowed for in arrival conditions, such weight in the case of timber deck cargo being taken to be 15 per cent by weight.

6. A diagram or scale showing the load line mark and load lines with particulars of the corresponding freeboards, and also showing the displacement, metric tons per centimetre immersion, and deadweight corresponding in each case to a range of mean draughts extending between the waterline representing the deepest load line and the waterline of the ship in light condition.

7. A diagram or tabular statement showing the hydrostatic particulars of the ship, including:
   (1) the heights of the transverse metacentre and
   (2) the values of the moment to change trim one centimetre,

for a range of mean drafts extending at least between the waterline representing the deepest load line and the waterline of the ship in light condition. Where a tabular statement is used, the intervals between such drafts shall be sufficiently close to permit accurate interpolation. In the case of ships having raked keels, the same datum for the heights of centres of buoyancy and metacentres shall be used as for the centres of gravity referred to in paragraphs 3, 4 and 5.

8. The effect on stability of free surface in each tank in the ship in which liquids may be carried, including an example to show how the metacentric height is to be corrected.

9.-(1) A diagram showing cross curves of stability indicating the height of the assumed axis from which the Righting Levers are measured and the trim which has been assumed. In the case of ships having raked keels, where a datum other than the top of keel has been used the position of the assumed axis shall be clearly defined.

(2) Subject to the following sub-paragraph, only (a) enclosed super-structures and (b) efficient trunks as defined in paragraph 10 of Schedule 5 shall be taken into account in deriving such curves.

(3) The following structures may be taken into account in deriving such curves if the Board are satisfied that their location, integrity and means of closure will contribute to the ship's stability:
  (a) Superstructures located above the superstructure deck;
  (b) deckhouses on or above the freeboard deck, whether wholly or in part only;
  (c) hatchway structures on or above the freeboard deck.

  Additionally, in the case of a ship carrying timber deck cargo, the volume of the timber deck cargo, or a part thereof, may with the Board's approval be taken into account in deriving a supplementary curve of stability appropriate to the ship when carrying such cargo.

(4) An example shall be given showing how to obtain a curve of Righting Levers (GZ) from the cross curves of stability.

(5) Where the buoyancy of a superstructure is to be taken into account in the calculation of stability information to be supplied in the case of a vehicle ferry or similar ship having bow doors, ship's side doors or stern doors, there shall be included in the stability information a specific statement that such doors must be secured weather-tight before the ship proceeds to sea and that the cross curves of stability are based upon the assumption that such doors have been so secured.

10.-(1) The diagram and statements referred to in sub-paragraph (2) of this paragraph shall be provided separately for each of the following conditions of the ship:-
  (a) *Light condition.* If the ship has permanent ballast, such diagram and statements shall be provided for the ship in light condition both (i) with such ballast, and (ii) without such ballast.

(b) *Ballast condition*, both (i) on departure, and (ii) on arrival, it being assumed for the purpose of the latter in this and the following sub-paragraphs that oil fuel, fresh water, consumable stores and the like are reduced to 10 per cent of their capacity.

(c) Condition both (i) on departure, and (ii) on arrival, when loaded to the Summer load line with cargo filling all spaces available for cargo, cargo for this purpose being taken to be homogeneous cargo except where this is clearly inappropriate, for example in the case of cargo spaces in a ship which are intended to be used exclusively for the carriage of vehicles or of containers.

(d) Service loaded conditions, both (i) on departure and (ii) on arrival.

(2) (a) A profile diagram of the ship drawn to a suitable small scale showing the disposition of all components of the deadweight.

(b) A statement showing the lightweight, the disposition and the total weights of all components of the deadweight, the displacement, the corresponding positions of the centre of gravity, the metacentre and also the metacentric height (GM).

(c) A diagram showing a curve of Righting Levers (GZ) derived from the cross curves of stability referred to in paragraph 9. Where credit is shown for the buoyancy of a timber deck cargo the curve of Righting Levers (GZ) must be drawn both with and without this credit.

(3) The metacentric height and the curve of Righting Levers (GZ) shall be corrected for liquid free surface.

(4) Where there is a significant amount of trim in any of the conditions referred to in sub-paragraph (1) the metacentric height and the curve of Righting Levers (GZ) may be required to be determined from the trimmed waterline.

(5) If in the opinion of the Board the stability characteristics in either or both of the conditions referred to in sub-paragraph (1)(c) are not satisfactory, such conditions shall be marked accordingly and an appropriate warning to the master shall be inserted.

11. Where special procedures such as partly filling or completely filling particular spaces designated for cargo, fuel, fresh water or other purposes are necessary to maintain adequate stability, a statement of instructions as to the appropriate procedure in each case.

12. A copy of the report on the inclining test and of the calculation therefrom of the light condition particulars.

Merchant Shipping (Safety Convention) Act, 1949

Section 18-(1) There shall be carried on board every British ship registered in the United Kingdom whose keel is laid after the commencement of this

Act such information in writing about the ship's stability as is necessary for the guidance of the master in loading and ballasting the ship.

(2) The said information shall be in such a form as may be approved by the Minister (who may approve the provision of the information in the form of a diagram or drawing only), and shall be based on the determination of the ship's stability by means of an inclining test of the ship:

Provided that the Minister may allow the information to be based on a similar determination of the stability of a sister ship.

(3) When any information under this section is provided for any ship, the owner shall send a copy thereof to the Minister:

Provided that the owner shall not be required to send a copy of any information to the Minister if a previous copy of the same information has been sent to the Minister.

(4) If any such ship proceeds, or attempts to proceed, to sea without such information as aforesaid on board, the owner or master of the ship shall be liable to a fine not exceeding one hundred pounds; and if the owner of any ship contravenes the last preceding subsection, he shall be liable to a like fine.

(5) It is hereby declared that for the purposes of section two hundred and fifty-eight of the principal Act (which requires documents relating to navigation to be delivered by the master of a ship to his successor) information under this section shall be deemed to be a document relating to the navigation of the ship.

Section 29-(l) Nothing in this Act:

    (c) requiring information about a ship's stability to be carried on board; shall, unless in the case of information about a ship's stability the Minister otherwise orders, apply to any troopship, pleasure yacht or fishing vessel, or to any ship of less than five hundred tons gross tonnage other than a passenger steamer or to any ship not propelled by mechanical means.

Appendix V
Department of Transport Syllabuses (Revised April 1995)*

Supplied kindly by Marine Safety Agency (MSA) of Southampton and Scottish Qualifications Authority (SQA) of Glasgow.

<u>CLASS 5 CERTIFICATE OF COMPETENCY</u>

General Ship Knowledge – MSA/SQA
(a) General ideas on ship construction and on plans available on board ship.
General pumping arrangements.
General definition of main dimensions.
The names of the principal parts of a ship.
(b) General understanding of:
Displacement;
Deadweight;
Buoyancy; Reserve buoyancy.

Use of displacement and tonnes per centimetre immersion scales to determine weight of cargo or ballast from draughts or freeboard.
Load line marks.
Effect of density of water on draught and freeboard.
Fresh water allowance.
(c)   (i) General understanding of:
Centre of gravity
Centre of buoyancy
Metacentric height
Righting lever
Righting moment
    (ii) The use of stability and hydrostatic data supplied to ships, including stability data in simplified form.

* All of these syllabuses to be reviewed and possibly revised by MSA in 1999/2000.

The effect of adding and removing weights. The danger of slack tanks.

(iii) Rigging a ship for loading and discharging cargo, the use of derricks, winches and cranes.

'Lining up' pipelines on oil products carriers.

The stowage and securing of cargoes including bulk cargoes. Grain cargoes, timber cargoes and ro-ro cargoes. A knowledge of the safety precautions to be taken during the loading and discharging of bulk oil, chemicals and other dangerous commodities.

Ventilation systems of holds and tanks. Entry into enclosed spaces.

CLASS 4 CERTIFICATE OF COMPETENCY

General Ship Knowledge – BTEC/SQA/HND Part 1

(a) General ideas on ship construction and on plans available onboard ship. General definitions of main dimensions.

The names of the principal parts of a ship.

The candidate will be expected to show his practical acquaintance with:

Longitudinal and transverse framing
Beams and beam knees
Watertight bulkheads
Hatchways and closing appliances
Rudders
Steering gear
Shell and deck plating
Double bottoms and peak tanks
Bilges
Side and wing tanks
Stern frames
Propellers and propeller shafts
Stern tubes
Sounding pipes
Air pipes
General pumping arrangements
The stiffening and strengthening to resist panting, pounding and longitudinal stresses.
Cause and prevention of corrosion in a ship's structure.

(b) General ideas on welding, riveting and burning and the precautions to be taken when such processes are carried out aboard ship.

(c) (i) The meaning of the terms: Block co-efficient; Displacement; Deadweight.

(ii) Density, relative density; Principle of Archimedes; flotation. Effect of density of water on draught and freeboard. Fresh water allowance. The marine hydrometer and its uses.

(d) Care and maintenance of all life saving and fire fighting appliances, lights and sound signalling apparatus.

(e) The computation of areas by Simpson's First and Second Rules.

<u>CLASS 4 CERTIFICATE OF COMPETENCY</u>

Cargo Operations and Stability – MSA/SQA

(a) Use of displacement and tonnes per centimetre immersion scales to determine weight of cargo or ballast from draughts or freeboard.
Load line-marks.
Buoyancy; Reserve buoyancy; understanding of fundamental actions to be taken in the event of partial loss of intact buoyancy.

(b)   (i) General understanding with definitions of:
      Centre of gravity, stable, unstable and neutral equilibrium.
      Centre of buoyancy
      Metacentric height
      Righting lever
      Righting moment

  (ii) The use of stability and hydrostatic data supplied to ships.
The effect of adding and removing weights.
The danger of slack tanks. Security of hatches.

  (iii) Rigging a ship for loading and discharging cargo, the use of derricks, winches and cranes.
'Lining up' pipelines on oil products carriers.
The stowage, separation and dunnaging of cargoes including bulk cargoes, timber cargoes; grain cargoes, ro-ro cargoes.
Causes of sweating, and precautions to be taken before, during and after stowing to prevent damage by sweat.
A knowledge of the safety precautions to be taken during the loading and discharge of bulk oil, chemicals and other dangerous commodities, Calculations of weight capacities taken up by part cargoes and of space remaining.
Conversion of weight measurement of cargo into space measurement and vice versa.
The making and use of cargo plans.
Ventilation and systems of holds and tanks.
Precautions to be taken before entering cargo and ballast tanks and void spaces. The carriage of passengers and livestock.

<u>CLASS 2 CERTIFICATE OF COMPETENCY</u>

Ship Construction – BTEC/SQA/HND

(a) Types of ships. General ideas on strength and construction in relation to particular trades, including specialised carriers.

The use of special steels, aluminium and fire resistant materials in ship construction.

(b) Midship sections of single deck and 'tween deck ships, including bulk carriers, container ships and specialised carriers. Functions, construction and stiffening of watertight bulkheads, including collision bulkhead. Structure at the stern, construction, stiffening and closing arrangements of hatchways and superstructures, tank openings, watertight and hull doors.

(c) General ideas on welding processes in construction and repair work, types of weld, common faults, visual examination of welded work.
Testing of tanks and other watertight work.
Methods of corrosion control.

(d) Stresses produced by shear and bending. To produce simple curves of load, shear force and bending moments. Torsional stress. Modern methods of determining the effect of different conditions of loading and ballasting on the ship's structure. Methods of compensating for discontinuity of strength. Local and specific stiffening.

(e) Classification of ships; periodic surveys for retention of class. The Cargo Ship Construction and Survey Rules and surveys required under the Rules.

CLASS 2 CERTIFICATE OF COMPETENCY

Ship Stability – MSA/SQA

(a) Determination of the position of the centre of gravity of a ship for different conditions of loading and ballasting. The effect on the position of the centre of gravity of adding, removing, shifting or suspending weights. To determine the virtual rise in the position of the centre of gravity due to slack tanks. Transverse and longitudinal metacentres, metacentric height. Initial stability and its limitation to small angles of inclination. Changes in stability during a voyage. Effects of a shift of cargo or solid ballast. Stiff and tender ships.

(b) Changes of trim and draught due to loading, discharging and shifting weights. Effects of list and trim on stability. Stability and trim when drydocking.

(c) Stability to moderate for large angles of heel; assessment of dynamical stability from GZ curve; angle of loll; shifting or adding weights with zero GM; effect of wind and wave excitation.

(d) Dangers to a ship with a heavy list. Precautions when righting. Deck cargoes, homogeneous cargo and cargo liable to shift. Ballasting for stability consideration. The effect of beam and freeboard on stability.

(e) The inclining experiment. A comprehensive knowledge of the hydrostatic, stability and stress data supplied to ships.

(f) An understanding of the factors affecting the shape of a curve of statical stability and the significance of the area under the curve, including its calculation. Use of simplified data. Grain shift moments.

(g) Principles of damage control in passenger ships and ro-ro vessels. Arrangement for restricting the spread of fire in superstructures.

(h) Requirements of the Load Line Rules, period and conditions of validity of certificate, an understanding of those aspects of the conditions of assignment which affect the stability and seaworthiness of a ship. Knowledge of the principles underlying the assignment of passenger ship subdivision load lines.

(i) Permeability of a compartment. The effect of bilging and flooding (end or midships' compartment, on or off the centre-line).

(j) Shallow water effect. Ship to ship and ship to shore interaction. The turning circle. Angle of heel when turning; effect on stability.

(k) Load line marks and zones; calculations involving their use.

MASTER (LIMITED EUROPEAN) ENDORSEMENT

Ship Construction and Stability – MSA/SQA

This syllabus is designed to cover only those aspects of ship stability which are of a practical nature and within the control of the master.

(a) Use of stability and hydrostatic data supplied to ships, including stability date in simplified form. Initial stability and its limitation to small angles of heel. An understanding of the factors affecting the shape of a curve of statical stability and the significance of the area under the curve.

(b) Determination of the centre of gravity of a ship for different conditions of loading and ballasting. The effect on the position of the centre of gravity of adding, removing, shifting or suspending weights.

(c) Transverse metacentre, metacentric height. Free surface of liquids (without proof) and its effect on stability.

(d) Change of draught and trim due to loading, discharging or shifting weights (MCTC and CF given). Effects of list and trim or stability.

(e) Changes in stability during a voyage, including the effect of a shift of cargo or solid ballast. Grain Regulations.

(f) Load Line; an understanding of those aspects of the conditions of assignment which affect the stability and seaworthiness of a ship.

MASTER (EXTENDED EUROPEAN) ENDORSEMENT

Ship Construction and Stability – MSA/SQA

(a) A fuller knowledge of the fundamentals of ship construction than is required in Class 4, General Ship Knowledge.

(b) Stresses and strains in ships in a seaway or due to loading and ballasting. A knowledge of the parts of a ship specially strengthened to withstand such stresses.

Methods of compensating for discontinuity of strength.

Testing of tanks and other watertight work. Methods of corrosion control.

(c) Use of stability and hydrostatic data supplied to ships.
Initial stability and its limitation to small angles of heel.
An understanding of the factors affecting the shape of a curve of statical stability and the significance of the area under the curve. Computation of areas by Simpson's first and second rules.
(d) Determination of the centre of gravity of a ship for different conditions of loading and ballasting. The effect on the position of the centre of gravity of adding, removing, shifting or suspending weights.
(e) Transverse metacentre, metacentric height. Free surface of liquids (without proof) and its effect on stability.
(f) Change of draught and trim due to loading, discharging or shifting weights (MCTC and CF given). Effects of list and trim on stability.
(g) Changes in stability during a voyage, including the effect of a shift of cargo or solid ballast. Grain Regulations.
(h) Load Line; an understanding of those aspects of the conditions of assignment which affect the stability and seaworthiness of a ship.
(i) Stability and Trim when drydocking.
(j) Methods of compensating for discontinuities of strength.

Appendix VI
Specimen examination papers

Supplied kindly by Scottish Qualifications Authority (SQA) in Glasgow.

General Ship Knowledge

2 hours. Attempt all questions. Marks for each question are shown in brackets.

1. A vessel has a Light Ship Displacement of 1625 tonnes. The vessel loads

175 tonnes of fuel oil	kg	0.60 m
60 tonnes of fresh water	kg	2.50 m
375 tonnes of steel	kg	3.60 m
910 tonnes of general	kg	4.80 m
555 tonnes of pipes on deck	kg	7.00 m

    The effect of free surface is 350 tonne metres

    On the Simplified Stability Information sheet provided (Worksheet Q. 1),* plot the condition of the vessel's stability and state whether the vessel has sufficient or deficient stability. (20)

2. (a) Define TPC. (5)

    (b) Explain why the TPC for a given draft will vary with the density of the water in which the ship floats. (10)

    (c) A ship has an even keel draught of 3.78 m and is required to change berth to one where the maximum draught allowed is 3.60 m.
    Calculate the amount of cargo that must be discharged before the ship can shift berth. (5)
    TPC = 5.5

*The worksheet provided with this paper is the same as that shown in Figure 44.1 on page 375 of this book (where simplified stability data relating to worked examples are plotted).

3. Sketch a half midship section through the weather deck of a cargo vessel, in the way of the hatch coaming. The vessel has combination framing. Name all parts.   (30)
4. List the main hazards and state the precautions associated with the carriage of concentrates.   (25)
5. List the safety precautions that should be observed when working cargo on a general cargo vessel using ship's gear.   (30)
6. An oil tanker is required to thoroughly clean cargo tanks prior to drydocking. Describe how this procedure is carried out using portable tank washing equipment. State all necessary safety precautions.   (25)

CLASS 4 DECK OFFICER

Operational Safety
$2\frac{1}{2}$ hours. Attempt all questions. Marks for each question are shown in brackets.

1. A vessel displacing 4500 tonnes has a constant KM = 6.2 m and a present KG = 5.8 m. The vessel loads 50 t of cargo on deck at Kg = 8.5, and then moves 100 t of cargo from the 'tween deck (Kg = 5.5 m) to the lower hold (Kg = 2.3 m), all weights being on the centre line.

   Calculate the final GM.   (15)

2. (a) A vessel is floating in water of R. D. 1.025
      The initial drafts are: 4.10 m forward and 4.85 m aft.
      Cargo is then loaded as follows:

      150 t at 80 m forward of the aft perpendicular.
      70 t at 25 m forward of the aft perpendicular.

      LBP = 100 M; TPC = 15; MCTC = 40.
      Centre of Flotation is 45 m forward of the aft perpendicular.

      Calculate the final draughts on completion of loading.   (25)

   (b) Is the final trim desirable? Give brief reasons for your conclusion. (5)

3. Outline the contents of the 'Code of Safe Practice for Merchant Seamen' with respect to cargo winches, derricks, and hatches.   (25)

4. (a) State what is meant by the term 'Unitised Cargo'.   (10)
   (b) Give three examples of unitised cargo.   (10)
   (c) State the advantages and disadvantages of this method of cargo handling.   (10)

5. (a) Draw a plan view of a single ring main pipeline system on an oil tanker having 5 sets of 3 tanks.   (13)
   (b) Show on your diagram how you would discharge three different products from No. 1 centre tank, No. 3 centre tank, and No. 4 centre tank, respectively.   (12)

6. Describe the causes of static electricity in tanker operations, and explain how this can be reduced or prevented.   (25)

CLASS 2 DECK OFFICER

DATASHEET Q.2(a)

(This Datasheet must be returned with your answer book)

TABULATED KN VALUES

KN values in metres

KN values calculated for vessel on an Even Keel and fixed trim.

Displacement (tonne)	Angle of Heel (Degrees)						
	12	20	30	40	50	60	75
15 000	1.72	2.98	4.48	5.72	6.48	6.91	7.05
14 500	1.73	2.98	4.51	5.79	6.58	6.95	7.08
14 000	1.74	2.98	4.55	5.85	6.68	7.00	7.10
13 500	1.75	2.99	4.58	5.90	6.73	7.08	7.13
13 000	1.77	3.00	4.62	5.93	6.78	7.14	7.16
12 500	1.78	3.03	4.63	5.98	6.83	7.18	7.18
12 000	1.78	3.05	4.65	6.04	6.88	7.20	7.20
11 500	1.80	3.12	4.70	6.10	6.93	7.25	7.22
11 000	1.82	3.15	4.75	6.15	6.98	7.30	7.24
10 500	1.83	3.19	4.79	6.18	7.02	7.35	7.27
10 000	1.86	3.23	4.83	6.22	7.07	7.40	7.30
9500	1.93	3.28	4.91	6.25	7.11	7.45	7.35
9000	2.00	3.36	5.00	6.28	7.18	7.50	7.40
8500	2.05	3.43	5.04	6.32	7.20	7.55	7.41
8000	2.10	3.52	5.10	6.36	7.22	7.60	7.42
7500	2.17	3.62	5.18	6.38	7.24	7.65	7.46
7000	2.22	3.70	5.25	6.40	7.26	7.70	7.50
6500	2.32	3.85	5.35	6.43	7.27	7.70	7.51
6000	2.42	4.00	5.45	6.48	7.28	7.70	7.52
5500	2.57	4.15	5.55	6.53	7.29	7.68	7.51
5000	2.72	4.32	5.65	6.58	7.30	7.66	7.50

KN values are for hull and forecastle only.

DATASHEET Q.2(b)

(This Datasheet must be returned with your answer book). Note: 'foap' denotes for'd of AP

Hydrostatic Particulars

Draught m	Displacement t		TPC t		MCTC tm		KM_T m	KB m	LCB foap m	LCF foap m
	SW RD 1.025	FW RD 1.000	SW RD 1.025	FW RD 1.000	SW RD 1.025	FW RD 1.000				
7.00	14 576	14 220	23.13	22.57	184.6	180.1	8.34	3.64	70.03	67.35
6.90	14 345	13 996	23.06	22.50	183.0	178.5	8.35	3.58	70.08	67.46
6.80	14 115	13 771	22.99	22.43	181.4	177.0	8.36	3.53	70.12	67.57
6.70	13 886	13 548	22.92	22.36	179.9	175.5	8.37	3.48	70.16	67.68
6.60	13 657	13 324	22.85	22.29	178.3	174.0	8.38	3.43	70.20	67.79
6.50	13 429	13 102	22.78	22.23	176.8	172.5	8.39	3.38	70.24	67.90
6.40	13 201	12 879	22.72	22.17	175.3	171.0	8.41	3.33	70.28	68.00
6.30	12 975	12 658	22.66	22.11	173.9	169.6	8.43	3.28	70.32	68.10
6.20	12 748	12 437	22.60	22.05	172.5	168.3	8.46	3.22	70.35	68.20
6.10	12 523	12 217	22.54	21.99	171.1	167.0	8.49	3.17	70.38	68.30
6.00	12 297	11 997	22.48	21.93	169.8	165.7	8.52	3.11	70.42	68.39
5.90	12 073	11 778	22.43	21.87	168.5	164.4	8.55	3.06	70.46	68.48
5.80	11 848	11 559	22.37	21.82	167.3	163.2	8.59	3.01	70.50	68.57
5.70	11 625	11 342	22.32	21.77	166.1	162.1	8.63	2.95	70.53	68.65
5.60	11 402	11 124	22.26	21.72	165.0	161.0	8.67	2.90	70.57	68.73

5.50	11 180	10 908	22.21	21.66	163.9	160.0	8.71	2.85	70.60	68.80
5.40	10 958	10 691	22.15	21.61	162.9	158.9	8.76	2.80	70.64	68.88
5.30	10 737	10 476	22.10	21.56	161.8	157.9	8.81	2.74	70.68	68.95
5.20	10 516	10 260	22.05	21.51	160.8	156.9	8.86	2.69	70.72	69.02
5.10	10 296	10 045	22.00	21.46	159.8	155.9	8.92	2.63	70.75	69.09
5.00	10 076	9830	21.95	21.41	158.8	154.9	8.98	2.58	70.79	69.16
4.90	9857	9616	21.90	21.36	157.9	154.0	9.06	2.53	70.82	69.23
4.80	9638	9403	21.85	21.32	156.9	153.1	9.13	2.48	70.86	69.29
4.70	9420	9190	21.80	21.27	156.0	152.2	9.22	2.43	70.90	69.35
4.60	9202	8978	21.75	21.22	155.1	151.3	9.30	2.38	70.93	69.42
4.50	8985	8766	21.70	21.17	154.2	150.5	9.40	2.32	70.96	69.48
4.40	8768	8554	21.65	21.12	153.3	149.6	9.49	2.27	71.00	69.55
4.30	8552	8344	21.60	21.07	152.4	148.7	9.60	2.22	71.04	69.62
4.20	8336	8133	21.55	21.02	151.5	147.8	9.71	2.17	71.08	69.68
4.10	8121	7923	21.50	20.97	150.6	146.9	9.83	2.12	71.12	69.74
4.00	7906	7713	21.45	20.93	149.7	146.0	9.96	2.07	71.15	69.81
3.90	7692	7505	21.40	20.88	148.7	145.1	10.11	2.01	71.18	69.88
3.80	7478	7296	21.35	20.83	147.8	144.2	10.25	1.96	71.22	69.94
3.70	7265	7088	21.30	20.78	146.8	143.3	10.41	1.91	71.25	70.00
3.60	7052	6880	21.24	20.72	145.9	142.3	10.57	1.86	71.29	70.07
3.50	6840	6673	21.19	20.67	144.9	141.3	10.76	1.81	71.33	70.14

THESE HYDROSTATIC PARTICULARS HAVE BEEN DEVELOPED WITH THE VESSEL FLOATING ON EVEN KEEL

SHIP STABILITY

Attempt ALL questions

Marks for each question are shown in brackets

1. A box shaped vessel, length 96 m, breadth 18 m, is floating on even keel draught of 5.70 m in salt water.
   KG 5.77 m.
   A full width forward compartment extending 13 m aft of the forward perpendicular is bilged.

   Calculate the resultant draughts.   (35)

2. Ship 'A', KG 8.20 m, is floating at an even keel draught of 6.80 m in salt water.
   With the aid of Datasheets Q.2(a) Tabulated KN values and Q.2(b) Hydrostatic Particulars, compare the ship's stability values with those required by the current Loadline Rules.   (35)

3. A vessel is floating at an even keel draught of 7.93 m in salt water.
   The vessel is to proceed to a dock where the water has a relative density of 1.003.
   Displacement 36 000 t   TPC 34   MCTC 220
   LBP 184 m   LCB 80 m foap   LCF 96 m foap

   Calculate EACH of the following:

   (a) the trim on entering the dock;   (18)
   (b) the draught aft on arrival.   (17)

4. (a) Explain why the values of trim and metacentric height in the freely afloat condition are important when considering the suitability of a vessel for drydocking.   (15)
   (b) Describe the effect on a vessel's buoyancy of removing water from a drydock after taking the blocks aft with a stern trim.   (8)
   (c) Describe TWO methods of determining the upthrust (P force) during the critical period.   (12)

5. (a) Show by means of suitable sketches how beam and freeboard affect the shape of the GZ curve.   (15)
   (b) Draw TWO curves of statical stability on the same axis to illustrate:

   • departure condition
   • arrival condition

   Explain the reasons for the differences between the two curves.   (15)

6. (a) Describe an 'A' Class Division as defined by the Merchant Shipping (Fire Protection) Regulations.   (15)
   (b) Describe the measures required for the protection of stairways and lifts.   (15)

DATASHEET Q.3

(This Datasheet must be returned with your answer book)

MAXIMUM KG (METRES) TO COMPLY WITH MINIMUM STABILITY CRITERIA
SPECIFIED IN THE CURRENT LOAD LINE RULES

Displacement (t)	KG (m)
19 500	7.85
19 000	7.93
18 500	8.02
18 000	8.10
17 500	8.17
17 000	8.20
16 500	8.19
16 000	8.18
15 500	8.18
15 000	8.19
14 500	8.20
14 000	8.22
13 500	8.24
13 000	8.28
12 500	8.34
12 000	8.42
11 500	8.50
11 000	8.60
10 500	8.71
10 000	8.85
9500	9.03
9000	9.24
8500	9.48
8000	9.73
7500	9.82
7000	9.62
6500	9.43
6000	9.18
5500	8.84
5000	8.40

SHIP STABILITY

Attempt ALL questions

Marks for each question are shown in brackets

1. A box shaped vessel, length 90 m, breadth 13 m, depth 8 m is floating at an even keel draft of 4.0 m. There is a deeptank amidships, length 18 m, breadth 13 m extending from the ship's bottom to a watertight flat 4.2 m above the keel.

   The deeptank is tightly stowed with cargo of relative density 1.14 and stowage factor 1.5 m³/t.

   Calculate the resultant draught if this deeptank is bilged.   (35)

2. (a) Define *dynamical stability*.   (5)
   (b) The righting levers of a vessel displacing 9500 t are as follows:

Heel:	0°	10°	20°	30°	40°
GZ (m):	0	0.04	0.14	0.40	0.55

   Calculate EACH of the following:

   (i) the dynamical stability at 40°;   (15)
   (ii) the residual dynamical stability at 40° if the vessel is subjected to a steady wind moment of 380 tm.   (15)

3. (a) The Loadline Rules require the master to be provided with stability particulars for various conditions. Detail the information to be provided for a given service condition and describe how this information may be presented.   (20)
   (b) A ship plans to depart from port at:

   Displacement 18 000 t   KG 8.02 m

   During the ensuing voyage the ship will consume 60 t of fresh water (Kg 0.8 m) and 240 t of bunkers (Kg 1.4 m) from full tanks causing a free surface moment of 2100 t m.

   Using Datasheet Q.3 'Maximum KG', determine the stability condition of the ship both on departure and on arrival.   (15)

4. Describe the Loadline Rules requirements governing the ability of Type B vessels with reduced freeboard to withstand flooding due to damage, and the stability in the final condition.   (30)

5. Discuss the stability problems associated with the operation of an oil rig supply vessel.   (30)

6. (a) List the precautions to be observed before and during an inclining experiment to find a vessel's KG.   (10)
   (b) State the maximum interval at which the inclining test must be carried out on a Passenger Ro/ro vessel.   (5)
   (c) From the following results of an inclining test, calculate the KG of the vessel in the *Lightship Condition*, KM 8.1 m.

Present displacement 5400 t, which includes the following:
Inclining weight 25 t, Kg 7.94 m.
Fuel oil 50 t, Kg 2.30 m, FSM 640 t m.
The inclining weight is moved 14.0 m transversely producing a
deflection of 27 cm in a plumbline of length 9.0 m.   (20)

DATASHEET Q.1

(This Datasheet must be returned with your answer book). Note 'foap' denotes for'd of AP

Hydrostatic Particulars 'A'

Draught m	Displacement t		TPC t		MCTC t m		KM$_T$	KB	LCB foap	LCF foap
	SW RD 1.025	FW RD 1.000	SW RD 1.025	FW RD 1.000	SW RD 1.025	FW RD 1.000	m	m	m	m
7.00	14 576	14 220	23.13	22.57	184.6	180.1	8.34	3.64	70.03	67.35
6.90	14 345	13 996	23.06	22.50	183.0	178.5	8.35	3.58	70.08	67.46
6.80	14 115	13 771	22.99	22.43	181.4	177.0	8.36	3.53	70.12	67.57
6.70	13 886	13 548	22.92	22.36	179.9	175.5	8.37	3.48	70.16	67.68
6.60	13 657	13 324	22.85	22.29	178.3	174.0	8.38	3.43	70.20	67.79
6.50	13 429	13 102	22.78	22.23	176.8	172.5	8.39	3.38	70.24	67.90
6.40	13 201	12 879	22.72	22.17	175.3	171.0	8.41	3.33	70.28	68.00
6.30	12 975	12 658	22.66	22.11	173.9	169.6	8.43	3.28	70.32	68.10
6.20	12 748	12 437	22.60	22.05	172.5	168.3	8.46	3.22	70.35	68.20
6.10	12 523	12 217	22.54	21.99	171.1	167.0	8.49	3.17	70.38	68.30
6.00	12 297	11 997	22.48	21.93	169.8	165.7	8.52	3.11	70.42	68.39
5.90	12 073	11 778	22.43	21.87	168.5	164.4	8.55	3.06	70.46	68.48
5.80	11 848	11 559	22.37	21.82	167.3	163.2	8.59	3.01	70.50	68.57
5.70	11 625	11 342	22.32	21.77	166.1	162.1	8.63	2.95	70.53	68.65
5.60	11 402	11 124	22.26	21.72	165.0	161.0	8.67	2.90	70.57	68.73

5.50	11 180	10 908	22.21	21.66	163.9	160.0	8.71	2.85	70.60	68.80
5.40	10 958	10 691	22.15	21.61	162.9	158.9	8.76	2.80	70.64	68.88
5.30	10 737	10 476	22.10	21.56	161.8	157.9	8.81	2.74	70.68	68.95
5.20	10 516	10 260	22.05	21.51	160.8	156.9	8.86	2.69	70.72	69.02
5.10	10 296	10 045	22.00	21.46	159.8	155.9	8.92	2.63	70.75	69.09
5.00	10 076	9830	21.95	21.41	158.8	154.9	8.98	2.58	70.79	69.16
4.90	9857	9616	21.90	21.36	157.9	154.0	9.06	2.53	70.82	69.23
4.80	9638	9403	21.85	21.32	156.9	153.1	9.13	2.48	70.86	69.29
4.70	9420	9190	21.80	21.27	156.0	152.2	9.22	2.43	70.90	69.35
4.60	9202	8978	21.75	21.22	155.1	151.3	9.30	2.38	70.93	69.42
4.50	8985	8766	21.70	21.17	154.2	150.5	9.40	2.32	70.96	69.48
4.40	8768	8554	21.65	21.12	153.3	149.6	9.49	2.27	71.00	69.55
4.30	8552	8344	21.60	21.07	152.4	148.7	9.60	2.22	71.04	69.62
4.20	8336	8133	21.55	21.02	151.5	147.8	9.71	2.17	71.08	69.68
4.10	8121	7923	21.50	20.97	150.6	146.9	9.83	2.12	71.12	69.74
4.00	7906	7713	21.45	20.93	149.7	146.0	9.96	2.07	71.15	69.81
3.90	7692	7505	21.40	20.88	148.7	145.1	10.11	2.01	71.18	69.88
3.80	7478	7296	21.35	20.83	147.8	144.2	10.25	1.96	71.22	69.94
3.70	7265	7088	21.30	20.78	146.8	143.3	10.41	1.91	71.25	70.00
3.60	7052	6880	21.24	20.72	145.9	142.3	10.57	1.86	71.29	70.07
3.50	6840	6673	21.19	20.67	144.9	141.3	10.76	1.81	71.33	70.14

THESE HYDROSTATIC PARTICULARS HAVE BEEN DEVELOPED WITH THE VESSEL FLOATING ON EVEN KEEL

DATASHEET Q.1

(N.B. This Datasheet must be returned with your examination answer book)

TABULATED KN VALUES 'A'

KN values in metres

KN values calculated for vessel on an Even Keel and fixed trim.

Displacement (tonne)	Angle of Heel (Degrees)						
	12	20	30	40	50	60	75
15 000	1.72	2.98	4.48	5.72	6.48	6.91	7.05
14 500	1.73	2.98	4.51	5.79	6.58	6.95	7.08
14 000	1.74	2.98	4.55	5.85	6.68	7.00	7.10
13 500	1.75	2.99	4.58	5.90	6.73	7.08	7.13
13 000	1.77	3.00	4.62	5.93	6.78	7.14	7.16
12 500	1.78	3.03	4.63	5.98	6.83	7.18	7.18
12 000	1.78	3.05	4.65	6.04	6.88	7.20	7.20
11 500	1.80	3.12	4.70	6.10	6.93	7.25	7.22
11 000	1.82	3.15	4.75	6.15	6.98	7.30	7.24
10 500	1.83	3.19	4.79	6.18	7.02	7.35	7.27
10 000	1.86	3.23	4.83	6.22	7.07	7.40	7.30
9500	1.93	3.28	4.91	6.25	7.11	7.45	7.35
9000	2.00	3.36	5.00	6.28	7.18	7.50	7.40
8500	2.05	3.43	5.04	6.32	7.20	7.55	7.41
8000	2.10	3.52	5.10	6.36	7.22	7.60	7.42
7500	2.17	3.62	5.18	6.38	7.24	7.65	7.46
7000	2.22	3.70	5.25	6.40	7.26	7.70	7.50
6500	2.32	3.85	5.35	6.43	7.27	7.70	7.51
6000	2.42	4.00	5.45	6.48	7.28	7.70	7.52
5500	2.57	4.15	5.55	6.53	7.29	7.68	7.51
5000	2.72	4.32	5.65	6.58	7.30	7.66	7.50

KN values are for hull and forecastle only.

SHIP STABILITY

Attempt ALL questions

Marks for each question are shown in brackets

1. Ship 'A' has a displacement of 14 000 tonne and a KG of 8.20 m.

   Using Datasheets Q.1 *Tabulated KN Values* and *Hydrostatic Particulars*, determine whether the vessel complies with the stability requirements of the current Load Line Rules. (35)

2. A box shaped vessel floating at an even keel in salt water has the following particulars:

   Length 75.00 m   Breadth 18.00 m   Depth 11.0 m
   Draft   6.00 m   KG 6.80 m

   An empty midship watertight compartment 15.00 m long is bilged.

   Calculate EACH of the following:
   (a) the new draft; (8)
   (b) the GM in the flooded condition; (12)
   (c) the righting moment at an angle of 16 degrees. (15)

3. (a) Describe, with the aid of a sketch, the forces that cause a vessel to heel when turning. (12)
   (b) A vessel turns in a circle of diameter 200 m at a speed of 16 knots. GM 0.78 m. BG 0.88 m. $g = 9.81 \, \text{m/sec}^2$ (Assume 1 knot = 1.8532 km/hr).

   Calculate the angle of heel due to turning. (18)

4. (a) Describe the hydrostatic, stability and stress data required to be supplied to ships. (30)
   (b) A maximum draft forward is sometimes stated in the above data when supplied to the ship under the Load Line Rules.

   State the reason for this limitation. (5)

5. A vessel with a high deck cargo will experience adverse effects on its stability due to strong beam winds on lateral windage areas.

   With the aid of a sketch, show the minimum stability requirements, with respect to wind heeling, under current regulations. (35)

6. With regard to the inclining experiment:
   (a) state its purpose; (5)
   (b) describe the precautions to be taken before and during the experiment; (16)
   (c) list the circumstances when the experiment is required to take place. (9)

COMMAND ENDORSEMENT (LIMITED EUROPEAN)

Ship Construction and Stability

2 hours. Attempt all questions. Marks for each question are shown in brackets.

1. A ship has a light displacement 435 tonnes with KG 3.25 m.

   On board this ship there are 40 tonnes of fuel, water, stores and crew effects at Kg 3.80 m with a free surface moment of 35 t m.

   The single hold is rectangular of length 40 m, width 9.4 m and depth 5.1 m and is to be filled with a bulk cargo (stowage factor 1.4 m³/tonne). When filled the Kg of the hold is 3.34 m.

   Calculate the GM of the ship in its loaded condition if the loaded KM is 4.05 m   (30)

2. A ship is at displacement 1700 tonnes with draughts 3.20 m forward 4.05 m aft. The following is the appropriate hydrostatic data:

   Length BP: 55 m TPC: 5.2 MCTC: 22.8
   Centre of Flotation 2.5 m abaft amidship.

   Calculate:
   (a) the drafts forward and aft produced by loading 100 tonnes 40 m forward of the aft perpendicular;   (20)
   (b) from the initial condition, the weight to load 37 m forward of the aft perpendicular to bring the ship to a trim of 0.6 m by the stern.

3. Use Worksheet Q.3: Simplified Stability − Deadweight Moment Curve. (Ensure that all points plotted on the diagram can be identified in the working).

   The load displacement is 1175 tonnes.
   The ships present condition: displacement 800 tonnes.
   Deadweight moment 600 t m.
   Cargo to be loaded: 250 tonnes at Kg 2.8 m.

   From the above condition:
   (a) Determine the maximum weight of cargo that can be taken at Kg 4.5 m so that stability is adequate.   (10)
   (b) It is anticipated that 30 tonnes of fuel and water at Kg 1.6 m will be used on passage producing a free surface moment of 100 t m. Determine the maximum weight of cargo that can be loaded at Kg 4.5 m so that stability is adequate on arrival at the discharge port.   (20)

4. (a) Explain clearly the meaning of the term 'reserve buoyancy'.   (15)
   (b) Describe the items that maintain the integrity of reserve buoyancy giving a brief indication of any maintenance that may be required.
                                                                          (15)

5. (a) (i) Sketch a typical GZ curve for a stable ship and indicate the features that may be found from it.   (15)
       (ii) The ship in (a) (i) is now further loaded with deck cargo. Show on the same curve how the GZ might change due to this.   (7)

(b) A ship is at a certain draught and displacement.
Sketch two GZ curves on the same axes to show this ship in a stiff
and a tender condition.

(8)

WORKSHEET Q.3

(N.B. The Worksheet must be returned with your examination answer book. Ensure that all
points plotted on the diagram can be identified in the working)

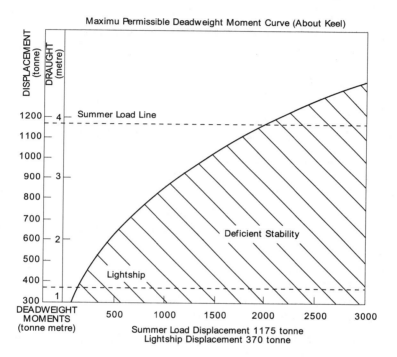

COMMAND ENDORSEMENT (EXTENDED EUROPEANS)

Ship Construction and Stability

3 hours. Attempt all questions. Marks for each question are shown in brackets.

1. A ship has a light displacement of 2700 tonnes and KG 6.50 m. The load
displacement of 11 800 tonnes has an associated KM 6.60 m. The
following are to be taken on board:

Fuel and FW: 520 tonnes at Kg 0.60 m
Stores: 100 tonnes at Kg 4.50 m

A full cargo is then to be loaded in the tween deck at Kg 8.20 m and
hold at Kg 5.00 m to give a sailing GM of 1.00 m.

Calculate how much of the cargo should be loaded in the:

   (i) tween deck;
   (ii) hold   (35)

2. The GZ values of a vessel at a certain displacement are as shown:

Heel ($\theta°$)	0	15	30	45	60	75
GZ (m)	0	0.27	0.73	0.95	0.61	0.06

KM: 9.00 m KG 8.20 m

  (a) Plot the GZ curve on the graph paper provided.   (10)
  (b) Calculate the area under the curve between 0° and 30° using Simpson's Rules.   (15)
  (c) Show that the curve satisfies the stability criteria required by the Load Line Rules 1968.   (10)

3. MV Mexna (2) is floating at draughts 6.40 m forward and 7.60 m aft. Using the hydrostatic data provided (Worksheet Q.3) calculate:

  (a) the amount of ballast to load into the forepeak tank (c.g. 60 m forward of amid-ships) so that the draught aft is 7.30 m;   (25)
  (b) the final draught forward.   (10)

4. Explain with reference to a well labelled sketch, how the effect of free surface can be considered as a reduction in a vessel's metacentric height.   (35)

5. (a) List the requirements of the Load Line Rules 1968, relating to weathertight doors.   (10)
  (b) Describe the maintenance and testing of a superstructure door in order to ensure weathertightness.   (20)

6. Illustrate by means of labelled half mid-section sketches each of the following framing systems:

   (i) Transverse;   (10)
   (ii) Longitudinal;   (10)
  (iii) Combination.   (10)

WORKSHEET Q.3 Hydrostatic Curves for Mexna (2)

(N.B. This worksheet must be returned with your answer book)

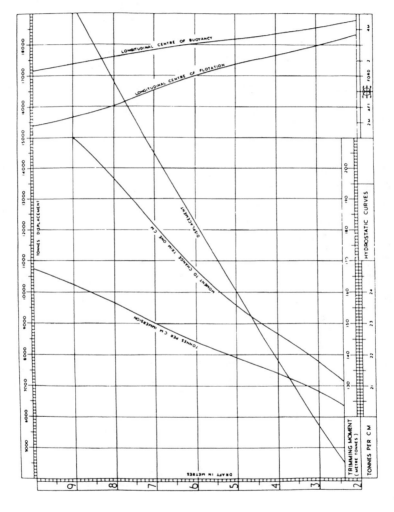

COMMAND ENDORSEMENT
(EXTENDED EUROPEAN)
DATASHEET Q.5
This Datasheet must be returned with your answer book
HYDROSTATIC PARTICULARS 'B'
(in salt water R.D. 1.025)
The hydrostatic particulars have been calculated for the vessel on Even Keel.

Draught (m)	Displacement (t)	TPC (t)	MCTC (tm)	LCB from amidships (m)	LCF from amidships (m)	KB (m)	KM_T (m)
4.00	1888.8	5.20	23.30	1.45 A	2.39 A	2.09	4.05
3.90	1836.8	5.20	23.20	1.42 A	2.43 A	2.04	4.05
3.80	1784.8	5.19	23.10	1.39 A	2.46 A	1.99	4.05
3.70	1733.0	5.18	22.99	1.36 A	2.49 A	1.93	4.06
3.60	1681.2	5.17	22.89	1.32 A	2.52 A	1.88	4.06
3.50	1629.5	5.16	22.77	1.29 A	2.55 A	1.83	4.07
3.40	1577.9	5.16	22.65	1.24 A	2.57 A	1.78	4.09
3.30	1526.4	5.15	22.52	1.20 A	2.59 A	1.72	4.11
3.20	1475.1	5.13	22.39	1.15 A	2.61 A	1.67	4.13
3.10	1423.8	5.12	22.25	1.10 A	2.62 A	1.62	4.15
3.00	1372.6	5.11	22.11	1.04 A	2.63 A	1.56	4.19
2.90	1321.5	5.10	21.96	0.98 A	2.64 A	1.51	4.22
2.80	1270.6	5.09	21.80	0.91 A	2.64 A	1.46	4.27
2.70	1211.4	5.07	21.64	0.84 A	2.64 A	1.40	4.32
2.60	1169.1	5.06	21.47	0.76 A	2.63 A	1.35	4.37
2.50	1118.6	5.05	21.30	0.68 A	2.63 A	1.30	4.44
2.40	1068.4	5.01	20.87	0.59 A	2.51 A	1.24	4.51

SHIP CONSTRUCTION AND STABILITY

Attempt ALL questions

Marks for each question are shown in brackets

1. A vessel of 5200 tonne displacement has a KG of 4.32 m and is listed 2.5° to starboard. KM 5.50 m (assumed constant).

   The following cargo operations take place:

   Load: 125 tonne Kg 2.45 m and 4.85 m to starboard of centreline.
   Discharge: 280 tonne Kg 3.55 m and 1.50 m to starboard of centreline.

   Calculate EACH of the following:

   (a) the resulting angle of list;   (25)
   (b) the angle of list if a slack tank containing salt water and with a fresh water free surface moment of 900 t m is also considered.   (10)

2. A ship is floating at drafts 7.25 m forward and 8.45 m aft and has to pass with an underkeel clearance of 0.5 m over a bar with a depth of 8.5 m.

   The following hydrostatic particulars apply:

   Length BP: 180 m
   LCF: 3 m aft of amidships
   MCTC: 200
   After peak tank: Lcg 2 m aft of AP
   Fore peak tank: Lcg 173 m for'd of AP

   Calculate EACH of the following:

   (a) the amount of water ballast to transfer from the after peak to the fore peak to enable the bar to be crossed with minimum clearance;   (25)
   (b) the final drafts forward and aft.   (10)

3. A rectangular shaped vessel of length 50 m and breadth 8 m floats on an even keel draft of 1.50 m in salt water at a KG of 2.50 m.
   500 tonne is now loaded at Kg 2.20 m.

   Calculate the vessel's righting moment at 5° heel for the loaded condition.   (35)

4. Explain, with the aid of sketches, how the stability of a vessel is affected by an increase in EACH of the following:
   (a) KG;   (15)
   (b) Freeboard.   (20)

5. (a) 'When a ship is floating out of design trim, the true mean draft (or draft at the centre of flotation) and not the arithmetic mean draft (or draft at amidships), must be used with the hydrostatic data in order to obtain the correct displacement.'

   For a ship floating with a trim by the stern and LCF abaft amidships, explain, with reference to a sketch EACH of the following:

    (i) how the true mean draft is obtained; (10)

    (ii) why it would be incorrect to use the arithmetic mean draft. (5)

(b) A ship of length BP 56 m is floating at draughts 2.70 m forward and 3.00 m aft.

Using Hydrostatic Particulars 'B' Datasheet Q.5:

Calculate the vessel's true mean draught and displacement. (15)

6. Illustrate EACH of the following with labelled sketches:

(a) the sheer/stringer strake connection at a deck transverse frame station; (10)

(b) a duct keel; (10)

(c) the watertight closing (or sealing) arrangements for a deep tank lid. (10)

DATASHEET Q.3

(N.B. This Datasheet must be returned with your examination answer book)

TABULATED KN VALUES 'A'

KN values in metres

KN values calculated for vessel on an Even Keel and fixed trim.

Displacement (tonne)	Angle of Heel (Degrees)						
	12	20	30	40	50	60	75
15 000	1.72	2.98	4.48	5.72	6.48	6.91	7.05
14 500	1.73	2.98	4.51	5.79	6.58	6.95	7.08
14 000	1.74	2.98	4.55	5.85	6.68	7.00	7.10
13 500	1.75	2.99	4.58	5.90	6.73	7.08	7.13
13 000	1.77	3.00	4.62	5.93	6.78	7.14	7.16
12 500	1.78	3.03	4.63	5.98	6.83	7.18	7.18
12 000	1.78	3.05	4.65	6.04	6.88	7.20	7.20
11 500	1.80	3.12	4.70	6.10	6.93	7.25	7.22
11 000	1.82	3.15	4.75	6.15	6.98	7.30	7.24
10 500	1.83	3.19	4.79	6.18	7.02	7.35	7.27
10 000	1.86	3.23	4.83	6.22	7.07	7.40	7.30
9500	1.93	3.28	4.91	6.25	7.11	7.45	7.35
9000	2.00	3.36	5.00	6.28	7.18	7.50	7.40
8500	2.05	3.43	5.04	6.32	7.20	7.55	7.41
8000	2.10	3.52	5.10	6.36	7.22	7.60	7.42
7500	2.17	3.62	5.18	6.38	7.24	7.65	7.46
7000	2.22	3.70	5.25	6.40	7.26	7.70	7.50
6500	2.32	3.85	5.35	6.43	7.27	7.70	7.51
6000	2.42	4.00	5.45	6.48	7.28	7.70	7.52
5500	2.57	4.15	5.55	6.53	7.29	7.68	7.51
5000	2.72	4.32	5.65	6.58	7.30	7.66	7.50

KN values are for hull and forecastle only.

DATASHEET Q.1(e)

(N.B This Datasheet must be returned with your examination answer book). Note: 'foap' denotes for'd of AP

Hydrostatic Particulars 'A'

Draught m	Displacement t		TPC t		MCTC t m		KM_T	KB	LCB foap	LCF foap
	SW RD 1.025	FW RD 1.000	SW RD 1.025	FW RD 1.000	SW RD 1.025	FW RD 1.000	m	m	m	m
7.00	14 576	14 220	23.13	22.57	184.6	180.1	8.34	3.64	70.03	67.35
6.90	14 345	13 996	23.06	22.50	183.0	178.5	8.35	3.58	70.08	67.46
6.80	14 115	13 771	22.99	22.43	181.4	177.0	8.36	3.53	70.12	67.57
6.70	13 886	13 548	22.92	22.36	179.9	175.5	8.37	3.48	70.16	67.68
6.60	13 657	13 324	22.85	22.29	178.3	174.0	8.38	3.43	70.20	67.79
6.50	13 429	13 102	22.78	22.23	176.8	172.5	8.39	3.38	70.24	67.90
6.40	13 201	12 879	22.72	22.17	175.3	171.0	8.41	3.33	70.28	68.00
6.30	12 975	12 658	22.66	22.11	173.9	169.6	8.43	3.28	70.32	68.10
6.20	12 748	12 437	22.60	22.05	172.5	168.3	8.46	3.22	70.35	68.20
6.10	12 523	12 217	22.54	21.99	171.1	167.0	8.49	3.17	70.38	68.30
6.00	12 297	11 997	22.48	21.93	169.8	165.7	8.52	3.11	70.42	68.39
5.90	12 073	11 778	22.43	21.87	168.5	164.4	8.55	3.06	70.46	68.48
5.80	11 848	11 559	22.37	21.82	167.3	163.2	8.59	3.01	70.50	68.57
5.70	11 625	11 342	22.32	21.77	166.1	162.1	8.63	2.95	70.53	68.65
5.60	11 402	11 124	22.26	21.72	165.0	161.0	8.67	2.90	70.57	68.73

5.50	11 180	10 908	22.21	21.66	163.9	160.0	8.71	2.85	70.60	68.80
5.40	10 958	10 691	22.15	21.61	162.9	158.9	8.76	2.80	70.64	68.88
5.30	10 737	10 476	22.10	21.56	161.8	157.9	8.81	2.74	70.68	68.95
5.20	10 516	10 260	22.05	21.51	160.8	156.9	8.86	2.69	70.72	69.02
5.10	10 296	10 045	22.00	21.46	159.8	155.9	8.92	2.63	70.75	69.09
5.00	10 076	9830	21.95	21.41	158.8	154.9	8.98	2.58	70.79	69.16
4.90	9857	9616	21.90	21.36	157.9	154.0	9.06	2.53	70.82	69.23
4.80	9638	9403	21.85	21.32	156.9	153.1	9.13	2.48	70.86	69.29
4.70	9420	9190	21.80	21.27	156.0	152.2	9.22	2.43	70.90	69.35
4.60	9202	8978	21.75	21.22	155.1	151.3	9.30	2.38	70.93	69.42
4.50	8985	8766	21.70	21.17	154.2	150.5	9.40	2.32	70.96	69.48
4.40	8768	8554	21.65	21.12	153.3	149.6	9.49	2.27	71.00	69.55
4.30	8552	8344	21.60	21.07	152.4	148.7	9.60	2.22	71.04	69.62
4.20	8336	8133	21.55	21.02	151.5	147.8	9.71	2.17	71.08	69.68
4.10	8121	7923	21.50	20.97	150.6	146.9	9.83	2.12	71.12	69.74
4.00	7906	7713	21.45	20.93	149.7	146.0	9.96	2.07	71.15	69.81
3.90	7692	7505	21.40	20.88	148.7	145.1	10.11	2.01	71.18	69.88
3.80	7478	7296	21.35	20.83	147.8	144.2	10.25	1.96	71.22	69.94
3.70	7265	7088	21.30	20.78	146.8	143.3	10.41	1.91	71.25	70.00
3.60	7052	6880	21.24	20.72	145.9	142.3	10.57	1.86	71.29	70.07
3.50	6840	6673	21.19	20.67	144.9	141.3	10.76	1.81	71.33	70.14

THESE HYDROSTATIC PARTICULARS HAVE BEEN DEVELOPED WITH THE VESSEL FLOATING ON EVEN KEEL

SHIP CONSTRUCTION AND STABILITY
Attempt ALL questions

Marks for each question are shown in brackets
1. All parts of question 1 carry equal marks.

(a) Define *Transverse Metacentre*.
(b) Define *Statutory Freeboard*.
(c) State the meaning of *watertight* as given in the Load Line Rules 1968.
(d) A ship of displacement 15 000 t is heeled 3°. Given KG 8.46 m and KM 9.36 m determine the Righting Moment.
(e) Use Datasheet Q.1(e).
The ship, length 145 m, is floating in fresh water at drafts 4.30 m Forward and 6.30 m Aft. Determine the ship's displacement.   (35)

2. Use Datasheet Q.1(e).
The ship, at displacement 6950 t, KG 7.80 m loads the following:

2800 t at Kg   3.79 m
3400 t at Kg   6.86 m
900 t at Kg   8.89 m
500 t at Kg 10.30 m

On passage it is anticipated that 950 t of fuel and fresh water will be used from Kg 2.85 m producing a free surface moment of 414 t m.

Calculate the GM on arrival.   (30)

3. Use Datasheets Q.1(e) and Q.3.
The ship is at displacement 11 750 t, KG 8.00 m.

(a) Draw the GZ curve for the ship in this condition.   (20)
(b) Using the curve drawn in Q.3(a), estimate EACH of the following:
(i) the angle of vanishing stability.
(ii) the angle of deck edge immersion.
(iii) the maximum GZ and the angle at which it occurs.   (10)

4. Use Hydrostatic Datasheet Q.1(e).
The ship, length b.p. 140 m, is at drafts 6.10 m Forward and 6.50 m Aft. 100 t of ballast, already on board, is to be moved 85 m forward.

(a) Calculate the position, with reference to amidship, at which 227 t of cargo should be loaded so that the ship finishes on an even keel.(20)
(b) Determine the final draught.   (10)

5. A ship of displacement 9500 t floats upright in still water with KG 8.84 m and KM 9.96 m.
On passage containers of weight 65 tonne are lost overside from a position Kg 12.0 m, 10.5 m to port of the centreline.

Calculate the list to be expected giving the direction.   (25)

(This Worksheet must be returned with your answer book)

HYDROSTATIC PARTICULARS 'B'

(in salt water R.D. 1.025)

The hydrostatic particulars have been calculated for the vessel on Even Keel.

Draught (m)	Displacement (t)	TPC (t)	MCTC (tm)	LCB from amidships (m)	LCF from amidships (m)	KB (m)	KM_T (m)
4.00	1888.8	5.20	23.30	1.45 A	2.39 A	2.09	4.05
3.90	1836.8	5.20	23.20	1.42 A	2.43 A	2.04	4.05
3.80	1784.8	5.19	23.10	1.39 A	2.46 A	1.99	4.05
3.70	1733.0	5.18	22.99	1.36 A	2.49 A	1.93	4.06
3.60	1681.2	5.17	22.89	1.32 A	2.52 A	1.88	4.06
3.50	1629.5	5.16	22.77	1.29 A	2.55 A	1.83	4.07
3.40	1577.9	5.16	22.65	1.24 A	2.57 A	1.78	4.09
3.30	1526.4	5.15	22.52	1.20 A	2.59 A	1.72	4.11
3.20	1475.1	5.13	22.39	1.15 A	2.61 A	1.67	4.13
3.10	1423.8	5.12	22.25	1.10 A	2.62 A	1.62	4.15
3.00	1372.6	5.11	22.11	1.04 A	2.63 A	1.56	4.19
2.90	1321.5	5.10	21.96	0.98 A	2.64 A	1.51	4.22
2.80	1270.6	5.09	21.80	0.91 A	2.64 A	1.46	4.27
2.70	1211.4	5.07	21.64	0.84 A	2.64 A	1.40	4.32
2.60	1169.1	5.06	21.47	0.76 A	2.63 A	1.35	4.37
2.50	1118.6	5.05	21.30	0.68 A	2.63 A	1.30	4.44
2.40	1068.4	5.01	20.87	0.59 A	2.51 A	1.24	4.51

GENERAL SHIP KNOWLEDGE
Attempt ALL questions

Marks for each question are shown in brackets

1. A combustible gas indicator (explosimeter) is used to check the atmosphere of a cargo oil tank.

    (a) Describe how the instrument is used.   (5)
    (b) State the information given by the instrument.   (5)
    (c) State THREE circumstances where a zero reading may give a false idea of the cargo tank atmosphere.   (15)

2. (a) Define TPC and explain its use.   (5)
   (b) Explain why TPC changes with the draft of a conventional ship.(10)
   (c) Explain how the TPC in fresh water may be found.   (5)

3. A ship has been laid up for four months. Before the ship re-enters service, a survey is necessary. The fore-peak tank which is empty, requires inspection.

   State the safety precautions that should be taken.   (25)

4. A ship has a load draft of 3.80 m in seawater.

   The present mean draft in seawater is 3.30 m and KG is 3.65 m.

   40 tonnes of bunkers are then loaded at Kg 0.50 m giving a free surface moment of 150 tonnes metres. The loading plan requires 100 tonnes of cargo to be loaded in the hold at Kg. 2.50 m and the remainder of the cargo to be loaded on deck at Kg 5.00 m.

   Using the Worksheet Q.4, calulate EACH of the following:

    (a) the weight of deck cargo;   (10)
    (b) the load KG;   (10)
    (c) the metacentric height when fully loaded.   (10)

5. A ship is upright. A 10 tonne container is then lifted with the ship's own derrick from the centre-line of the lower hold and is re-stowed on the port side of the weather deck.

   Explain, with suitable sketches, the movement of the ship's centre of gravity when the container:

    (a) is first lifted;   (10)
    (b) is swung to the port side;   (10)
    (c) is landed on the weather deck.   (10)

6. Describe FIVE main hazards which can occur with the carriage of solid bulk cargoes.   (20)

OPERATIONAL SAFETY
Attempt ALL questions

Marks for each question are shown in brackets

1. (a) A vessel on even keel is at anchor outside a port in SW of RD 1.025 at a Summer Load draught of 10.24 m.
   TPC 18 (constant);   Summer Load displacement 13 176 t.
   Calculate the quantity of cargo to discharge into barges in order that the vessel can pass over a bar at the river entrance (RD 1.025) with an under keel clearance of 1.5 m. Depth of water available at the bar = 9.25 m. (10)
   (b) Calculate the FWA of the vessel mentioned in Q.1(a). (7)
   (c) Explain why, when loading a vessel, it is necessary to know the Dock Water density. (8)

2. A vessel is initially displacing 6650 t.

   KG 8.40 m;   KM 8.90 m (constant).

   A 38 t weight is to be discharged from a position on the centreline Kg 5.2 m using the vessel's own derrick. The derrick head is 32 m above the keel.
   Calculate the vessel's GM value when:

   (a) the weight is lifted just clear of the initial stowage position; (15)
   (b) the weight is finally discharged ashore. (10)

3. (a) Explain the formation of EACH of the following:
      (i) ship's sweat; (6)
      (ii) cargo sweat. (6)
   (b) List FIVE reasons for ventilating the holds of a general cargo vessel. (5)
   (c) (i) List SIX *hygroscopic* cargoes. (6)
      (ii) List TWO *non-hygroscopic* cargoes. (2)

4. (a) State the meaning of EACH of the following abbreviations:
      (i) FLT; (1)
      (ii) ISO. (2)
   (b) List the methods by which cargo can be secured onto pallets. (5)
   (c) State the advantages and disadvantages of unitising cargo. (17)

5. (a) With respect to the carriage of bulk or packaged Dangerous Goods, state the meaning of EACH of the following abbreviations:
      (i) EmS No; (1)
      (ii) MFAG No; (1)
      (iii) UN No. (2)
   (b) List the main headings found under an EmS entry. (10)
   (c) Detail the symptoms resulting from exposure to increasing concentrations of *Benzene*. (3)
   (d) List the principal sources of information when carrying any type of dangerous cargo. (8)

6. (a) Define EACH of the following terms:

     (i) upper flammable limit (UFL);   (3)

     (ii) lower flammable limit (LFL);   (3)

     (iii) flammable range (also referred to as 'explosive range').   (3)

  (b) Draw a diagram which shows the relationship between EACH of the terms in Q.6(a).   (6)

  (c) State the limitations when using a combustible gas indicator (explosimeter).   (10)

Appendix VII
Revision one-liners

The following are sixty-five one-line questions acting as an aid to examination preparation. They are similar in effect to using mental arithmetic when preparing for a mathematics exam. Elements of questions may well appear in the written papers or in the oral exams. Good luck.

1. What is another name for the KG?
2. What is a hydrometer used for?
3. If the angle of heel is less than 10 degrees, what is the equation for GZ?
4. What are the formulae for TPC and MCTC for a ship in salt water?
5. Give two formulae for the Metacentre, KM.
6. How may Free Surface Effects be reduced on a ship?
7. What is another name for KB?
8. List four requirements before an Inclining Experiment can take place.
9. With the aid of a sketch, define LOA and LBP.
10. What are Cross Curves of Stability used for?
11. What is the longitudinal centre of a waterplane called?
12. Adding a weight to a ship usually causes two changes. What are these changes?
13. What is Simpson's First Rule for a parabolic shape with seven equally spaced ordinates?
14. What is KB for (a) box-shaped vessel and (b) triangular-shaped vessel?
15. What are Hydrostatic Curves used for onboard a ship?
16. Using sketches, define the Block, the Waterplane and Midship form coefficients.
17. Sketch a Statical Stability curve and label six important points on it.
18. What are the minimum values allowed by D.Tp. for GZ and for transverse GM?
19. List three ways in which a ship's end drafts may be changed.
20. GM is 0.45 m. Radius of gyration is 7 m. Estimate the natural rolling period in seconds.
21. What is a Deadweight Scale used for?

22. What is the formula for Bending Stress in terms of M, I and y?
23. Sketch a set of Hydrostatic Curves.
24. List three characteristics of an Angle of Loll.
25. Define (a) a moment and (b) a moment of inertia.
26. Sketch the first three curves for a set of ship's Strength Curves.
27. What is the 'theory of parallel axis' formula?
28. What are the effects on a Statical Stability curve for increased Breadth and increased Freeboard?
29. Sketch a Metacentric Diagram for a box-shaped vessel and a triangular-shaped vessel.
30. Block coefficient is 0.715. Midship coefficient is 0.988. Calculate Prismatic coefficient.
31. Describe the use of Simpson's Third Rule.
32. What is the wall-sided formula for GZ?
33. Define 'permeability'. Give two examples relating to contents in a hold or tank.
34. Give the equations for BM, box-shaped vessels and triangular-shaped vessels?
35. List three characteristics of an Angle of List.
36. Sketch the Shear force and Bending Moment curves. Show their inter-relation.
37. For a curve of seven equally spaced ordinates give Simpson's Second Rule.
38. What is the formula for pressure of water on a lockgate situation?
39. When a weight is lifted from a jetty by a ship's derrick whereabouts does its CG act?
40. Sketch a set of Freeboard Marks and label dimensions as specified by D.Tp.
41. Sketch a Displacement curve.
42. What is Morrish's formula for VCB?
43. For an inclining experiment how is tangent of the angle of list obtained?
44. What do 'a moment of statical stability' and 'dynamical stability' mean?
45. Show the range of stability on an S/S curve having a very small initial negative GM.
46. Breadth is 45 m. Draft is 15 m. What is the increase in draft at a list of 2 degrees?
47. What is the formula for loss of GM due to free surface effects in a slack tank?
48. For what purpose is the Inclining Experiment made on ships?
49. What is the 'true mean draft' on a ship?
50. When drydocking a ship there is a virtual loss in GM. Give two formulae for this loss.
51. With Simpson's Rules, give formulae for M of I about (a) Amidships and (b) Centre line.

52. Discuss the components involved for estimating an angle of heel whilst turning a ship.
53. What is a 'stiff ship' and a 'tender ship'. Give typical GM values.
54. With the Lost Buoyancy method, how does VCG change, after bilging has occurred?
55. Sketch a Deadweight Moment curve and label the important parts.
56. Sketch a Bending stress diagram for a vessel that is in a Sagging condition.
57. What are 'Bonjean curves' and for what purpose are they used?
58. Define 'Ship Squat' and 'blockage factor'.
59. Draw the line diagram for Murray's method for maximum Bending Moment.
60. What is the formula for shear stress for an H-girder?
61. What happens to cause a vessel to be in Unstable equilibrium?
62. What causes Hogging in a vessel?
63. Which letters signify the Metacentric Height?
64. Give typical C_b values for fully loaded VLCC, general cargo ships and passenger liners.
65. What happens when a ship passes from one density of water to another water density?

Appendix VIII
How to pass exams in Maritime Studies

To pass exams you have to be like a successful football team. You will need: Ability, Tenacity, Consistency, Good preparation and Luck!!

The following tips should help you to obtain extra marks that could turn that 36 per cent into a 42 per cent + pass or an 81 per cent into an Honours 85 per cent + award. Good luck.

In Your Exam
1. Use big sketches. Small sketches tend to irritate examiners.
2. Use coloured pencils. Drawings look better with a bit of colour.
3. Use a 150 cm rule to make better sketches and a more professional drawing.
4. Have big writing to make it easier to read. Make it neat. Use a pen rather than a biro. Reading a piece of work written in biro is harder, especially if the quality of the biro is not very good.
5. Use plenty of paragraphs. It makes it easier to read.
6. Write down any data you wish to remember. This makes it easier to retain in your memory.
7. Be careful in your answers that you do not suggest things or situations that would endanger the ship or the onboard personnel.
8. Reread your answers near the end of the exam. Omitting the word 'not' does make such a difference.
9. Reread your question as you finish each answer. Don't miss, for example, part (c) of an answer and throw away marks.
10. Treat the exam as an advertisement of your ability rather than an obstacle to be overcome. If you think you will fail, then you probably will fail.

Before Your Exam
1. Select 'bankers' for each subject. Certain topics come up very often and

these you will have fully understood. Bank on these appearing on the exam paper.

2. Don't swat 100 per cent of your course notes. Omit about 10 per cent and concentrate on the 90 per cent. In that 10 per cent will be some topics you will never be able to understand fully.

3. Work through past exam papers in order to gauge the standard and the time factor to complete the required solution. Complete and hand in every set coursework assignment.

4. Write all formulae discussed in each subject on pages at the rear of your notes.

5. In your notes circle each formula in a red outline or use a highlight pen. In this way they will stand out from the rest of your notes. Remember formulae are like spanners. Some you will use more than others but all can be used to solve a problem.

6. Underline in red important key phrases or words. Examiners will be looking for these in your answers. Oblige them and obtain the marks.

7. Revise each subject in carefully planned sequence so as not to be rusty on a set of notes that you have not read for some time whilst you have been sitting other exams.

8. Be aggressive in your mental approach to do your best. If you have prepared well there will be a less nervous approach and, like the football team, you will gain your goal.

Appendix IX
Draft Surveys

When a ship loads up at a port, departs from this port and travels to another port, a Draft Survey is carried out. This is to check that the cargo deadweight or 'constant' is satisfactory for the shipowner at the port of arrival.

It is virtually a check on the amount of cargo that left the first port against that arriving at the second port. This Draft Survey may be carried out by a Master, a Chief Engineer or a Naval Architect.

Prior to starting on a Draft Survey the vessel should be in upright condition and on even keel if possible. If not on even keel then certainly within 1 per cent of her LBP would be advantageous.

When the ship arrives in port ready for this Draft Survey, there are several items of information that have to be known by, say, the Naval Architect. They include:

LBP and C_b relative to the ship's waterline or actual loaded condition.
Lightweight.
Density of the water in which the vessel is floating.
Draft readings port and starboard at the stern, midships and at the bow.
Distance from aft perp to Aft draft marks.
Distance from amidships to midship draft marks.
Distance from forward perp to forward draft marks.
Distance of LCF from amidships.
Cargo deadweight or 'constant', for example, say 10 766 t.

Using above data the Naval Architect will modify the actual draft readings to what they would be at AP, amidships and FP. These values are then used to determine the mean draft at the position of the ship's LCF (see chapter on Trim).

To take into account any Hog or Sag a 'mean of means' formula is used. Suppose the drafts at the AP, amidships and FP were 8.994 m, 8.797 m, 8.517 m and LCF was 0.37 m forward of amidships with an LBP of 143.5 m. Then the mean of means draft is:

$$\text{Means of means draft} = (d_{AP} + (6 \times d_{AM}) + d_{FP})/8$$

$$= (8.994 + (6 \times 8.797) + 8.517)/8$$

Thus, mean of means draft $= 8.787\,\text{m}$

When corrected for LCF position, <u>the mean draft is 8.786 m.</u>

The Naval Architect uses this draft of 8.786 m on the ship's Hydrostatic Curves or tabulated data to obtain a first estimate of the displacement and TPC. These are of course for salt water density of 1.025 t/m^3. Assume this displacement was 17 622 t and the TPC was 25.86 t. The Naval Architect can now evaluate the Fresh Water Allowance and proceed to make a correction for density.

$$\text{FWA} = W/(4 \times \text{TPC}) = 17\,662/(4 \times 25.86)$$

$$\text{FWA} = 171\,\text{mm}$$

The density correction is then made (see chapter on Density correction). Assume the water was of 1.019 t/m^3. Consequently this correction would be minus 0.041 m.

Thus, the <u>final true draft</u> would be $8.786 - 0.041 = $ <u>8.745 m.</u>

Interpolating once more the Hydrostatic data the final Displacement at the time of the Draft Survey is obtained. Pressume this final Displacement is 17 537 tonnes.

From this figure must be deducted the Lightweight and all other deadweight items (except the 'constant' or Cargo deadweight). Assume this Lightweight was 5675 t and the residual dwt of oil, fresh water, stores, crew and effects, water ballast etc. was 1112 t. This residual dwt would have been estimated after all tanks had been sounded and all compartments been checked for contents. Then the final Cargo dwt or 'constant' is:

$$\text{Cargo deadweight} = 17\,537 - 5675 - 1112 = \underline{10\,750\ \text{tonnes}}$$

This compares favourably with the Cargo dwt given at the port of departure, that is 10 766 tonnes, a difference of 0.15 per cent. In a perfect world the Cargo dwt at the arrival port would have been 'constant' at 10 766 t. However, ships are not built to this degree of accuracy and measurement to this standard is very hard to achieve.

Summary:

Corrections have been made for:

Draft mark positions.	Trim and LCF position.
Hog or sag.	Density of water.

<u>True mean draft is 8.745 m</u>   True displacement is 17 537 t

<u>Cargo deadweight or 'constant' is 10 750 t (-0.15 per cent)</u>

A well-conducted survey is capable of achieving an absolute accuracy of within plus or minus 0.50 per cent of the Cargo dwt. This is as good, if not better, as other systems of direct weighing.

Error can creep in over the years because of the ship's reported Lightweight. This is due to the ship herself gaining about 0.50 per cent Lightweight each year in service. Hence over a period of ten years this ship would have gained about 280 tonnes since her maiden voyage.

Lightweight will also alter slightly depending on the position of the anchors and cables. Obviously, with anchors fully housed the Lightweight will be more. Adjustment may have to be made but it is better if at both ports the anchors are fully housed.

Error can also be made if the draft readings were taken in a tidal current. The speed of the tide would cause the ship to sink slightly in the water (squat effects) and so give draft readings that were too high in value. One reported instance of this occurring resulted in a cargo reduction of over 300 t. Initially this was put down to excessive pilfering until further checks discovered that drafts had been taken in moving water. At departure and arrival ports draft readings must be read when water speed is zero.

One suggestion for improving accuracy of measurement is to have draft marks also at 1/4L and 3/4L from aft. In other words at stations 2.5 and 7.5. They would reduce errors where there is an appreciable hog or sag at the time of the Draft Survey.

Answers to exercises

Exercise 1
1. 1800 Nm   2. 2 kg m, anti-clockwise   3. 0.73 m from the centre towards the 10 kg weight   4. 45.83 kg   5. 81 kg m

Exercise 2
1. 11.05 m   2. 10.41 m   3. 4.62 m   4. 6.08 m   5. 0.25 m

Exercise 3
1. 98.78 tonnes   2. 114.13 tonnes   3. 172.8 tonnes
4. 108 tonnes   5. $83\frac{1}{3}$ tonnes   6. 861 tonnes

Exercise 4
1. 0.484 m   2. 0.256 m   3. 1.62 tonnes   4. 11.6 tonnes
5. 0.04 m, 32 per cent   6. 900 kg, S.G. 0.75
7. 0.03 m   8. 1.02   9. 0.75 m, 182.34 tonnes
10. (a) 125 kg (b) 121.4 kg   11. 64 per cent
12. (a) 607.5 kg (b) 4.75 cm   13. 1.636 m   14. (a) 1.2 m
(b) 70 per cent   15. 9.4 per cent

Exercise 5
1. 7 612.5 tonnes   2. 4352 tonnes   3. 1.016 m   4. 7.361 m
5. 0.4875 m   6. 187.5 tonnes   7. 13 721.3 tonnes   8. 6 406.25 tonnes
9. 6.733 m F 6.883 m A   10. 228 tonnes   11. 285 tonnes
12. (a) 8515 tonnes (b) 11 965 tonnes   13. 27 mm   14. 83.2 mm

Exercise 6
5. 2604 tonnes metres

Exercise 8
1. (b) 3.78 tonnes 4.42 tonnes (c) 2.1 m   2 (b) 6.46 tonnes 7.8 tonnes
(c) 3.967 m   3. 4.53 m   4. (b) 920 tonnes (c) 3.3 m (d) 6.16 tonnes
5. (a) 2.375 m (b) 3092 tonnes (c) 1125 tonnes   6. (b) 3230 tonnes

(c) 1.625 m   **7.** (b) 725 tonnes (c) 4.48 m (d) 5 tonnes
8. (b) 5150 tonnes 4.06 m (c) 5.17 m

Exercise 9
1. (b) 12.3 tonnes   **2.** (b) 8302.5 tonnes   **3.** 12 681.3 tonnes
4. 221 tonnes   **5.** 180 tonnes   **6.** 95   **7.** 53

Exercise 10
1. (a) 508 m^2 (b) 5.2 tonnes (c) 0.8 m aft of amidships   **2.** (a) 488 m^2
(b) 5 tonnes (c) 0.865 (d) 0.86 m aft of amidships   **3.** (a) 122 mm
(b) 43.4 m from forward   **4.** (a) 30 476.7 tonnes (b) 371.4 mm (c) 15.6 m
5. 5062.5 tonnes   **6.** (a) 978.3 m^2 (b) 15.25 cm
(c) 2.03 m aft of amidships   **7.** (a) 9993$\frac{3}{4}$ tonnes (b) 97.44 mm (c) 4.33 m
8. (a) 671.83 m^2 (b) 1.57 m aft of amidships
9. 12.125 m^2 **10.** 101 m^2 **11.** (a) 781.67 m^3 (b) 8.01 tonnes
12. (a) 2 893.33 m^3 or 2965.6 tonnes (b) 3 m

Exercise 11
1. 2.84 m   **2.** 3.03 m   **3.** 3.85 m   **4.** 5.44 m   **5.** 0.063 m
6. 1466.67 tonnes   **7.** 1525 tonnes
8. 7031.3 tonnes in L.H and 2568.7 tonnes in T.D.   **9.** 1.2 m   **10.** 1.3 m
11. 55 tonnes   **12.** 286.3 tonnes   **13.** 1929.67 tonnes

Exercise 12
1. 5 m   **2.** (a) 1.28 m (b) 4.56 m   **3.** (a) 1.78 m (b) 3 m
4. No. Unstable when upright.   **5.** (a) 6.2 m, 13.78 m (b) 4.9 m
6. (a) 10.6 m, 5.13 m (b) 4.9 m at 4.9 m draft **7.** (a) 6.31 m, 4.11 m
(b) 4.08 m   **8.** (b) GM is +1.8 m, vessel is in stable equilibrium
(c) GM is zero, KG = KM, so ship is in neutral equilibrium

Exercise 13
1. 6° 03' to starboard   **2.** 4.2 m
3. 216.5 tonnes to port and 183.5 tonnes to starboard   **4.** 9° 30'
5. 5.458 m   **6.** 12° 57'   **7.** 91 9 tonnes
8. 282.75 tonnes to port, 217.25 tonnes to starboard
9. 8.52 m to port   GM = 0.864 m   **10.** 14° 4' to port   **11.** 13° 24'
12. 50 tonnes   **13.** 3.8°

Exercise 14
1. 674.5 tonnes metres   **2.** 7.773 m   **3.** 546.2 m
4. 6.027 m, 2000 tonnes metres   **5.** (a) 83.43 tonnes metres
(b) 404.4 tonnes metres   **6.** (a) 261.6 tonnes metres
(b) 2647 tonnes metres   **7.** (a) 139.5 tonnes metres
(b) 1366 tonnes metres   **8.** 0.522 m
9. Angle of Loll is 14.96°, KM is 2.67 m, GM is −0.05 m

Exercise 15

1. 218.4 tonnes in No. 1 and 131.6 tonnes in No. 4.   2. 176.92 tonnes
3. 5.152 m F 5.342 m A   4. 6.162 m F 6.726 m A
5. 668.4 tonnes from No. 1 and 1331.6 tonnes from No. 4.
6. 266.7 tonnes   7. 24.4 cm   8. 380 tonnes, 6.785 m F
9. 42.9 tonnes in No. 1, and 457.1 in No. 4   GM = 0.79 m
10. 402.1 tonnes from No. 1 and 47.9 tonnes from No. 4
11. 3.118 m F 4.340 m A   12. 5.50 m F 5.56 m A
13. 5.679 m F 5.901 m A   14. 4 metres aft   15. 3.78 metres aft
16. 4.44 metres aft   17. 55.556 metres forward
18. 276.75 tonnes; 13.6 metres forward   19. 300 tonnes; 6.3 m
20. 200 tonnes; 7.6 m   21. 405 tonnes in No. 1 and 195 tonnes in No. 4
22. 214.3 tonnes   23. 215.4 tonnes; 5.96 m F   24. 200 metres
25. 240 metres   26. Draft aft is 8.23 m. Draft forward is 7.79 m. Dwt is
9195 t. Trim by the stern is 0.44 m

Exercise 16

1. GM = 2 m, Range 0–84.5°, Max. GZ = 2.5 m at 43.5° heel.
2. GM = 4.8 m, Max. Moment = 67 860 tonnes metres at 42.25° heel,
Range 0–81.5°   3. GM = 3.07 m, Max. GZ = 2.43 m at 41° heel,
Range 0–76°, Moment at 10° = 16 055 tonnes metres. Moment at
40° = 59 774 tonnes metres   4. Moment at 10° = 16 625 tonnes metres,
GM = 2 m, Max. GZ = 2.3 m at 42° heel, Range 0–82°
5. GM = 3.4 m. Range 0–89.5°, Max. GZ = 1.93 m at 42° heel.
6. 6.61 m   7. 8.37 m   8. 25.86 m forward
9. 39 600 tonnes; 513 tonnes metres; 40.5 tonnes; 9.15 m
10. 3.15 m F 4.53 m A   11. (a) 0–95°, (b) 95°, (c) 3.18 m at 47.5°
12. (a) 0–75°, (b) 75°, (c) 2.15 m at 40°   13. 1.60 m 40°, 12°, 72.5°
14. 1.43 m, 39.5°, 44 000 tonnes metres, 70°

Exercise 17

1. 1.19 m   2. 1.06 m   3. 0.64 m   4. 7 m   5. 4.62 m

Exercise 18

1. 1.545 m   2. 6.15 tonnes/m^2 3. 7.175 tonnes/m^2, 1,435 tonnes
4. 6.15 tonnes/m^2, 55.35 tonnes   5. 9 tonnes/m^2, 900 tonnes
6. 6.15 tonnes/m^2, 147.6 tonnes   7. 1 tonne
8. 386.76 tonnes on side with density 1010 kg/m^3
9. 439.4 tonnes on side with density 1016 kg/m^3 10. 3075 tonnes
11. 128.13 tonnes

Exercise 19

1. Transfer 41.94 tonnes from starboard to port, and 135 tonnes from
forward to aft.
2. Transfer 125 tonnes from forward to aft, and 61.25 tonnes from port to
starboard. Final distribution: No. 1 Port 75 tonnes, No. 1 starboard

200 tonnes, No. 4 Port 63.75 tonnes, No. 4 starboard 61.25 tonnes
3. 13° 52' 3.88 m F 4.30 m A   4. Transfer 133.33 tonnes from each side
of No. 5. Put 149.8 tonnes in No. 2 Port and 116.9 tonnes in No. 2
starboard

Exercise 20
1. 0.148 m   2. 0.431 m   3. 1.522 m
4. 7° 2'   5. Dep. GM = 0.842 m, Arr. GM = 0.587 m   6. 3° 0'
7. 112.4 tonnes   8. 6.15 m   + 0.27 m

Exercise 21
1. 5.12 m   2. 0.222 m   3. 0.225 m   4. 0.558 m   5. 0.105 m
6. 0.109 m   7. 0.129 m   8. 3.55 m F 2.01 m A   9. 7.529 m F 5.267 m A
10. 6.25 m F 2.96 m A   11. 5.598 m F 3.251 m A
12. 5.305 m F 4.859 m A

Exercise 22
1. 1344 m tonnes   2. 2038.4 m tonnes   3. 1424 m tonnes
4. 13.67 m tonnes   5. 107.2 m tonnes

Exercise 24
1. No; 35° 49'   2. 39° 14'
3. Probable cause of the list is a negative GM
4. Discharge timber from the high side first.

Exercise 25
1. 33 tonnes   2. 514 tonnes   3. 488 tonnes   4. 146.3 tonnes. Sag 0.11 m
0.843 m

Exercise 26
1. 15.6 cm   2. 1962 tonnes 4.087 m   3. 4.576 m   4. 5000 tonnes
5. 39.1 cm   6. 10.67 m   7. 2.92 m   8. 4.24 m
9. 0.48 m, 1.13°, 8050 tonnes, 8.51 m

Exercise 27
1. 1.19 m   2. 69.12 tonnes 1.6 m

Exercise 28
1. −0.2 m or − 0.25 m   2. + 0.367 m or + 0.385 m
3. + 0.541 m or + 0.573 m. Safe to drydock vessel.
4. + 0.550 m or + 0.564 m. Safe to drydock vessel.
5. Max trim 0.896 m or 0.938 m by the stern.

Exercise 29
1. 0.707   2. $\dfrac{8a^4}{3}$ 3. 9 : 16   4. 63 281 cm^4 5. (a) 3154 m^4
(b) 28 283 m^4 6. (a) 18 086 m^4 (b) 871 106 m^4
7. BM$_L$ 206.9 m   BM$_T$ 8.45 m   8. I$_{CL}$ 35 028 m^4 I$_{CF}$ 1 101 540 m^4

9. I_{CL} 20 267 m^4 I_{CF} 795 417 m^4 **10.** I_{CL} 13 227 m^4 I_{CF} 396 187 m^4

Exercise 30
1. 658.8 tonnes 4.74 m   **2.** 17.17 m   **3.** 313.9 tonnes 2.88 m
4. 309.1 tonnes 1.74 m   **5.** 5.22 m

Exercise 31
1. (a) 366.5 m (b) 0.100 (c) 0.65 m (d) 0.85 m
2. (a) W of I is 418 m > 350 m (c) 9.05 kt   **3.** 10.56 kt

Exercise 32
1. 4° 34′   **2.** 6° 4′   **3.** 5° 44′   **4.** 6.8° to starboard

Exercise 33
1. 20.05 s   **2.** 15.6 s   **3.** 15.87 s   **4.** T_R is 28.2 s – rather a 'tender ship'

Exercise 34
1. 3.6°   **2,** 11.57°   **3.** 5.7°   **4.** 4.9°   **5.** 8°

Exercise 36
1. Passenger liner (0.78 m) and general cargo ship (0.66 m)

Exercise 37
1. 4.1 m F 8.2 m A   **2.** 2.44 m F 4.39 m A
3. Draft aft is 6.91 m, draft forward is 6.87 m

Exercise 38
1. 14° 33′   **2.** 13° 4′   **3.** 9° 52′   **4.** 5° 35′

Exercise 40
1. Max. BM 2.425 tonnes m at 5.8 m from A
2. (a) Max. BM 29.2 tonnes m between the positions of the two
masses. (b) At $\frac{1}{3}$ L from L.H. side SF = 4.87 tonnes BM = 24.34 tonnes m.
At $\frac{1}{3}$ L from R.H. side SF = 0.13 tonnes, BM = 28.65 tonnes m

Exercise 43
1. Max. SF = ±40 tonnes Max. BM = + 145.8 tonnes m, −62.5 tonnes
m
2. Max. BM = 150 tonnes m at amidships.
3. Max. SF = ± 250 tonnes at 25 m from each end. Max. BM = 6250
tonnes m at amidships
4. Descriptive
5. SF_{max} is 128.76 MN, BM_{max} is 10 220 MN m at station 5.2, just forward
of mid-LOA

Exercise 44
1. 420 tonnes

Index